SOLDIERS OF THE CROSS,
THE AUTHORITATIVE TEXT

Atlanta Campaign. Army of the Cumberland. Divine Service by Rev. P. P. Cooney, C.S.C. Chaplain Gen. of Ind. Troops in the field (Library of Congress Prints and Photographs Division, Washington, DC)

SOLDIERS *of the* CROSS,
the Authoritative Text

The Heroism of Catholic Chaplains
and Sisters in the American Civil War

DAVID POWER CONYNGHAM

Edited by
David J. Endres and William B. Kurtz

UNIVERSITY OF NOTRE DAME PRESS

NOTRE DAME, INDIANA

University of Notre Dame Press
Notre Dame, Indiana 46556
undpress.nd.edu

Published in the United States of America

Library of Congress Cataloging-in-Publication Data
Names: Conyngham, David Power, 1840–1883, author. | Endres, David Jeffrey,
    1979– editor. | Kurtz, William B. (William Burton), editor.
Title: Soldiers of the cross, the authoritative text : the heroism of
    Catholic chaplains and sisters in the American Civil War / David Power
    Conyngham ; edited by David J. Endres and William B. Kurtz.
Other titles: Heroism of Catholic chaplains and sisters in the American Civil War
Description: Notre Dame, Indiana : University of Notre Dame Press, [2019] |
    Includes bibliographical references and index. |
Identifiers: LCCN 2019012694 (print) | LCCN 2019012873 (ebook) | ISBN
    9780268105310 (pdf) | ISBN 9780268105327 (epub) | ISBN 9780268105297
    (hardback : alk. paper) | ISBN 0268105294 (hardback : alk. paper)
Subjects: LCSH: United States—History—Civil War, 1861–1865—Participation,
    Catholic. | United States—History—Civil War, 1861–1865—Religious
    aspects. | Military chaplains—Catholic Church—History—19th century. |
    Nuns—United States—History—19th century. | United States.
    Army—Chaplains—History—19th century. | United States.
    Army—Chaplains—Biography.
Classification: LCC E540.C3 (ebook) | LCC E540.C3 C66 2019 (print) | DDC
    973.7/78—dc23
LC record available at https://lccn.loc.gov/2019012694

Contents

Acknowledgments   ix

Editors' Introduction   xi

SOLDIERS OF THE CROSS   1

Introduction   13

THE FEDERAL CHAPLAINS

Chapter I. Rev. J. F. Trecy: Chaplain 4th U. S. Cavalry   37

Chapter II. Rev. J. F. Trecy, Continued   51

Chapter III. Rev. J. F. Trecy, Continued   67

Chapter IV. Rev. Joseph C. Carrier, C.S.C.: Chaplain 6th
Missouri Cavalry   79

Chapter V. Rev. Joseph C. Carrier, C.S.C., Continued   91

Chapter VI. Rev. Joseph C. Carrier, C.S.C., Continued   101

Chapter VII. Rev. Joseph C. Carrier, C.S.C., Continued   111

Chapter VIII. Rev. R. C. Christy: Chaplain 78th Pennsylvania
Volunteers   121

Chapter IX. Rev. Thomas Scully: Chaplain 9th Massachusetts
Veteran Volunteers   141

Chapter X. Rev. Thomas Scully, Continued 153

Chapter XI. Rev. Peter Tissot, S.J.: Chaplain 37th New York
Volunteers 163

Chapter XII. Rev. Thomas Willett, S.J.: Chaplain 69th New
York Volunteers 171

Chapter XIII. Rev. C. L. Egan, O.P.: Chaplain 9th Massachusetts
Volunteers 181

Chapter XIV. Rev. Paul E. Gillen, C.S.C.: Chaplain 170th
New York Volunteers 187

Chapter XV. Rev. Innocent A. Bergrath 205

Chapter XVI. Rev. Peter P. Cooney, C.S.C.: Chaplain 35th
Indiana Volunteers 211

Chapter XVII. Rev. Thomas Brady: Chaplain 15th Michigan
Volunteers 225

Chapter XVIII. Rev. William Corby, C.S.C.: Chaplain 88th
New York Volunteers 233

THE CONFEDERATE CHAPLAINS

Chapter XIX. Rev. Louis-Hippolyte Gache, S.J.: Chaplain
10th Louisiana Volunteers 249

Chapter XX. Rev. Charles P. Heuzé 263

Chapter XXI. Rev. James Sheeran, C.Ss.R.: Chaplain 14th
Louisiana Volunteers 269

Chapter XXII. Rev. James Sheeran, C.Ss.R., Continued 283

Chapter XXIII. Rev. James Sheeran, C.Ss.R., Continued 293

Chapter XXIV. Rev. James Sheeran, C.Ss.R., Continued 295

Chapter XXV. Rev. James Sheeran, C.Ss.R., Continued 307

THE SISTERS

Chapter XXVI. The Sisters in the Army   323

Chapter XXVII. The Sisters of Mercy, Charleston   329

Chapter XXVIII. The Sisters of Mount St. Vincent, Cincinnati   353

Chapter XXIX. Mount St. Vincent, St. Joseph's Military
Hospital, Central Park Grounds   363

Chapter XXX. The Sisters of Mercy, St. Louis   379

Chapter XXXI. The Sisters of Mercy, New York   389

Chapter XXXII. The Sisters of Mercy, New York, Continued   397

Chapter XXXIII. The Sisters of the Holy Cross   409

Chapter XXXIV. The Sisters of the Holy Cross, Continued   421

Notes   435

Selected Bibliography   487

Index   491

Acknowledgments

A century and a half ago, David Power Conyngham began writing *Soldiers of the Cross*. His untimely death placed the not-quite-finished manuscript in limbo, and despite attempts to have it published, it remained among the archival collections of the University of Notre Dame, waiting for its first printing. In 2012, we first discussed undertaking the project of transcribing and editing the work, convinced of its great worth for scholars of the Civil War and American Catholic history.

This long-awaited publication of *Soldiers of the Cross* has been the work of many. The University of Notre Dame Press, especially Eli Bortz, acquisitions editor, was instrumental in bringing this work to publication. Our thanks are also due to Elizabeth Sain at the press who did a tremendous job in copyediting the book, frequently checking our transcription against the original manuscript. She made many helpful suggestions that greatly improved the quality of our finished work. We are also grateful for the assistance of the staff of the University of Notre Dame Archives, especially Peter Lysy, William Kevin Cawley, and Charles Lamb, for providing permission to publish the manuscript, for digitizing it for our use, and making available images to complement the text. Dr. Cawley helped us acquire correspondence at the archives that explained how Conyngham's manuscript came to reside at Notre Dame, and he went above and beyond to help our work throughout the editorial process. We would also like to thank Kathleen S. Cummings, director of Notre Dame's Cushwa Center for the Study of American Catholicism, for her support and endorsement of the project.

Many archivists, librarians, and historians provided assistance or consultation, including Gary W. Gallagher, John L. Nau III Professor

Emeritus in the History of the American Civil War at the University of Virginia. Dr. Gallagher provided useful advice on editing an unpublished manuscript. His *Fighting for the Confederacy: The Personal Recollections of General Edward Porter Alexander* (University of North Carolina Press, 1989), served as a model for our own work. Patrick Hayes of the Redemptorist Archives in Philadelphia also offered helpful suggestions and his *The Civil War Diary of Father James Sheeran: Confederate Chaplain and Redemptorist* (Catholic University of America Press, 2016) proved invaluable in editing the chapters on Father Sheeran. Susan H. Perdue, former director of Documents Compass and veteran documentary editor, also gave advice and training in the field of documentary editing to Dr. Kurtz. Alex T. Dugas of Mount St. Mary's Seminary in Cincinnati served as a research assistant, uncovering the biographies of sometimes-obscure chaplains. Dr. Jeffrey Zvengrowski, current editor at the Papers of George Washington, provided an extra set of eyes during our initial proofreading and helped to transcribe some of the more difficult portions of the text.

Each of us is thankful for the support of our own respective communities of fellow scholars, friends, and family. Father Endres is grateful to the priests, seminarians, and faculty at the Athenaeum of Ohio/Mount St. Mary's Seminary of the West in Cincinnati. Dr. Kurtz wishes to acknowledge the professors and staff of the University of Virginia and the John L. Nau III Center for Civil War History. Finally, he is grateful to his wife, Erin, for her support and patience through the years it took to finish this project.

Editors' Introduction

The story of Catholic chaplains and sister nurses during the Civil War (1861–1865) is generally underappreciated, known mainly to historians of Catholic America. Yet as soon as the war ended, efforts were made to record their wartime contributions and make known their service to historians and the wider public. Their wartime roles were seen as among the most important contributions of Catholics to American society in the nineteenth century, a testimony to selfless service that often transcended regional and religious differences. In the late nineteenth and early twentieth centuries, Catholics remembered the accomplishments of both priest chaplains and sister nurses in celebratory books and speeches, by erecting a statue of chaplain William Corby in Gettysburg in 1910, and by building a monument to the "nuns of the battlefield" in Washington, DC, in 1924. American Catholic historians have analyzed, detailed, and celebrated their contributions in a number of articles and a few scholarly books.[1]

Yet historians' efforts remain incomplete. The role of chaplains and sister nurses is still underappreciated in the academic world outside of the subfield of American Catholic history. With very few exceptions, they are largely ignored by historians of the conflict and those specializing in gender and social history are often unfamiliar with the religious archives that hold the stories of Catholic chaplains and sister nurses.[2] Consequently, their role is usually absent from the general historical narratives of the war. It is hoped that this scholarly edition of David Power Conyngham's unpublished work, *Soldiers of the Cross*, will help to bring greater recognition for Catholic chaplains and sister nurses on both sides during the Civil War and help inform future scholarship.

"HOLY JOES" AND "SISTERS OF CHARITY"

The service of priest chaplains, on both sides of the conflict, began with the war's commencement. During the four years of conflict, about fifty priests, often called "Holy Joes" by the soldiers, ministered to the Union's Catholic soldiers. Another thirty priests ministered to Confederate regiments, providing the sacraments to Catholic soldiers from the South. Other chaplains stationed near battlefields or in proximity to hospitals served in an unofficial capacity, sometimes providing spiritual care indiscriminately to Federal[3] and Confederate soldiers.[4]

The Catholic clergy faced most of the same hardships as their Protestant and Jewish counterparts, not the least of which was the lack of standard regulations for chaplains in the Union and Confederate armies at the conflict's beginning. Clergymen working in Union hospitals, for example, were not officially considered military chaplains until May 1862. Union regimental chaplains received two rations a day and were paid the same as captains of the cavalry while their Confederate counterparts received only $80 a month. In both cases, chaplains were generally nominated by their regiment's troops or commander, pending an official commission by the Union or Confederate government. While better paid than enlisted men and treated as officers without an official command, chaplains on both sides shared the tedium of camp life, the difficulty of long muddy or dusty marches, and, occasionally, the possibility of violent death at the front with the men of their regiments. Even hospital chaplains far from the front suffered and even died from diseases they contracted from hospital patients. Chaplains on both sides were generally expected to look after the morale of their men, provide spiritual instruction and preaching, and help take care of the sick and dying. According to one recent study, 3,694 men served as chaplains on both sides of the conflict. The approximately 80 Catholic priests were only a very small part of that number.[5]

The role of Catholic women religious as nurses was more numerically significant than that of the Catholic clergy who served as chaplains. Perhaps twenty percent of all American nuns served as nurses in the war, totaling nearly seven hundred from at least twenty different religious communities. One historian estimated that one in six female nurses during the war was a Catholic sister. The sisters, invariably called "Sisters of Charity" or "Sisters of Mercy" no matter their membership in a particular religious congregation, served in proportionally higher numbers than any other group of American women, irrespective of region of origin or denomination. In addition to the Daughters of Charity and Sisters of Charity who comprised more than half of all female religious nurses, significant numbers of Sisters of the Holy Cross, Sisters of St. Joseph, Mercy Sisters, Dominicans, and Franciscans also served. Many of these sister nurses remain unknown, omitted even from the historical record out of a sense of modesty. In some cases, especially when abbreviations were used in records, further research has determined their identities.[6]

While many Catholic sisters were better trained in nursing than Protestant lay women in the mid-nineteenth century, the sister nurses shared many of the duties and experiences as other women nurses in the Union and Confederacy. When compensated at all, female nurses or hospital workers were poorly paid. To obtain work they required letters of reference from local politicians, prominent civilians, or military officials, and to keep their places they needed to win the trust of the male surgeons and doctors in charge of most Civil War–era hospitals. Many male doctors on both sides initially opposed the appointment of female nurses, preferring instead to employ convalescing male soldiers as helpers around hospital wards. Nonetheless, the famous examples of the English nurse Florence Nightingale and the Sisters of Mercy in the Crimean War (1854–1856) paved the way for Civil War female nurses like Kate Cumming in the South and Clara Barton in the North. Nurses cared for the sick, washed clothes, cleaned hospital wards, assisted at surgeries, wrote letters to loved ones, distributed rations and care packages, and did whatever was necessary to comfort their patients. In addition to their filthy and exhausting work, many women contracted diseases from their patients and some died as a result. Despite such dangers, the good service Catholic sisters and Protestant lay women rendered during the war helped pave the way for women's greater participation in nursing and health care to the present day.[7]

In the later decades of the nineteenth century, Catholic historians and leaders began to herald publicly the service of Catholic chaplains during the war. Among chaplains on both sides, the most famous is Father William Corby, C.S.C., two-time president of the University of Notre Dame and long-serving chaplain of the Union's famous Irish Brigade. A member of several veterans' groups including the Grand Army of the Republic, Corby wrote a memoir of his service in 1893 that was well received by his fellow veterans and the Catholic community. Corby is memorialized with a bronze statue on the Gettysburg battlefield at the spot where he famously gave absolution "under fire." A copy of the statue and a large painting depicting the event can be found on prominent display on the University of Notre Dame's campus.[8]

James B. Sheeran, C.Ss.R., among the best-known Confederate chaplains, served the many Irishmen of the 14th Louisiana Infantry. The Irish-born father of three was an unusual candidate for the chaplaincy, entering the priesthood after his wife died. During the war the self-assured Sheeran famously informed his general, Stonewall Jackson: "As a priest of God I outrank every officer in your command. I even outrank you." Sheeran's extensive wartime journal, first published in excerpted form in 1960, has been recently published in its entirety, helping to assure that Sheeran will continue to be remembered.[9]

Despite the fame of a few of the chaplains, the experiences of the rest of the approximately eighty government-recognized priest chaplains and many of the seven hundred sister nurses who served are not well known to Civil War scholars or students of American history. Several recent works detail the contributions of individual chaplains or communities of nuns, but many of their contributions remain obscured because of a lack of published sources.[10]

DAVID POWER CONYNGHAM

David Power Conyngham (1825–1883), an Irish American journalist, author, and Civil War veteran, sought to preserve the deeds of Catholic chaplains and sister nurses forever in a work he titled *The Soldiers of the Cross*, an unpublished manuscript compiled between the late 1860s and his death in 1883. Born in Crohane, County Tipperary, Ireland, Conyngham arrived in the United States in 1861 shortly after the beginning of the conflict as a war correspondent for the *Dublin Irishman*. In late 1862, armed with letters of introduction, he joined General Thomas Meagher and the Irish Brigade before the Battle of Fredericksburg. In early 1863, Conyngham became a member of Meagher's staff and served with the brigade at the battles of Chancellorsville, Gettysburg, and Bristoe Station. In the spring of 1864, he was sent by the *New York Herald*'s editor, James Gordon Bennett, to cover Union General William T. Sherman's Atlanta campaign. He not only wrote for the *Herald* but served as a volunteer aide-de-camp to General Henry M. Judah during the Battle of Resaca in mid-May 1864. Even after Judah was relieved from command, Conyngham continued with Sherman's forces through their famous March to the Sea and subsequent invasion of the Carolinas. He briefly contemplated a career as a captain in the U.S. Army, for which generals Joseph Hooker and Judah heartily recommended him. Not receiving the appointment, Conyngham returned to life as a journalist and author in New York City. He was officially naturalized on October 19, 1866, with the endorsement of his friend, the Irish American postmaster of New York City, James Kelly.[11]

Both a committed Irish nationalist and a devout Catholic, Conyngham wrote a number of novels or historical accounts about Irish saints, Irish history, and his experiences during the Civil War. His *Sherman's March Through the South* (1865) provided a first-hand account of his service during the war with General Sherman. His most famous work, however, was *The Irish Brigade and Its Campaigns* (1867). Conyngham wrote from personal experience and his own research into the famed brigade's wartime exploits. The book established the heroic sacrifice of Irish Catholics on behalf of the Union cause, as represented by those who died or were injured in the brigade's many bloody battles, and his work has been useful to historians ever since. If *Soldiers of the Cross* had been published shortly after the war, it would have been a complimentary volume to this work, establishing the loyalty, sacrifice, and Christian virtues of the Catholic clergy and sisters on both sides of the conflict.[12]

Soldiers of the Cross is the fullest record of the Catholic Church's involvement in the war written during the nineteenth century. Many of Conyngham's chapters contain new insights into the clergy during the war that are unavailable elsewhere, either during his time or ours, making the work valuable to Catholic and Civil War historians.[13] The introduction contains over a dozen letters written between 1868 and 1870 from high-ranking Confederate and Union officials praising the services of Catholic priests and nuns during the war. Such figures as Confederate General Robert E. Lee, Union Surgeon General William Hammond, and Union General George B. McClellan all heaped praise on the religious of the Catholic Church for their selfless devotion to Union and Confederate soldiers. Chapters on Father William Corby, Father Peter Paul Cooney, and the Sisters of the Holy Cross cover subjects relatively well known to Catholic scholars, but others are so useful and unique that they prompted this project to annotate and publish his entire work. The Sisters of Mercy of St. Louis and their wartime efforts on behalf of the sick and imprisoned, for example, are unknown to historians as are the careers of such chaplains as Fathers Innocent A. Bergrath, Paul E. Gillen, C.S.C., and Thomas Scully. Father Jeremiah Trecy, an Alabama resident at the start of the war, soon became the favorite of Catholic General William S. Rosecrans. Trecy's exploits are well chronicled by Conyngham and present a prime example of the larger manuscript's worth to historians. Letters from soldiers who had received excellent care from the Sisters of Mercy of Charleston and New York attest to the good work sister nurses did during the war in healing broken bodies and dispelling long-held prejudices toward Catholics and their faith.

The apologetic tone of Conyngham's work throughout, as well as its occasional anti-Protestant bias, reveals much about the state of the Church and its uneasy place in American society at the time. Although Conyngham portrays many examples of Protestants repenting of their anti-Catholic ways during the war, antipathy to the Church and its largely immigrant and Democratic membership remained strong, especially in the North, among many Protestants, Republicans, and nativists. They tended to remember anti-war Catholics' criticism of President Abraham Lincoln's wartime policies or Irish Catholic participation in the infamous New York City Draft Riots instead of their service in the Union Army. As a New Yorker, Conyngham would have been familiar with the anti-Irish, anti-Catholic cartoons regularly penned during Reconstruction in *Harper's Weekly* by famed Republican cartoonist Thomas Nast.[14] Thus Conyngham clearly was determined to portray the Church in the most positive light possible, and his great reverence for the chaplains and especially the sisters may strike modern readers as overly sentimental, too positive, and not sufficiently critical. Thus, both scholars and readers should approach Conyngham's text with the understanding that his work is part history, part hagiography.

Still, most Catholic scholars agree that the sister nurses and chaplains generally left behind a positive legacy.[15] Putting aside the many letters praising priests and sisters in this volume's introduction, there is even more evidence of Protestant contemporaries appreciating what these Catholic men and women did during the war. For example, General Benjamin F. Butler praised Catholic chaplains before a congressional committee in January 1862, stating that he had "never seen a Roman Catholic chaplain that did not do his duty. . . . They have always been faithful, so far as my experience goes." Similarly, Mary Livermore, an ardent pro-Union, anti-slavery member of the U.S. Sanitary Commission, praised the Sisters of the Holy Cross for "their devotion, faithfulness, and unobtrusiveness" in tending to patients in Union hospitals.[16] If Conyngham was prone to filiopietistic exaggeration, he nonetheless grounded his account in historical reality.

Conyngham compiled parts of *Soldiers of the Cross* from various newspapers, books, and other published sources dealing with Catholic chaplains and sisters during the war. For example, his chapter on Father Peter Paul Cooney, C.S.C., is taken largely from David Stevenson's *Indiana's Roll of Honor* (1864). In such cases, we have used indentation or other formatting changes to indicate Conyngham's use of previously published material. Still, much of the work is original, based on his conversations and correspondence with former chaplains and nurses and drawing upon unpublished primary sources. His chapters on another Holy Cross priest, Father Joseph Carrier, contain the only known excerpts of Carrier's diary from his service in General Ulysses S. Grant's army at Vicksburg, Mississippi. Likewise, letters of thanks from soldiers or their families to the Sisters of Mercy of New York, who served in hospitals on the North Carolina coast in 1862–1863, are invaluable sources unavailable elsewhere. The five chapters of the book dedicated to

Confederate Chaplain Father James Sheeran were based on a much larger diary written by the priest during the war. Had Conyngham published his book during his lifetime, these chapters would have been the first time this important diary had ever been made available to the larger public. Although a modern and scholarly edition of the entire diary was recently published, Conyngham's use of the diary is presented herein as he intended it to be published.[17] After all, the inclusion of Confederates like Sheeran was essential to Conyngham's argument that the Church had selfless heroes serving soldiers on both sides of the war.

Unfortunately, Conyngham died unexpectedly from pneumonia on April 1, 1883, while serving as the editor of the Catholic weekly *New York Tablet*. The manuscript then passed into the hands of his brother-in-law, Michael Kerwick, then living in Ireland. In 1897, Kerwick sent it to Father Daniel Hudson, C.S.C., the editor of *Ave Maria*, a journal published at the University of Notre Dame. Kerwick hoped that Hudson would help him edit and publish the work for sale in the United States. Little of Hudson's and Kerwick's correspondence exists, but it is clear the manuscript was not published and was simply archived among the growing collection of Catholic historical items at the university. It received no special attention until rediscovered by Father Thomas McAvoy, C.S.C., a historian and priest at Notre Dame who published important transcriptions of letters written by Father Peter Paul Cooney, C.S.C., a former Notre Dame priest and Civil War chaplain. McAvoy seems to have entertained publishing *Soldiers of the Cross* himself, for he wrote numerous letters to scholars and historical societies seeking more information about Conyngham's life. Along with a typescript of the manuscript prepared in the 1940s, the original work still resides at the University of Notre Dame Archives, seldom consulted beyond a handful of Catholic and Civil War scholars.[18]

STATE OF THE MANUSCRIPT AND EDITORIAL METHOD

Soldiers of the Cross, as it exists in manuscript form at the University of Notre Dame, is an early revised draft in Conyngham's hand and that of another, probably a secretary or aide with better handwriting.[19] The manuscript shows evidence of Conyngham or an aide having edited the work. Many spelling and grammatical mistakes remained uncorrected, however, and Conyngham was inconsistent in the way he spelled names, capitalized nouns, and abbreviated various places or military ranks. In addition, the table of contents and a few of the chapters, specifically those on the Sisters of the Holy Cross, still exist as multiple drafts.[20]

While it is difficult to tell when the draft was written, Conyngham clearly began his research by sending inquiries to Catholic authorities and famous Union and Confederate generals between 1868 and 1870. The title page does not include any of Conyngham's later works such as *O'Mahoney, Chief of the Comeraghs* (1879), *Rose Parnell, the Flower of Avondale* (1883), or *Ireland: Past and Present* (1883). Based on these omissions and the draft's initial descriptions of where various chaplains lived or worked after the war, the work appears to have been substantially drafted by 1873. Thereafter, the manuscript contains minor edits by Conyngham and a few other hands made between 1880 and 1882— just a year before Conyngham's untimely death. Most of these edits updated the status of chaplains after the war (to their new positions or whereabouts in the early 1880s), trimmed the narrative to make it shorter, or softened the tone of the writing, eliminating offensive speech and some of his (or his subjects') harsher criticisms of Protestants or soldiers on the other side of the war.

Unfortunately, some of the manuscript has been lost or frayed at the edges over the years, necessitating the use of the 1940s-era typescript of the manuscript to fill in the blanks. There are many errors in this typescript, which often left in large sections of text that Conyngham had deleted from the handwritten manuscript. The use of this later typescript has been carefully indicated with either square bracketed text or footnotes.

The manuscript has been presented as faithfully and with as little intervention as possible in order to let Conyngham and his writing style speak for itself. Like many writers of his time, he capitalized words like "Sister" or "Chaplain" that are generally lowercased today, quoted primary sources such as letters in their entirety, and used em dashes, commas, and semicolons liberally. Some of his sentences and passages, therefore, will appear stilted or as run-ons to readers. Our original goal was to alter the text only by including short introductory and concluding paragraphs to chapters and explanatory footnotes. Despite these intentions, however, there were many instances where corrections to punctuation and spelling were necessary to make the work more readable and useful to scholars and modern readers. There were numerous grammatical and spelling errors throughout, made by the original manuscript writers or later editors. Given the more polished nature of Conyngham's spelling and grammar in other works published during his life, it was decided to make silent changes to the manuscript when absolutely necessary. These changes included silently correcting slight misspellings, adding missing punctuation such as periods at the end of sentences or apostrophes in possessives, standardizing inconsistent capitalization, standardizing the way regiments and corps were named, expanding abbreviated military ranks and most place names to their full spelling, creating consistent and uniform chapter titles, and breaking up very long run-on sentences and paragraphs.

Occasionally, a phrase or word was restored when a deletion from the manuscript removed words necessary for the sentence's meaning. In these cases, or when there was a significant spelling error or a missing word was supplied to improve clarity, the intervention was noted with a footnote or square brackets. In choosing to honor Conyngham and his editors' revisions, text deleted from the manuscript was not included except in the cases noted above or when the text omitted was of potential use to scholars. Because the manuscript was an early draft, personal names were often represented in various spellings, and have been standardized whenever possible. For example, various spellings of Father Jeremiah Trecy's surname as Trecy, rather than Tracy or Tracey, were standardized since the name's spelling was not uniform throughout. Finally, a few words could not be deciphered. These are noted in square brackets with a question mark to indicate an indecipherable word and its most likely substitute. In some cases, illegibility or damage to the manuscript prevented us from making a guess, and such cases are indicated as [. . .].

Since *Soldiers of the Cross* is primarily a religious history of the war, minute details of battles or army movements described by Conyngham or his sources were not verified or corrected. If, however, there was a clear mistake such as dating the Battle of Gettysburg to 1862 instead of 1863, the error was corrected by inserting the correct word, name, or date in square brackets or in a footnote. Grammatical mistakes, unusual punctuation, and misspellings were usually left unaltered when they occurred in quotations, such as when Conyngham was attempting to represent the Irish brogue phonetically. Just as in his work on the Irish Brigade, Conyngham utilized distinctive Irish accents and diction to add moments of humor to his depictions of the horrific suffering and bloodshed of the Civil War.

While our primary focus and the bulk of our time as editors was spent on presenting a faithful transcription of Conyngham's manuscript, we have included additional, brief contextual information throughout our edited edition. In addition to short introductory and concluding paragraphs for each priest or female religious community, footnotes have been provided where appropriate to explain events and persons likely unfamiliar to general readers. Although every person mentioned in the text could not be positively identified, short biographical annotations for significant religious or military figures and those appearing more than twice in the text were added. In some cases, where information was sparse or the individual's rank, command, or position are explicitly stated in the text, we provide only a very short footnote with name and life dates. Conyngham generally identified officers, doctors, clergy, civilians, and others only by their surnames, and we have endeavored to provide first names and middle initials in square brackets where the individual first appears in the text. Sources utilized for identification included biographical reference works, studies of chaplains in the war, state and regimental histories, rosters of officers and soldiers, many local histories, clergy directories, an online database of Union surgeons, and digitized military records.[21] When employed for identification, the use of these sources was not ordinarily noted in the footnotes.

Discursive discussions about military history or the accuracy of battles or military maneuvers as represented by Conyngham or his sources are not included here. Rather, the work's primary usefulness is the window it provides into the unique and underexplored Catholic experience of the war. The introductions, source citations, and annotations are thus aimed at this end: to present a useful edited version of Conyngham's last great work that furthers the public's and historians' understanding of the important contributions of Catholic chaplains and sister nurses to the war effort on both sides of the Mason-Dixon line.

David J. Endres
William B. Kurtz

THE SOLDIERS OF THE CROSS

or

HEROISM OF THE CROSS

or

NUNS AND PRIESTS ON THE BATTLEFIELD

or

THE HEROISM OF THE CATHOLIC CHAPLAINS AND SISTERS IN THE AMERICAN WAR

BY

D. P. Conyngham L.L.D.

AUTHOR OF

"The O Donnell's of Glen Cottage," "Sherman's March through the South," "The Irish Brigade and its Campaigns," "Sarsfield, or the last great Struggle for Ireland," "Lives of the Irish Saints and Martyrs"

—

This work embraces a full account of the services rendered, both on the field and in the hospital, by the Catholic chaplains and sisters, in both the Federal and Confederate Armies during the late Civil War.

Contents

INTRODUCTION

The chaplains of the Federal and Confederate Armies [and the sisters]—
Testimony to their work and services by leading officers of both armies.

THE FEDERAL CHAPLAINS

CHAPTER I

REV. J. F. TRECY
Chaplain 4th U. S. Cavalry

His early life—Adventures among the Indians—The Garryowen settlement—
The Knights of the Golden Circle—Down in Dixie—His first adventures
with Federals and Confederates.

CHAPTER II

REV. J. F. TRECY, CONTINUED

Father Trecy's arrival at General Rosecrans's Headquarters—His reception
and mission—General Stanley's conversion—Father Ireland—Attending to
the dying and wounded—Stones River—Mass on the battle field—
The wounded Confederate.

CHAPTER III

REV. J. F. TRECY, CONTINUED

Father Trecy commissioned as chaplain in the regulars—The pious
penitent—Enjoying Morgan's breakfast—A large family—The Battle of

Chickamauga—His service under Sherman and Thomas—His resignation—
He returns to his old mission at Huntsville.

CHAPTER IV

REV. JOSEPH C. CARRIER, C.S.C.
Chaplain 6th Missouri Cavalry

The order of the Holy Cross—What it has done—Sketch of Father Carrier's
early life—He joins Grant's army in front of Vicksburg—His reception by
Generals Grant, Sherman, and Ewing—His visit to the camps and hospitals.

CHAPTER V

REV. JOSEPH C. CARRIER, C.S.C., CONTINUED

Few Catholics and a number of infidels in hospital—Pious soldiers saving
their temporary church from destruction—On board the Red Rover—His
reception and services there—Celebrating Mass under fire.

CHAPTER VI

REV. JOSEPH C. CARRIER, C.S.C., CONTINUED

Father Carrier visits a sick priest—His labors and services among the
soldiers—Moralizing over a dead soldier—The explosion of a mine—
A negroe's surprise—A surgeon brought to his senses—A fair Convert.

CHAPTER VII

REV. JOSEPH C. CARRIER, C.S.C., CONTINUED

Father Carrier's diary—Welcome intelligence—Surrender of Vicksburg—
His letter to his Father Provincial—Father Carrier and his "birdies"—
A fatiguing march—The conclusion.

CHAPTER VIII

REV. R. C. CHRISTY
Chaplain 78th Pennsylvania Volunteers

The chaplains entitled to their share of the glory of victory—Father
Gallitzin—Father Christy's early life and missionary labors as a priest—

*Selected chaplain of the 78th Pennsylvania—His services to the sick
and wounded in and around Louisville—His voyage in the dugout—
Sufferings at Stones River—The influence of the chaplains on Protestant
officers and soldiers—A feeling conversion—Complimentary notices—
An involuntary bath—He returns with his regiment and is mustered out
of service.*

C H A P T E R   I X

REV. THOMAS SCULLY

Chaplain 9th Massachusetts Veteran Volunteers

*A pen picture of Catholic persecution in Massachusetts—Grand attitude of
the Catholic Church and people of Massachusetts—Colonel Cass and the 9th
Massachusetts—Father Scully volunteers to be their chaplain—Father Scully's
birth, education, and ordination—At Arlington Heights—Governor Andrew's
visit—The chapel tent.*

C H A P T E R   X

REV. THOMAS SCULLY, CONTINUED

*Vespers and confession in camp—Burial of Sergeant Regan—Praying under
difficulties—Hearing the confessions of the men under fire—Services on the
Peninsula—His address to the "Home Guard"—His capture and escape—
A night in the swamps—A prisoner again—A brutal officer—Taken to
Richmond—His release and return to army life—Amusing incidents—
His failing health—He leaves the army and returns to Boston.*

C H A P T E R   X I

REV. PETER TISSOT, S.J.

Chaplain 37th New York Volunteers

*The application to Archbishop Hughes for a chaplain to the 37th—
Father Tissot appointed—His zeal in the service and obedience to orders—
His narrow escape at Fair Oaks—His capture—His duties in camp and
services in the field—Raising a new flag—Father Tissot's prayer and
address—His exertions to raise money to send to Ireland—How the soldiers
loved and reverenced him.*

C H A P T E R   X I I

REV. THOMAS WILLETT, S.J.
Chaplain 69th New York Volunteers

His reception by the officers and men—How he cheered the men on board the transport—Mass at Alexandria, Virginia—Solemnity of the scene—His raids against gambling, cursing, and drinking—Sending the soldiers' money home—Father Willett in the field—Preparing the men before battle—His services under Foster—A high compliment—He returns to the 69th again— His zeal and services—Leaves the army at the close of the war.

C H A P T E R   X I I I

REV. C. L. EGAN, O.P.
Chaplain 9th Massachusetts Volunteers

His mission to the army—Prepares men under sentence of death—He is appointed chaplain—His school of logic—He visits the 5th Corps and exhorts the men to attend to their duty—Father Egan at the Wilderness—The 9th suffered dreadful loss—The soldier priest at his post—Mustered out with the regiment.

C H A P T E R   X I V

REV. PAUL E. GILLEN, C.S.C.
Chaplain 170th New York Volunteers

He joins the army at the commencement of the war—His services in and around Washington—His services in the field—His attention to the sick and wounded—Mass in camp—The 42nd [New York] Tammany [Regiment]— The Corcoran Legion—Dr. Dwyer's sketches of Fathers Gillen, Dillon, and Mooney—Chaplain's life in camp—Heroic endurance and forbearance.

C H A P T E R   X V

REV. INNOCENT A. BERGRATH

Born in Prussia—His parents emigrate to America—His early career— His desire to go as a chaplain opposed by his bishop—His mission among the Federal and Confederate soldiers—He is cut off from communication with his bishop—The celebration of Mass in the little church of S.S. Peter and Paul in Chattanooga the morning of battle—His services given to Federals and Confederates alike.

CHAPTER XVI

REV. PETER P. COONEY, C.S.C.
Chaplain 35th Indiana Volunteers

*His birth and early education—His connection with Notre Dame, Indiana—
The order of the Holy Cross—He joins the 35th Indiana as chaplain—His
popularity with the troops—He saves a man from being shot—His mission of
mercy—Carrying funds for the soldiers under difficulties—A perilous trip to
Nashville—Irish wit and humor—The march—Its trials, dangers, and
hardships—Gallant charge of the 35th Indiana—Father Cooney's conduct
in the camps, the hospital, and the field.*

CHAPTER XVII

REV. THOMAS BRADY
Chaplain 15th Michigan Volunteers

*At the request of a deputation from the regiment he becomes their chaplain—
His services in the field night and day—A war of words—His services in
Vicksburg and Chattanooga—After the battle of Nashville his regiment pro-
ceeds to North Carolina—His regiment disbanded at the close of the war—
Father Brady's death from disease contracted in the service.*

CHAPTER XVIII

REV. WILLIAM CORBY, C.S.C.
Chaplain 88th New York Volunteers

*His connection with the Irish Brigade—A rustic chapel in the field—
The service—How faithfully the men attended to their spiritual duties—
The priests as the soldiers' banker and amanuensis—Father Corby at the
battle of Fredericksburg—The wounded chaplain—The officer's indignation
at finding Father Corby in the front of battle—His failing health—He resigns
and returns to his university in Indiana.*

THE CONFEDERATE CHAPLAINS

CHAPTER XIX

REV. LOUIS-HIPPOLYTE GACHE, S.J.
Chaplain 10th Louisiana Volunteers

*His services in and around Richmond—He attends the Federal prisoners—
At the desire of Bishop Odin he joins the army as chaplain of the 10th
Louisiana—He visits the camps on the Peninsula—His forbearance,
meekness, and kindness subdue his enemies—A grateful penitent—Father
Gache's account of scenes around Richmond—Interesting incidents and
anecdotes—A soldier anxious to be baptized in the "Sisters' religion"—His
account of the treatment of the Federal prisoners in Richmond and Lynchburg.*

CHAPTER XX

REV. CHARLES P. HEUZÉ

*His mission in Vicksburg—The account of the siege and of the suffering and
hardships accompanying it—The horrors at Vicksburg surpassing those at
Sebastapol—A shell among the worshippers at Mass—Heart rending scenes
in the field and hospitals—Sad picture of want and suffering.*

CHAPTER XXI

REV. JAMES SHEERAN, C.Ss.R.
Chaplain 14th Louisiana Volunteers

*His regiment joins Ewell's Corps—His reception—First appearances in
Virginia battles—Stonewall Jackson—A night scene on a battle field—
Jackson's marches—Sufferings and hardships of army life—Father Hubert—
At Manassas—The Second battle of Bull Run—Scenes and incidents in
Frederick City—How the Fathers of the Society of Jesus and the sisters
acted—The battle of Antietam and its horrors.*

CHAPTER XXII

REV. JAMES SHEERAN, C.Ss.R., CONTINUED

*Father Sheeran falls back with Lee's army—His visit to Richmond—
His return to the army—Gambling in the army—A surprise—His services in*

Winchester—En route to Fredericksburg—Caught in a snow storm—The battle of Fredericksburg—Scenes and sufferings in the field and hospital—A generous donation—A day of fasting and prayer—Easter days in camp—The piety of the poor soldiers—The slaughter pen of the Irish Brigade.

C H A P T E R   X X I I I

REV. JAMES SHEERAN, C.Ss.R., CONTINUED

Father Sheeran's account of Stonewall Jackson's death—The battle of Chancellorsville—Jackson's council adopted—The attack on Hooker's right—Jackson wounded—The terrible sufferings—His last orders on the field—"You must hold your ground, General Pender."—Jackson's last words—"Let us cross over the river and rest under the shade of the trees!"—His death.

C H A P T E R   X X I V

REV. JAMES SHEERAN, C.Ss.R., CONTINUED

Father Sheeran celebrates Mass in camp—March of the army—He takes charge of the hospitals around Winchester—Father Smulders—The march to Gettysburg—The battle—The retreat and its hardships—Father Sheeran goes to Mobile—He visits Bragg's army in Tennessee in order to attend to the Catholic soldiers there—His visit to Savannah sad Charleston—A terrible scene—Shells on all sides—He returns to the Army of Virginia.

C H A P T E R   X X V

REV. JAMES SHEERAN, C.Ss.R., CONTINUED

Father Sheeran's missionary labors continued—An important convert—An officious officer—The horrors of a battle field—A visit to the grave of Stonewall Jackson—The march toward Washington—Battle of Winchester—General Mulligan's death—Father Sheeran and Sheridan—His arrest and imprisonment—His release—He leaves the army and returns to Richmond and witnesses its surrender.

THE SISTERS

CHAPTER XXVI

THE SISTERS IN THE ARMY

*How their services were at first received—All prejudices soon disappeared—
True charity knows neither creed, station, or persons—The charity that
teaches us to love our neighbor as ourselves—What the sisters have done and
how gratefully their services have been appreciated.*

CHAPTER XXVII

THE SISTERS OF MERCY, CHARLESTON

*Their attendance on the Federal prisoners—Their best donors—Their
influence on the soldiers—Anecdotes and incidents in hospital—The sisters
provided with a general pass—Letters from Federal officers and soldiers—
Their generous testimony to their services and kindness—Protestants and
Catholics alike bear testimony in their behalf—Their Christian charity and
incessant labors.*

CHAPTER XXVIII

THE SISTERS OF MOUNT ST. VINCENT, CINCINNATI

*The sisters at Camp Dennison—Sister Sophia and her assistants—With the
Army of the Cumberland—Their services in Virginia—Their devotion and
attention to the Indiana soldiers—The sisters fired upon—Their return to
Cincinnati—They attend the wounded after Shiloh and Pittsburg Landing—
Honorable testimonials of service—The sisters not subject to general orders
issued to nurses &c.*

CHAPTER XXIX

MOUNT ST. VINCENT,
ST. JOSEPH'S MILITARY HOSPITAL,
CENTRAL PARK GROUNDS

*Resolution of Common Council—The services of Mother Jerome and the
Sisters of Charity accepted—Our sick and wounded soldiers—E. M. Stanton*

on the sisters' services—The chaplains of Mount St. Vincent—Dr. McGlynn's attention—Death and imposing obsequies of Sister M. Prudentia Bradley— The benefactors of the establishment—Thanksgiving day at the hospital— Feeling letters to the sisters—The fruits of the good sisters' labor—Mount St. Vincent of today.

CHAPTER XXX

THE SISTERS OF MERCY, ST. LOUIS

Their convent and school—The hospitals crowded with sick and wounded during the war—Prisoner and refugees—One priest baptized over five hundred prisoners—Liberality of the citizens—Instructing soldiers in the principles of religion—Soldiers asking to be baptized in the "sisters' religion"—How they supplied the soldiers with books—Physicians anxious to secure the services of the sisters—The soldiers' gratitude to the sisters— Their humility and obedience—An interesting patient.

CHAPTER XXXI

THE SISTERS OF MERCY, NEW YORK

The sisters of the Houston Street Convent in the hospitals—Their services in New Bern—Sufferings of the patients before the arrival of the sisters—Strong religious prejudices against them at first—The sisters after landing—Strange surmises as to who and what they were—Things soon changed—Touching instances of love and confidence—The grief of the patients and Negroes at the departure of the sisters.

CHAPTER XXXII

THE SISTERS OF MERCY, NEW YORK, CONTINUED

A Unitarian minister's tribute to the sisters—The life of Christ exemplified— Writing letters for the soldiers—What a dying man wanted—Prejudice and religion at variance—Anecdote of the battle of Gettysburg—How Paddy buried the chaplain—A soldier's faith—How Mackey lost his leg—The story of a dead soldier—A father's gratitude—A wife's thanks—The grief of a loved one for her betrothed.

CHAPTER XXXIII

THE SISTERS OF THE HOLY CROSS

Their response to the call of suffering humanity—Their devotion, their services, and their sacrifices—Governor Morton of Indiana gratefully accepts the offer of the sisters' services—The sisters under charge of Mother Mary Angela in care of the hospitals at Paducah—Their zeal not abated by their hardships—Scenes and sufferings in the hospitals—The sisters' trials and triumphs—How they conquered prejudice by meekness, charity, and good works—Touching incidents—Mother Angela at Mound City.

CHAPTER XXXIV

THE SISTERS OF THE HOLY CROSS, CONTINUED

Removing from the hospital—Gratitude to the sisters—Incidents and scenes—Fort Charles and the Mound City affair—The men in hospital going to kill Colonel Fry—The sisters interfere—Colonel Fry vindicated—Captain Kilty fully exonerates Colonel Fry from all blame relative to the firing on the men blown up with the Mound City—Close of the hospital labors of the Sisters of the Holy Cross.

Introduction

The chaplains of the Federal and Confederate Armies
[and the sisters]—Testimony to their work and
services by leading officers of both armies.

During the late war I had frequent opportunities of observing with what unflinching zeal, fortitude, and Christian charity the Catholic chaplains and sisters ministered both to the spiritual and temporal wants of the sick, the dying, and wounded soldiers. Whether on the battle field or in the hospital, their attention and services were freely given to all alike, regardless of their religion, their complexion, or their nationality. Few, who have passed through these trying times, but recollect the patient priest, who was always to be found in the front shriving the dying soldiers if a Catholic, or assisting and comforting him if a member of a Protestant denomination. Always at his post, always doing his duty regardless of hardship and danger, the Catholic chaplain soon came to be regarded with respect and veneration even by men brought up in the most straight-laced and exclusive Puritanism. The man who pours [balm][1] into the wounds of his fellow man, and who in his service ventures his life is sure to come [by] the respect and admiration of good and generous men, no matter what their religion, conviction, and opinions. It was [so] with the Catholic chaplains and nuns; and the highest tributes paid to their charitable services and unremitting zeal in the discharge of their duties have been rendered to them by Protestant writers, officers, and privates.

As for the sisters, their labors and services were only equaled by their meekness and charity; and no one who has spent weary weeks and months in a hospital, can forget the tender care and soothing influence of the quiet gentle sister who stood by his bed side, like an angel of mercy and light, ever ready to cool his aching brow, to moisten his parched lips, or to minister to him the prescribed medicine or nourishment. What sweet angelic influence they exercised over the patients is only known to those who have passed under their care. Many a soldier, with coarse words and jibes on his lips, soon became docile as a child, and modest in his language, through the sweet example and gentle influence of the sisters.

Knowing and seeing all this, I resolved, at the close of the war, to set about collecting the necessary materials to add to the history of the great American contest, the record of these Soldiers of the Cross, both in the Federal and Confederate armies. I do this not with any intention of disparaging the labors and services of the chaplains of other denominations, for there were many noble self-sacrificing Christian men and zealous workers among them; but in order that the odor of sanctity and good works might descend to posterity to stimulate others to take up their cross and follow in the footsteps of their Divine master.

When I had made some progress in collecting materials, I communicated with the late learned and truly pious archbishop of Baltimore, the most Reverend Dr. [Martin J.] Spalding,[2] and laid my project before him. He thoroughly approved of it as appears from the following letter.

Baltimore, November 5th 1868

D. P. Conyngham, Esq.

Dear sir,

I applaud your effort to rescue from oblivion the glorious deeds of our sisters and chaplains in the late war. I will do whatever I can to aid you by speaking to those who are likely to know most, and by writing the preface as you desire. Do not be too much in a hurry; gather your facts carefully and be sure of them before you write. I would advise you to write to Mother Euphemia [Blenkinsop], Sisters of Charity, Emmitsburg, and to the

Revd. [Angelo] Paresce S.J., Provincial, Baltimore, as well as to
Revd. Father [Joseph] Wissel, St. Alphonsus Church, Baltimore,
requesting facts.

You may use my name as reference.

Yours truly

M. J. Spalding
Archbishop

The mission to Rome as a member of the Oecumenical council,
and the subsequent illness and death of this Christian bishop and
learned divine, deprived me of the advantages of his great influence
and support.[3]

A very serious difficulty that lay in my way arose from the fact that,
as soon as the war was over, the Catholic chaplains returned to their
various missions, some to die by disease contracted from the hardships,
exposure, and privations of army life; others to be scattered on their
missionary labors throughout different countries. As a consequence, it
was no easy task to get facts or materials directly relating to them.

Believing that true Christian charity knows no sectarianism, religious or political, and that the Catholic chaplain was the Soldier of
the Cross, and not of the sword, I was also anxious to procure sketches
of the chaplains and sisters serving with the Confederate as well as
with the Federal armies. If in some cases the partiality of the chaplains
for the success of the army with which they were serving appears, we
must not forget that we are all more or less influenced by surrounding
circumstances and associations, and that the chaplain with the Federal
army was just as ready to minister to a Confederate soldier as to one of
his own, and *vice versa.*

It is a well-known fact that many of our officers and men in Confederate hospitals and prisons owed their lives to the care, the attention,
and devotion of the sisters, a fact that is confirmed by the statements
and letters published in this work, many of which have been furnished
by Protestants. The sisters of the different orders, with the meekness
and modesty of true charity, shrunk from bringing their humble labors
before the public gaze, and many of them refused to furnish sketches
or materials, so that I had to rely on other sources for the information.

In reply to a personal application for materials the superioress of one house said, "I am sorry, sir, we cannot help you but whatever we have done, we have done for the love and glory of God, and we neither seek nor desire earthly praise or glory. If God is satisfied with our humble services and labors, we are content, and shall calmly and hopefully await His reward. If, on the other hand, we have not pleased Him it will profit us nothing to gain the praise and admiration of mortals. We have labored for the salvation of souls, and the good of our fellow creatures, not for worldly praise or distinction, we, therefore expect to reap our reward only in Heaven."

The superioress of another house, writing, says: "During the war the constant occupation of the sisters with the sick and dying left them scarcely time to attend to their necessary exercises, consequently they had none to devote to the recording of deeds of charity they ever esteemed themselves privileged to perform."

I did not despair, but went to work with the more zeal and vigor, and finally succeeded in collecting sufficient materials for very interesting sketches of the devoted and self-sacrificing sisters and their services to the sick and wounded in hospital.

The following were the most prominent of the Catholic chaplains who served with the Federal armies; namely: Rev. Father J. F. Trecy, chaplain of the 4th U.S. Cavalry, and private chaplain to General Rosecrans. Father Trecy is now pastor at Bayou la Batre,[4] Alabama. The record of his services and checkered career as a missionary priest, is full of stirring and interesting incidents.

The Congregation of Holy Cross supplied to the army the following able and energetic chaplains: Revd. William Corby, C.S.C., now at Notre Dame, Indiana;[5] Rev. Joseph C. Carrier, C.S.C., professor at St. Laurents College, Montreal;[6] Rev. Paul E. Gillen, C.S.C., deceased;[7] Rev. Peter P. Cooney, C.S.C., now in Waterton, Wisconsin;[8] Rev. James M. Dillon, C.S.C., deceased, and the Revd. Julian Bourget, C.S.C., also deceased.[9]

The Revd. R. C. Christy, chaplain to the 78th Pennsylvania, is now pastor at Freeport, Pennsylvania; the Rev. Father Willett, S.J., [is] now in St. John's [New Brunswick, Canada].

Rev. Father [Peter] Tissot, S.J., chaplain of the 42nd [New York Infantry], [10] Tammany Regiment, deceased.[11]

The Rev. Michael Nash, S.J., chaplain to Wilson's Zouaves,[12] now in Troy, New York.[13] The Rev. [Francis] McAtee, S.J.,[14] and the Rev. Father [Constantine L.] Egan and several other missionary priests, who served as chaplains, are scattered over the country. The Revd. Thomas Scully, chaplain to the 9th Massachusetts, is at present pastor of Cambridgeport, Massachusetts. Father [Thomas] Brady, chaplain to the 15th Michigan Vol., died soon after the close of the war; as also Father Brown.[15] Father [William T.] O'Higgins of the 10th Ohio, returned to Ireland whilst others were sent by their bishops and superiors on different missions throughout the world.[16]

These are a few of the soldiers whose mission was not that of hate and strife but of peace and good will among mankind. Besides these, several clergymen, who were not attached as paid chaplains to the army, rendered invaluable services to the sick and wounded in the hospitals in Washington and elsewhere.

As far as I have been able to ascertain, the following reverend gentlemen were the regularly appointed Catholic chaplains with the Confederate armies.

Rev. Darius Hubert, S.J., was appointed in April 1861, chaplain to the 1st Louisiana Regiment, and served with the army in Virginia to the close of the war.

Rev. E[gidius] Smulders,[17] of the Redemptorist Order was chaplain of the 8th Louisiana and served with it until the end of the war. Father H[ippolyte] Gache, S.J., served as chaplain to the 10th Louisiana partly in the field and partly in hospital, to the close of the war. The sketch of his services is very full and interesting. Revd. James Sheeran, of the Redemptorist Order, served as chaplain to the 14th Louisiana to the end of the war. The sketch of his services is varied and interesting embracing, as it does, the campaigns of Stonewall Jackson and a full and accurate account of the manner in which that Confederate leader came by his death. Revd. Joseph Prachenski, S.J., was chaplain to an Alabama regiment.[18]

Revd. Dr. John Teeling of Richmond served as chaplain to the 1st Virginia.

Revd. A[ndrew] Cornette was for some time with the troops in Mobile, Alabama.[19]

Rev. C[harles] Boglioli, now of New Orleans, Louisiana, though not regularly appointed, followed, as chaplain, the Donaldsonville Battery.[20] Rev. F. X. Leray,[21] now coadjutor bishop of New Orleans, attended the troops in Vicksburg during the siege.

The Revd. Father [Anthony] Carius served for some time with the troops in Tennessee.[22]

The following chaplains with the Confederate armies, have since died.

Revd. Isidore Turgis, whose fearless and gallant services at Shiloh, earned for him the esteem of all, died at New Orleans in March, 1868.[23]

The Revd. Father [Emmeran] Bliemel was killed at the battle of Jonesboro, Georgia, while ministering to a dying soldier.[24] The Rev. Francis Nachon,[25] S.J., chaplain to the soldiers in the fort on the Mississippi and in Washington, Louisiana, died in 1867.

The Revd. Dr. [Anthony] [de] Chaignon died in 1867; he served with a Louisiana regiment at Corinth.[26]

In addition to these regularly appointed chaplains, the local clergy were assiduous in their attentions to the wants, spiritual and temporal, of the soldiers in and around the cities of Charleston, Savannah, New Orleans, Richmond, and elsewhere; and to their credit be it said, that the Federal prisoners and sick soldiers found them and the sisters their kindest and best friends.

It would take volumes to give ample details of the zeal and self-sacrificing devotion of the chaplains and sisters in both armies during the war.

On this account, and believing that the work should not extend beyond one volume, I confine myself to those presenting the most interesting features and the most attractive points.[27]

In order to lay before my readers the views and opinion of the generals and medical gentlemen under whose eyes the chaplains and sisters officiated, I wrote to many of the most prominent of them requesting their impartial and candid opinions, relative to the services rendered during the war by the Catholic chaplains and sisters. In reply I received many encouraging letters speaking of the good done by them in the most laudatory terms.

As these letters speak for themselves, I here give the most prominent of them.

Hoboken, [New Jersey], October 26th, [18]69

Maj. D. P. Conyngham

My Dear Sir,

I cordially approve of your intention to publish a work on the services of the Catholic chaplains and sisters with the army during the recent war. My attention was very frequently drawn to their disinterested and most valuable efforts in the cause of humanity, and I think that it is eminently proper that a prominent record should be made of their efforts.

Very truly yours,

George B. McClellan[28]

❀   ❀   ❀

New York, May 28th, 1870

My Dear Sir,

Unusual press of business affairs for the past two months have prevented my earlier attention to your letter requesting my views as to the work of the Catholic clergy and sisters in the army during the late war.

As far as my observations extended, the Catholic clergy engaged in army work were eminently distinguished for the self-sacrificing and zealous manner in which they performed their duties.

They spared no pains and shrank from no exposure or hardships in their labor for the relief of the sick and wounded.

Wherever there is sympathy for suffering, there will be gratitude for the self-sacrificing labors of these devoted men.

Of the Sisters of Mercy there is little need for me to speak. Their good deeds are written in the grateful hearts of thousands of our soldiers, to whom they were ministering angels. I heartily approve of your design to put these benefactors upon record. It is due to those engaged therein, and cannot fail to inspire others to like deeds of love and mercy.

Very truly yours,

A. E. Burnside[29]
Late Major General

❀   ❀   ❀

To Major D. P. Conyngham

New York, June 16th

D. P. Conyngham, Esq.

My Dear sir,

I heartily approve of your intention of writing a work on the Catholic chaplains and sisters, and their services, in our army during the late civil war. As to my personal experience I must say that I always found the Catholic chaplain faithful, attentive, and zealous in the discharge of his duties. His mission seemed to be to devote himself solely to the spiritual and temporal wants of the soldiers.

In camp, by his pious example and religious teachings, he greatly softened and Christianized the tone and actions of the men; while, in the field, he was ever found, regardless of danger, where his duty called him and where the wounded or dying soldiers needed his ministrations.

Personally I have had but little acquaintance with the labors and good works of the sisters, as they were mostly confined to hospital duties, but on all sides, and by persons of various religious denominations I have heard them spoken of in terms of praise and respect.

Truly yours,

Joseph E. Hooker[30]
Late Major General

❀   ❀   ❀

Headquarters Military Division of the Atlantic
Philadelphia, January 24th, 1870
Dear Sir,
My position as commanding general of the army of the Potomac, did not afford me the opportunity for personal knowledge by intercourse with regimental chaplains so that though I
know that the chaplains of the Catholic Church did good service,
and are deserving of all commendation, my memory does not
enable me to speak of individuals.

I have no doubt if the names and services of some of them
were recalled to my mind I could say more than I can of them
personally. All I can say of them is in general terms and to the effect that they faithfully discharged their duties to the credit of
their church and the service.
Respectfully yours,

George [G.] Meade[31]
Major General

❀   ❀   ❀

New York, November 5th, 1868
D. P. Conyngham, Esq.
Sir,
Your letter of the 25th ult. received today; I always expected
from the Catholic chaplains and sisters works stamped with the
impress of that Divine Charity which has God for its author and
final end and do not remember an instance in which I felt
disappointed.

If you wish to compare the fruits of various kinds of charity,
displayed during the late war, I think considerable contrast may
be found between those which spring from natural and those
which spring from supernatural motives. Those of the clergy

were marked but less conspicuous, owing to their religious training and retiring modesty.

I shall not be able to give you details for the work you propose. I also think it would be the best thing, when you do charity, do it secretly if possible, for such is the maxim of our religion.

Yours respectfully,

W. S. Rosecrans[32]

❀   ❀   ❀

Headquarters military Division of the Missouri
Chicago, Illinois, January 29th, 1870

D. P. Conyngham, Esq.
Dear Sir,

In reply to your note of the 22nd inst. in regard to my opinion as to the efficiency of the Catholic chaplains and sisters in the army during the late war, I beg to state that so far as my experience is concerned they were both active and efficient in their several callings, and rendered good services both in the field and in the hospital.

Respectfully etc. etc.,

P. H. Sheridan[33]
Major General

❀   ❀   ❀

Headquarters Department of the East
New York City, February 25th, 1870

D. P. Conyngham
My Dear Sir,

I beg your pardon for delaying so long in answer to your note of the 23rd ultimo. It was received during my absence and was overlooked after my return.

I did not chance personally to be brought into contact with the chaplains and can only of my own knowledge speak in a general way as to the services of the sisters. The latter I met in the course of my visits to the hospitals, where I found them as they are ever all over the world, ministering to the sick and wounded in a way to command the respect gratitude and affection of all who saw them, or had the benefit of their pious services. I am respectfully, etc. etc.

Irvin McDowell[34]
Major General
Comdg Depart.

❀   ❀   ❀

Hd. Qrs. Dept. of Dakota
St. Paul, Minnesota, February 3rd, 1870

D. P. Conyngham, Esq.
My dear sir,

I have received your letter of the 23rd ultimo informing me, that with those of other Generals, you were desirous of getting for publication my views as to the services of the Catholic chaplains and sisters during the late war.

Having the good fortune during the war to have in my command the "Irish Brigade" and the "Corcoran Legion" as well as other bodies of troops having chaplains who were Catholics, I had favorable opportunities of observing the manner in which the chaplains performed their duties and I can safely and with pleasure assert that none were more useful or could have been more devoted to their duties under all circumstances of the service—in the camp, in the conflict, or in presence of the enemy.

They had too the respect of the troops, without regard to their religious views, from the general highest in command down to the drummer boy. The sisters of the Catholic Church

did not I believe at any time in the field, come under my observations.

I am very respectfully etc. etc.,

[Winfield Scott] Hancock[35]
Major General

❁   ❁   ❁

St. Louis, Missouri, January 31st, 1870

Dear sir,

In reply to your letter of 23rd inst. it affords me great pleasure
to say that from my own observation and the unanimous testimony of all whom I have heard speak on the subject, I regard the
conduct of the Catholic Sisters associated with the army during
the late war as one of the highest and noblest exemplifications of
the Christian religion, of which we have any knowledge in our
age of the church. The missionaries among the heathens give us,
perhaps, the only higher example of practical Christianity.

It was not my fortune to be thrown much in contact with
Catholic chaplains, but their individual reputation was, so far as I
know, that of faithful devotion to their duty.

Yours truly,

J. M. Schofield[36]
Major General

❁   ❁   ❁

Hd. qrs. Artillery School U.S.A.
Fortress Monroe, Virginia, January 25th, 1870

Major D. P. Conyngham
My dear sir,

I have the pleasure to acknowledge the receipt of your note
of 23rd inst.

It would afford me sincere gratification to comply with your
request, but strange to say, the beneficent labors of the clergy and

sisters of the Church of Rome—which I have so often heard spoken of as being so faithfully bestowed in the army during the war of the Rebellion—never chanced to fall under my personal observation.

That they were unremitting and self-sacrificing must of course to be true, for the concurrent testimony in that direction is very strong.

I am dear sir etc. etc.,

William F. Barry[37]
Col. 2nd Regiment Artillery
Brevet Major General U.S.A.

❀   ❀   ❀

Washington, D.C., February 11th, 1870

D. P. Conyngham
My dear sir,

I have the pleasure this morning of receiving your note of January 23rd.

During the rebellion my duties did not throw me so much with the troops as to become familiar with the services rendered by the Roman Catholic priests but I have heard them spoken of in the highest terms of praise by all. In St. Louis I watched a hospital containing many of our sick soldiers. The sisters there were assiduous in their attentions and careful to relieve the necessities of our sick soldiers.

At New Orleans also I know that the sisters were ever ready to extend the hand of sympathy and words of comfort and consolation to our suffering soldiers. This is their record on all sides.

Respectfully yours etc. etc.,

L. Thomas[38]
Brvt. Major General
U.S.A.

❀   ❀   ❀

Army Building New York
January 27th, 1870

D. P. Conyngham, Esq.
Dear sir,

I am in receipt of yours of the 23rd inst. informing me that you are preparing a work on the Catholic chaplains and sisters in the army during the late war and asking my views regarding their efficiency.

My duties during the late war were of a character to bring me but seldom in contact with the labors of the chaplains and sisters, but so far as my personal knowledge goes it fully sustains the reports constantly made to me of their valuable services, and of their zeal and self-denial, and the comfort which their services so largely conferred on the sick and the wounded.

I am glad that you are preparing a work upon a subject of so much interest, not only to the thousands who were benefited by their labors, but to the public at large.

Very respectfully etc.,

H. G. Wright[39]
Brevt. Major General U.S.A.

❊   ❊   ❊

Hd. qrs. Dept. of the Platte
Omaha, Nebraska, January 26th, 1870

My dear sir,

I have the honor to acknowledge the receipt of your note of the 23rd inst. desiring my opinion of the efficiency and services of the Catholic chaplains and sisters during the late war.

It was not my good fortune to be brought into close relations with the Catholic chaplains, or to have any personal knowledge of their services or their work. But I heard constantly of the latter, and always in terms of the highest praise and commendation. But this is no more than is and has always been said of that band of devoted and self-denying women.

Your book cannot fail to be interesting and will be welcomed as an act of justice to a class who does not blazon their own deeds or tell their right hand the doings of their left.

I am very respectfully etc.,

C. C. Augur[40]
Brev. Major General

❀   ❀   ❀

What nobler compliments were ever paid to duty and Christian charity than they convey? Here are men of the highest standing and unimpeachable honor, differing in religious opinions and connections from the Catholic chaplains and sisters; yet paying the fullest tribute to the zeal and purity and self-sacrificing devotion of our noble band of Soldiers of the Cross.

These letters are a history in themselves and do honor, not only to the subjects of their just need of praise, but also to the tolerant and generous spirit of the writers. To these we might add General Ben Butler's[41] testimony; when giving evidence on the conduct of the war he said that the Catholic chaplains were the only real chaplains in the army.

If the generals of the Federal armies fully appreciated the good offices and services of the Catholic chaplains and sisters, they were equally respected and honored in the Confederate Army. As a proof of the high estimation in which they were held by the Confederate leaders as well as by the rank and file, I give the following letters.

One is from General Robert E. Lee, a man whose bravery and military knowledge and genius, commanded the respect and admiration even of those who fought against him. The other is from General Beauregard, one of the ablest engineers and strategists whom the late war has produced.

Lexington, Virginia, 8th February, 1870

D. P. Conyngham, Esq.
Dear Sir,

In reply to your letter of the 22nd ult. it gives me great pleasure to state that the Catholic chaplains in the army of Northern

Virginia, so far as my knowledge extends, were kind and attentive to the temporal and spiritual wants of the men of their brigades, and were assiduous in their attentions in encouraging the well and comforting the sick of the army. There were three regular chaplains attached to General [Leroy A.] Stafford's and [Harry T.] Hay[s]'s Louisiana Brigades,[42] namely Father[s] Sheeran, Hubert, and Smulders. Other Catholic clergymen occasionally visited the army, conspicuous among whom were Bishop Gill[43] of Richmond.

The Catholic sisters in Richmond devoted themselves to the sick and wounded in the hospitals and I was told were unremitting in their attentions to the soldiers generally.

Respectfully yours,

R. E. Lee[44]

❀   ❀   ❀

New Orleans, March 25th, 1870

Dear sir,

Your favor of the 22nd ult. has been received but not answered sooner, in the hope of being able to obtain positive information as to the services rendered on the Confederate side, by the Catholic chaplains and Sisters of Charity in the field and hospitals during the late war. I regret that I can only transmit you herewith the names of the chaplains who served with Louisiana regiments; those of the sisters who attended Confederate State Hospitals, cannot now be obtained by me.

The services of both chaplains and sisters, were most devoted and invaluable during the most trying periods of the war; their efforts to alleviate the sufferings of the wounded and sick (Federals as well Confederates) were indefatigable and unremitting. Even Protestant commanding officers were always happy to avail themselves, in our hospitals, of the self-sacrificing, untiring and generous assistance of the "sisters" who were so kind and devoted to the poor, helpless, sick, and wounded soldiers placed under their care, that these heroes of many hard fought battles, looked upon them as their own sisters or mothers.

I sincerely hope that you may succeed in collecting all the facts necessary to enable you to carry out your praiseworthy design.

I remain yours truly,

P. G. T. Beauregard[45]

    ⚘   ⚘   ⚘

As an evidence of the Christian feeling and tolerant spirit that inspired the chaplains of various denominations in the army, I give the following letter from the Revd. Geo[rge] W. Pepper, a clergyman of the Methodist Episcopal Church, and a chaplain of the regular army, who was all through the war, and who, for his zeal, his devotion, and purity of life and actions, commanded the respect and esteem of men of all classes and denominations.

Wellington, Loraine Co., Ohio
October 20th, 1869

Major D. P. Conyngham
My dear Major,

I am glad that you are preparing a volume on the Roman Catholic chaplains and Sisters of Charity. The task is a worthy and noble one. I was well and intimately acquainted with many Catholic chaplains, and truly express the sentiments of thousands of my own faith, when I say, that, a more unselfish, more devoted, and a more courageous set of men never served in any army. In battle, they splendidly defied the bullets of the enemy and were always present in the front among the bravest of the brave.

I have beautiful memories of the Revd. Fathers Trecy, Cooney, and also of the brave Chaplain Brady of the fifteenth Michigan; my estimate of these stainless men of God, you will find in my volume entitled "Recollections of Sherman's Campaign."

The last time I saw these gifted and gallant priests, was at the battles of Atlanta, with the chivalrous [General David S.] Stanley, where they displayed rare heroism and patriotism. I earnestly hope that you will meet with encouragement and sympathy in your praiseworthy enterprise.

Truly and sincerely,

Geo W. Pepper[46]
Chaplain U.S.A.

❀   ❀   ❀

The Revd. Mr. Pepper paid worthy tribute to the Sisters of Charity, in an address delivered during the war, and published in the *Catholic Telegraph*, from which I take the following extract.

The war has brought out one fine result, it has shown that numbers of the weaker sex, though born to wealth and luxury, are ready to renounce every comfort and brave every hardship, that they may minister to the suffering, tend the wounded in their agony, and soothe the last struggles of the dying. Scores of these devoted ladies—Sisters of Charity—are consecrating themselves, heart and soul, spending and being spent, in the service of God and of humanity. If we look at the army of the Potomac, at the army of the Tennessee, we find these angels of piety diffusing gladness and joy in every hospital. Follow them where you will, and you track them not as you track war's conquerors by cities laid in ruins, and plains whitened with the bones of the slaughtered; but you track them by their deeds and monuments of love, peace, and good will toward men. God bless the Sisters of Charity in their heroic mission! I had almost said their heroic martyrdom! And I might have said it, for I do think that in walking those long lines of sick beds, in giving themselves to all the ghastly duties of the hospitals, they are doing a harder thing than was allotted to many who mounted the scaffold or dared the stake.

Though the introduction to this work has extended much longer than I intended, the letters and matter are too interesting to be in any way curtailed.

I will conclude with the following letters from two medical directors of the army and then[47] proceed with my work. Dr. Hammond stands so high in his profession, and had such opportunities of judging of the efficiency of the chaplains and sisters while Surgeon General of the Army, that his views are of the utmost importance. In reply to my letter he writes,

New York, February 27th, 1870

Dear Sir,

My experience with the nurses and chaplains of Catholic faith, who served during the war, was in the highest degree favorable to their skill, devotion, and faithfulness.

No one had better opportunities of judging than myself, for I inspected nearly all the hospitals, and admired the gentle influence and tender care exercised over the sick and wounded soldiers by the sisters. I can therefore speak in the most unqualified manner of the good they have done.

I understand that in order to meet the demand for their services in the army that Archbishop [John] Hughes[48] had to get a supply from Canada.

I should like to write more fully on this subject but my time is so occupied at present that I cannot say all on the subject I would wish in order to do justice to these noble and truly Christian women.

Yours truly,

William Hammond[49]

❀   ❀   ❀

The following letter from Dr. [Samuel De] Camp[50] shows how the sisters were appreciated by the medical faculty out West.

Saratoga Springs, October 26th, 1870

D. P. Conyngham, Esq.

Dear sir,

I received your letter here desiring information respecting the services of the Sisters of Charity to the sick soldiers of the United States Army, during the late civil war.[51] Feeling disposed to comply as far as I can with your request I give you a brief sketch of matters which came under my own observation while I was medical director in the city of St. Louis.

Soon after Major General J[ohn] C. Fremont assumed command of the army of the West, he wrote me a note saying that fourteen Sisters of Charity had kindly offered their services as nurses in the hospital and expressed a wish that I would receive them and assign them to duty. My office was in the city, but the hospital was four miles distant. The sisters being ignorant of military rules and being also unacquainted with me, went direct to the hospital and presented General Fremont's note which was intended for me, to the surgeon in charge. By some strange error, the surgeon instead of directing these ladies to me, took it upon himself to say to them that he had no occasion for their services, as he was supplied with nurses.

The sisters returned to General Fremont and reported what I have stated.

As was natural the general was disappointed and vexed that his polite request had been so little appreciated, and that the services of such valuable nurses had been lost to the government. He visited the hospital at once, and in no pleasant state of mind, opened the eyes of the offending surgeon to the error he had committed. The surgeon without delay came to me, and gave me the facts. [I]n a military point of view, the surgeon's offense was one of grave import.

He being a valuable man to the service, I determined to see General Fremont at once and secure the services of the sisters in the hospital. I satisfactorily arranged the whole matter and then proceeded to the [. . .][52] where I wrote out and issued the following order.

General Hospital, House of Refuge

August 23rd, 1861

Order No. 1

With the view of carrying out the wishes of Major General Fremont, as expressed in his letter to me, dated August 21st in which I am informed that the Sisters of Charity have offered to nurse the sick and wounded in the general hospital: I herewith direct the Senior Medical officer in charge to see that they are treated kindly and respectfully, and that every facility be afforded them for the performance of their official duties, and for their personal comfort. The sisters will be distributed among the sick, by the sister who is principal among them.

The surgeon in charge will give them such a number of male attendants as they may require.

(signed) S. G. [J].[53] De Camp

Medical Director

U. S. Army of the West

The sisters took entire charge of the sick soldiers and the surgeon in charge often times told me that *one of the sisters was worth more to the sick than all the former attendants put together.*[54]

From this [time] forward I had frequent opportunities of judging of their efficiency and services and I must say that they did more, by their kindness, their gentleness, and cheerful devoted attention to restore the sick and wounded to convalescence than all the medicine administered to them.

The influence of kind, cheerful nurses on the sick can only be fully appreciated by the patients themselves, and their medical attendants.

As a proof of the influence, the truly Christian charity, and faithful services of these good ladies had on me *I have since become a member of the Holy Roman Catholic Church* as also my little daughter. In all gratitude I say that next to God, I owe this conversion to Sister Florence and her thirteen associates.

S. G. [J]. De Camp

❀   ❀   ❀

The author of this work is greatly indebted to several Catholic clergy-men, officers, and private citizens for materials, notes, and sketches.

Among the number he would gratefully mention the names of Dr. [John] Dwyer,[55] Dr. Charles B. Gillespie, Freeport, Pennsylvania,[56] Dr. William O'Meagher, Harlem;[57] Colonel James E. McGee, New York;[58] and Captain M[ichael] H. MacNamara,[59] Boston. In conclusion the writer would state that though the terms "Yank" and "Rebs" frequently occur, that they are not intended in an offensive sense, but merely as colloquial phrases.

The Author

THE FEDERAL CHAPLAINS

CHAPTER I

Rev. J. F. Trecy

Chaplain 4th U.S. Cavalry

---

*His early life—Adventures among the Indians—
The Garryowen settlement—The Knights of the Golden
Circle—Down in Dixie—His first adventures with
Federals and Confederates.*

INTRODUCTION: Father Jeremiah F. Trecy[1] (1822–1888) became pastor of St. Mary of the Visitation Catholic Church in Huntsville, Alabama, as the war began. Born in Drogheda, County Louth, Ireland, he immigrated with his parents and two siblings in 1836. His family settled in Lancaster, Pennsylvania, and afterwards he began studies for the priesthood at Mount St. Mary's Seminary in Emmitsburg, Maryland. He was recruited to serve as a missionary in the West and was ordained in 1851 for service in the diocese of Dubuque, Iowa.

Father Trecy was very interested in the prospect of westward expansion and Catholic colonization. He ministered to a Catholic settlement near Dubuque named Garryowen before enticing some of his parishioners in 1856 to leave with him to found a colony at present-day Jackson, Dakota County, Nebraska, named "St. John's City."

Ostensibly to help him recover his health, Father Trecy sought to move to the South. He arrived in the Diocese of Mobile,

Alabama, in 1861 and was assigned to the Catholic community at Huntsville. During the Federal occupation of Huntsville, the city's public buildings were transformed into hospitals and Trecy ministered to the sick and wounded on both
sides of the conflict, prompting concern from each side that he
was aiding the other. Attracting the attention of two Catholic
converts, Union Generals William S. Rosecrans and David S.
Stanley, Trecy was invited—some say coerced—to serve as a
chaplain for the Federals. After serving in an unofficial capacity
for months, Trecy was appointed the 4th U.S. Cavalry's chaplain on April 17, 1863. Conyngham relates Father Trecy's perilous crossings over enemy lines, his near-death experiences
ministering to soldiers during battle, and the humorous mis-
apprehensions regarding his identity as a priest. While Conyngham clearly relied on the *Annals of the Army of the Cumberland* in writing his account, his frequent quotations of
Trecy's personal military passes and other detailed knowledge
of the priest's activities indicate he personally interviewed
Trecy as well.

Rev. J. F. Trecy, was born in Ireland in the year 1825, and came with his
parents to the United States in 1836.[2] His father, who settled in Pennsylvania, had his son educated for the ministry, and in 1851, the young
man was ordained at Dubuque, Iowa, where he remained some time
on the mission. As the organizer of the "Garryowen" Settlement, twenty
miles back of Dubuque, Father Trecy[3] labored during a period of four
years, drew around him a congregation, and built a nice stone church.
This little Irish colony came by its name in the following manner. A
meeting was held for the purpose of christening the settlement, but as
everyone present wanted it called after his native place, there seemed
little chance of an agreement, until a Limerick man called out why in
the name of St. Patrick don't ye call it "Garryowen"? The compromise
was at once adopted and the colony was called after this celebrated sub-
urb of Limerick.

In 1854, Father Trecy was sent by Bishop [Mathias] Loras[4] to the country along the line between Iowa and Nebraska, where he labored for four years and established several congregations and colonies. While in this section of the country he made repeated visits to the military posts of Fort Randall, Fort Pierre, Fort Kearney, and Fort Leavenworth, and to several of the Indian tribes, amongst whom he became a great favorite.

His health being greatly affected by his labors and exposure in the rigorous climate of the Northwest, Father Trecy at his own request was ordered to the South in 1859. The winter previous to his departure the Yankton[5] and other Indian tribes, located near the Missouri, sent delegates to the father requesting him to look after their annuities of which they were shamefully defrauded by government agents. He charitably took the matter in hand, and was kept running from one official to another for nearly three months, until he found that he could offer no good, as the whole affair was controlled by men whose avarice exceeded their sense of justice or mercy.

Whilst in Washington, on this Indian business, he made numerous acquaintances, among them many members of the "Knights of the Golden Circle" and the "Knights of Malta."

Being a shrewd observer and seeing that some secret movement was on foot he went to work to find out their object, but with all his labor and ingenuity he could only derive the information that their aim was an intended movement on Cuba or South America. Fortifying himself with numerous letters of introduction he left Washington for the South. On his route he visited the principal cities in Virginia, North Carolina, South Carolina, Georgia, Florida, Alabama, and Louisiana and then started up the Mississippi as far as St. Louis. Everywhere he found the same veiled movement as in Washington, everywhere the "Knights of the Golden Circle," and the "Knights of Malta" were ready to move when called on. He made a brief sojourn in St. Louis and then went north into the Indian Country. After a short stay among the red men he made up his mind to return to the South where he intended to make his future home.

As we are now about to follow the good father to the South, we beg leave to introduce the following anecdote of his sojourn in the Indian

Country as related by himself. While at Fort Pear with General H——,
in 1855, when the latter was holding council with the Indian chiefs,
Father Trecy was one day conversing with a Sergeant of Co. B., 2nd
Dragoons when suddenly a stentorian voice among the Indians called
out in Irish: "A yerhaar will Gaelic agut?" (Brother, do you understand
Gaelic?) Turning to find out who asked such a question, Father Trecy
was surprised to see only the Indians in their war-paint and blankets.
He and the sergeant were no little astonished. They looked at each
other, and then, smiling, resumed their conversation. They were permitted to enjoy their *tête-à-tête* but a few moments, when the same
voice interrupted them again, with: "A yerhaar mo hree will Gaelic?"
(Brother of my heart, do you understand Gaelic?) This was more than
the priest could stand, and mustering up the few Irish words he knew,
he replied, "Ta cuid de" (I do, some of it). At this, one of the braves
stepped out from among the Indians, and extended his hand. The feelings of the priest can be imagined better than described. There stood
one of his countrymen, his face daubed with paint, his body wrapped
in deerskins and blankets, and to all appearance, as much an Indian as
any of the tribe! The illusion was gone, however, the moment he spoke,
for there came rolling from his mouth a brogue as rich and as racy of
the soil as any heard in Ireland.

During the conversation between the chief and the priest, the latter
learned that the "Indian" was a Tipperary man—a landlord killer—
who was obliged to fly his country in the year [18]38. He and a companion in crime were both followed to New York, which they were
forced to leave. They were hunted to Reading, Harrisburg, and Pittsburg, Pennsylvania, thence to St. Louis and St. Joseph, Missouri. There
the chase becoming too hot, they resolved to make known their circumstances to the Molly Maguires, who at once went to work and
placed the future Indian chiefs on board a fur company's boat.[6] On arriving at Fort Union[7] they joined the trappers. They soon acquired the
Indian dialect, became great friends with the natives, and constantly
joined them in their Buffalo hunts. During these sports our Tipperary
men distinguished themselves by brave deeds and active exploits, the
result of which was they were soon made chiefs. They then took unto
themselves wives of the daughters of the forest. Before the good father

departed, he baptized not only the squaws and children of his countrymen, but also forty other Indian families, and united the fathers and
mothers in the sacrament of matrimony.

Having thus consoled them with the sweets of religion Father
Trecy took his leave, followed by their regrets that he could not remain
with them. We have since learned that these Irishmen and their families, subsequently settled inside the lines of civilization, and that their
children have become wealthy.

In the fall of 1858, Father Trecy left to take up his abode in the
South. He went by steamboat via the Missouri and Mississippi Rivers
to New Orleans, where at St. Patrick's Church, he spent some time;
thence to the Diocese of Mobile. By order of Rt. Rev'd Bishop [John]
Quinlan[8] he was assigned to duty as Missionary priest throughout the
state of Alabama. At Huntsville, Northern Alabama, he found fully half
of the inhabitants Catholics and Irish, but with no church within hundreds of miles. He resolved to try to do something for their spiritual
welfare.

His first care was to restore peace to the souls of almost all who
professed the Catholic faith, his next step was to erect a church. He
went to work with a will and had it well advanced when the terrible
tocsin of war sounded throughout the length and breadth of the land,
and he was in consequence obliged to defer its completion. Huntsville
was made a camp of instruction for the Confederate troops, and Father
Trecy seeing that his services, in a spiritual way, were needed, freely
tendered them.

His first duty therefore as army chaplain in the late war, was among
the Confederate soldiers encamped in and around Huntsville. He next
extended spiritual consolation to the troops stationed around Mobile
Bay, particularly those at Fort Morgan and Fort Jones. When the troops
were moved from these places to North Mississippi he returned to
Huntsville where he remained until after the surrender of Fort Donelson, in Tennessee, by the Confederates. The Southern soldiers wounded
in the attack on the fort were transferred to Huntsville and as Albert
Sidney Johnston's[9] army which was falling back to North Mississippi
passed through that place in its retreat, Dr. [Yandell],[10] the Medical Director attached to General Johnston's Staff, called on Father Trecy and

requested him to take charge of the hospitals, and to look after their sanitary condition. This the priest was at first reluctant to do, but on seeing the wretched treatment of the wounded, he charitably consented.

Taking with him some Irishmen who were working on the church before the breaking out of the war he gave all the hospital wards a thorough cleansing, and providing tubs, had the patients bathed, thereby greatly refreshing them. He forbade the indiscriminate visits of ladies with delicacies to particular friends, as he wished all the charities sent to the hospital to be distributed in as fair a manner as possible. This gave offense and the cry was raised that Father Trecy issued the order only for the purpose of proselytizing and further that it was for this same purpose that he had schemed to get the hospitals under his charge. Hearing himself thus calumniated, Father Trecy attended a meeting of the relief society for wounded soldiers and charged the persons who circulated such calumnies with being willful maligners, and stated that he had taken charge of the hospitals with reluctance and was ready at any moment to abandon them to other hands; but that he would attend to the spiritual wants of the invalided Catholic soldiers at all risks and hazards. Dr. Ross, a Presbyterian minister, and several other Protestant clergymen who were present denounced the maligners and prevailed on Father Trecy to continue in charge of the wounded. Thenceforth everything was left entirely under the care of the priest who continued in charge until the battle of Shiloh when the following dispatch was received from Dr. Yandell. Revd. Father Trecy "prepare at once to come to Corinth. Bring all the hospital stores you can: Such as brandy, whiskey, lint, bandages, etc. All the wounded able to bear transportation send to Atlanta, Georgia, the balance to Courtland, Alabama. Bring with you all the nurses you can. Trains are ordered to report to you immediately, D. W. Yandell, S & M.D."

In due time that afternoon the trains arrived and the transportation of the invalids and stores at once took place. Besides the inmates of the hospitals there were numbers of applicants for transportation, among whom were several ministers of the Episcopal, Methodist, and Presbyterian churches. The trains started for Corinth which they reached the following morning. On his arrival, Father Trecy turned over to Dr. Yandell all the stores and receiving the following pass was ordered for duty.

Corinth, April 10th, [18]62

No. 110—Pass and repass Father Trecy in and out of hospitals in and about Corinth at will, until further orders.
D. W. Yandell, S. & M.D.

Dr. Yandell then informed him that Huntsville was in the hands of the Federals.[11] On receiving this news Father Trecy at once started to see his bishop who had just come to Corinth from Mobile with priests and Sisters of Charity. He communicated to Bishop Quinlan the intelligence he had received from Dr. Yandell, and expressed a determination to return to his people in Huntsville, to which the bishop at once replied "go and God bless you and do all you can for the salvation of souls." Father Trecy then called on Dr. Yandell to tell him of his determination and received the following pass.

No. 132

Corinth, April 13th 1862

Pass Rev'nd Father Trecy through, outward and back, our lines until further orders.

D. W. Yandell S. & M.D.W.L.

Thus fortified, the priest started on foot along the railroad for Huntsville. When about three miles from Corinth he was fired on by a soldier on picket duty, about a quarter of mile distant, who wished to examine his pass. After the examination he was allowed to proceed. On arriving at Burnsville his pass had again to be shown. Five miles east of Burnsville he was once more shot at, but not being able to discern the sentry or the smoke of the gun, he hurried into the thicket undergrowth along which he travelled for more than a mile, when he again took to the railroad to avoid the mud and swamps. He then passed on through the town of Iuka, until he reached Bear Creek, where he found the railroad bridge in flames and the valley on the opposite side literally covered with Federal troops.[12] Father Trecy at once left the road, not unnoticed by the soldiers, who sent him their compliments in [the] shape of a shower of bullets. Fortunately, they missed him, although branches of trees in close proximity to his person were cut off.

Finding the place too hot for him he waded through the creek for about a mile when he came to a crossing south of the old Tuscumbia road. Here he forded the river, waist deep, and started off keeping the south side of a rocky and broken range of hills until he reached near Buzzard's Roost, Alabama. From this point, he directed his course north until he ascended to the summit of the highest adjacent hill whence he could view the valleys all around him. In that which lay to the west, the Federal troops mustered very strong. They were marching over the grounds he had passed, and were advancing toward him. Eastward the valley was covered with the Confederates. Finding it unsafe to remain longer and not wishing to be a prisoner to either side, Father Trecy made his way along the mountain ridge until he came in the rear of the Southern cavalry. Having a full view of the valley before him he struck for Cherokee, where he remained over night with Dr. D—— who in the morning furnished him with a mule, on which bare-backed he rode to Tuscumbia where he spent the night with Mr. B——.

After Mass the next morning his friend loaned him a horse which carried him to the Tennessee River at Florence. The bridge at this point had been burned the day before by a regiment of Kentucky cavalry and Father Trecy was obliged to cross the river in a dugout. On reaching the opposite shore he paid a negro ten dollars to take him on an old mule to Athens, and, on the following morning, ten dollars more to guide him to the Federal camp. When the negro[13] came in sight of the Blue jackets he cried out "Say Massa, dar be dar-des be. Massa I goes no farther de hang me I goes no farther Massa." Suiting the action to the word the guide turned around and started off as best he could. Father Trecy then entered the lines of General [Ormsby] Mitchel[14] unnoticed and unmolested, passed the general's marquee, and went directly home. As soon as he made himself presentable, he proceeded to the headquarters of the general, in order to report himself as having come inside his lines.

On announcing his presence in camp to the general the latter asked, "What guard brought you in, Sir?" "In coming I have not seen any guard, General." "What road did you come in on Sir?" "On the Athens old road." "Have I no guards or pickets on that road Sir?" "I have not seen any, General." Here the general rang his little bell violently, and an orderly instantly entered. "Tell the Inspector I want to see him," said the general. The soldier saluted and left and the general and the priest were again alone. "You are from Corinth," said the general, "Yes, General," answered the priest. "Is Beauregard there?" "He is, General." "Did you see him?" "I did." Here an officer entered, "Capt D——," said the general. "Is it possible that I have no pickets on the Athens Road?" "We have, General, I just came in from there." "Why, this gentleman came from Corinth and did not see a picket." "I don't believe it, General." "There is the man that came in." The officer turning to Father Trecy asked, "What road did you come in upon?" "I came direct from Athens on the mud road." "Did you see no Guards on that road?" "No Sir, about a mile and a half back as I was approaching the hill I saw a soldier crossing the road at the top of it, but on arriving there I did not see any." "I don't believe you, Sir. You are like the rest of those d——d Secesh,[15] you skulked off the road into the bush when you came to the post." At this insolence Father Trecy mildly, yet firmly, replied, "You state an untruth with regard to me, and do me injustice Captain. I am not aware that I ever did an act that should cause me to flee the face of men. What I have stated, Sir, is true." At this firm assertion the general jumped up and sternly said, "Captain go and see to that road and every road around, leading to the camps of my men, I do not want to be taken by surprise, sitting in my tent." The officer left. The general then addressed the priest, "Your name is Trecy. They call you Father Trecy. How many men has [General Braxton] Bragg?"[16] "I do not know General." "How much Artillery have they?" "I cannot say." "What can you say?" "On this subject General I can say but little." "You know I have those other D——d Sesech preachers locked up and that I can lock you up too." "You have the power General, but do you want me to lie to you?" "No Sir." "Then what I have said is true, I do not know. But were I permitted by you to leave your lines, what would you think of me if I went to your enemy and gave him such information as I might have acquired in your camp, while attending to a sacred and religious duty?" "By G—— Sir if I ever caught you I would hang you." "That then is my position in your camp today. Any knowledge that I may have acquired respecting the Confederate lines was while attending to my duties as a priest. Apart from all this I know nothing of what you have asked me." "Well Sir," responded the general, "you speak like a sensible man, you don't set our authority at defiance like those other fellows,[17] who call themselves ministers of the Gospel. I have them locked up and I am going to keep them so. I have a great number of your people in my camp, and I wish you to see to them." "I shall do so General, with the greatest of pleasure." "Call and see me often Mr. Trecy." "General I need a pass." "You shall have it." The following pass was then made out.

Guards & Pickets

May 21, [18]62
Required and will pass Father Trecy until further orders in and out lines and through the camps.

J. S. Ford, A.A.G.
by Command Major Genl. Mitchel
Commanding

Thus fortified Father Trecy saw open to him an extensive field wherein he could render himself efficient for the honor and glory of God. On the news of Father Trecy's arrival reaching the Confederate hospitals wherein were located those who were not able to bear transportation to Corinth, there was a general rejoicing. One poor fellow from Louisiana, named Williams, a non-Catholic, who was in a rather precarious state, raised himself up in his bed and exclaimed, "Thank God our friend at least is allowed us," and as he fell back on his pillow the tears rolled down his cheeks.[18] A like feeling pervaded every inmate of the hospital. Several gentlemen who were present expressed their surprise at the love and respect shown to Father Trecy by the invalids. Before then some of them looked on him as a haughty, over-bearing man, but from that day all esteemed him as highly as did the poor wounded soldiers.

A few days after he baptized Williams and administered to him the sacraments of the Church, and a week later he followed his remains to the City Cemetery. The funeral was attended by the elite of Huntsville and, through the influence of Father Trecy and Captain [William] Halpin of the 15th Regular Kentucky Infantry, also by the Confederate prisoners then in Huntsville. These poor fellows felt and acknowledged the favor conferred upon them, of being permitted to accompany the remains of their brother to their final resting place, without guard of any kind whatever, save their word to Father Trecy.

In about an hour after the internment of poor Williams Father Trecy was called upon to attend the funeral of a Federal soldier.[19] How unlike, those two funerals were! The one attended by a death like silence; the other with martial pomp, and gaudy decorations. Father Trecy preached at both. The sermons were so effective and the ceremonies so impressive that Captain Halpin sent an elaborate account of the affair to the *Cincinnati Enquirer*, which was published on receipt, with laudable comments.[20] On the day following the funeral ceremonies, Father Trecy was requested by the Protestant chaplains, whom General Mitchel had locked up in the courthouse, to visit them. He called upon them and on inquiring if there was anything he could do for them, one, a bishop, replied that there was not, but he would like to know how he got along with "the old bear Mitchel." Father Trecy replied that he had no trouble whatever with the general, that he always treated him as a gentleman. "Well," said the other, "he has been more favorable to you than to us."

Father Trecy untiringly attended to his arduous duties throughout the camp and hospitals until the end of August when General [Don Carlos] Buel[l][21] fell back into Kentucky from North Alabama. There were some residents of Huntsville who considered Father Trecy's attention to the spiritual wants of the Federals a sufficient cause for branding him a traitor, and as one who should not be allowed to remain among them. In consequence of this state of affairs the priest was advised by some of his friends to leave Huntsville for a short time; consequently in the 2nd day of September he started on a mission to Tuscumbia in Alabama. Before reaching his destination, he had to cross the Tennessee River in a flat boat, and when about midway in the stream, the sergeant in charge of the boat squad noticed the address: "J. F. Trecy, Mobile, Alabama" on his valise. "So you are from Mobile!" said he. "I was in Mobile some time ago," answered the priest. The circumstance was considered suspicious, and on reaching the bank, Father Trecy was informed that he could not land but should consider himself a prisoner. He at once asked to be brought before the officer in charge. In about an hour afterwards the officer condescended to see him, and accosted him as follows, "What business have you within our lines?" "I am a Catholic priest and on my mission attending to my duty." "The h-ll you are, All you d——n preachers are Secesh. I like to catch you fellows." "Captain," said the priest "don't be so fast, you might mistake your man," producing as he spoke, two passes, one from General Buell and the other from General Mitchel; on looking at these the officer asked, "Why did you not show them to me at first?" "No matter," he continued, assuming a defiant attitude, "they are of no account, you must stay here tonight." "I greatly desire to see the commandant of the post at Tuscumbia," said Father Trecy. "Have you any orders for him; if so let me see them." "I cannot let you see them." "Well give them to me and I will send them up." "If you can send them up, you can send me up." "If I did I should send a guard with you, and I have not the men to spare as I do not know how soon I may be attacked." After a little further conversation, however, a sergeant was sent with the priest to the quarters of the post commandant, a Colonel Murphy of a Wisconsin regiment.[22]

This Murphy, as on other occasions besides the present, gave the priest to understand that he was not a Catholic and during their conversation did his best to hurt his feelings. In the heat of Murphy's vituperations, General D[avid] S. Stanley[23] entered, to learn from the priest, if possible, something regarding Buell's movements. When informed that Buell's army had left North Alabama and General Morgan's Brigade had changed its route from Huntsville to Nashville, and that all their couriers had been captured, General Stanley at once telegraphed all the particulars to Major General Rosecrans, then at Iuka, and also of Father Trecy's presence at Tuscumbia. General Rosecrans telegraphed back to send the latter at once to his headquarters. While these dispatches were passing General Stanley and Father Trecy became engaged in conversation, and such a favorable impression was left on the general, that he invited the priest over to his headquarters to spend the night. This invitation stung Colonel Murphy and he endeavored though unsuccessfully to persuade the general to allow the priest to remain with him. General Stanley ordered Murphy to send sufficient forage for the horses that night, which order the infidel colonel did not obey. The next morning Father Trecy said Mass for the few Catholics in Tuscumbia, and then started for Iuka. On the way he spent a night at [Cherokee]²⁴ at the residence of Dr. D.'s, celebrating Mass in the morning which was attended by all the Catholics of the place and by almost all the soldiers stationed there. Of the latter quite a large number approached the Holy Sacraments. During that whole morning before Mass it was both pleasing and praiseworthy to see the Protestant chaplain of one of the regiments going round among the Catholic soldiers, urging them to their religious duties.

CHAPTER II

Rev. J. F. Trecy, Continued

*Father Trecy's arrival at General Rosecrans's Headquarters—
His reception and mission—General Stanley's
conversion—Father Ireland—Attending to the dying and
wounded—Stones River—Mass on the battle field—
The wounded Confederate.*

When Father Trecy arrived at the headquarters of General Rosecrans, he was met and welcomed by the general in person. Quarters were at once furnished him and an orderly appointed to care for his horses. The next day a large hospital tent was pitched on the grounds near the Iuka Springs and a chapel was established therein. Word was at once sent to the regimental officers to notify their men of the arrival of a priest. That afternoon and night the latter was kept busily engaged hearing the confessions of penitents, both officers and men. That same afternoon also General Stanley arrived with all his command except that portion left with Colonel Murphy, who was to transport the stores, etc., from Tuscumbia.

On the following morning, however, the valiant colonel ran away, leaving a large quantity of supplies to the enemy.[1] This disgraceful action on Murphy's part caused great indignation in the camp and loud and bitter were the threats on all sides. One stalwart grenadier on learning how the dastard had treated Father Trecy exclaimed: "Ah then! None but a poltroon[2] would do that, and sure, he must be that, to be

ashamed of his religion and to deny his country for he was a disgrace
to her anyway."

For five days, until September 12, Father Trecy was kept busily engaged hearing confessions. On that day he received General Stanley
into the church and on the following day five others. On the 14th
he desired to return again over his missionary grounds; but General
Rosecrans would not permit it, as they were about falling back to
Corinth, and expected some fighting, and would therefore require his
services. That night and the next morning the army moved for a point
between Corinth and Jacinto, called the Big Springs, and on the 19th
they commenced moving back again to Iuka, where General [Sterling]
Price[3] was in force. About three o'clock skirmishing commenced, and
by four the battle raged. Father Trecy was up with[4] the advance, and at
one time when there was considerable confusion, it is reported he rode
forward, and, in his masterly and powerful voice, commanded a halt,
which was obeyed. He then began upbraiding the officers and men for
turning their backs to the enemy and by his firmness on the occasion,
it is said, he stopped a panic at this particular place. However, confusion reigned everywhere else and the enemy's artillery made havoc in
the demoralized ranks. The priest's attention was now called to the
wounded men who were to be seen in swarms going to the rear and on
these he remained in incessant attendance until darkness set in, when
he repaired to the hospital where he gave his services to such of the
wounded as needed them.

It was two o'clock the next morning before, tired and weary, he was
able to seek some repose. He went to Father Ireland's regiment[5] which
was bringing up the reserve line, and found their chaplain busily at
work hearing the confessions of the soldiers who, poor fellows, did not
know but that their doom might be sealed in the morning. After getting something to eat, Father Trecy lay down to sleep. Shortly after daylight the two fathers proceeded to the hospital to look after the
wounded. Father Ireland remained there while Father Trecy went to the
front. Price had fled during the night. The wounded were moved into
Iuka, and both priests had then plenty to do. They were careful to show
no favor to Federals or Confederates, but to give their services equally
to all. The army then moved back towards Jacinto from which place Fa-

ther Trecy was permitted to return to North Alabama, supplied with the following pass.

No. 879

I, J. F. Trecy of Madison County, State of Alabama, do solemnly affirm before God, the Sovereign Judge, that during the war with the so called Confederate States, or any of them that I will truly and strictly behave myself as a peaceable citizen; that I will neither do myself, nor incite others to do, by word, writing, or act, anything prejudicial to the military forces of the U.S. nor give information about them which will enable others to do them harm or interfere with their operations, nor will I pass within or without the Federal lines except by permission of the military authorities. So help me God.

J. F. Trecy, Catholic Priest
W. M. Wiles,[6] Captain, 44th Indiana Vol.
Provost Marshal General
By Command Major General Rosecrans
September 23rd, [18]62

On the morning of the 24th, Father Trecy started from Jacinto for Iuka, where he arrived during the day and by permission, and spent a couple of hours with the wounded.

When about to proceed on his journey, a man by the name of Condon made his acquaintance and on learning which way the priest was going stated that he too was going the same as far as Tuscumbia. The priest was pleased to have Condon's company though surprised to see him with a Government horse and saddle. He explained how he came by them, however, by stating that the soldiers stole his and that the provost marshal had given them to him in their stead. When crossing Bear Creek they met a squad of Captain [Philip] Roddey's Cavalry,[7] and as Condon became alarmed, the priest asked him what he had to fear. The cavalry passed on and when about a mile distant, Condon, suddenly turning his horse around, started back for Iuka by another road. He had not gone far when he met the same squad of Cavalry who took him prisoner, [and] brought [him] to the camp of Captain

Roddey's Brigade, where he was charged with being a spy. When Father Trecy reached Cherokee, he too, was arrested and would have been taken to the camp had it not been for Dr. D——. He was however kept under guard all night. The sentinel, who was placed on guard over him was more than astonished when he saw his prisoner, and with an oath said that he would never do duty over him. The priest remonstrated, told him he was a soldier and requested him to do his duty and not get himself into difficulty. "I would sooner have you here," said the priest, "than anyone else; it will be all right in the morning." Then changing the conversation he asked: "E—— how long is it since you have been to your duty?" "Not since I was with you Father, when I made my first communion over two years ago." "Well now," said the priest, "prepare yourself while you are walking up and down. See what God has done for you. Obey always my child in what is not sin." The soldier complied with the request and settled his accounts with Almighty God. The next morning Captain Roddey called on Father Trecy who showed General Rosecrans's pass and thus made all things satisfactory, after which the captain offered to give him a pass in case he again entered the Federal lines. Thereupon the following parole was presented to him to sign.

> I hereby pledge my parole of honor that I will not convey any information to the enemies of the Confederate States, this 25 September/[18]62 J. F. Trecy.
> Pass J. F. Trecy in and out.
>   P. [D].[8] Roddey Captain Commanding
>   September 25th /62

Condon was sent to Price and condemned as a spy to be hung, but escaped.[9] Father Trecy reached Huntsville on the 28th. The battle of Corinth began on the third day of October, 1862, the Confederates under Price and [Earl] Van Dorn[10] being the attacking party. That day they seemed to have the advantage. The following day the contest was renewed at daybreak, and for some hours continued to be waged with indifferent success. At length the great struggle followed, a struggle exhibiting the master workings of modern generalship in a high degree.

For a time the Confederates lay quiet in the angle of the woods near the railroad. Presently two lines were formed, one at right angles to the other—the one destined with its reserves to sweep over the railroad, through the abatis into the village—the other with its reserves to attack battery "Robinett,"[11] which was the key to the whole position. If once taken and held, Corinth was undeniably in possession of the South. The line destined for the occupation of the village came rapidly forward at a charge across the railroad, over the fallen timber, driving the Federal line before them like chaff. All that grape and canister could do to impede their progress was attempted, but in vain. They still came onward until they reached the public square, where they formed in line of battle. The Federal line of battle was formed directly opposite.

The two armies advanced. A terrible hand-to-hand fight ensued, and for a time the destruction of the Federal line seemed inevitable. It gradually yielded, and fell back until the enemy had nearly reached the Corinth House. Here General Rosecrans rode along the line, and with a few cheering words, revived the courage of the men. The Confederate reserve at this time was directly in range of the guns on the redoubts to the left, and huge shells began to drop in their midst, creating great confusion and loss of life. At the same time, the order was given to *charge bayonets*, and the Federal soldiers springing to their work with a will, the enemy were soon flying across the public square. The fiery missives from the two batteries hastened their movements, and by the time they reached the cover of the timber their retreat was a rout.

The other line with their reserves were well advanced in the direction of battery Robinett.

In the meantime, General Price and his principal officers held a consultation to devise means to take the battery. The importance of its capture was admitted, and the danger of the attempt thoroughly considered. General Price not being willing to assume the responsibility of ordering the attack, called for volunteers, and Colonel [William P.] Rogers of Arkansas at once tendered his brigade as the forlorn hope, and Colonel [Lawrence S.] Ross, his brigade as a support. They massed their troops eight deep and advanced under a heavy fire of double charges of grape and canister. A terrible enfilading and flanking fire was poured upon them from every battery bearing in that direction, aided by incessant volleys of musketeers from the supports for the batteries and the Federal regiments drawn up in line parallel with them.

The first shell from battery William exploded in the center of the advancing column, killing thirty or forty. Every discharge caused great gaps in their ranks, but they still pushed on. Twice did they approach almost to the outer works of the battery, and twice were they compelled to fall back. The third time they reached the battery, and planted their flag upon the edge. It was shot down—raised again—again shot down. They swarmed about the battery, they climbed over the parapets, and for a time it seemed as if victory was theirs. But the Federals who were working the battery fell back behind the projecting earthworks, out of reach of the Federal shells, and immediately all the [Federal] batteries bearing upon the position were turned upon battery Robinett, and a shower of missiles came hailing down upon the brave [Confederate] invaders. Mortal men could not stand the fire and they retreated. As they slowly turned their steps towards the forest, from which they had started, the order was given to the two regiments supporting the battery to charge, and the miserable remnant of gallant men who had escaped the batteries was now almost annihilated. The dead bodies of the Confederates were piled up in and about the entrenchments, in some places eight and ten deep. In one place directly in front of the point of assault, two hundred and sixteen dead bodies were found within a space of a hundred feet by four, among them the commanders of both brigades making the assault: Colonel Rogers and Colonel Ross.

So ended the battle of Corinth, leaving General Rosecrans the victor.

The Southern people were called on to attend to the wounded but they responded very poorly as they were afraid of the Yankees. Finally, Father Trecy was appealed to, and answered as promptly as ever in the work of charity. He went to Corinth to see General Rosecrans, obtained the necessary permission to bring the Confederate wounded to Iuka, and to buy such stores and hospital clothing as he wanted. Having made the purchases he returned to Iuka to find that the hospitals were more like places of amusement for the young surgeons and their[12] friends than a place where nurses were needed. For days the beds of the patients were not cleaned nor were their wounds dressed. Father Trecy sent a full account of the state of affairs to General Rosecrans who soon had everything made right. After remaining a week attending to the spiritual and temporal welfare of these patients the good priest left for Corinth. On the day he arrived there General Rosecrans was ordered to Cincinnati to take command of the 14th Corps,[13] and requested the priest to accompany him which the latter promised to do as soon as he saw to the welfare of these invalids in the hospitals in Corinth. Here he remained two weeks at his good work, during which time he baptized thirty-two soldiers, ten of whom died, and then, on the 5th of November, he joined Rosecrans at Bowling Green, Kentucky. A week after he accompanied the general to Nashville, to which place the order of march was given for Sunday; but at the suggestion of Father Trecy, as there was nothing pressing in the affair the march was postponed until Monday. During this route the priest had the pleasure of being escorted by his old regiment of the plains, the 4th Regulars (who were principally Irish). A few days after arriving in Nashville Father Trecy received the following special field order.

Headquarters 14th Army Corps Dep
Cumberland, Nashville, Tennessee, November 24, [18]62

Special Orders No. 25.
XI

The Rev J. F. Trecy Chaplain at these headquarters is authorized and directed to visit the various camps hospitals and garrisons of this army for the purpose of allowing the Catholics belonging to the same an opportunity of fulfilling their religious obligations. Every necessary facility for the becoming discharge of his duty will be afforded him by the commanding officers at each point.
By command of Major General Rosecrans
M. Ledlee, Major 15th U.S. Infantry

Father Trecy was at once provided with ambulances, drivers, and orderlies from the 10th Ohio Infantry and first visited the 14th Michigan Infantry then doing duty at Stones River near the Hermitage. He stayed with the regiment six days and during that time was kept very busy hearing confessions, giving Instructions and attending in general to the spiritual wants of the soldiers. While here he received five persons into the Church and made numerous esteemed acquaintances, among them a Dr. Sporting[14] of the 10th Michigan. This gentleman the priest always accosted by the sobriquet of Charley O'Malley, or the Irish Dragoon, which name stuck to him while he remained in the army. The next mission was to the Regular Brigade, camped west of the penitentiary. There he spent ten days as he found both officers and men were almost entirely Catholics. His next visit was to the cavalry with whom he spent a week. Christmas being near at hand Father Trecy returned to the city to spend the holidays. On arriving at headquarters he was informed that a move on the enemy was about to be made in a few days. At this news, he went around amongst the camps to hear confessions. On Christmas Eve, he was out along the lines as usual, and came in late expecting to have a pleasant Christmas, but to his great astonishment was told that a move was to be made at 4 o'clock in the morning. To satisfy himself as to the truth of the report he repaired to the general who confirmed his information. "General," said Father Trecy, "tomorrow is the greatest day in the Christian era, tomorrow is the birthday of man's Redeemer!"

"I did not think of it, Father," answered the general turning to Colonel [Julius P.] Garesché,[15] chief of staff, who was the only person present, he said, "Colonel, can we countermand it?"

"Oh yes, general," answered the colonel, "Send orders to the corps commanders, and all will be right."

The order was countermanded and on the morning of the 26th the army moved forward at daylight. When about eight or nine miles from Nashville on the Murfreesboro pike the Southern army could be seen and shots were exchanged during the whole of that day and the following one, with very few casualties. The next day, December 28, was Sunday, and the general opposed operations unless it became a necessity. He attended Mass that morning and spent the greater part of the forenoon in religious devotions. After Mass Father Trecy attended to the wounded throughout the rest of the day, not returning to headquarters until night weary and tired. On Monday he went to Stewarts Creek, stopped there overnight, and the next morning after Mass went to the front to find the general, whom he met within two miles of Murfreesboro. The day was spent in heavy skirmishing all along the line, and the priest rode everywhere to see after the wounded, who, however, were few in number. It was in the arduous discharge of his duties on that day that he first met Father Christy, chaplain of the 78th Pennsylvania Infantry, who was ever afterwards a very fast friend of Father Trecy's. On the following morning, December 31st, the deadly strife was expected, and on the night of the 30th the scenes around some of the camp fires were sad to behold. At one in particular, around which the poor fellows were clustered, the impending battle was the all absorbing topic. "Which of us boys," said a stalwart fellow, "will go up tomorrow?" "Not I," said one. "Not I," said another. "Nor I," said each and all. However in spite of their assurance some were downcast, and others would glance at a token of friendship presented by some fond friend at home; others again would carry on their games, and even curse and swear just as if they were seated in some New York gambling house.

The morning dawned. A few minutes past 4 o'clock Father Trecy said Mass and General Rosecrans, Colonel Garesché and some others went to Communion. That Communion was destined to be poor Garesché's last. After Father Trecy having finished the holy sacrifice, Father Cooney said another Mass. A short time after the conclusion of the latter service Father Trecy celebrated High Mass in a little tent opposite to the general's marquee. The general knelt humbly and devoutly in the corner of the tent, and Garesché, no less devout by his side. Soldiers meekly knelt in front of the tent and groups of officers, booted and spurred for battle, with heads reverently uncovered, stood outside, and mutually muttered their prayers. What grave anxieties, what exquisite emotions, what deep thoughts moved the hearts and minds of these pious soldiers unto whom God and their country had delivered, not merely the lives of thousands of men who on that day died, but the vitality of a principle the cause of self[-]government and of human liberty! Mass being over the general called the priest to breakfast but they were scarcely seated when firing began.

The general cried "mount gentlemen." The staff were in an instant in their saddles, and galloped away at break neck speed to [Colonel Charles] Harker's front. Every member of this little band was a conspicuous target on the occasion. A tremendous cannonading was then heard and the battle was fairly opened. Father Trecy left the general and staff, to look after the wounded. After the lapse of a few minutes his faithful orderly's horse was struck and Father Trecy was left to himself amongst the wounded and dying. At one time during the day the army was giving way and Father Trecy was obliged to fall back and join the general. A new line was formed by the men, and, in spite of an incessant shower of shell and rifle balls, the general dashed along it encouraging the men. About this time Father Trecy rode to the front, raised himself in his saddle and with a stentorious voice cried out: "Men prepare yourselves. I will give you the general absolution." It happened that the command in front of whom the priest stood were almost all Catholics. He recited the *Confiteor*[16] aloud for them, and then told them to make an act of contrition while he pronounced the words of absolution. In an instant all the hats were off and the soldiers were on their knees. The scene was indeed striking! The ceremony over, the priest dashed through the line to the rear of the batteries where he joined a portion of the staff. The battle raged, wounded men were carried to the rear and the priest was again at his work. But it was only of the mortally wounded that he took notice, those slightly hurt he did not notice. He carried with him two canteens one containing whiskey and the other water. During this struggle, as in many others, he was frequently seen with some poor fellow's head on his knees giving him a reviving draught so as to enable him to make his confession, and prepare himself for eternity. The water which he carried with him was for the purpose of baptism, for numbers of the Protestants in the army were never baptized and a great many of them required the services of the priest on the battle field.

At the final charge, Father Trecy joined the general and staff. The carnage was terrible and Fathers Trecy and Christy worked near each other till after dark. After attending to the wounded till late in the night, they both lay down together on a pile of wet canvass to take a sleep, there being no tents pitched that evening, as the following day was expected to be another of slaughter. The morning dawned. It was January 1st 1863. The two fathers had a cup of coffee and were off for the field. They went to places they had not visited before. There lay the Blue and Gray Jackets side by side. As there was little or no fighting that day it afforded the fathers an opportunity to pass around the hospitals. There were five priests doing duty on that day. The other three were Fathers [Peter] Cooney, [William] O'Higgins, and [Francis] Fusseder.[17]

While in the hospital Father Trecy was called by Major [William D.] B[ickham], correspondent of the *Cincinnati Commercial* to see a countryman of his, a rebel, who was wounded on the previous day. On the priest being introduced the soldier scanned him from head to foot. The priest then asked him if he were an Irishman. "Yes, captain," was the reply. "What part of Ireland are you from?" "Faith, from all parts." "What county were you born in?" "Kerry." "What is your name?" "James O'Driscoll, Captain." "I am not a captain, I am a priest." "Bad luck to the bit of me you can fool that way! A priest eh? with top boots spurs and soldiers coat and hat." The priest here opened his overcoat and James saw the black clothes. "James where do your people live?" "In Pittsburgh." "In Pittsburgh, Pennsylvania?" "Yes, Father." "With your people living in the North how came you to be in the Southern army?" "Well faith, Father, I will tell you that, I was ditching all winter for a planter and he would not pay me unless I would go into the army, and he said he would present me with $300 as was well if I did so." "Well did he give it to you?" "No, sure when I was going he said he'd keep it till I'd go back." "Was that the only thing that induced you to join the army?" "Well now faith I liked a bit of fun, and I saw all the boys going, so I thought to myself I'd go too." "Then you were not forced into service?" "No your Reverend I went into it with a good will, as I'd let no man get fornest me in that." Father Trecy then bid James goodbye and as the latter's wound was not serious, and the doctor taking a liking to him, he made a nurse of him and as such he drew pay from the government till the end of the war.

On the next morning, January 2nd, at about 11 o'clock a sharp musketry fire took place on the left center. It gradually increased till 3 o'clock in the afternoon, when a terrific battle raged. It only lasted an hour but the carnage was fearful. The Confederate loss was far in excess of that of the Federal. Father Trecy did his Christian work that night with his usual alacrity. Mass was said early next morning, and immediately after the priest started off with his posse of mounted men from the 4th Cavalry to see that the wounded were removed to hospital. On reaching a high knoll he took out his field-glass and took a glance over the ground between the lines. In so doing he espied an object in the furrow of a corn field, which the officers who accompanied him thought to be a log. It however soon moved. In spite of the remonstrance of the officers the priest proceeded to find out what the object was. On reaching it he found it to be a Confederate soldier. "Who are you?" said the priest. The soldier rolled back the blanket that covered him with his right arm, thereby exhibiting three bars on the collar of his coat; he looked at the priest for a moment and then said "My name is Ryan, Sir."[18] "Are you an officer?" "I am." "You are a Catholic I presume. To what regiment do you belong?" "To the 12th[19] and 13th Consolidated Louisiana." "Have you a priest with you?" "Not for the last six months or more." "Well, poor fellow, I am a priest and I suppose during the past night, lying here in this mud, you have made as good a preparation as ever you made in your life. I will hear your confession." The officer at first did not believe that his visitor was a priest from the dress worn by the latter, and he raised his eyes and looked at him in such a manner, as if to say "you can't fool me that way old fellow." The priest dismounted, pulled out his canteen and handing it to the wounded man said, "There Captain, take a draught of whiskey. You must indeed stand in need of it after lying here all night." The captain put it to his lips took a gentle sip and was about returning it, when the priest insisted that he should take a good drink. At the same time the priest produced his stole and threw it around his neck, which on beholding, the soldier actually shed tears. After hearing his confession the priest again handed him the canteen. After drinking the Captain said "I wish I were sitting up by that tree" (pointing to one about fifty yards distant). "I will help you there," said the priest. The officer then threw one arm around the priest's neck and limped along dragging a broken limb after him and placing him beside the tree he made him as comfortable as possible. No sooner was he seated by the tree than several shots were fired at the priest from the Confederate ranks. Two of the bullets entered the tree not far from his head, which caused Ryan to exclaim "Oh the damned Rascals, what are they shooting at you for?" The priest immediately got into his saddle and fled over the crest, followed by a volley. Having made the rounds of the lines he returned to head-quarters to report. Having mentioned the affair about the captain, the general said, "Father get an ambulance and have that man taken off the field to hospital at once." "General it would be impossible without losing men," said the priest. "Never mind," responded the general, "by the time you get there our line will have advanced to drive them out of that skirt of woods." Father Trecy instantly started off and had Captain Ryan placed in the ambulance and sent to the rear.[20] That night General Bragg left Murfreesboro and on the following morning General Rosecrans entered and established his headquarters there. Father Trecy was assigned the Masonic hall for a chapel and on that same morning after Mass the good priest, as usual, visited all the hospitals. The first was that of the wounded enemy left by Bragg in Murfreesboro. The greatest number of Catholics and Irish whom he found here were from the commands of [Patrick] Cleburne[21] and [Benjamin] Cheatham.[22] After seeing to all the Confederate soldiers in danger, he turned his attention to the wounded men of the command in which he was chaplain, who were just being brought in from the field.

After passing through the hospitals without finding Captain Ryan, whom he sent to the rear on Saturday, he called on the Dr. Swift to know of his whereabouts, but the doctor could not account for him. Father Trecy then started off in order to find if he were yet alive. He rode back two and a half miles to the field hospitals, searched every cabin and tent without finding him. He returned to Murfreesboro and examined the hospitals again. On passing through those occupied by the Confederate soldiers he asked aloud in each if anyone knew of Captain Ryan. He met with no response until he reached that occupied by the wounded of General Cheatham's command. There in answer to his inquiry a truly Celtic voice replied, "Yes sure that is my Captain one of the best men that ever God let live and he was wounded on Friday."[23] "Where is he now?" said the priest, "I had him taken off the field and sent to hospital on Saturday morning and I want to see that he is cared for as his wound is a dangerous one." "Ah then Father he is where he will be cared for. He is at General Morgan's father-in-law's house, Colonel [Charles] Ready's."[24] "I thank you my man, may God bless you and keep you from sin."

Instantly Father Trecy started for Colonel Ready's. On arriving there he went in and said that he wished to go upstairs when he was informed that he should see Mrs. [Martha] Ready.[25] The latter at first denied that Captain Ryan was in the house and said that she was ignorant of the existence of any sick man in her house at all and showed every anxiety that he should not enter. At her back stood a negro woman who raised her hand and pointed to the room where the captain was. Here Father Trecy requested the lady to let him pass as he was a friend of Ryan's, but it was of no avail. Then said the priest, "Madam, I never wish to be rude with ladies I am always inclined to let them have their way when it does not interfere with me in the discharge of my duty. I am a Catholic priest and must see that sick man." The lady instantly stepped aside and he walked up stairs into Ryan's room who, it is needless to say was in ecstasies on beholding the priest. After examining the wound the priest found that as yet it had but a field dressing and that mortification was likely to set in. He at once reported the circumstances to General Rosecrans who ordered the captain to be instantly removed and attended to. Father Trecy saw that every attention was paid him but in order to save his life it was found necessary to amputate the limb just above the knee.

When out of danger, the priest obtained permission for him to return home. A few months afterwards a sister of his, on a visit to Nashville, sent a letter to Father Trecy expressing a desire to see him. As he thought it was passport business, he paid no attention to it being annoyed to a great extent that way by ladies. On the same day he received the letter he accompanied General Stanley on an expedition. When they returned at the end of four weeks the army was being paid off, and the father was called upon to go to Cincinnati with money from numbers of men around headquarters and on his return he was to conduct to the seat of war five sisters who were ordered to attend the hospital by Archbishop [John B.] Purcell.[26] On arriving in Nashville he was handed a note by Father [Joseph A.] Kelly, then administrator of the Diocese of Nashville. It was from Miss Ryan. He Called at Mrs D—— to see the young lady. After giving his name to a negro servant who opened the door, the latter announced it. Almost instantly she ran back and ushered him into the parlor, where he was scarcely seated until three ladies entered. The first two politely bowed, but the other dropped on her knees at the feet of the priest and asked his blessing. She arose saying, "Father, from my brother I know you, and as a Father I revere you and love you." After some convers[at]ion Miss Ryan handed Father Trecy a letter which she requested him not to open till he reached home. The next morning after Mass he read enclosed which was as follows:

Baton Rouge, Louisiana

Very Revd. Father Trecy,
Sir,
          Under God to you I am indebted for my life. I would like dear Father to say much to you. But as I believe you a man of deeds more than words, I will be brief by asking you to accept the assurance of one who shall ever cherish and pray for the name of Father Trecy. As my watch and gold you spurned please accept this small token of regard, the emblem of our salvation and which united you and I. My Ma sends her loving regards to you and hopes she will have an opportunity in person to thank you. My Sister Mary Ann who will hand you this will say much I cannot.

J. S. Ryan, late Captain, 12th
Louisiana Reg.

Thursday January 29th, [18]63

The token of friendship mentioned in the letter was a diamond cross valued at $700, which we have ourselves seen. Father Trecy proceeded the next day to Cincinnati, forwarded the money as directed and returned to the front with five sisters (Sister Anthony [O'Connell] and four others).[27] The sisters were at first stationed at the hospital near the Chattanooga depot, after which they were distributed between hospitals 4 and 12. The good sisters in a few days were found to be so efficient that the surgeons made urgent requests for more of them. After Father T[recy] reporting at headquarters he went with Colonel [Robert] Minty's Brigade to McMinnville, Tennessee, in pursuit of some Confederate battalions. In McMinnville the enemy was reinforced and Minty had to return in double quick.

CHAPTER III

Rev. J. F. Trecy, Continued

Father Trecy commissioned as chaplain in the regulars—
The pious penitent—Enjoying Morgan's breakfast—
A large family—The Battle of Chickamauga—His service
under Sherman and Thomas—His resignation—He returns
to his old mission at Huntsville.

On the retreat from McMinnville, Father Trecy got sick and had to give up his horse and saddle and take an ambulance. The road was so rough and he got such a terrible shaking that he was quite exhausted when he got back to Murfreesboro. Arriving at headquarters he made known his will to quit the army as up to that time he had served without pay. He was requested by many of the general officers not to leave, but to take a chaplaincy in one of the regiments then in the field. He would not however accept such in one of the volunteer regiments as he then would be required to take an oath to some particular state. Up to that time he had never been asked to take an oath and if compelled to take one at all it should be to the United States at large, as he acted as chaplain to the 4th U.S. Cavalry previous to the war. He therefore accepted the chaplaincy of the 4th U.S. Cavalry with the understanding that there would be no objections to him in attending at the headquarters of the Army of the Cumberland and of visiting those of his persuasion in the regular brigade, or other commands, whenever the same might come within his reach. On the morning of the 28th of April Father

67

Trecy received a note from General Rosecrans telling him to bring his papers from the 4th U.S. Cavalry with him to headquarters that evening and that he would see about them. Shortly after arriving at headquarters the following order was issued which again put the zealous priest on detached service.

> Headquarters, Dep. Cumberland, Murfreesboro
> May 2nd 1863
> Extract,
> **Special Orders No. 75**
> Father J. F. Trecy, Chaplain 4th U.S. Cavalry, is hereby detached for duty in General hospitals in the City of Nashville and will report without delay to Surgeon A. H. Thurston Asst. Med. Dir.
> By Command Major General Rosecrans
> C. Goddard Lt. Col. A. A. Genl.[1]

After remaining a month in Nashville he was again called to the front. Shortly after returning to the camp Fathers Trecy and Christy gave a mission to the men of the brigade. One night Father Christy preached on the necessity of Holy Communion. The sermon was so very effective, that the next morning a young man, a non-Catholic, on seeing the large number of his comrades going to Communion, thought that he should go too. The orderly sergeant of his company, a good and a pious man, was terribly shocked at the occurrence and called the soldier to an account. The poor fellow wept like a child. The sergeant communicated the facts to the priest who at once sent for the young man and asked him about the affair. The soldier said "Father, I want to save my soul as well as the other men." "Yes, but you are not a Catholic." "Well Father, I believe all you and that other priest have said, just the same as any other man in the regiment." "Be not troubled my young friend," said the priest, "God has given us his own wise ways of doing things often times." Father Trecy then gave the young man a catechism, every word of which he committed to memory in a few days. He was baptized the following Sunday and General Stanley became his godfather. He belonged to the 16th U.S.I. and was either killed or taken prisoner a short time afterwards.

About the same time an unfortunate artillery man who deserted sometime previous and joined the rank of the enemy was captured with the enemy's uniform upon him. He was tried and sentenced to death. The provost marshal Captain Williams of the 19th U.S.I. asked him if he wished to see any minister. The condemned man replied with an oath that he did not. After a few kind words from the captain, he however said, "If I were to have any preacher he should be that old man Trecy for I think he is the d——st sensible one amongst them." The provost marshal at once sent word to headquarters to General Rosecrans, who without delay sent Father Trecy to them. Arriving at General Rouper's[2] headquarters the priest was conducted to the condemned man. The latter was at first indifferent and denied having sent for the priest. "He then said I don't know you, I never saw you but I have heard of you." Father Trecy then had the bracelets taken off and the provost marshal had him brought into his own tent in order that he and the father might converse freely. In a short time, he wept so that the guard looked to see what was the matter. The priest spent the greater portion of the evening with the condemned man and in the next morning baptized him, and accompanied him to the place of execution.

There were two others about to be executed at the same time, one of whom was blaspheming in the most horrid manner and the other was apparently indifferent but the penitent as he moved forward recited after the priest the Litany of the Holy Name. When he arrived at the place where his coffin lay he asked pardon of all around him and asked all to pray for him as he said he should then meet a just God he had often outraged. He then knelt by his coffin and the blind was adjusted over his eyes; the good father spoke the last words of consolation in his ears and withdrew. The signal was then given, the volley fired and all was over.

A few days after the army moved from Murfreesboro to Shelbyville, where the general expected to encounter Bragg. The latter however fell back across the Tennessee River. After three days' heavy march the army halted one morning in order to take breakfast and feed their horses. In one of the mounted infantry regiments was a tall Irish captain.[3] He was rather a jocose and generous fellow but was fond of a row particularly with an Orangeman[4] and was familiarly called throughout the regiment "the bloody Tip." When ready for breakfast he seated himself on a log and began eating his hard tack and pork. He was not long in enjoying himself when a volley of solid shot was fired by the enemy and passed over his head. A few minutes elapsed when another volley was fired. This was war being disastrous, as one of the balls struck the log on which the captain sat and drove it away with such velocity that it swept along with it the skirts off his coat and the seat out of his pants. He instantly leaped to his feet made the sign of the cross with his left hand and exclaimed, "In the name of the Blessed Virgin Mary wasn't it the Lord saved me. May the devil be far from us, Father Trecy!" "To mount" was sounded and on that day the brave 14th Irish Michigan did their work magnificently. They took more prisoners than they had men.

During the day the father was at one time riding to the rear, [where he] met the captain. "Father," said he, "those gray friends of ours are likely to get it hot today." "If," said the priest, "you call them friends they have a poor way of showing their friendship by shooting the behind out of a fellow's breeches and make him look like showing the white feather." "Ah Father you know me too well for that, and you must know that with God's assistance I'm not afraid of the devil." Seeing that the captain did not like his bravery questioned the priest apologized and left.

During the day the army pressed on and pursued Bragg to Winchester; [John] Morgan the Guerilla[5] and Dick McCann[6] joined Bragg on his retreat. On reaching Winchester the army pursued the retreating Confederates to McMinnville, and early one morning captured their rearguard and just at the limits of the town. Among others Dick McCann was here taken. As usual Morgan got away. In the house where he made his headquarters was found a magnificent breakfast placed on the table. The Yanks entered so quickly and so unexpected that the Confederates had not time to resist an attack nor to enjoy the luxurious repast laid out for them. The caterer to the general was not slow in discovering Morgan's breakfast, which he secured for the chief and staff. After a few minutes they all entered followed by Father Trecy. As the good father entered the officers saluted him in various ways such as

"Father, are you tired?" "Good morning, Father," etc. All the ladies of the house were present and looked wondrously at the father of so large a family of sons. The old lady of the house seated herself close by the general and exclaimed, "God be blessed and are all you men sons of that man. Is he indeed your father?" "Indeed" said the general, "he is my father, and these are his children." "Glory be to God," she exclaimed, "I would like to see his wife." "Oh then," said the general, "you can see her." "Well then she is along."

By this time the eyes of all the ladies were turned upon Father Trecy who could not any longer withstand from bursting out with a fit of laughter, which he smothered by another fit of coughing. He then left the room for a few minutes but the general and staff enjoyed the fun until breakfast was announced. When all were seated the old lady deputed herself as a committee of one to see to Father Trecy and his wants at table. As soon as a vacancy occurred she seated herself alongside him and began a conversation with him, as follows. "Your son the general says your wife is along with you." "Oh yes, madam, I never travel without her." "The Lord be praised some of your sons look as old as yourself." "Oh, it is nothing uncommon to see a son as old looking as his father, or a daughter as old looking as her mother." "Oh dear me, that is true there is my Nelly; my second eldest how old she looks." Then turning to the priest and staring him in the face, she said, "Now I want you to bring your wife till I see her." "Oh yes, oh yes," exclaimed the daughters, "bring her up to see us. We would like to see her very much."

The priest having some business to attend to at headquarters started off but returned in a few hours. He was then asked why he did not bring his wife along with him, to which he responded that he was a Catholic priest, and that his wife was the Church. "Spiritually," said he, "Those you see as well as those with whom you conversed this morning are my children." The countenance of the old lady fell, the daughters rose and left the room greatly disappointed. The priest and the old lady remained some time in conversation with which she expressed herself as delighted and invited him if ever he came the way again to be sure and call to see her. She then hinted if his sons accompanied him that he would request them to leave their shooting irons at home. During the conversation lively skirmishing was heard. Father Trecy bid the ladies good bye, and all the soldiers are in their saddles in an instant and are off.

The enemy retreated and the general was ordered with his command to Alabama. On the way Father Trecy saved several buildings destined for destruction and also frustrated the arrests of numbers of persons whom enmity had caused to be suspected. On entering the city of Huntsville the negroes who knew Father Trecy during his residence there ran along the streets, exclaiming "Press[7] de Lord," "Lord be praised," "Dar is Massa Trecy," and they ran off the sidewalks to shake hands with him. While shaking hands they would say, "Massa Trecy is my friend." "Massa gave me books." "Massa, Father tells me what's right." "Press[8] God I loves him!" "Massa Father you stay now." "Teach nigger again." "You's our friend." The priest had to leave the line at the head of which he was with the general to speak to the negroes. The officers as they passed laughed heartily and while numbers of them exclaimed, "Father is a prisoner in the hands of his friends,"[9] others would say, "Save me from my friends."[10]

It was his kindness to these negroes previous to the war that caused this attachment. The Sunday previous to leaving Huntsville an order was issued to allow all negroes inside the picket lines, but none to go outside. The consequence was the negroes flocked into the city in swarms and all dressed up in their best attire. One of them who was a preacher, finding that he could not return approached Father Trecy with tears in his eyes beseeching his interference to get him permitted to return and bring with him his wife and children. "You knows Massa Trecy," said he, "I likes you and believes all you tell me. You knows I goes your church when you preach for we niggers, and whiles you away I preaches. You tells us Bless God Massa. I [did] dis Massa. I loves be free but I loves my babies Massa, hable de Genl. bring my wife and children!" Father Trecy interfered in his behalf and an escort was furnished him to go five miles in the country for his wife and children.

The next route of the army was for Winchester. On nearing Salem, Father Trecy observed as he passed by a house some ladies screaming at the windows. Inquiring [as to] the cause, he learned that some soldiers were inside and were acting rudely. The priest remonstrated with the soldiers and endeavored to remove them. His entreaties were of no avail, they would not stir. He then had them arrested. In a few hours they were tried by court martial, disarmed, stripped of their uniforms and one half of their beards and head were shorn, and they [were] drummed out of service.

Near Bridgeport, Alabama, a rather amusing scene took place between an old Irish woman and the priest. The latter had some occasion to call at her residence. On entering it he said, "God save all here." "And you too," responded the old woman. After the salutation, Father Trecy passed around and shook hands with the children saying to each as he did "God bless you." "Arrah then maybe you are an Irishman and a Catholic?" said the old lady. By this time a soldier had said to one of the boys, "That's a priest." The young lad instantly stole over to the old lady and said in a loud whisper. "Granny that's a priest." "Arrah musha begor then be coming none of your tricks on me," exclaimed Granny striking the boy on the shoulder. "Grandmother," said Father Trecy speaking up, "The boy tells you the truth I am a priest." "Ah then you may quit your blathering, and have off your blasphemy, shure no one would take you for a priest with that long black goat's beard on you" (then making the sign of the cross she continued). "A priest, ah God stand between us and harm but you are the purty priest." Her son who met the priest the day previous at the general's headquarters now entered and addressing the old woman in Irish told her that he really was a priest. This put an end to her doubts. She instantly fell on her knees clasped her hands and raised her eyes to heaven in the most fervent prayer, then turned to the priest and asked him in the most suppliant tone to forgive her for what she had done and said. During that day Father Trecy baptized two of her grandchildren, and next morning said Mass and had many of the residents to Holy Communion.

Early next morning the army moved across the Raccoon Mountain and rested the following night at Trenton a small town in Wills Valley, Georgia. About the middle of the night, the Most Reverend Archbishop Purcell of Cincinnati and Father [John Mary] Jacquette[11] arrived. At 3 o'clock next morning word was received that Bragg had fled to the Pigeon Mountains in Georgia and orders were instantly given to move without delay for Chattanooga. His Grace expressed a desire to say Mass in Chattanooga. Father Trecy accompanied by Colonel [Arthur C.] Ducat and Captain Kelly of the general's staff went in advance of the column in order to have the church in readiness. On arriving at the sacred edifice they were horrified to learn that it had been entered the night before by soldiers of General [George D.] Wagner's Brigade and rifled of everything. The Tabernacle was broken open, the altar stone smashed to pieces, the stations of the cross and the crucifixes broken and strewn around, the vestments torn to pieces and the altar linens were carried off. The archbishop and general arrived and witnessed the spoliation. Father Trecy then instituted an active search for the pastor, the Rev. Father Nealis, [O.P.].[12]

After some time he was found on a sick bed suffering from a dangerous wound received at the hands of two miscreants while in the discharge of his duty amongst his countrymen in the coal mines on the Raccoon Mountains. Passing between two houses about a mile apart he was met by two ruffians who called themselves soldiers of the Confederate army. They ordered him to a halt and inquired who he was, what he was and what was his business there? In response he inquired of them who they were who thus demanded him to give such an account of himself. "If," said he, "by authority you are here I will show you my pass. My name is Nealis, I am a Catholic priest—" Before he could utter another word one of them[13] seized him by the collar of the coat, and drew out a long corn cutting knife and raised it over his head and swore he would cut his head off.[14] Father Nealis tore away from his grasp and was about to defend himself when the other raised his gun and shot him through the side.[15]

At Father Nealis's house the vestments were had, and the archbishop celebrated Mass with Father Trecy assisting. After Mass a guard was placed in ambush near the church in order to discover if possible who the sacrilegists were. While they were watching seven persons entered. Word was sent to Father Trecy who with a squad of men proceeded to the church. On entering they found seven men about to renew their work of spoliation. They were arrested and brought before the general. He was about to have them Court-martialed but Father Nealis begged them off. Two of them were found to be Irish Protestants.

The evening of the day following this occurrence the army moved from Chattanooga south along the Pigeon Mountains. At about ten miles off the army was joined by General [Thomas L.] Crittenden[16] commanding the 21st Corps. General Bragg was about this time reinforced with troops from Virginia and Alabama and drew up in line of battle at Chickamauga. General Rosecrans advanced to the attack. The battle was bloody and fearful. During it Father Trecy had many narrow escapes. On Saturday the first day three bullets passed through the cape of his great coat and his vestments were captured but retaken during the day. He did not however get them for eight days after, when they were sent to headquarters. On Sunday the hat was blown off his head by a solid shot while attending a patient. The wounded were so numerous that the chaplains had not a moment's rest during the engagements or for several days afterwards. A few days after the battle General Rosecrans was relieved from duty and proceeded to Cincinnati.[17] Father Trecy accompanied him. When the latter was returning, General [George H.] Thomas[18] sent him an order to attend the wounded then lying in hospital at Nashville. He did so and found them in many instances very much neglected by the persons appointed as hospital stewards by General Thomas. During the days of the battle and within the following two weeks, Father Trecy baptized over one hundred and fifty persons.

The battle field of Chickamauga, was in every sense, a desperate and bloody one. Father Trecy and the other chaplains found their hands full in attending to the spiritual wants of the Catholics, as well as in trying to alleviate the sufferings of the wounded. A routed army— a lost battle field—all fearful sights to contemplate. The one presents to you a disorganized mass of men, without hope, vainly seeking safety in flight: the other the fearful spectacle of dead and dying men, the former shattered and torn out of all human semblance; the latter gasping in all the fierce agony of terrible torture.

Such were the scenes that the chaplains and doctors, who remained on the field after the retreat of the army witnessed. Here our chaplain was near losing his life while preparing a dying man; he remained behind the troops until the enemy had just come up to him. Having heard the man's confession he rose to go. When a sharpshooter took aim at him and sent the bullet through the breast of his coat. The priest hurriedly mounted his horse, but as he did so a perfect shower of bullets rained around him but he miraculously escaped with a few slight scratches on his horse.

The services of the chaplains were sorely tried in attending the hospitals in and around Chattanooga and in offering up the Holy Sacrifice for the soldiers.

At the opening of [William T.] Sherman's[19] remarkable campaign, Father Trecy attached himself to his old command, the 4th Regular Cavalry, but soon after, and at the request of General Stanley, he joined his headquarters as chaplain.

General Stanley, as stated elsewhere, became a convert and was ever after remarkable for his truly Christian piety and zeal. Though Father Trecy enjoyed a kind of roving commission in the army, passing from command to command attending to the spiritual duties of the soldiers, he had his headquarters with General Stanley. He also spent much of his time with his old command, the 4th Regular Cavalry. The further history of Father Trecy with the army is the history of Sherman's brilliant march and campaign against Atlanta.

During the hundred days campaign the father was incessant in his ministrations to the sick, the dying and the wounded, and was as well-known and in a manner as much respected by the troops as "Old Sherman" himself.

After the capture of Atlanta, while we lay encamped there preparing for the March to the Sea, Father Trecy was devoted in his attendance and duties and frequently said Mass both for the benefit of the troops and citizens.

When [John Bell] Hood[20] struck out for Nashville, with Thomas in pursuit, Father Trecy accompanied Thomas's army with General Stanley. He rendered invaluable services to the wounded along the line of march, particularly after the battles of Franklin and Nashville.

At Franklin he was beside General Stanley when a bullet tore across the latter's neck, just touching the carotid artery. The general put up his hand and felt that the string of his scapular was cut by the bullet; in his faith and religious belief, he turned to the priest and said, "Father, this blessed scapular, through God's mercy, has saved my life."[21]

After the surrender of the Confederate armies, though Father Trecy held a commission as chaplain in the regulars, he at once resigned and returned to his mission at Huntsville, Alabama, where he set to work to repair the injury done to his church and to reestablish his mission. He has been so far successful, and before long, the Catholics of Huntsville, owing to the labors and exertions of their energetic pastor, will possess a church worthy of their zeal and piety and of the service of the Most High.

❧   ❧   ❧

EPILOGUE: After taking a leave of absence in December 1865, Trecy finally officially resigned from his regiment in August 1866. After the war, Father Trecy continued his service to the Diocese of Mobile, pastoring St. Mary of the Visitation Catholic Church in Huntsville, Alabama, during the years of reconstruction. About 1873, he was appointed to serve the parish of St. Michael at Bayou La Batre, Alabama. He suffered a stroke that left him partially paralyzed and he retired from ministry in 1881. He died in 1888 at the Alexian Brothers' Hospital in St. Louis, Missouri. He was buried in the Catholic section of Maple Hill Cemetery, Huntsville, Alabama.

SOURCES: "Jeremiah F. Trecy," Appointments, Commissions, and Promotions file, Records of the Adjutant General's Office (RG 94), U.S. National Archives, Washington, DC; Henry C. LaBudda, F.S.C., "A Study of Father Jeremiah F. Trecy, Civil War Chaplain" (master's thesis, University of Notre Dame, 1935); Catherine Jones Twohig, "An Epic of Early Iowa: Father Trecy's Colonization Scheme," *Iowa Catholic Historical Review* 3 (Spring 1931): 3–13; Pat Tumminello, ed., *A Mighty Fortress of Faith: A History of St. Mary of the Visitation Church, 1861–2011* (Quitman, MS: Specialty Publishing and Printing Co., 2012), 3–18, 329–32, 426–28; Robert J. Miller, *Both Prayed to the Same God: Religion and Faith in the American Civil War* (Lanham, MD: Lexington Books, 2007), 115–16.

See also John Fitch, *Annals of the Army of the Cumberland: Comprising Biographies, Descriptions of Departments, Accounts of Expeditions, Skirmishes, and Battles; Also Its Police Record of Spies, Smugglers, and Prominent Rebel Emissaries. Together with Anecdotes, Incidents, Poetry, Reminiscences, Etc. and Official Reports of the Battle of Stone River* (Philadelphia: J. B. Lippincott & Co., 1863), 326–30.

CHAPTER IV

Rev. Joseph C. Carrier, C.S.C.

Chaplain 6th Missouri Cavalry

*The order of the Holy Cross—What it has done—Sketch of
Father Carrier's early life—He joins Grant's army in front
of Vicksburg—His reception by Generals Grant,
Sherman, and Ewing—His visit to the camps and hospitals.*

INTRODUCTION: Father Joseph Celestine Carrier, C.S.C.
(1833–1904), served as chaplain to the 6th Missouri Infantry.
Born in Saint-Jeoire, France, on July 14, 1833, Carrier was the
youngest of ten children.[1] He received an excellent education
at the College of Belley. He excelled in mathematics and science and received an appointment (while still a teenager) as
professor of natural philosophy to the faculty of a college in
Ferney, near Geneva, Switzerland.

Carrier joined the Brothers of the Holy Family of Belley, a
community dedicated to the education of boys, taking the
name Brother Cyrille. When, in 1855, Bishop Joseph Crétin of
St. Paul, Minnesota, requested the service of the brothers in
his American diocese, Brother Cyrille was sent as superior.
The brothers' school project was ill-fated. The bishop, who
died only two years later, seemed to be displeased with the
brothers' teaching abilities and few showed interest in joining

79

their community. There was also infighting with the other brothers viewing Cyrille as a poor superior—paranoid and despotic. The Brothers of the Holy Family remained in Minnesota only until February 1860 when they were called back to France.

At this time, instead of returning, Carrier journeyed to Notre Dame where he entered the Congregation of Holy Cross. He was ordained in early 1861 and commenced teaching at the university. After the 1862–1863 academic year, Father Carrier left Notre Dame for General Ulysses S. Grant's army, which was besieging Vicksburg, Mississippi. He was enrolled on July 1, 1863, as chaplain to the 6th Missouri. His service was not long. Carrier found the work taxing and traumatic. He resigned on October 3, 1863, and returned to his community having secured the government's promise not to draft any of Notre Dame's priests or brothers.

Despite the short duration of his service as a chaplain, Conyngham here relates in great detail Carrier's wartime efforts devoting four chapters of his manuscript to him. His sources include Carrier's diary, though admittedly fragmentary, and information supplied by a childhood friend. He relates Carrier's interactions with various high-ranking officers, including Generals Sherman, Ewing, and Grant, and their obvious esteem for the priest. The text also highlights Carrier's ministry to those who had experienced the horrors of war: the sick and wounded in military hospitals. The account concludes with excerpts from Carrier's diary following the surrender of Vicksburg on July 4, 1863.

❀   ❀   ❀

Perhaps no other Catholic order in the country supplied so many chaplains to the army as that of the Holy Cross of Notre Dame, Indiana, while its co-religious establishment gave a long list of faithful sisters, who fervently devoted themselves to the attendance of the sick and wounded in the various hospitals.

The Rev. Father Carrier, who is at present superior of the House of Studies at Notre Dame and professor of chemistry, physics, and the natural sciences in the university there, is a native of France. He was born in the year 1833 of very respectable parents in one of the southeastern departments of that country, and from his tenderest age, he manifested sentiments of deep piety and religious thoughtfulness. One of the most striking characteristics of his early youth was an unceasing desire to acquire knowledge. From a sketch furnished us of the early life and career of the reverend gentleman, whose name heads this article, by an old friend and fellow student of his we take the following extracts:

When not more than six or seven years old, he made it a special object to ransack every private library in his native town, at the same time as he would spend every penny he could procure in buying books, particularly works treating of things not generally known in the physical sciences, or natural history. Nor were his readings fruitless, for he was always careful to read attentively, and to take copious notes of what he wished to remember. At the age of four years, he was a good and fast reader, and wrote a beautiful small hand. He also could speak French, Italian, or rather Piedmontese (his maternal ancestors were Italians, as the name of his mother Maria Canelli indicates) and a kind of patois which he had picked up in the company of other children. For the three following years, he was placed under the direction of a private tutor. When eight years old his father sent him to the College of Belley—a famous institution founded more than two centuries before by the Oratorians, but directed, at this time, by priests of the secular clergy. Such were his diligence and progress during the eight succeeding years that he invariably carried off the first honors of his class. And at the age of 19, [having]² finished his course of studies, he traveled through France, Switzerland and part of

Italy. [He] received, that year, an appointment as professor in a college, not having as yet determined to embrace the ecclesiastical state.

The late bishop of St. Paul, [Minnesota]—Dr. [Joseph] Crétin prevailed on the young professor to accompany him to America, and to prepare himself for the sacred ministry. Mr. Carrier made up his mind, then, to become a missionary priest. Accordingly he arrived in the episcopal city of his protector and friend in the early part of the year 1855—being only 21 years of age—The bishop had long cherished the idea of forming a "Petit Séminaire," or small college, in his episcopal city; he laid the foundation stone and he naturally cast his eyes on Mr. Carrier to take the direction of it as he had some experience in teaching, and could speak English quite fluently having learned the language in France.

The Catholic schools for boys, taught by some brothers lately arrived from France, were also placed under his direction. Shortly after, the bishop died. This together with the long vacancy of the See ruined the projects of Mr. Carrier with regard to establishment of a great house of education in the Northwest. On the other hand, observing that the condition of the secular clergy in this country was extremely precarious, he felt loath to lead the life of a secular priest.

He accordingly sought, and readily found admittance in a religious order. In the beginning of the year 1860 he entered the Congregation of the Holy Cross, made his profession at Notre Dame the following year, and since that time has been almost constantly connected with the university of that name.

Father Carrier has filled various and responsible positions in the order and in the university but none proved more acceptable and congenial to him than his present position.[3] For offices of mere honor and preeminence, or of responsibility, he feels, and always felt, an invincible repugnance. Father Carrier is a strong hater and an unforgiving foe of all hypocrisy, shallowness, and humbuggery. His sympathies are true, strong, and enduring, and it is as difficult to lose his confidence and friendship when once secured as it is unavailing to regain his esteem when once forfeited for good and sufficient causes.

Thus writes his friend, of his early life, his studies, his success, and of his great ability as an accomplished scholar and brilliant professor.

Though these qualities are, no doubt, meritorious and laudable in themselves, still I have to deal with his career simply as a chaplain in the army.

Nothing but a strong sense of duty to his God, his fellow man and to his adopted country could induce a man of his scholastic retired habits, to resign the lecture hall for the field, and the day's abstruse researches of science for the war and din of battle, accompanied by all the hardships and privations of army life.

Obedient to the call of duty and to the cry of distress, he and several other members of his order joined the army as chaplains, while the good sisters poured forth from the silence of their cloisters to tend the wounded, soothe the afflicted and to minister to the dying, and even to pay the last tribute to the dead.

A very well written but broken and decommuted journal of Father Carrier's was placed in my hands by the friend aforesaid to whom he had transmitted it for safe keeping, in the shape of letters during the war. The journal or diary was occasionally broken by the intermission of several weeks. This is accounted for by the fact that much of it was lost in its transmission and more of it captured on the march. I have used it as far as practical but for the most of my facts I am indebted to other sources. If the diary were only complete it would make a most valuable work in itself, but as it is, I occasionally make extracts from it.

From the notes in my possession, it would appear that Father Carrier did not join the army as chaplain until 1863, when Grant's[4] army lay in front of Vicksburg. The following are the copies of the approbation or order of his bishop as also of the general pass given to him by General Grant.

The bishop writes:

This is to certify that the bearer of this, the Reverend Joseph C. Carrier, C.S.C., goes with my full approbation and consent to attend to the spiritual wants of the soldiers in the army of General Grant as well as of all others who may need his services.

As he is a clergyman of excellent standing I hereby recommend him most cordially, and sincerely trust that he will meet with that attention and kindness which he merits and the cause which he is engaged in deserves.

John Henry Luers[5]
Bishop of Fort Wayne

After receiving this complimentary letter of approbation from his bishop, Father Carrier immediately started to join Grant's Army, then in front of Vicksburg. On his way he remained a few days at Mound City, [Illinois,] where the good Father [Julian] Bourget[6] had just fallen a victim to his devotion and attention to the sick in the hospitals and where some fifteen of the Sisters of the Holy Cross were left without a priest; and consequently without spiritual ministrations. During his stay here Father Carrier was the guest of Dr. [Newton] Casey and his amiable lady.[7]

He joined the army in a few days and the high opinion entertained of him by General Grant is evident from the unlimited pass in the general's own handwriting given him of which the following is a copy.

Headquarters, Dept. of the Tennessee
Near Vicksburg, June 15th, 1863

The Rev. J. C. Carrier will be permitted to pass all guards and visit through all the camps of the "Investing Army" of Vicksburg, and the troops at Haines's[8] Bluff until otherwise directed.

U. S. Grant
Major General

For a commanding general to write and issue such an order himself was no small compliment and must have been deeply appreciated by the reverend recipient of such a mark of favor and confidence.

As a proof that General Sherman and the various corps and division commanders entertained the same high regard for Father Carrier as General Grant did, we have before us letters written by them in which they speak of him and his valuable services in terms of the highest respect and admiration. As we have said it is greatly to be regretted that Father Carrier's valuable diary of events and operations in front of Vicksburg previous to the surrender, have been, for the most part, lost or destroyed. However, the following sketch, the materials for which has been partly supplied by the friend aforesaid and partly taken from notes, will be found most interesting.

To this are added his letter to the Father Provincial and some [lines] from his own diary which have been placed in our hands. The following sketch goes back to his first connection with the army as chaplain.

On the 14th May (Ascension day) 1863 the Rev. Father Carrier then residing at the College of Notre Dame, Indiana received orders from the Very Reverend Father Provincial (Reverend Father Sorin) to hold himself in readiness to start at a moment's notice for the Army of the Mississippi in the capacity of chaplain. After receiving the orders Father Carrier apprised his parishioners at Lowell[9] that his connection with them as their pastor was at an end. The children whom he had been preparing at that place for some time had made their first Communion and after two lengthy sermons to his beloved parishioners, he started to the college there to meet the students whom he had prepared also for their first Communion. He took dinner with them at the priest's novitiate. Towards the close of the repast the Rev. Father Provincial entered and announced that a chaplain was wanted in Sherman's command, that he had just received a letter from Mrs. [Ellen] Sherman[10] requesting him to yield to the oft expressed desire of several generals in sending priests to Vicksburg.

The Father Provincial then requested Father Carrier to read the letter aloud.[11] After dinner he took Father Carrier and Father [Alexis] Granger[12] to another apartment, and there said there was much good to be done in the army around Vicksburg and requested the former to go at once.

Father Carrier consulted and at the request of the Father Provincial wrote instantly to Mrs. Sherman, stating that he had accepted the proffered position in her husband's command and requesting her to forward him a letter of introduction and a pass from General Burnside. On the 28th a package directed to Father Carrier was handed to him. It was from Mrs. Sherman and contained the pass and letters of introduction to Generals Grant, Sherman, and [Hugh] Ewing, and to Captain Ch[arles] Ewing,[13] together with a kind letter from herself enclosing a $20 bill. Father Carrier immediately carried the package to the Father Provincial who was then in St. Mary's with Bishop Luers. Having found everything satisfactory Father Carrier was told to hold himself in readiness for his departure to the army the following day. The next morning the father in order to be prepared for any eventuality made a general confession, and, after requesting the blessing of the bishop and Father Provincial, he took leave of his confreres and friends and started to minister to the spiritual wants of the Catholic soldiers serving in Sherman's command and then engaged in deadly strife around the entrenchments at Vicksburg.

The next afternoon he arrived in Mound City (8 miles from Cairo), visited the hospitals heard the confessions of the sisters in charge and prepared some of the wounded soldiers for death. He preached that evening in the church which was crowded principally by soldiers and started next morning for Cairo. During the day he visited General [John] Buford [at] the Cairo hospital then in charge of the sisters, and Father [Louis] Lambert the parish priest.[14] On the afternoon of the following day he left for Memphis where he arrived the next morning. As soon as the steamboat was moved to the wharf, Father Carrier directed his steps towards the Overton hospital where the sisters were.[15] Meeting with Sister Flavina he announced to her that he wanted to say Mass. As [it][16] was a great festival (Corpus Christi), she showed him where the Catholic Church was. Going there Father Carrier met Father Kelly who kindly told him that he should make his house his home for the time he should remain in Memphis. After Mass Father Carrier took breakfast with Father Daly, and then went to see General [Stephen] Hurlbut[17] who received him with great politeness and granted him, with the utmost readiness, free transportation to Vicksburg.

After taking leave of the general he returned to the Overton Hospital, saw all the sisters (ten in number) and addressed to them a few encouraging words as he had also done to those in Mound City. There were about eight hundred wounded in the hospital here of different religions, but all were glad to see the Catholic priest. After bidding the sisters and Dominican Fathers good bye, Father Carrier left for the boat, which started that evening for Vicksburg. On the 6th of June they arrived at a place called Chickasaw Bayou on the Yazoo River, where men, provisions, ammunition, etc. destined for Sherman's army, were disembarked. Innumerable wagons and mules were constantly stationed there on an open prairie for the purpose of transporting the materials to the different corps then around Vicksburg. On landing Father Carrier directed his steps to the general commanding at that point for the purpose of procuring the necessary pass as well as an ambulance to convey him to Sherman's headquarters. The drivers of the wagon were Irishmen and had of course every respect for their priest. The wagon master (a sergeant) was the nephew of the Rev. Father [James] Curley of Georgetown College. The distance to Sherman's headquarters was about six miles, and during that short ride the sufferings from thirst and dust which Father Carrier endured were indescribable. His lips were fearfully parched and he dared not drink the turbid water the men had with them for fear of getting sick. In spite of its extreme muddiness the soldiers highly relished it and pronounced it excellent, and were quite astonished when the father begged to differ with them. "Ah Father," they would say, "happy we if we could have such fine water," and they drank of it with real gusto. Near Vicksburg they had only mud hole water. Thirst however was not the father's greatest torment. He was continually enveloped in a high dense cloud of dust that extended around to such an extent that the foliage of the trees was of sally brown instead of its natural lovely green.

When he arrived at Sherman's headquarters he was quite exhausted and his appearance quite altered. His would be black clothes had turned to a dirty yellow brown and his features could scarcely be recognized. As soon as he saw the general's flag waving in the breeze he jumped out of the vehicle and without thinking or caring of washing himself he entered into the tent and exclaimed, "General, for God's sake give me something to quench my thirst and I will tell you, after, whom I am!" "Porter or wine?" said the general. "Porter," said the father. At the same time the general saw his large cross protruding on his breast and said, "You are Father Carrier. I have been expecting you for the past few days. You left Notre Dame on the 29th did you not?" By this time a fine glass of porter had cleared the father's throat and he answered the general's queries. They then indulged in a general friendly conversation for over an hour. After the general inquiring about his wife and children, Father Sorin, etc., etc., he, without waiting [for] enquiries concerning the operations of the army before Vicksburg, kindly explained to the father the positions of the troops, what they had done and what they expected to do.

The general then introduced him to Dr. [Charles] McMillan,[18] the Medical Director of the corps, who at once informed him that he had been for several years the physician of Fordham College, N.Y. After being introduced to the staff, Father Carrier started to General Ewing's headquarters in order to see that worthy soldier. Entering his tent he said "Here is a soldier, general, a soldier of the cross." "Hea! Hea!" he exclaimed rising to greet him. "You are Father Carrier!" "Yes, General," said the father. "Very well," replied the general, "You shall remain with me, and share with us whatever our peculiar situation can furnish. Tomorrow morning early, I shall have a tent erected for you to dwell in and say Mass in." "Tomorrow is Sunday, General," said the father. "I desire to say Mass for your men." "Very well," the general replied. "I will send word to all the colonels of my brigade to that effect." After a pretty long conversation the general ordered two horses to be saddled and both rode to Captain Charley [Ewing]'s tent. After a short conversation with the captain, they returned to the general's headquarters.

Early in the morning twelve men were engaged in leveling a place on the hill side close by the general's tent, and fitting up two tents adjoining each other, one for the sanctuary and priest's residence and the other for the church. At 10 o'clock all was ready and a great many soldiers had assembled to hear Mass. Mass was commenced. The general and his brother and some other officers and several soldiers were present. During the Holy Sacrifice the father delivered a splendid military exhortation which had a telling effect. After Mass a sergeant stepped forward and told the father that there was another priest in Grant's command who was sick for some time past. On hearing this the father resolved to go and see him instantly, and after a great deal to do found Father [Napoleon] Mignault[19] (the sick Father) in one of [General James] McPherson's[20] hospitals. He was very much enfeebled and was suffering badly from chronic dysentery. After remaining sometime with the sick priest Father Carrier left for headquarters. The following morning he said Mass and gave Communion to several soldiers.

After breakfast he wrote a letter to the sisters on board the Red Rover to apprize them of his arrival and of his intention to visit them in a few days. He had scarcely finished it when General Sherman came to invite him and General Ewing[21] to visit him. Father Carrier greatly desired to obtain from the Governor of Ohio a regular commission as chaplain in one of the regiments of the 3rd Brigade with full liberty of ministering where he pleased within the limits of the 15th Army Corps or throughout Grant's Command. His objects were manifold, 1st to remain in the army and be recognized by the army at large as a commissioned officer acting in an official capacity,

2nd to defray his own expenses, with the salary which such a position would bring him as his means and those of his order were limited. Having made known his wish to General Ewing the latter not only approved of it but said that he was thinking the same matter over himself and that he would attend to it immediately. The general then had Father Carrier's name proposed to the officers of the 6th Missouri who unanimously elected him their chaplain, although all the officers (numbering 20) who signed the petition to the Governor of Ohio were non-Catholic. The afternoon of the election General Ewing called on the father and asked him if he did not wish to be introduced to General Grant. Having received an affirmative answer the general ordered four horses to be harnessed, one for himself, one for the father, and the others for two officers of staff. On the way towards General Grant's headquarters they passed General Sherman's tent. The party called on the general but he was absent being on business of importance at Grant's headquarters. Under these circumstances General Ewing thought better not to proceed any further and the party resolved to spend the day with General Frank Blair.[22]

CHAPTER V

Rev. Joseph C. Carrier, C.S.C., Continued

Few Catholics and a number of infidels in hospital—
Pious soldiers saving their temporary church from
destruction—On board the Red Rover—His reception and
services there —Celebrating Mass under fire.

Father Carrier having been fortified with the following pass commenced to visit all the hospitals.

Rev F. Carrier will be permitted to visit all hospitals of the 15th army corps until further orders.
By command of Major General Sherman
H[ugh] Ewing, Brigadier General

Having reached the division hospital the surgeon in charge received him kindly and was polite when he showed him General Sherman's pass. He accompanied the father through the different wards and explained the diverse complaints or wounds of the sick soldiers. The father approached every patient, and inquired of him how he felt, where he was wounded, or what was the nature of his ailment, his name, the regiment he belonged to and the like, at the same time, giving him a chance to see the large cross suspended on his neck. No sooner would the cross be seen than the patient would recognize him as a Catholic priest; if a Catholic, he would say so, and if an Irishman he would say, "Oh your Reverence is a Catholic clergyman, God bless you, I have not seen a priest [for] so long." After going through all that ordeal, he only found out of one hundred and thirty-five patients, twelve Catholics whose confessions he heard. The great majority of the rest were complete infidels who were never baptized and who were deprived of all religion, instructions, or ideas.

Among these whose confessions he heard was an Irishman who after receiving absolution said: "Oh! Father what a happy day for me, I would have given the whole world when I fell wounded on the battle field to have a priest at my side for a few moments only. Thanks be to God, and to you, Father. I am now at peace with my Maker and with myself. I desire nothing more." After returning from the hospital the general kindly offered the father his chief of staff to accompany him on a visit to the surrounding country. The trip was delightful and the party returned about dusk laden with the most choice floral selection of every kind and description.

That same evening a terrific tempest took place, notwithstanding which, numbers of soldiers attended the confessional, and were it not for the presence of these Christian soldiers the chapel tents would have been blown away. They held fast to the cords and held them in spite of the hurricane of rain, flashes of forked lightning, and peals of terrific thunder which were then raging. After a short time the fierce storms ceased but the rain kept falling in such torrents that the floods threatened to carry into the bottom of the ravine, which was a short distance off, all the tents contained. The pious soldiers who held fast by their temporary, yet sacred edifice during the hurricane, now turned out and dug deep trenches around the tent and succeeded in preventing its utter destruction.

Having had a letter of introduction from the Rev. Father Lambert, pastor of Cairo, to General Lalor,[1] Father Carrier resolved to call on that worthy soldier, and General Ewing and

Captain Cornyn[2] volunteered to accompany him. The trio had a smart ride before reaching his headquarters, where they found the gray haired and good natured old general in his dishabille. He received the party as old friends and felt highly gratified at their visit. In addition to seeing the general personally, who was a fervent Catholic and an exemplary and true soldier, Father Carrier wished to find out if there were many Catholics in his brigade and to make known his presence among them so that in case of need they might know where to find him. After about two hours' conversation with the general the party left for home.

That evening and morning a large number of confessions were heard and in the afternoon General Ewing invited the father for another ride, viz. to visit [General Frederick] Steele's[3] fortifications, in order, he said, to inure him to the hardships of war, and to make him proficient in the art of horsemanship. The following company started riding two abreast, Generals Sherman and Steele, General Ewing and Major Hammond, Captain Cornyn and Father Carrier, Captain Sofland and Lieutenant Eddington, and three orderlies. The company rode up to the very works, though the firing on both sides was brisk. They rode all around the fortification under the lead of acting Brigadier General [Charles R.] Woods, 'till they arrived at a defile quite unprotected from the enemy's sharpshooters. When some soldier shouted at them not to stop there they immediately turned to the other side of the defile where they halted and took a peep at the enemy's breastworks. The father having an eager desire to see the enemy's works put his head over the parapets when a bullet from the rifle of a sharpshooter struck the parapet within a foot of him. Having to cross the defile again, the father turned to General Sherman and said, "General, one who is not accustomed to the music of the balls and finds no entertainment in them, would as well not hear them at all." "Well," said the general laughing, "Such music is rather strange and unusual for professors or civilians, but to old troopers there is still a good deal of harmony in it." All the party agreed in the general's remarks except the "civilian" who begged the privilege to differ from them in "toto."

The ride to headquarters was a perfect race and the father was much jaded, not being skilled in equestrianism. On entering the tent he threw himself on his cot and fell into a sound sleep from which he did not awaken till the following morning, and then he found himself scarcely able to leave the bed. While he was considering the possibility of arising, there came peeping into his tent an Irishman who said, "Be there Mass this morning your reverence, there are four of us here who wish to go to confession." Here all possibility of further repose vanished from the good father and he arose said Mass and heard numerous confessions. At dinner (which took place at noon) General Ewing again invited him to another ride, in the afternoon to General [John A.] Logan's headquarters which he hesitatingly accepted on the condition that the general would ride slower than he did the day previous. They rode under the cover of the breastworks but their course was marked by showers of bullets the whole way with an occasional shell bursting over their heads. On entering General Logan's tent, the father, to his great surprise, was introduced to Major General U. S. Grant, the able commander of the Department of the Tennessee. The father was also introduced to General McPherson, General Logan and numbers of other officers. As the father shook hands with General Grant, he said, "I am happy to meet a great soldier and a successful general. Victory follows you wherever you go. The nation's hopes are now on you General Grant." The general in reply thanked him two or three times in a quite embarrassed and modest manner.

The general then made the father sit by him on a little cot and both engaged in a somewhat lengthy conversation. He asked the father if he came directly from the North. On receiving an affirmative answer he said, "You are attached as professor to a college in Indiana." "Yes, General," replied the father, "I have been years in the college of Notre Dame and I am still attached to it." "Well," said the general, "You will find that the life of a soldier is quite different from that of a professor and that our tents are not so comfortable as the halls of a college." "General," replied the father, "I understood that before I left Notre Dame. I did not expect to find in the soldiers' camp all the comforts the conveniences and ease of home." "Very well," responded the general, "I am glad to find you prepared to meet the hardships of war. I hope you will remain with us as long as you can." Then changing the conversation he asked the father how he liked the Federal breastworks to which the [father] responded, "Very well, General, I am perfectly astonished to see how much has been done in so short a time." The father then took the liberty of asking the general when he hoped to be in Vicksburg, to which the latter responded by saying that as everything was working well he hoped the siege would not be long. When the father expressed his fears with regard to [Confederate General Joseph E.] Johnston's[4] army coming upon them in the rear, he said with great composure, "There is nothing to apprehend from him I have troops enough on the Big Black and at Haines's Bluff to prevent his further advance towards Vicksburg."

After some further conversation the father handed him a letter of introduction from Mrs. Sherman. After reading it he said, "I thank you Rev. Mr. Carrier for the letter. I will be happy to afford you every facility to fulfill your praiseworthy purpose. I am going to give you a full pass." Suiting the action to the word he stepped into the adjoining tent to the adjutant's office and wrote with his own hand a general pass.[5] When the general was handing the order to the father he said, "Reverend Sir, I will be always happy to give you every facility in my power." "Thank you General, you are extremely kind," responded the father. The general then said, "Let us see what General Logan has been doing of late." The four generals walked first and the rest accompanied by the father followed. They went along the extensive lines of approaches and fortifications built by General Logan. Having visited every nook of General Logan's fortifications all the party went away in different directions.

General Grant returned to his headquarters and accompanied only by one orderly and one aide-camp, General McPherson went to inspect some other works in his division, and Father Carrier and General Ewing retraced their steps towards their tents taking care to avoid certain dangers which might await them at different passes on the road.

The following day being Sunday, the father heard numerous confessions before Mass which he offered up at 10 o'clock. He preached after the first Gospel, and after the conclusion of the Holy Sacrifice he vested with the scapular those who had that morning received Holy Communion. After dinner he visited the hospitals of the 2nd Division and addressed to every patient a few cheering and consoling words regardless of his creed. They all kindly thanked him except one dark despairing infidel who desired to be left alone. "I come here," said the father, "as a friend who desires to cheer, with the consoling truths of religion those who like you are suffering and infirm (he had lost one of his legs) and who soon might experience the realities of a future life." The wretched and hopeless man then turned toward the wall and said not a word.

After remaining three days at headquarters hearing confessions, writing communications and the like, Father Carrier resolved to visit the sisters on board of the hospital boat, the "Red Rover." Having procured an ambulance he started for the landing point viz. Chickasaw Bayou, in order to take the boat for Young's Point. It was about 3 P.M. when the boat reached Young's Point, and there was the "Red Rover" lying just at the junction of the Yazoo and Mississippi Rivers. Being landed on the Louisiana side of the Mississippi and not a single craft being about the place Father Carrier did not know what to do in order to reach the "Red Rover." A thought then struck him and he hoisted his handkerchief as a signal to the boatmen of the Red Rover to come for him but all in vain, as they did not see him. A stalwart Irishman was passing by and the father requested him to hail with all the powers of his lungs the boatmen of the Red Rover. Although the Irishman made the surrounding hills echo and re-echo repeatedly it was of no avail, the distance was too great. Again he resumed the waving of the handkerchief and again he despaired and was about to fold and pocket the unrecognized flag, when two navy surgeons approached and seeing the colors floating in the air, one of them with great politeness and pointing to the direction of the Red Rover said, "We belong to the boat, Sir, and have a bark on this side and will ferry you over if you so desire." "I thank you very much gentlemen," responded the father. "You greatly oblige me in taking me with you."

On reaching the place where the bark was lying the kind physicians took the father's travelling bag and umbrella and placed them in the boat and then helped himself in just as if he had been a lady. Four vigorous marines, armed with oars, soon landed them on board the "Red Rover." There the same surgeon who had spoken to him first on the bank of the river took hold of his baggage and bade him to follow and conducted him directly to the sisters' parlor. Although the father up to that time had manifested no desire to see them nor indeed had he even told who he was; but the physician readily guessed it and introduced him to the sisters, having asked the father's name just before entering the parlor. None of the sisters knew of the existence of a Father Carrier, nor were they expecting a priest from Notre Dame, nor had the letter which he wrote them the day after his arrival at General Sherman's headquarters reached them. So they were quite taken by surprise; yet, it was an agreeable surprise.

Although the father had lost his credentials from the Provincial still the good sisters believed him to be a priest and made their confessions under such an impression. Towards evening, he went to the surgeon, Dr. [George H.] Bixby,[6] who the father had by this time learned was director and acting head surgeon of the boat hospital, and asked him the privilege of remaining in his floating hospital till the Friday following. "Certainly," he answered, "any length of time. We would be glad to have you remain with us for a much longer period."

The father then expressed a wish to see the captain of the boat, who by the way, was only third officer on board. Dr. [Ninian] Pinkney[7] the medical director of the Mississippi flotilla was the first in rank and Dr. Bixby the chief surgeon was the second. Dr. Pinkney generally stayed onboard the steamer but at that time was absent in Memphis. The captain was a jolly old sailor talkative and would be witty, a great historian with having read little apparently.

Dr. Bixby, having assigned a splendid room for the father he retired there early and slept soundly during the night. The next morning the father arose early, and said Mass at 5 o'clock on a neat altar the sisters had prepared. After Mass he breakfasted with Dr. Bixby and his assistant surgeons. The father asked permission of the chief surgeon to visit the sick on board. The request was instantly granted, so he went to every bed and spoke a few consoling words to every man. After dinner, which he also had with Dr. Bixby, he returned to the sisters' parlor where several sailors and invalids were waiting for him to hear their confessions and it was late at night when he got through with them. Early next morning the father after reciting his prayers went to hear the confessions of some poor bed stricken sailors. After which he celebrated Mass, and gave Communion to some forty persons. The large majority of them had not been at confession for years, some for ten or twenty and one for forty-eight years. All the Catholics that were on board went to their duty excepting two, and even one of them asked the father to hear his confession just as he was going away.

The singular and wonderful workings of the grace of God which was witnessed that day in many a remorseless yet guilty heart was beautiful to behold. It was one of the greatest, if not absolutely the greatest, harvest days of the father's life. After bidding his friends good bye, and imparting a blessing to the sisters and promising to return again in about a month, he jumped into the little boat and started off. Six robust darky sailors rowed the little craft, and soon landed him on the opposite bank of the river by the packet boat "Diligent" which was returning to Chickasaw Bayou. At the latter place he found one of General Ewing's orderlies with his horse, which he immediately mounted and rode to headquarters.

Early the following morning, the father was awakened by the noise of a constant and heavy cannonading. All was in a blaze. Hundreds of pieces of artillery all along the extensive line of the Federal fortifications, and many thousand discharges of musketry from innumerable covered rifle pits, stockades, etc. were vomiting destruction, desolation, and death on the Confederates and undoubtedly spreading consternation and terror throughout the doomed city of Vicksburg. The father instantly dressed himself and ran full of excitement to the general's tent but there was no one there. All the tents in fact were deserted, and the horses gone excepting the father's own, which stood solitary and restless.

Meanwhile, the cannons were playing most briskly and dreadfully their savage music, and the father thinking, no doubt, that a terrible fight was going on determined to go wherever his men were. During his uncertainty he met one of the general's men and asked where his chief was, [and the man][8] told him that the general was at the head of his brigade leading his men to another assault on the enemy's works. The father instantly took his hat and some holy water for baptizing purposes and started off with all the enthusiasm of a Frenchman "born to be a soldier of the cross." He had not proceeded far when he met with a lieutenant of the general's staff, who asked him where he was going so hurriedly, to which the father responded that he was of course going to the battle field and to "follow the men into Vicksburg." "Stop, Stop, Father Carrier, we are not ready yet to go there," said the lieutenant. "There is no engagement." "What," replied the father, "are you not fighting now?" "Oh, we are only shelling the city and firing at the enemy's works." "Well even so my presence is probably required there." "Not at all, not at all, there is no danger of our men, the rebels keep pretty silent." As the lieutenant was soon to return with the general the father requested him to tell him that if he could be of any use here he was to let him know it by one of his orderlies as he was holding himself in readiness to go wherever his duties would call him.

Meantime the father thought he could not do a better action than to offer up the Holy Sacrifice of the Mass, for the souls of those who were falling under the murderous fire. Suiting his thoughts to actions he did so in the presence of some soldiers and amidst the continual and deafening discharge of the artillery and musketry on both sides.

CHAPTER VI

Rev. Joseph C. Carrier, C.S.C., Continued

Father Carrier visits a sick priest—His labor and services among the soldiers—Moralizing over a dead soldier— The explosion of a mine —A negroe's surprise—A surgeon brought to his senses—A fair Convert.

At 10 o'clock the firing ceased, and shortly after the general and staff returned. On meeting with the general Father Carrier asked him, "What was that infernal noise about?" and was informed that General Grant had issued an order the day previous that all the batteries of the investing army should open that morning from 3 to 10 o'clock a brisk and continued fire on the Confederate fortifications. The general further told the father that he was about taking him with him to witness the effect of the bombs on the enemy's works, but it being so early in the morning he thought proper not to disturb him from his sleep.

The following day was St. Aloysius day (June 21), a day of rejoicing to the father on account of it being the anniversary of a happy event in his life. He rose early in the morning and heard confessions till 9 o'clock when he celebrated Mass and preached and distributed medals to all the soldiers who had received Communion on that day. In the afternoon he paid a visit to Father Mignault who he heard was worse and on the eve of leaving the army. He found him very weak, prostrated by fever and dysentery and preparing to leave for Montreal in a day or two. Not knowing when he would have another chance to see a priest Father Carrier availed himself of Father Mignault's presence and made a confession after which they bid each other goodbye.

On the way home Father Carrier visited the division hospital. During the short time he remained there he met two Catholics, one an Italian and the other a German, who desired to go to confession; he heard the latter but as the former had not been at his duty for upwards of twenty years, he could not undertake to hear him that evening, but went the following day to do so. After attending to the spiritual welfare of the Italian, the father, who had been suffering from dysentery for a couple of days thought he could rest himself during the remainder of the day but he had no sooner reached his tent than he was sent for in a great hurry to attend a dying soldier who had been wounded a few hours before. The dying man he found to be a Canadian and a Catholic. After hearing his confession, anointing him and vesting him with the scapular he consoled him as best he could and finally left him in the agonies of death.

When the father returned he found a gentleman in his tent. On being interrogated he gave his name as R. Purcell Bomer[1] and said that he was surgeon of the 41st Ohio, that he was a Catholic and baptized after the name of the Archbishop of Cincinnati, that he had not seen a priest for two years, that he was desirous of going to his duties for he had always been a practical Catholic, and was still anxious to fulfil the obligations of the Roman Catholic Church.

At Mass the following morning, there was a large number of communicants, among them General Ewing. The afternoon of the following day a soldier, a mere boy, was shot through the lungs by a stray bullet while he was standing at a grave reading the epitaph of his former captain who was killed at a charge made on the 22nd of May before Vicksburg. The wounded boy, being a Catholic, and knowing the gravity of his wound, sent immediately for the father who hastened to where he was lying unconscious, and almost lifeless. He could not utter a word, yet when he was aroused from his lethargy and made to look at the father, he evidently manifested signs of recognition, but he would fall asleep immediately and just as the father had finished giving him the absolution and extreme unction, the poor wounded lad gave up the ghost.

Early the next morning Captain Smith of the regulars sent the father a note requesting him to perform the funeral rites, as used in the Catholic Church, over the remains of a young drummer who had been killed the day before by a negro. The burial was to take place at 2 P.M. and the father did not know what answer to give. The dead youth had been baptized in the Catholic Church, but he never went to confession and of course never made his first Communion; besides the father had heard that he was not a very edifying youth in the camp. However, as he was young (not over 14 or 15 years of age) and as he used to call himself a Catholic the father thought proper to accept the invitation of the Protestant Captain Smith, and at the appointed time went. The body was laid in a rude coffin and surrounded by all the men composing the company, to which the boy belonged. They were under arms and in grave and profound silence. The father put on his stole and commenced the recitation of the usual prayers after which he addressed a short exportation to those present principally on the necessity of being always prepared to appear before God. After the usual ceremonies both spiritual and military, a cross was placed over the grave, and all returned to their quarters.

That evening the father, not having much to do, wrote a petition to President Lincoln to have him appointed as chaplain in Grant's army, no action having been taken so far on his previous application. This step was taken in order to give the father a larger field for his labors and place him in a position in which he need not be dependent on any one. He also wrote a letter to the Archbishop of Cincinnati requesting him to endorse it, and showed both to General Ewing before forwarding them. The general highly approved of the father sending them without delay and wrote a letter himself to the archbishop for the purpose of recommending the measure in question and also requesting him to send them without the least possible delay to the president in Washington. During that afternoon and all the forenoon of the following day, almost a solemn silence reigned in both armies.

During dinner the latter day the general said to the father jokingly, "Monsieur Carrier, if you come with me this afternoon at 3 o'clock yon will see something grand." "What is it, and where is it to be?" "Oh, I won't tell you now, just make up your mind to come." "Well, be it so then." At 3 o'clock the horses were brought to the tents and the party mounted and galloped away towards an eminence inside of General [Joseph A. J.] Lightburn's fortifications. Before starting however, the general told the father the scene they were to witness was the explosion of an undermined fort, under General Logan's supervision whose men had been working at it for several days. The explosion was to take place at 4 P.M., but it did not come off before 5 on account of the fuse being made of materials that burned much slower than was anticipated. The Confederate soldiers, who were in the fort, never suspected anything of what was going on underneath them. When the party approached the eminence commanding Fort Hill they left their horses at its foot under shelter, and then ascended the steep acclivity at a double quick.

As they were directing their steps towards a certain observation of ground General Lightburn, who was standing at some distance beside a tree cried out, "Leave that road, gentlemen, quick. I just had one of my men killed on that spot." The party at once cleared out and Father Carrier went to see the man hoping that he was not absolutely dead; but [in] vain hope [as] he had been shot through the brain, and never uttered a word after. The father was much moved by the terribly sudden and perhaps unprovided [for] death of the soldier and sadly turned away and went and sat at the foot of a tree. There instead of gazing on the doomed fort and holding himself ready to witness fully the effect of the explosion, as all those present were doing, he fell into a deep and irrepressible reverie, for the scene he had a minute before witnessed had too strongly impressed his mind to worry about explosions or the like. Finally becoming disgusted by being in such a place, he abruptly left and returned home on foot and when he reached the tent threw himself on his cot. He, however, did not remain long there when he felt some remorse of conscience. Not knowing but his services might be required, he returned to witness the explosion. It was now near 5 o'clock and no explosion yet. General Blair came and sat by him and offered him his field glasses in order to view the Confederate troops in the fort. The father witnessed them moving leisurely and apparently as unconcerned about danger as if they stood on an unshakable rock, and yet it frightened him to think how many of them would, in a moment, be hurled into eternity.

Still viewing them he commenced to tell the general the result of his observations when all at once a loud explosion accompanied by a huge upheaving of the earth took place and bales of cotton, mules, men, and implements of every sort were cast into the air; then a dreadful dust and smoke followed which almost shrouded the remainder of the scene. Although the mine succeeded well, yet it failed to meet the expectations of the bystanders. Among the incidents which occurred during the explosion was that of a negro who was thrown from the fort inside the Federal lines and when asked how he came there replied, "I don't know Massa, some machine carried me off." "How far up were you thrown?" "Oh, about three miles." He was not the least hurt. There were altogether only a few killed and the Federals gained little advantage by it.

The following morning as the father was going to General McPherson's hospital to attend a number of soldiers belonging to the 7th Missouri (an Irish Catholic regiment) who had been wounded the day before at a charge made upon the enemy after the fort had been blown up, he was met on the way by a young boy mounted on a mule, who gracefully and politely saluted him saying, "Good morning, Father, you are a Catholic priest are you not?" "Yes, my little friend, but how did you recognize me as such?" "Oh, I saw your cross, only Catholic priests carry it." "Are you a Catholic yourself my fine fellow?" "Oh, yes Sir, and my mother, too." "Where do you live?" "In the country five miles from here. My father is a planter but he is not a Catholic. We have a chapel in our house; the priest of Vicksburg and[2] Bishop [William Henry] Elder[3] of Natchez used sometimes to come before the war and say Mass for us. My mother would like to have you come to say Mass too in our chapel." "Did your mother know that I was here?" "Oh! No, we did not know that there were Catholic priests with the Yankees. We only thought that they had preachers with them." "Why, I am a preacher too." "Oh! But you are not a Protestant preacher," answered he laughingly. "You are a Catholic priest— A Catholic preacher." "But I am a Yankee." "Oh, I know all about that," said he smiling. "Catholic priests are not Yankees." "So you would like me to go and say Mass at your father's house." "Yes, Father." "Well, I will go tomorrow." "Well, all right I will tell my mother of it and my father, too." "Do so, good bye, my little fellow," and both parted.

On entering McPherson's hospital the first thing that caught the father's attention were numbers of hands, legs, fingers, toes, etc., thrown about in the courtyard. A human limb cut off from the body, and kept with decency is even then painful to look at, but when it is thrown away to be eaten up by dogs or hogs, human nature shrinks and revolts at such an abominable affair. Father went into the house full of indignation and horror and immediately inquired for the chief surgeon. After being shown his room he entered and as he appeared before him said with an air of severe rebuke, "Are you aware, Sir, that the amputated limbs of our soldiers are cast into the courtyard exposed to be devoured by dogs or swine?" Vexed sorely at this inquiry the surgeon dryly and abruptly answered, "Yes Sir, what about it?" "What about it? Sir it is

shameful and criminal on the part of a hospital superintendent to leave a leg, an arm, or a hand sacrificed in the service,
and for the good of the country, before a dog! Why not bury
them?" This severe rebuke made the doctor very impatient and
he angrily answered, "Chaplain, if you care so much about,
amputated legs and arms, go and bury them yourself." "Doctor," replied the father, "your inhumanity is only excelled by
your impudence." "If," he continued, "there were no one to do
it, I would not come to you to see about it, but I must tell you
one thing I am going to visit this hospital with or without your
permission. These orders (showing him General Grant and
Sherman's passes) from high authorities leave the hospitals of
the army open to me at all times and if these amputated limbs
are not removed from the courtyard before I leave this place, I
shall go direct to General Grant and if I do not obtain any satisfaction there, I shall most assuredly write to the Surgeon
General of the U.S.A., or even to the Secretary of War."

The doctor never said a word and the father retired. He
had however scarcely left the ward when the surgeon stepped
towards him and apologized saying that he did not know a
thing about the amputated limbs being carelessly thrown away
and unburied, and that it was the business of the ward master
to attend to that. "Perhaps, I have given orders for their immediate removal and burial." "Very well," said the father and that
was the end of it.

The next morning, according to [his] promise, the father
started to see the family of Major [McKinney L.] Cook.[4] Following the direction which the little boy had given him the day
before, he experienced no difficulty in finding out the plantation and entered a large and splendid mansion that stood
alone in the middle of a fine and extensive farm, containing
at least two thousand acres. Upon inquiring if that was Major
Cook's house he was answered in the affirmative, and at the
same time was ushered into the parlor, where he found the
major engaged with an officer of the army. The major received
the father very kindly, offered him some refreshment, said he

was happy that to have him in his house, and that he was expecting him since morning. Mrs. Cook came next, and seemed full of joy at seeing the father at her house. She said, "We were in hopes, Father, that you would have come this morning to say Mass for us at our little chapel and am sorry you did not bring your vestments with you. Won't you come another day to say Mass for us all, for we are quite a number of Catholics in our house? Oh, do come." The father promised if possible to do so. "Thank you very much, but won't you see our chapel?" [asked] the lady. The father was struck with the beauty of the chapel and the taste with which it was decorated.

After returning to the parlor the major asked him how he liked Mrs. Cook's chapel. "Very well indeed," replied the father. "It is neat, tasty, and fragrant." The father was then introduced to several members of the family including Mrs. Bolles and Miss Heines, sisters of Mrs. Cook and a Protestant young lady, a sister-in-law of Mrs. Bolles, and all Mrs. Cook's children. After spending a pleasant day and promising to call the following Monday and say Mass for them, the father left. As he was going away through the garden accompanied by all the folks in the house, Miss Bolles,[5] the Protestant young lady, expressed a desire to speak to him in private. The father at once consented and bade Miss Fanny to go with them. Miss Bolles then told the father that she had read of late many good religious books, that she was not satisfied with the Protestant sects, that she had for some time a strong desire to see a Catholic priest who might explain to her some points of the Catholic Church that were not very clear to her and that she had a strong tendency to become a Catholic. The father then told her that he was at her disposition and would be glad to render her any services especially when such would be the means of her conversion to the Catholic Church. Continuing he said, "If you are earnest sincere and single-minded in seeking after the truth, and at the same time, you pray to God and the Blessed Virgin Mary, you will find the truth and will yet be in the Catholic Church." After advising her to prepare herself, and telling her that he would call tomorrow and stay two days, he mounted his horse and rode off to camp.

The following day (June 29) he rose early and heard numerous confessions, preached, and after Mass distributed medals to the communicants. The firing was very brisk, but particularly from the Confederate side. Their musketry was especially disagreeable and annoying. A few balls fell harmless within one or two feet of the father's tent, one even fell in it, and several struck the tree to which the tent was attached and buried themselves a couple of inches in it. A cannon ball fell within fifteen feet of the tent, and another struck a large sycamore tree with such violence that it cut it in two, and a broken limb in falling came very near killing the general and Captain Cornyn who were sitting in their tent. As the father had promised to go to Major Cook's this day to instruct the neophyte, he started accompanied by Captain Cornyn.

As soon as the father arrived there he commenced his instruction to Miss Bolles, which continued for three hours, after which she said she was fully convinced that the Catholic Church was the only true Church of Christ. The next morning the father heard the confessions of all the Catholic inmates of the house, and none appeared near so penitent as Miss Bolles. Just as the priest had finished imparting an instruction for her benefit the general arrived. All then assembled in the chapel where the baptism took place, Miss Fanny being godmother for nearly all the converts for fifty miles around. Mass was then celebrated and the general served it, after which the new convert was invested with the scapular. After breakfast the major took the party to his garden to show them his floral selections. The garden contained fully two acres of land, and was laid out with the greatest taste and skill. The party bade farewell to Major Cook, his wife and the other persons that were in the house, and rode off at a brisk pace to the camp. The next day the father and the general paid a visit to General Frank Blair, the general commanding the division. General Blair never before manifested so much kindness and familiarity than on this occasion. He felt evidently flattered by the visit and tried to show his appreciation of it by a great display of wines as well as politeness, amiability, and goodness generally.

It is to be regretted that the writer has not had materials to follow this sketch all through the memorable siege of Vicksburg. The following is a portion of Father Carrier's diary and evidently commences with the reception of the news of the surrender of the city of Vicksburg. As it is the only portion placed in our hands and as the writer has not materials to follow Father Carrier's career with the army to its close, our sketch of the reverend gentleman, in consequence, ends rather abruptly.

CHAPTER VII

Rev. Joseph C. Carrier, C.S.C., Continued

---

*Father Carrier's diary—Welcome intelligence—Surrender
of Vicksburg—His letter to his Father
Provincial—Father Carrier and his "birdies"—
A fatiguing march—The conclusion.*

---

*July 4th [1863]—Immediately after this most welcome announcement
(towards evening of that day and whilst I was in General Sherman's tent
with General Hugh Ewing and several other general officers, the news
reached us that the Confederate General Pemberton had sought and had
an interview with General Grant and agreed to surrender unconditionally
Vicksburg and her garrison of 32,000 men), nearly all the general officers
and their staff went to Vicksburg, for the purpose of getting as soon as possible an insight into the works and witnessing the damage which our guns
had done to the city. General McPherson was appointed governor of the
city with General Logan's division to protect and guard it. All the Confederate soldiers had been previously[1] ordered to stack their arms and occupy
the new quarters assigned them (in a little pleasant valley in the rear of
the fallen city and outside the corporation limits). General McPherson
had no sooner taken possession of his important office than he vigorously
commenced the operation of paroling the whole Confederate forces and at
the same time distributing rations to the prisoners and the starving inhabitants of the city.*

*I did not go to Vicksburg that day, notwithstanding many pressing in-
vitations to do so, as I wanted to write some letters (to my old father in*

France, and to my superior and friends at Notre Dame) besides I desired to pack up my things in order to be ready to move early the next day. I wrote to N. N. to whom I had promised to write when Vicksburg would fall. The following is a copy of the letter to my superior written on wall-paper.

Rev. and Dear Father Provincial:

I send you this trophy from Vicksburg. I obtained it from the pious and devoted assistant pastor (the pastor is following the Confederate army somewhere in Alabama) of the Catholic church of the city. Please to preserve this memento of a beleaguered but now fallen stronghold: it will show to all future generations to what extremities the Confederates were reduced— having to print their only paper (daily) on wall paper!! This was the last No. issued.

The Catholic church of the city—the largest and best edifice of the place, was but slightly injured, but the priest's house is very much shattered; the barn and stable are completely destroyed. Good Father Heuzé [2] lived for 15 days in his cellar not daring to occupy his ordinary apartments for fear of the shells. There is not (at least we have not seen any) one single house in the whole city which has not been more or less damaged. It really saddens [us] [3] to see so many ruins. Father Heuzé is a Breton, and esteems our congregation. He even has some notions of joining our House. We fraternize most agreeably and amiably he provided me most generously, with a bottle of genuine wine and some hosts. The bottle of wine cost him $15.00! Today the "Red Rover" was just before Vicksburg, at anchor, but I had no time to pay a visit to our sisters who are still on board of her; we have just been ordered to move immediately towards Jackson, Mississippi.

I take advantage of a halt to finish, and forward, my letter to you. [4] We are now camping on back of that sluggish dirty river called Big Black. General Sherman is the commander in chief of all the moving forces. I took supper with him last night with a crowd of general officers; we had marched that day twenty miles under a scorching sun, and through a most dense column of fine dust that penetrated our very pores! I felt very much exhausted. Nevertheless, my health is pretty good, and am in excellent spirits. I passed the night under a tree without other bedding than the bare ground, and other covering than the canopy of heaven. So did Genl. Ewing, and all. We shall march again today. Every one treats me, here, with the greatest distinction and respect. I don't know why, but it is really so.

I have to correct a statement sent to Notre Dame two days ago, regarding the capture of Vicksburg.

We actually took 30,000 prisoners, 50,000 muskets, 136 field guns, 104 siege guns, and a large am[oun]t of powder and other small ammunition. The Confederates have lost it is asserted 55,000 men since Grant moved in May last. We are going on . . . on to Mobile maybe. I have sent several letters to you and other persons at Notre Dame; did you receive them all? Send your letters in care of General Sherman.

Yours respectfully,

J. C. Carrier

July 5th—At 4 o'clock A.M. I awoke with the thought uppermost in my mind—that the keys of the rebel city were in our hands; but it took me several seconds of time to fully realize that that thought was a reality, a fact, and not a dream or the result of a dream. I immediately got up, dressed quickly, and prepared myself to say Mass (a duty I never missed during my stay in the army). It was Sunday, a good many soldiers were outside of my tent, sitting on a little knoll, about fifteen or twenty feet from the entrance of my double tent (one serving as a chapel and the other as a residence). Awaiting for his "Reverence," to awake of the "portals" of the Holy of Holies and hear their confessions. All this having been duly done, I celebrated the Holy Sacrifice of the Mass—good Captain Cornyn serving at the altar. I addressed a very brief discourse to my congregation and dismissed them with my blessing. It was seven o'clock when I took my breakfast. Having supplied my soul and my body with their respective needs, I directed my faithful orderly (an excellent Irishman) to saddle my fine black mare and get ready to accompany me to Vicksburg. This was done instantly. As General Ewing was expecting orders to move his brigade towards Jackson, he could not accompany me to Vicksburg, but he gave me, besides my mounted orderly, a young man, a civilian, the son of the Hon. Mr. Hunter of Lancaster, Ohio, and a convert to the Catholic Church. We started together at a rapid speed towards Vicksburg where we arrived about 9 o'clock.

My first object in reaching the city was to pay visit to the pastor, but I was told that he left the city in April with the Sisters of Mercy and gone to Selma, Alabama. However, I found in the pastoral residence his worthy assistant, a pious young priest, who had suffered terribly during the siege both for want of sufficiently nutritious food and of care during a severe and protracted attack of malarious fever. He received me with open arms. His poor emaciated countenance brightened up instantly as I told him I was a Frenchman (he had left France but a few months before) and a religious of the Congregation of the Holy Cross. He introduced me to a "confrere," Father [John] B[annon][5] of St. Louis, and chaplain of a Missouri Confederate regiment, who was about to say the high Mass in the fine and imposing Catholic church, and which had been but slightly damaged by our guns. Father B[annon] struck me as much by his stalwart form and distinguished features as by the intensity of his abhorrence of the Yankee and of Yankeedom.[6] He said a low Mass and I preached the sermon. (I several weeks afterwards had occasion to preach and lecture many times in Vicksburg having gone to recover from an attack of malaria that had threatened my life.) In the afternoon of that day I received a note from General Ewing apprizing me that he had received orders to move immediately his brigade towards the "Big Black" (a small river not far from Vicksburg) and that I should meet him there the next day.

July 6th—At 6 A.M. General Ewing began to move his brigade and by 10 o'clock when I returned to our former pleasant headquarters, nothing remained save the beautiful little terrace we had made on the declivity of the deep ravine for our tents.

Well shall I say it? It really had been painful for me to pull down my tents and leave my nice cozy quarters! I had become strongly attached to the place: its wild aspect, the beautiful and spacious terrace built by our Catholic soldiers for the tent-chapel and their "Father's" tent, the winding foot paths through the deep precipitous ravine; the shade of the grand magnolias and the large forest trees which had not been totally shattered by

*the enem[y's] bomb shells, (not a few were sadly wrecked mere skeletons
of their former gorgeous foliage and transcendent glory) and most especially a nest—the nest of the cliff-swallow which the birds had built on the
southwest corner of my tent; besides the many pleasant associations which
the spot recalled, all contributed to render the place most dear to me . . .
and I really felt loath to depart. For instance, it seemed cruel to pull down
my tent and leave unsheltered the little family of five newly hatched little
birds. But I had to do it! Then farewell my little birdies! I left Vicksburg
at 1 o'clock P.M. to the great sorrow of good Father Heuzé who had most
urgently implored me to stay with him and aid him in the ministerial duties of a priest, which his imperfect knowledge of the English language
made it difficult for him to discharge properly; but I owed my services to
our Catholic soldiers, especially to the soldiers of the 15th army corps, and
I resolved to accompany them wherever they would go, [for] I was bound
to do so. So, giving a warm hand and a hearty farewell to my friend, I
turned my face from hospital Vicksburg and proceeded towards Jackson, whither our army had been ordered to rendezvous. But where was the
15th army corps? Where were the headquarters of either Sherman, or
Ord, or Blair, or Ewing (for anywhere I would have been at home)? That
was indeed the question. Well! I trusted to my star, but more particularly
to the devotedness of my big hearted orderly, and the indefatigable zeal
of my young scout Mr. Thomas Hunter, who had become much attached
to me.*

   *Before leaving the city we visited many of the Confederate works; then
we passed through a cluster of big trees, not one of which had a single
branch left, besides being all decapitated at various heights. Those trees
stood just between the guns of the two armies and of course had passed
through the terrible and truly "fiery" ordeal of a two months constant fire.
No wonder that they were dismally shattered. It was indeed a sight most
striking and most painful to behold, I cannot forget it! I had yet a longing
desire to see the place of our long and somewhat eventful encampment; we
turned from the Jackson road in order to view, a last time, the spot where
we had pitched our tents. But all was gone and deserted; and where the
day before all was life and bustle there now reigned the silence of death.
Not one soldier, not one horse, not one wagon, not one tent, could be
now[7] discerned where hundreds could be seen twenty four hours before.
How grandly dismal the scene now appears. An indescribable sense of*

melancholy oppresses you; you dream vaguely, the world seems empty and life itself undesirable; you are half enshrouded in a mantle of death.

We go hence slowly, silently, musing until we come to Jackson's road, and then our drooping spirits revive, for we again meet life in various forms: a straggling soldier here; and a Negro there; a four mule ambulance yonder—dust everywhere—dust so fine so impalpable, that it rises high in the air, like a column of smoke, and penetrates through the texture of your clothes and coming in contact with the abundant perspiration of your body, makes a kind of dirty and irritating deposit on the skin, which makes you long for a pail full of clear and cool water! It is dark, nearly nine o'clock, and we are told that Sherman's headquarters are close by. Turning to our right under the guidance of a friendly colonel, we pass through a little grove, and presently we are before General Sherman's tent, who immediately rises and heartily greets me there. "How do you do Father Carrier we thought you had fallen into the hands of the enemy. Come in and have supper."

Having passed a pleasant hour or so with the general I enquired of General Ewing where were our wagons (regimental wagons). "I am sorry to say I do not know where they are Father." "But General, what will I do, my breviary is with my effects and I must say my office for tomorrow; besides, I certainly desire to say Mass tomorrow; and my cot!" "Well Father I have sent several orderlies to inquire where our wagons are and, when found, to bring them here. I expect them every moment." But they were not to come before three or four o'clock next morning and consequently, I as well as the general had to sleep "à la belle étoile" (in the open air and on the ground) with our saddles for pillows!

July [7th–8th]—I will content myself with simply copying a long letter written in French to my Provincial describing my journey to Jackson covering a period of five days. I wonder if that letter will ever reach its destination, as it is not pre-paid, not having any stamp with me, and nobody has any!

(Here it is: "Tout n'est pas rose ici bas, tant s'en faut." "All is not color of rose here below, far from it.")

The heat becomes so excessive and so oppressive that our soldiers could hardly bear it. Often were we obliged to halt in order to betake ourselves under the shade of thicket of wood or solitary trees by the way side. But we cannot always do so for we have frequently to pass through immense fields of maize (no cotton has been planted this year in the South: only corn and beans, and nothing else) and of course not a tree could we find to rest a while under the shade of its foliage.

We made but little progress the second day of our march (the 7th of July) either on account of the fervid heat, or because of a crossing we had with the 9th army corps (General [John G.] Parke's) which had anticipated us a little. It took at least five hours for that army corps to defile before us, with its long columns, wagons, and field artillery.

We then resumed our march; but we had not advanced two hundred furlong when an order came to us from General Blair to halt: the enemy had engaged the division of [Peter J.] Osterhaus.[8] Whilst we were waiting for further orders, the rumor spread that Osterhaus had had many of his men killed or wounded. Thereupon, I felt it my duty to immediately proceed to where the skirmish had taken place; and that was not far from where we stood as I learned from General Steele. I consequently went off with an aid-de-camp of General Ewing; but when we reached the field of combat, Osterhaus had moved on, and we could not learn what had been done with the wounded (only four or five of his men had been killed, for the engagement had been most grossly exaggerated). I was forced therefore to return to camp without doing anything. When I reached General Ewing's brigade I found them all encamped. We lit a little fire (for it was forbidden to make large fires as such might serve as signal for the enemy to attack us during the night). We supped; I said a little of the office of the day and went to sleep all dressed under the broad canopy of heaven, and with mother earth for a mattress. I fell asleep almost immediately, for I was half dead with fatigue.

July 9th We had not last night our headquarters commissariat wagons up—we had neither tents nor beds but we had the canopy of heaven for tent and the bare ground for a couch! I could have borne it better had I been fatter; but alas! every joint

in my frame forms a most acute angle! Still, I can assure you, that
"*Terra*" is not so hard a mother after all, that a body cannot rest
upon her, and sleep soundly. Yet so tall and thin a man as I am
cannot find a position where his pointed bones do not cause him
a sensation most unpleasant.

Bah; this is, for a follower of the Holy Cross a mere bagatelle.
The following morning, not a cracker to crack; no provisions and
no cook. As good Christians we took our departure, or rather resumed our march, strictly fasting, although it was neither Lent,
nor Ember Day, nor vigil. We had made the preceding day sixteen
miles and were nearing the river ("Big Black"). Arriving on its
right bank, we were detained nearly a full day, awaiting the completion of the bridge. Our "*corps de genie*"⁹ was thrown across it.
Towards morning we crossed the celebrated river (a muddier
river I never saw in my life) and bivouacked a few miles off at one
o'clock in the morning of the next day. It took us not less than six
hours to reach a certain position where we were to pass the
night—three miles only east of the Big Black. Never in my life
have I been so exhausted for want of food, sleep, and rest. Oh!
Those interminable halts! Well we slept as we did the night before, *minus* a supper and *plus* a little bed of leaves which my excellent and devoted orderly (a good and pious Irish soldier)
made for me.

At 6 o'clock we got up, I said a little of my breviary and went
to take a little breakfast which consisted of a few ears of fresh
corn, cooked on a slow fire, and a few hard crackers, and departed shortly afterwards. A day of extreme heat, several soldiers
were sun struck, and also many horses, and nearly all who were
struck died. We dined on hopes but not victuals, and reached
Bolton—the midway railroad station between Vicksburg and
Jackson—at about six o'clock P.M. It was indeed high time to
stop, for I verily believe, I could not have gone any farther, so
exhausted did I feel. Five days on horseback had stiffened me like
a piece of dry wood. I had yet nearly all of my office to say; I
bravely took hold of my breviary, and, God aiding, finished the
office for the day. Our good God sent us rain that night, a verit-

able deluge. Happily we had foreseen the storm and were able to put up two tents—and two only: one for the general, Captain Cornyn and myself, and the other for the rest of the staff officers, which tent being low built was entirely submerged during the night and put the poor fellows in a most pitiable if not actually ludicrous position! The following day was devoted to rest (although it was not Sunday) and we needed it, most of the men were as wet as drowned rats.

General Ewing and Captain Cornyn were also pretty thoroughly drenched, as they had put their little cots too near the borders of the tent. As for me, I was nearly all right. At 4 o'clock P.M. an order came to resume the "march." We stopped for the night, two miles this side of Clinton. This night's march was if possible still more harassing than that of the 7th.

Again we went to sleep supperless and bedless. I was no sooner stretched out on the bare ground, than a terrible intestine war was being waged within me. Hunger wrangling against sleep, at last after many sharp "passes" the latter got the victory: famine surrendered unconditionally. "*Ventre affamé n'a point d'oreilles*,"[10] says the French adage. The following day the 10th July we started at 10 o'clock en route again for Jackson.

Adieu! dear Father. Yours in Christ,

J. C. Carrier

EPILOGUE: Although Father Carrier's journal ends in early July 1863, he remained in the South until October when he returned to the University of Notre Dame. After the war, Father Carrier taught courses in chemistry, botany, and physics at the school. He had a special interest in collecting scientific specimens, having started his collection, which would become the university's natural history museum, while on a trip to Paris in 1866. In 1874, he became president of St. Mary's College in Galveston, Texas. He next taught at St. Laurent College, near Montreal, where he died in 1904.

SOURCES: Records and papers related to Carrier's priest-hood can be found in Notre Dame, Indiana, at the Congrega-tion of Holy Cross United States Province Archives Center (USPAC) and at the University of Notre Dame Archives.

See also Arthur J. Hope, C.S.C., *Notre Dame: One Hundred Years* (Notre Dame, IN: University of Notre Dame Press, 1943), 133–35, 156, 225–26; Edward Sorin, C.S.C., *The Chronicles of Notre Dame du Lac,* ed. James T. Connelly (Notre Dame, IN: University of Notre Dame Press, 1992), 284, 286–87, 302–3; James M. Schmidt, *Notre Dame and the Civil War: Marching Onward to Victory* (Charleston, SC: The History Press, 2010), 35–37, 66–68; Tangi Villerbu, "Early Catholic Minnesota: New Sources and New Questions," in *The State We're In: Reflections on Minnesota History,* ed. Annette Atkins and Deborah L. Mil-ler (St. Paul, MN: Minnesota Historical Society Press, 2010), 184–90.

Rev. R. C. Christy

Chaplain 78th Pennsylvania Volunteers

*The chaplains entitled to their share of the glory of victory—
Father Gallitzin—Father Christy's early life and missionary
labors as a priest—Selected chaplain of the 78th Pennsylvania—
His services to the sick and wounded in and around Louisville—
His voyage in the dugout—Sufferings at Stones River—The
influence of the chaplains on Protestant officers and soldiers—
A feeling conversion—Complimentary notices—An involuntary
bath—He returns with his regiment and is mustered
out of service.*

INTRODUCTION: Father Richard Callixtus Christy (1829–
1878) was born in Loretto, Pennsylvania, to Peter and Catherine Christy, early Catholic pioneers of this all-Catholic
community ministered to by Father Demetrius Gallitzin, the
"Apostle of the Alleghenies." Christy studied at St. Michael's
Seminary in Pittsburgh before continuing his studies at St.
Mary's Seminary in Baltimore. Ordained in 1854 in his home-
town of Loretto, Christy's first assignments were to minister to
the congregations of Freeport and Clearfield, Pennsylvania.
With the eruption of hostilities, Christy was assigned as chaplain to the 78th Pennsylvania Volunteer Infantry, a mainly
non-Catholic regiment, and joined on October 18, 1861.

Christy suffered from frequent illness during the war, resulting in some absences from duty. This may have led to the charge that he was absent without leave from July 10, 1863, to November 13, 1863. He pled not guilty. The court believed otherwise, yet agreed to restore him to duty.[1] He served until November 4, 1864.

Conyngham's correspondence with Dr. Charles B. Gillespie, a captain in the 78th Pennsylvania Infantry, was the chief source of information on Father Christy. The author here describes the hazards of war, including near-death experiences for Father Christy, one after capsizing a canoe in the Tennessee River. Conyngham includes the humorous story of the priest pitching in during battle, taking up the role of a commanding officer. He explains the dutiful response of Father Christy in battle and the closeness that the soldiers felt to their chaplain, especially when he was falsely charged with desertion.

If it be praiseworthy to rescue from oblivion the names of those who fight valiantly, or do great deeds for the sake of their country; it cannot be the less commendable to hold up for public gratitude, the labors of these who worked for the salvation of souls, and the greater glory of the Kingdom of God.

The warrior finds his guerdon, and receives his laurels from the hands of an admiring and applauding people; the other, whose deeds are hidden from the eyes of men, neither seeks, nor scarcely cares for the thanks of an admiring world. The one, looks for, and receives his reward in this world; the other, humbly hopes for a recompense hereafter.

If it be the duty of the historian to write the actions of these who deserve well of their country, especially in great emergencies like that of the late Civil War, then all who took part in it should be equally portrayed. Great battles are fought and won, not by the soldier only; the humble teamster often plays a part as important and necessary as he who wears a sword or shoulders a rifle.

An army carries in its midst, all the essentials that go to build up a nation. The soldier, the lawgiver, the artisan, the laborer, the doctor, the divine, have each their appropriate duties to perform. All labor in unison and for a common result; and where the battle is fought, the victory obtained, a due share of praise should be attributed to him, who by his prayers and council, and burning zeal for the soul's welfare, bore up the weak, and gave hope to the despairing, strengthening and encouraging all, so that in the day of trial, there should be fearless hearts, and strong arms, ready to dare, and do.

To the subject of this sketch, especially ought the thanks be given of a united people. For, among the many worthy Catholic chaplains of the army, none labored more steadfastly and zealously for the soldier's welfare; none, showed more energy and determination in laboring to crown the contest with a glorious victory.

The subject of this memoir, was born October 14, 1829, in the mountain village of Loretto, Cambria County Pennsylvania; a place forever to be remembered as the home of the illustrious Prince Gallitzin;[2] the second priest ordained in the United States, and one of the pioneers of Catholicity west of the Alleghenies. [Christy] was baptized by Father Gallitzin, who was also his sponsor; under whose care the embryo missionary was brought up, and was living with him as his altar boy, when his sainted teacher and guardian, died, May 6, 1840.

Young Christy was partly educated at the common schools of the borough. The classics were commenced under the care of the Revd. H. P. Gallagher,[3] now of San Francisco, California, and were continued under the charge of the Franciscan Brothers, who then lived in a little hut, but now occupy a magnificent college on the summit of the Alleghenies. In the year 1849, the youthful mountaineer entered St. Michael's ecclesiastical seminary; where he finished the classics and philosophy. Afterwards, he spent three years in St. Mary's, Baltimore and was finally ordained [a] priest, in Loretto, August 29, 18[54],[4] by the Rt. Rev. M[ichael] O'Connor, being the first American priest of the new diocese of Pittsburgh.

His first mission was in Freeport, Armstrong Co., Pennsylvania, where he labored zealously and successfully, and where his name is still loved and remembered, not only by those among whom he ministered, but by Protestants likewise, who soon learned to appreciate the noble qualities of the young Catholic priest.

The breaking out of the late war[5] found him in Clearfield, Butler County, Pennsylvania, where he had been for some years, laboring as usual, with untiring energy in the cause of religion. Here, far removed from the busy marts of men he was passing his days in quiet usefulness, and busy labor; serving, and ministering to a large and devoted congregation.

Though shut up in the woods of Butler County, Father Christy was a constant reader of the literature of the day. Being consequently well informed on all the great public questions, he was well prepared for the shock, and uncertainty that paralyzed the popular mind, when the late war was inaugurated under the battlements of Fort Sumter.

When the news of the first disaster at Bull Run was flashed throughout the country, all seemed paralyzed with consternation. The church bell rung out an alarm that startled the whole country side, and soon, from far and near, came gathering in the wonder stricken country folks,

"What tidings did these brazen lips foretell."

So soon as the people had assembled, Father Christy told them the news, and then spoke to them of their duties as Christian, and Catholic citizens; of the peril of the hour—of the necessity for exertion and of the right of the country to the services of her children. Under his direction, all the warlike spirits gathered into a company, and an old militia captain was employed to teach them the rudiments of military evolutions. Dr. Charles B. Gillespie of Freeport, Pennsylvania,[6] writing of Father Christy says,

When, in the summer of 1861, I visited San Ricardo, the home of Father Christy, in order to raise recruits for Colonel [William G.] Sirwell's[7] regiment then forming at Kittanning, my eyes were delighted to see a company of stalwart young men, drilling on the green. The old captain was putting them through the mysteries of "right and left face," keeping time with the "left foot foremost," and wheeling and countermarching to the music of Johnny Green's martial and effective band.

As soon as my errand was made known, Father Christy avowed his determination of going to the field himself, and, owing to his example, numbers of stalwart soldiers volunteered from among the hills of Butler County, to swell the ranks of the regiment then forming at Kittanning.

At the organization of the regiment in October 1861, such was the popularity of Father Christy that he was almost unanimously selected by the officers as their chaplain, though he had for competitors many Protestant divines, who were noted for their virtues and accomplishments. This selection, appears the more surprising, when we consider, that out of the thousand men comprising the regiment, there were not over fifty Catholics. In the history of the regiments comprising the armies of the republic, I do not believe there is an instance like this. It speaks well not only for the wisdom and imprejudice of the soldier of the valley of the Allegheny, but also, for the character and qualifications of the Catholic priest, whom the popular voice had selected as chaplain of the 78th.

The appearance and manners of Father Christy were well calculated to win the public heart. Of a fine, and manly presence, a candid and youthful countenance, resolute and determined, fearless of all personal danger, always cheerful and hopeful, in sickness the best comforter, and kindest of nurses, a genial companion. No wonder that the soldiers of all denominations, soon learned to love and revere him, as their best counsellor, and kindest friend.

Among the officers of the regiment, there was only one that expressed sentiments unfriendly to the selection of Father Christy. It was not however through any fault of his, for he came from a neighborhood where a Catholic was seldom seen, and where all knowledge of their faith, and teaching, was gleaned from "Foxe's Book of Martyrs," or works of like character.[8] This officer, as good and kind a soul as ever lived, expressed himself to many that the only cause of regret he had in leaving his home and family was that he was going away in company with a Catholic priest! Poor fellow; before he was many months in company with a Catholic priest he threw aside his prejudice and was eventually one of Father Christy's warmest friends.

The 78th, in company with the 77th and 79th, also of Pennsylvania, were, formed into a brigade at Pittsburgh, under the command of the chivalrous and gallant [James S.] Negley.[9] This brigade, for a long time known as "Negley's Brigade," left Pittsburgh about the middle of October 1861, for Louisville, Kentucky, which was then threatened by the Confederate Army, under [General Simon] Buckner. Several months were spent in drilling, and in camp duties, at Nolin, and Woodsonville.[10] The weather towards the middle of the winter was bad, and inclement; the soldiers badly fed, and housed, [with] eight [or] ten occupying a wedge-tent that was only intended to accommodate six.

Disease soon grew into a pestilence, and death followed after, striking down many who had lately appeared to be the healthiest and strongest in the regiment. At Camp Negley, near Nolin, hundreds were prostrated with sickness, and when the regiment was finally ordered to Green River, it left with wasted and depleted ranks. Father Christy was sent back to Louisville in company with the sick, and on this journey by rail and after their arrival, he it was on whom the soldiers relied for relief and succor. The surgeon in charge, whose business it should have been to have provided for all their wants, neglected his duty, and when the train arrived at Louisville, was too helpless to be of any use. The consequence was that the sick had to be laid out upon the floor of the depot, and there, through the cold of a long winter's night, had to remain until morning. So soon as the chaplain, who had gone into the city, found out how matters were, he hurried back to the depot, and soon, with the assistance of the hospital steward, Mr. Barnaby, had them all carried to the different hospitals and properly cared for.

At Munfordville, the brigade was suddenly ordered back to the Ohio River, to embark on steamboats at West Point and hurry to the assistance of General Grant at Fort Don[el]son.[11] A great many sick were here left in the field hospitals and such was the confidence in the energy and ability of Father Christy, that everything was placed in his charge. Not only had he to move the sick, and procure transportation, but he had also to provide for their necessities, acting in the triple capacity of priest, quartermaster, and commissary.

On the forced march to Bowling Green and Nashville the lusty chaplain had no horse and consequently had to paddle his own canoe; [this was] not, however, a very easy job, when they had such men as Negley to hurry them on. An officer speaking of this advance, writes,

> Our first hard march was from Bowling Green, starting at 1 o'clock P.M. and marching continuously till 12 o'clock at night. Hundreds of soldiers fell off by the wayside, utterly done up. Only sixteen out of my company of eighty men came into camp, and but three of the line officers of the regiment. What became of Father Christy, during that terrible race towards Nashville I never knew. But after resting a day and a night at Edgefield, when I crossed the river to the city, but just evacuated by the Confederates, I found Father Christy safely domiciled with the bishop, having got into the city before us.

The greater portion of the year 1862, was passed in Tennessee, with occasional expeditions into Alabama. Father Christy, when not with his regiment, was attending the different hospitals at Franklin, Columbia, and Pulaski.

At one time, the regiment was encamped for a while at Rogersville, Alabama. Whilst there, an event transpired that nearly put a sudden end to the useful career of our Catholic chaplain. The Confederate General [William Wirt] Adams, with his cavalry, occupied the country on the other side of the river, their headquarters being at Courtland, about seven miles away. Two companies of the 78th were sent one day across the river in boats, in order to make a reconnaissance of the surrounding country. Father Christy, who always accompanied such expeditions, happened at that particular time to be otherwise engaged. As soon as possible, however, he hurried after them, hoping that he would be in time to cross with the soldiers. When he arrived he was too late, for he saw them climbing the opposite bank of the river.

The only vessel left was a small dugout, or canoe, in which the venturesome priest resolved to attempt the passage. The Tennessee, at this place is deep, and fully a mile wide; even to an old and experienced boatman, it would have been a serious undertaking. As the chaplain had never before made any attempt at navigation, the results could have easily been foretold. He had gone but a few yards from the shore, when being entirely ignorant of the science of aquatics, the canoe began to turn to all points of the compass; as he afterwards expressed himself, "the light headed thing, would not go the right way," and over it went, submerging the rash voyager in the turbid waters of the Tennessee. The canoe floated away, Father Christy could not swim, [and] there was no one within sight or call. [But] despair gave him energy [and] the shore was almost within reach. He struck out manfully, but all would not do [and] down he sank, still struggling hopelessly against the overwhelming water. After what seemed an age he struck the bottom. Straightening himself upright for another effort when to his unspeakable relief he found that the water was but just up to his chin. He succeeded in wading out and forever afterwards had a perfect disgust for dugouts and a wholesome dread of the Tennessee.

At another time, when seated at the foot of a tree and quietly gazing out upon the water, a rebel sharp shooter, on the other side of the river, happened to perceive him, and taking deliberate aim, succeeded in planting a minie ball in the trunk, only a few inches above his head. These are but two, of the many incidents that befell our worthy chaplain, during his many journeys from one part of the state to the other.

At the battle of Stones River, Father Christy was with his regiment during the whole of that terrible week of continuous fighting. The weather was dreadful. Through sleet and snow, wading through mud and mire, the army struggled gloriously on, fighting the elements as well as the enemy, wet, shivering with cold, hungry; without fires at night, lying down on the muddy ground to snatch a short and hurried sleep; their supply trains hopelessly away in the rear. No wonder that the soldiers at times were almost ready to give up in despair. Our worthy chaplain by word and example helped to encourage and sustain the spirits of the wearied soldier. He trudged away to the quartermaster's wagons in the rear, and brought blankets and overcoats to the shivering soldiers. Regardless of shot and shell, he went back and forth over the blood-stained field, attending to the wounded, and in many instances carrying them away himself to the extemporised hospitals in the rear.

This being the first great battle in which the regiment was engaged, the soldiers, who always admire pluck, especially in their officers, were delighted with their heroic chaplain. "What a pity," said they, "[that] he is a priest. Wouldn't he make a bully general?"

During the first months that the army remained in the neighborhood of Murfreesboro, Father Christy busied himself attending to the spiritual wants of the Catholic soldiers. In Negley's division he was the only Catholic chaplain, and consequently had a great deal to do. In connection with Fathers Cooney, Trecy, and O'Higgins of the 10th Ohio, a church was procured in town where Mass was celebrated every day by one or the other, and, on Sundays, sermons preached in addition. The soldiers of Rousseau's[12] division had erected a large rustic pavilion, covered with hemlock and cedar, with circular seats capable of accommodating almost the entire division. Here, Fathers Christy and Trecy (the latter being lately assigned to the 4th Regulars) held divine service on alternate Sundays.

The religious fervor of the army was much strengthened and quickened by the zeal of these good men. Many careless ones were recalled and not a few converted. The good example of their general,[13] and other prominent officers who were zealous and practical Catholics, did much to quicken the zeal of the Catholic and disarm the prejudices of the Protestant soldiers. Sundays always found hundreds of the latter assembled to attend Mass and listening with the greatest attention to the practical exhortations of the good missionaries.

The few years of the war did more to allay the bigotry of the Protestant mind than fifty years of civil life could have possibly done. The few Catholic chaplains that were in the army were zealous and efficient men. The Protestant soldiers, at first distrustful and suspicious, soon learned to respect and love the priest, [who] knowing no difference labored so faithfully for the comfort and welfare of the sick and wounded. He found that whilst the Protestant chaplain rarely exposed himself to danger, in order to succor the helpless or wounded, the

Catholic priest was always at his post, laboring night and day in the hospital and in the field, with an entire abnegation of self that soon made the Protestant soldiers regard him as their best and warmest friend. This feeling the soldier has carried with him home, and the good seed thus sown in war and pestilence has grown and matured beneath a peaceful sky until it has multiplied itself, and is now scattered into all the hidden nooks and corners of this great country.

When the army left Murfreesboro for that brilliant campaign against the Confederates in Tennessee, Father Christy was assigned to the brigade then commanded by Colonel Sirwell. The campaign was short and effective.[14] There was no general battle until after the passage of the Tennessee River. Dr. Gillespie says,

> During the march across the state, for fourteen days we had an almost uninterrupted rain. The streams were all changed to raging torrents; the army, like a huge animal, was floundering in the mud; the quartermaster and commissary trains were totally engulfed in the vicinity of Tullahoma. Officers had to dismount and help their struggling horses out of unfathomable quagmires. Each field piece had a double team, and then could scarcely swim along. Officers swore lustily; the men grumbled. The only pleasant and genial face to be seen was that of Father Christy. Always in good humor himself, he managed to impart some of his equanimity to those immediately around him. The first good laugh we had was when Father Christy's horse suddenly wakened up a nest of yellow jackets. How that horse leaped and plunged among the bushes! The rider calmly smiling all the time, sat perfectly at home, notwithstanding all the animal's frantic efforts to dislodge him. Finally, when the horse with a scream of agony broke out into a gallop and dashed over a six rail fence into a corn field, his rider still erect, the cheers of the soldiers attested their admiration for the intrepid horseman.
>
> At Dug Gap, Pigeon Mountain, Georgia, almost the first notice we had of the approach of the enemy was the sudden opening of a rattling fire upon our chaplain who had ridden

out in the morning to a house immediately in the rear of our pickets. The sharp shooters, from [Father Christy's] appearance, mistook him for a general officer, and silently crept up under the shelter of the woods, until they had him apparently completely at their mercy. I was among a group of officers on a little hill, in an open field, when the firing attracted our attention in front. The first thing we saw was our gallant chaplain on his black charger, dashing to the rear. The bullets were striking and kicking up a dust all around him. Fortunately, neither rider nor horse were touched, and when he reined his horse in our midst we all felt greatly relieved at his narrow escape. Dismounting, he hurried back to the picket line and succeeded in bringing back the wounded, tearing his handkerchief and underclothing into bandages; by his energy and personal strength succeeding in saving them from capture by an advancing and exultant foe.

In a day or two afterwards, one of these same men happened to be captured. He was an Irishman and Catholic, and when he found out that the big officer on the black horse, whom he had tried so zealously to kill, was a Catholic priest! his look of holy horror, caused us all to burst out into uproarious laughter, and no one seemed to enjoy it more than Father Christy himself.

In the battle of Chickamauga, his daring zeal as usual carried him out to the front where he was busy attending wounded men and became separated from his friends and for a considerable time was between the fire of the opposing armies. A good Providence watched over him, and he came out of that "*feu de l'enfer*"[15] entirely unscathed!

When the army took up a new position at Rossville the day after the battle, a touching incident occurred in the conversion and baptism of a dying Confederate. He and half a dozen of others were shot down, a few yards in front of the 78th. This soldier was still alive when brought in, a beardless stripling of fourteen! When asked why he had entered the army, he said his mother had made him go! Father Christy was as usual on [hand],[16] and when the wounded boy found out there was a priest in the crowd, he desired him to be brought. It was a sad yet consoling sight, the baptism of that dying boy on the field of battle.

In Chattanooga, Father Christy had a Catholic church in which to officiate; however, he was everywhere, whenever needed. His ministrations were not confined to his own brigade or division, but he was often called upon to visit the sick in the different army corps. He was exceedingly popular throughout the whole Army of the Cumberland, [and] the soldiers all knew him by sight, and were always rejoiced at this appearance. A mission of a week's duration was given, during which time he labored unceasingly in the confessional when not otherwise engaged on the altar.

At the battle of Missionary Ridge, the 78th being thrown into Fort Negley, Father Christy would not remain when there was no fighting and consequently no wounded to attend to. He accompanied the 14th Corps in its magnificent charge up the mountain slope and continued on as far as Ringold, Georgia, giving his services to Federals and Confederates alike.

After the battle of Missionary Ridge, the regiment was put into winter quarters on the summit of Look Out Mountain. The duties of the chaplain were here very light in comparison with what had been done when the army was cooped up in Chattanooga. Colonel Sirwell had taken command of the brigade at Murfreesboro, and wishing to have Father Christy with him had ordered him to remain at his headquarters, from which he could more readily attend to all the sick calls of the command. Through some oversight of the commanding officer, or owing to a little leaven of prejudice, or both, Father Christy was reported as absent without leave. In consequence of this report, his pay was detained by the paymaster, until the charge could be brought before a court martial. During all this time, for a period of several months, Father Christy being without pay, was rather "hard up."

It was at this time that the boys of the 78th, without distinction of creed, clubbed together and raised him a handsome sum of money; which succeeded in keeping him afloat until his pay was restored by the highest official authority.

The following is taken from the *Democrat & Sentinel* publication in Ebensburg, Pennsylvania:

Loretto, Pennsylvania, April 7th 1864

Mr. Editor
Dear Sir,

    The following which I take from the "Louisville Journal" of March 23 is certainly a very nice compliment to one of "Little Cambria's" sons and one of which we can feel proud.

    When the war broke out, Father Christy notwithstanding his delicate state of health was among the first to sacrifice the endearments of home and brave the hardships and exposures of the battlefield for the sake of his country and, I am happy to say his labors have been appreciated.

    The Resolutions below speak for themselves.

    Father Christy is a native of this place born and raised and ordained in this village. But at the time the war broke out he was residing in Butler Co. when he joined the army.

Loretto

Honor to whom honor is due—Rev. R. C. Christy
Chaplain 78th Pennsylvania Volunteers.

    From the annexed proceedings it will be seen that the non-commissioned officers and privates of the 78th Pennsylvania Volunteers have presented their worthy chaplain Rev. R. C. Christy with a substantial proof of the sincere regard and esteem with which they appreciate his many sterling qualities. Rev. R. C. Christy of the Catholic Church is well and favorably known to many of our citizens for his acquirements as a scholar, his zeal in his holy calling, and his unfaltering devotion to the sacred cause of his country. We regret to learn that Mr. Christy is at present suffering from rheumatism but hope that a kind Providence will soon grant him power to recommence his mission of usefulness.

Lookout Mountain, Tennessee
March 11th 1864

Honor to the Iron Soldier

    The following preamble and resolutions accompanied with a purse well filled with greenbacks were presented to the Rev. R. C. Christy, chaplain of the 78th Pennsylvania Volunteers by the non-commissioned officers and privates of that Gallant (Iron) Regiment.

Whereas Reverend Sir we the non-commissioned officers and privates of the 78th Pennsylvania volunteers have heard that you have been deprived of some of your pay on the misconceived idea that you were absent from the regiment during the march from Murfreesboro to Chattanooga, we, knowing that you accompanied the regiment and desiring to acknowledge our estimate of your valuable services do hereby put on record our sincere and honest convictions.

Resolved, that the 78th Pennsylvania Volunteers do hereby acknowledge the beneficial services the unremitting zeal and constant attention which has at all times characterized you.

Resolved, that we will ever treasure up in our heart of hearts your kind and charitable labors in care of the sick at Camp Negley, Kentucky, in the winter of '61 as well as at all other places where duty called.

Resolved, that we will ever keep green in our memory your valuable services on the bloody field of Stones River where unmindful of the storm of iron hail that rained on that day you stood manfully as a Christian soldier in the discharge of your duty: and not alone on the blood-stained field of Stones River but on every battlefield that the Army of the Cumberland trod since October '61.

Resolved, that we tender you the accompanying purse filled with greenbacks as a small, but sincere, tribute to your worth as a clergyman, a scholar, patriot, and soldier, and we fervently pray that your present disability will soon end and restore you to your sphere of usefulness.

Resolved, that these resolutions be published in the *Louisville Journal*.

Taken from *Armstrong Democrat*, Kittanning, Pennsylvania:

Chaplain of the 78th Complimented

The Louisville *Journal* says: "Rev. Mr. Christy, Chaplain in General Negley's Brigade, preached to a very large congregation at St. Patrick's Church, Thirteenth Street, on yesterday. The discourse was highly spo-

ken of for its solidity and clearness of argument and its felicity of chastened language; in a word, as typical of the Quintillian standard of the
public speaker—*Dociut et Placiut.*[17] The Rev. gentleman is en route for
his brigade, having just returned from a short visit to his relatives in
Pennsylvania. No chaplain in the great armies of the west is a greater
favorite among his acquaintances, military or civil, than the Rev. Mr.
Christy, who, to the graces and virtues of the Christian minister, adds the
accomplishments and acquirements of the scholar." Mr. Christy was formerly [. . .][18] to St. Paul's Cathedral, in Pittsburgh, and at the time he
was chosen chaplain, had charge of a congregation in Butler county. He
is a mild, unassuming gentleman, and calculated to make friends wherever he goes.

On the morning of the second of May 1864, the regiment de-
scended from the heights of Look Out Mountain, and rejoined its brigade at Graysville, in the vicinity of which, General Sherman's veteran
army was concentrating, preparatory to its great march to Atlanta.
There was a battle almost every day. Three months of constant fighting
made a terrible gap in that army of over one hundred thousand men.
As a matter of course, there was much suffering among the wounded
and a great deal to do for those who had charge of them. Chaplains,
surgeons, and nurses, were kept constantly on the go night and day.
Among the daily events there happened sometimes incidents that
cheered the soldier and made him laugh even in the heat of battle. An
event that befell our chaplain was the cause of much merriment among
the soldiers of the brigade.

Whilst fording the Etowah River, which was wide and swift, there
were many involuntary dunkings, that, however unpleasant to the sufferers, were a source of much amusement to the lookers on. The water
was quite muddy, with a very swift current, from three to four feet
deep; the bottom being covered with boulders which made the footing
very insecure. Most of the officers were mounted, two on a horse, in
order to get across without the necessity of wading. The horse of Father
Christy being a very diminutive, weak kneed animal, was scarcely able
to carry his weighty master; but to be of some service to the soldiers,
the chaplain took several of their muskets on the saddle before him. All

went very well, until the middle of the river was reached, when his horse stumbled on one of those hidden boulders, and over he went, headforemost into the boiling current, carrying his helpless rider with him! For a while, there was an immense splashing in the water and a great struggling of man and beast. Father Christy, having a wholesome fear of rivers ever since his plunge into the Tennessee, thought he had fallen into a deep hole, far beyond his depth. He therefore made some desperate efforts to keep himself from the bottom. The river was alive with officers and soldiers, who, at first, were a little concerned for the chaplain's safety. But when they saw him finally raising his head Tantalus like above the turbid waters, shout after shout of hearty laughter greeted his appearance, and many a witty jest was made at the expense of the good-natured chaplain and his baptism in the Etowah River.

On the 27th of May, the Battle of [New] Hope Church was fought. The 78th Pennsylvania and 37th Indiana were on the extreme left, and suffered terrible from repeated charges of a confident and overwhelming foe. An officer writes,

> During the whole of the afternoon, there was not a staff officer to be seen; we had no communication with our general, save through the chaplain of the 78th. The enemy was swarming in our front and overlapping us on the left. There were no surgeons, no stretcher bearers, to attend to the wounded. Father Christy, undeterred by the terrible cross fire, was continually moving along our line, helping the wounded into the woods in our rear; and those men too badly hurt to help themselves, he took up in his arms and bore to a place of safety. About sunset, our ammunition began to fail; we, on the right, were advanced into the middle of an open cornfield, and if the enemy made another charge, it was doubtful about the result.
>
> I called to Father Christy, and urged him to hunt up Colonel [Benjamin F.] Scribner, our brigade commander, and make known our situation, and the absolute necessity for an instant supply of ammunition. All this time, the firing was becoming every moment heavier, on our front, and left. Our chaplain, soon returned with the information, that the ammu-

nition was far in the rear, and that the colonel said we must do the best we could. Father Christy, however, had begged some ammunition from a regiment in our rear and his pockets and handkerchief were stuffed with the much-needed supply. Along the line he went eking out his cartridges to those who needed them most. The enthusiasm of the soldiers was raised to its utmost, at this brave conduct of their chaplain, through whose assistance we were enabled to maintain our position until night put an end to the battle.

From Marietta, the regiment, along with the 104th Ohio, was sent back to Chattanooga to act as train guards on the railroad. It was a dangerous and laborious duty. All of the supplies for Sherman's grand army were conveyed over one line of railroad, one hundred and forty miles in length running through a mountainous, and thickly wooded country, in the recesses of which were many bands of guerillas, whose constant aim was to capture and destroy supply trains.

When Sherman entered Atlanta, the capacity of the road was stretched to its utmost in order to rush in supplies sufficient for his army before his contemplated march to the sea. In this duty, officers and men were constantly on the go night and day. Officers were scarce, and when one became sick it was hard to fill his place.

On one occasion, a train was waiting for its guard; the men were drawn out in front of the regimental headquarters, but there was no commissioned officer to take command. Father Christy, seeing the dilemma, buckled on a sword and reported to the colonel for duty. His services were thankfully accepted. He faced his men, and marched them off with as much *esprit* as any officer in the regiment. He conducted his train safely to its destination and brought his men home in good condition. The boys who were with him were so delighted with his conduct that they besought the colonel, to let them have the chaplain for their commanding officer on all subsequent expeditions.

"What would you have done?" asked someone of Father Christy, "if the rebels had attacked your train?"

"Why," said he complacently, "I would have told the boys to *pitch in!*"[19]

In November, 1864, the regiment was mustered out at Kittanning, Pennsylvania, after three years of active and laborious service in the field. In the final separation, officers and men expressed for Father Christy the warmest wishes for his success and prosperity. Certainly there was no other officer in the regiment that took home with him so many prayers and wishes for a happy future. The boys still enquire for him, and when a few get together to recount the dangers of the past, of all other officers Father Christy's name is mentioned the oftenest. It is certain that as long as one of the old 78th remains, its chaplain will not be forgotten.

After the war, Father Christy was sent to Ebensburg, [Pennsylvania], where he still remains, an honored, and a well-loved pastor. Resolute, and energetic, loathing ease, he began, and with but little assistance, has already almost completed a magnificent church; which for size and architectural beauty, promises to excel every other in the diocese.

EPILOGUE: Following the mustering out of the 78th at the conclusion of the war, Father Christy returned to his pastoral duties in the Diocese of Pittsburgh. He was assigned to the Church of the Holy Name in Ebensburg, where he remained until the last years of his life. During his time as pastor, he set about constructing a new and impressive church, highly praised at the time though sadly no longer standing. He also oversaw the construction of Mt. Gallitzin Seminary, a boys' boarding school, and invited the Sisters of St. Joseph to teach there. In his last years, he assisted at St. Patrick's Church in Pittsburgh before accepting a post in Columbus, Ohio. He died in Columbus on October 16, 1878. His body was returned to Ebensburg for burial, a testament to the importance that place served in his ministry.

SOURCES: "Necrology of the Diocese of Pittsburg," in *Catholic Historical Researches* 2, no. 3 (January 1886): 98–99;

Society of the Army of the Cumberland, Eleventh Reunion, 1879 (Cincinnati: Robert Clarke and Co., 1880), 260–63; *Souvenir of Loretto Centenary, October 10, 1899* (Cresson, PA: Swope Brothers, 1899), 372–74; J. T. Gibson, ed., *History of the Seventy-Eighth Pennsylvania Volunteer Infantry* (Pittsburgh: Press of the Pittsburgh Printing Co., 1905), 20, 140, 148, 184.

CHAPTER IX

Rev. Thomas Scully

Chaplain 9th Massachusetts
Veteran Volunteers

A pen picture of Catholic persecution in Massachusetts—
Grand attitude of the Catholic Church and people of Massachusetts—
Colonel Cass and the 9th Massachusetts—Father Scully volunteers
to be their chaplain—Father Scully's birth, education, and
ordination—At Arlington Heights—Governor Andrew's visit—
The chapel tent.

INTRODUCTION: Father Thomas Scully (1833–1902) served as chaplain to the 9th Massachusetts Volunteer Infantry. Born in Ireland on March 24, 1833, to Jeremiah and Mary Scully, he was educated in Ireland, England, and Italy before immigrating to the United States around 1858. He was ordained for service in the Archdiocese of Boston on September 18, 1860.

He enlisted in the war on April 15, 1861, and served until October 31, 1862. During his time as chaplain to the 9th Massachusetts, he was several times in the midst of battle and ministered to the dying and wounded. He was twice captured by the Confederates, taken prisoner on June 27, 1862, at the Battle of Gaines Mill (first battle of the Seven Days Battles) and on

141

June 29, 1862, at the Battle of Savage Station. He was held for a time in Richmond. He resigned from the military because of ill health at the end of October. Michael H. MacNamara, an officer in the 9th Massachusetts who had written a book about his regiment called *The Irish Ninth in Bivouac and Battle* (1867), was probably the source for Conyngham's chapters on Father Scully.

Conyngham highlights Father Scully's diverse ministry, including attempts to lead worship in less than ideal conditions, helping to form a soldier choir for the celebration of High Mass, hearing confessions "in the saddle," and transporting large amounts of cash for soldiers wishing to send their pay to loved ones back home.

We are impelled by the peculiar nature of our work to refer to a period anterior to the late war, in order that we may present the Irish priest and the Irish soldier, not in his strongest but in his purest and highest light. This necessity is peculiarly apparent from the fact that this chapter on "Catholic Chaplains in the Army" will be devoted exclusively to the sedate old Commonwealth of Massachusetts where once was made a most rigorous attempt to ostracise the foreign element, and especially the Irish and Catholic portion of it in the well-remembered years of 1852 and '53. Indeed, did we wish, we might go back a few decades and present scenes of evil, riot, wrong, and horror as might well embitter the Catholic heart against a state which has since been so well and bravely defended by the Irish and Catholic citizens of the old commonwealth.

   We might picture in these pages the lurid glare of burning convents—the awful desecration of religious houses; of holy nuns flying from sanctuaries sacred no longer in the eyes of a bigoted mob; of churches assailed; priests hunted—hunted as fiercely as ever they were, by the wildest of Cromwell's soldiery—ay, we might present pen pictures so degrading and so infamous as would fill the most callous human heart with horror and make the very wretches, who occasioned them, were they living today, crazed to look back upon their frightful deeds. The demolished convents of Massachusetts, however, are part and parcel of the history of the commonwealth, and the bloody crimes of those benighted days have left upon the once bright brow of Massachusetts a mark as indelible as that which disfigured the forehead of Cain![1]

But thank heaven, the times have changed! To picture such scenes is not for us—to mar the pages of our book with the unholy deeds of lowly minded bigots is not the purpose of our pen; we simply design to write of the later times when the warm and kindly hearts of Irish Catholics were filled with indignation at the narrow minded conduct of a state legislature, which authorized the mission of a [Joseph] *Hiss*— whose name is infamous—to search the Catholic female seminaries for mysterious trap doors and subterranean passages, where it was supposed were immured unwilling *religieuse* and implacable enemies of our holy religion.[2]

The embers of the Know-Nothing fire were still aglow with life when the mutterings of war came down to Massachusetts from the South. The Tubal Cains[3] of the nations began to fashion the spears and swords for the coming combat—the rattle of arms in the arsenals, and the rumbling of artillery upon the streets proclaimed that war had allied himself with death; that soon the private and public buildings of the land would be draped in mourning! The grave digger sharpened his tools and increased his force; and, in a sudden moment, the black thunder of war fell upon the nation, and the nation looked to her sons for protection!

What was the attitude of the plundered and insulted Catholic Church of Massachusetts in that hour of national peril?

Where stood the Irishmen of the state at that solemn moment of the Union's life? Though they still smarted with the fierce wounds inflicted upon them by the bigots of New England, they were not idle spectators of the drooping folds of "old glory"—they beheld the grand young flag which had never gone down in defeat before a foreign foe, falling to the ground to be trampled under the feet of men who had sworn they loved it well! It was then that the sons of Ireland leaped to the front—insults and ostracism—burned convents—and hunted priests—*all* were forgotten; and, when the grand old Irish 9th of Massachusetts prepared to march forth, to stand before and defend the life of the Republic, the Catholic Church of Massachusetts—all grand and forgiving—forgetting the past, and fervently praying for the future, stood behind her Irish heroes and with uplifted hands flowered their footsteps with prayers and benedictions!

Such was the attitude of our Church and people when the Irish 9th, as it was familiarly called, was organized by Colonel Thomas Cass,[4] and when its officers shortly afterwards applied to His Excellency [Massachusetts Governor] John Albion Andrew[5] for a chaplain to accompany them to the field; the application of the officers was referred by Governor Andrew to Bishop [John B.] Fitzpatrick[6] who was sadly puzzled how to comply with the request, owing to the scarcity of priests at that time in the diocese.

It chanced, however, that the Rev. Thomas Scully, the subject of our memoir, was then on a visit to the bishop, and, learning the desire of the 9th, immediately relieved the Right Reverend Father in his difficulty by volunteering to fill the place in question.

The bishop was both astonished and pleased at the alacrity of the young disciple, as well he might be, having himself a large knowledge of the dangers and trials which his young priest was certain to encounter—for how many times had he listened to the stories and military anecdotes of venerable Father [John] McElroy,[7] when he recounted the terrible trials he experienced in his own person in the romantic but bloody campaigns of Mexico!

The Right Reverend Bishop did not allow the ardor of the young priest to cool; he accompanied him almost immediately to the statehouse and he was there sworn into the service of the Union. Almost before he knew the situation, the unfaltering soldier of the Cross, became a soldier of the Great Republic. Governor Andrew was as much pleased as the bishop was overjoyed; but the joy of the bishop and the pleasure of the governor did not exceed the satisfaction of the boys of the 9th when they learned that their application had been successful.

When the knowledge arrived at the camp at Long Island in Boston Harbor, the boys felt themselves soldiers in every sense. By a thousand excuses they would get down to the transport when it arrived and, if asked what they were doing there, would reply:

"Arrah, sure we want a look at our *Sagart Aroon* [dear chaplain]!"

"Do ye know Jim, is he an ould man?" one would query.

"How should I know; ave coorse he's an ould man; why shouldn't he?"

"Yes, my banchal; but an ould man can't stand a sodger's life."

"Bah! What do ye know about it—Sure God looks out for his own—An' we can look out for him too!"

To say that the lads of the 9th were astonished when they beheld their priest for the first time, would hardly express their sensations. Instead of an old man, they beheld a slender, modest looking young gentleman, little more, if any, than a hundred and forty pounds in weight, with a bright eye, a handsome face, and general physique, which eminently well fitted him for the position to which he had been assigned.

The critical eyes of our boys soon took his measure.

"Well, he's a quiet looking man God bless him, but it's quare to me if he hasn't a mighty stiff back bone!"

Not only the 9th boys, but even Southern officers, afterwards found that he *did* have not only a "stiff back bone," but a heart as replete with courage, and a spirit as uncomplaining of suffering as the best man that ever battled under the flag!

We say no more than the facts warrant when we assert that a better tone permeated the regiment; a higher and nobler spirit animated the men; a finer idea of discipline took possession of them after Father Scully arrived than ever the brave fellows had experienced before.

Prior to the celebration of the first Mass, the camp of the 9th presented a curious scene. The soldiers were engaged in cleaning their clothes, pipe claying their brasses, "putting a polish" on their boots, every face shining with a new light—preparing to worship at the altar of God, before laying down their lives on the altar of their country— for the preservation of the Union—and for human liberty!

The camp was crowded with hundreds of visitors. No edifice in the world held a truer or more fervid congregation, than the magnificent church of Long Island! The brush of Michelangelo[8] aided by the most brilliant of human imaginations had not adorned the dome of Saint Peter's at Rome, a tithe as wondrously, as that which looked down upon the assembled thousands at that Island Camp. The roof of the church was a sky of glorious beauty! The green fields and the vast expanse of sun-sheened waters was the floor fashioned by God's own hand! Twas there, about their brave priest, the soldiers knelt, and in their gleaming brasses and uniforms of blue worshipped the everliving God, as they had never worshipped Him before. Around them, forming an outer circle, stood the visitors, friends and relatives of the kneeling braves, garbed in a thousand colors, with bowed heads adding beauty to the solemn scene. The voices of the choir sweetly ascending; the strange and, otherwise, solemn silence of the scene; the young priest equipped for his sacred office. Ah, it was a scene for a Michelangelo to paint, not for a feeble pen to picture.

The altar held no work of art. It was ornamented simply by the flowers of the field; and, at the elevation of the host, by a strange coincidence, was heard the solemn roll of drums, as if music too had bowed her head in solemn joy that Mass was served where Mass had never been served before!

In writing of the associations of our priest, our pen sometimes hesitates, as if to remind us, that we should say a kindly word of the dead who appreciated him so well, and upon whom *he* looked with a priestly and martial affection.

So then, let our pen ramble on; we are curious ourselves to see what it will tell of the dead Tom Mooney! He was the leader of the little choir. He, in his own unassuming way, would suddenly improvise, "Quartermaster Mooney of the 9th." How familiar the words—we hear them echo from a hundred camps—we hear them sounded after a score of battles—and we remember that the gallant fellow could never say twenty words consecutively without breaking in with—

"But boys, that's nothing to do with it—where's Father Scully?" Few priests in this world have a better or more devout friend, than had the subject of this memoir in poor, kindly hearted Tom Mooney, killed at Stoneman's Switch[9] on St. Patrick's Day [1863], by being thrown from his horse during the festivities of that occasion.[10] Truly he was a good son of the Church, and a finer priest than Father Tom, or a nobler regiment than the "Bloody Ninth," in his estimation never existed!

We have felt it necessary in this memoir of the chaplain of the 9th Regiment, Massachusetts Vols. to dwell somewhat upon matters which may appear anti-biographical; we have felt it necessary however, from the fact we are writing here of that most exclusive of states, Massachusetts, and of a citizen of it who as a member of the 9th is in a measure identified with its past and its present history.

For that reason if we have proved prosy our readers will excuse us, and for another reason, that we are now about to enter into the active life and military experiences of its chaplain.

The Rev. Thomas Scully was born in the City of Limerick—the grand old city of the "broken treaties"—on the 24th day of March, 1833. This youth was schooled in two of the finest cities of Ireland—Cork and Dublin and, probably, that is the reason why he is so lacking of the fine Irish brogue. He began and finished his collegiate career in England at one of the principle colleges, completing his education in philosophy and theology under the beautiful skies of Italy. A desire to practicalize the studies of the [Church][11] led him to visit America, where he arrived early in 1859, and was shortly afterward ordained priest in Saint James Church in Boston by the Rt. Rev. Bishop Fitzpatrick.

The first mission of our young priest was in Roxbury (now known as Boston Highlands) and Dedham; which, at that time, comprised his parish. Here he remained arduously engaged in fu[r]thering the interests of his flock until the breaking out of the war, in which, as recorded before, he immediately assumed a place. We can have no better proof of the remarkable energy of Father Scully, than the fact, of his short sojourn in the country and his immediately volunteering to leave a comfortable mission, and a well beloved flock, to encounter perils fierce sufferings and probably death in order that the brave men who went forth to defend the Union, might not die without the rites of their Church. We can have no better proof of the appreciation of his bishop than the simple fact that he was immediately assigned to the grave and responsible position he voluntarily assumed—a thousand times more responsible than the cares of a mission, and in which he won for

himself a name if equaled, certainly unsurpassed, by the brave and devoted Soldiers of the Cross, who so grandly associated themselves with
the battles, miseries, and tribulations of the sons of the Church.

The appreciation of his bishop was still further indicated by his
visit to Long Island shortly after Father Scully had assumed his duties
as pastor of the camp. On the occasion of his visit the bishop seemed
impressed with the onerous undertaking of the young clergyman, and
felt more than ever satisfied with his selection of a chaplain—for in Father Tom he saw all the necessary elements combined for this peculiar
phase of his holy vocation—youth, courage, indomitable [energy];[12] a
thorough contempt for difficulties and a natural faculty for winning
the affection of his men. During that visit the bishop bestowed his
benediction on the troops, encouraged the men of the 9th to be true
soldiers of *Jesus Christ*, as well as of the Republic, and distributed to
every man a medal of the blessed virgin Mary. He instructed them to
love and obey their young chaplain, who had sacrificed more than they,
in honor and preferment in his Church, to be with them in their times
of danger, and who would calmly follow them through every peril. In
every possible way the good bishop of Boston showed his anxiety for
the young disciple and for the future of the gallant men with whom he
had embarked his fortunes.

The story of the departure of the chaplain and his regiment until
their arrival at Fortress Monroe we need not tell. The pathetic incidents
of separation; the cheers; the "good byes"; the sweet and thrilling music
of the bands; a week's life aboard the *Cambridge* and *Ben de Ford*[13]—
the names of the transports—all this our readers may imagine but our
pen would fail to describe.

Upon the arrival of the transports at Fort Monroe, chaplain Scully
accompanied Colonel Cass and his officers to the fort and was then introduced to General Ben. F. Butler, since governor of the state, at that
time in command. The general was greatly pleased to see a Catholic
priest in the army, and expressed the wish that he had one with his
men, saying that "an army blessed with priests could always fight well."
The following Saturday the regiment debarked at Washington, marched
to the arsenal yard and then encamped. The 9th at that place went to
the church of the Dominican Friars, where Mass was said by Father
Scully and devoutly attended to by the officers and men.

We cannot pass this portion of our narrative without relating a comical incident, which illustrates the position occupied by the different chaplains (Protestant and others) in the army during that early period of the war.

While in Washington, at the time above referred to, Father Scully received an invitation to be present at a meeting of chaplains. The purposes of the meeting were not stated. Father Tom of course imagined that it was a gathering of Catholic clergymen to organize a system and uniformity of congregation which might be of moment to themselves and their military flock after entering into active service in the field. In this belief he attended the gathering—or, it might be better styled convention—and was somewhat surprised to meet a great number of Protestant ministers holding council together upon the following, to them, truly important issues; to wit:—

I.   Army chaplains should be graded as follows. Lieutenants, Captains, Majors, Lt. Colonels, Colonels, Brigadier Generals (none of them to be privates however!)
II. Said chaplains to be paid according to rank.
III. The uniform to be similar to that worn by the army—the insignia of *rank* however, to be worn *embroidered* upon the breast.

Such was the basis of the call of this convention, such the platform upon which they had, in caucus, determined to stand.

Having elected a president and other necessary officers the meeting was *formally* called to order.

"*Mr. President!*" were the first words that fell upon the ears of the assembly. A tall, gaunt, dark visaged man, robed in garments somewhat the worse for wear, with a soiled white linen gathered under his chin, syllabled the above and portentous words.

Mr. President: of the importance of this occasion no man among us can doubt. The country is in a difficult situation; who is right or who is wrong none of us need take the responsibility of judging—the Amerikin bird is in danger—our lives air precious and having a stake in the kintry we air bound to look out for that stake—rank an' money—that's the stake, an' feller ministers, that stake must come from the rump of the country! Generals air gettin' big pay; politishuns air speculatin'—an' if we keep on, our meat will come from the horn of the keow! This meetin' is called for elevatin' ourself, an' Lord knows we need elevatin'! So I purpose the follerin petition:

And the Rev. Gentleman presented a paper asking to be graded as above and paid according to grade. He had no sooner resumed his seat than another assumed his place.

There's nary a time tew fix oneself better than whin the enemy is in danger—Whar's the danger an whar's the enemy? I hev lift a congregation of nigh on a hindred folks who air charmed with my gospil talk and who'd give me a selery of 'bout three hundred dollars—but I'd rether come here an fight for the kentry than take it. Neow I agree with Brother Silas—we hev the country on the hip—Now's the time to strike for pay en rank—*I* indorse them air resolves!

Others followed in the same strain; but the importance as well as the grave matter of this chapter will not allow us to dilate upon what followed; our design being simply to present the reader with the part taken in this convention by Father Scully who was an amused spectator of the scene.

During the debate upon the petition many eyes had been turned toward him; every man in the meeting saw in a moment that he was not one of themselves—but they imagined that the almighty dollar influenced him as well as the other members of that memorable body. The president of the convention finally called upon the Rev. Mr. Scully, chaplain of the 9th M[assachusetts] V[olunteers]. Father Tom arose; he spoke as solemnly as if he were addressing his people from the altar:

Gentlemen: I cannot join you in your movement upon the government. She has enemies without—I am sorry to learn that she has foes within. *I* have a higher rank than the president or the congress of the United States can give to man! *I am a Catholic priest!* I labor in the service of God. *He* is my pay-master. My men will support me, and I need not to trouble the government of this nation—now sadly troubled indeed—to do that which my Church commands me to do without money and without price; but if my vote will be of any use to you gentlemen, for I know you have families depending upon you, I hope that you may be all generals and be paid as such!

And with a quick bow and quizzical smile, Father Tom went from among them.

The stay of Father Scully and his regiment in Washington was of short duration; for, a day or two after their arrival, they took up their march for an available spot called Emmart's Farm,[14] and afterwards, Wool's Hill; here the men soon fixed themselves comfortably and awaited events.

In a few days they were startled by the thunder of the guns at Bull Run. The news came to them that the Union arms had experienced an overwhelming and disastrous defeat!

We remember well the condition of Washington at that time. The stores were deserted and the doors flung open, nobody to sell goods and nobody to steal them. Wounded soldiers lying about on every hand. Where the people had disappeared to it was impossible to tell. The day too was wet and dismal when the news of the defeat reached the 9th Regiment. It had but little effect on the boys however; they were only anxious to come in contact with the enemy and give an additional touch to the magnificent picture painted by the glorious 69th Regiment of New York, under the gallant [Michael] Corcoran,[15] upon the memorable occasion referred to.

At Emmart's Farm the 9th was visited by Governor Andrew of Massachusetts. It is no wonder that this distinguished man was a general favorite with Irish officers and soldiers. The domestics in his family were Irish and Catholic, he would employ no others, and when he called upon the regiment in this camp he brought with him blessed medals and prayer books to present to the brothers of two of his domestics enlisted in the 9th. He visited the tent of Father Scully who sent for the men, to whom his excellency presented the sacred emblems and expressed the great pleasure it gave him to bring them to the boys in person; he then entered into conversation with them, and when he departed he shook them cordially by the hand, and was loudly cheered as he left the camp.

From Emmart's Farm the regiment crossed the Potomac, pitching its camp at Arlington Heights, where the boys were received with bonfires, lighted by the gallant 69th New York, with cheers and other tokens of joy. Here *Fort Corcoran* and *Fort Cass* were built for the better protection of the Capitol. In these labors the two Irish regiments worked side by side harmoniously together and at one time expected and wished to be brigaded. This was not to be, however, much to the disappointment of both.

Shortly after their arrival at this camp the men of the 9th Regiment got together a generous fund which they presented to their beloved pastor, requesting him to purchase a chapel tent. This was soon done and the regiment became the owner of as fine a chapel tent as was in the army of the Potomac. The men were never backward in coming to the assistance of the young priest, rather anticipating than awaiting an expression of his wishes. Quartermaster Mooney, after the purchase of the tent, became more active than ever, and was soon engaged in organizing a *choir*; and, as he came from a family of musicians, this work he accomplished most successfully, for the 9th could boast many excellent singers. The chapel tent was dedicated at Falls Church by a High Mass; and it was a grand and solemn celebration.

It was not only attended by the soldiers of the 9th Regiment, but brave men gathered from all quarters to worship God and witness the holy ceremonies of the True Church. With the low tones of the priest would sometimes mingle the clash of arms, the roll of drums, the quick sharp word of command from some marching squad performing a necessary duty. Sometimes the sharp crack of a picket rifle would fall upon the ears but above and beyond all the rich and powerful voices of the soldier *choir* would ascend to the heavens—its solemn strains affecting every heart witnessing that martial scene.

❀

CHAPTER X

Rev. Thomas Scully, Continued

Vespers and confession in camp—Burial of Sergeant Regan—
Praying under difficulties—Hearing the confessions of the men
under fire—Services on the Peninsula—His address to the
"Home Guard"—His capture and escape—A night in the
swamps—A prisoner again—A brutal officer—Taken to
Richmond—His release and return to army life—Amusing
incidents—His failing health—He leaves the army
and returns to Boston.

The arduous duties of Father Scully went on without cessation. In the afternoon [the] Rosary was said in camp and the holy utterances of the man of God [were] gravely attended to by the men. In the evening confessions would be heard—indeed the good priest's time was fully taken up in this, and a score of other ways, in a manner foreign to the duties of his sacred work.

Falls Church in Virginia was succeeded by the desperate fields of the Peninsula; by Camp California, better known as Camp Misery; by Yorktown's bloody front; and the battle of Hanover Court House where fell the first victim of the 9th Regiment, Sergeant [Daniel] Regan who was eminently a good soldier and a good man.[1] Of course being the *first* victim of the war, so far as the 9th was concerned, he was buried with military honors. His funeral was grand and impressive; his grave was blessed and an affecting discourse delivered by the chaplain. A short time before he was killed, as if anticipating his approaching end,

153

he took from his finger an engagement ring, which he beseeched the Rev. Father to forward to his betrothed in the event of his death, and Father Scully complied with his request.

At Yorktown our unflinching chaplain continued the services of the Church—Rosary being said every evening in honor of the Blessed Virgin. Cannonballs fell thick and fast about the man of God; death held carnival in the air and on the ground; and here and there the groans of the wounded and dying might be heard—but the voice of the priest, could be heard as calmly uttering the divine word as if he had been securely ensconced in his own church in Roxbury.

We recall another instance of this calm heroism at the first Bull Run, to which friend Father Scully had been invited by Colonel Corcoran. Here, in a dry ditch he heard the confessions of the men of the 69th—nor budged his body nor bowed his [head], except to the name of Jesus, more potent than bullets—though the deadly missiles of war shrieked and struck around him all impotent to harm.

This calm, enduring bravery, witnessed upon scores of occasions, could not fail to win the admiration and respect of Protestant officers and men. In fact, it did much to elevate the character of these men of God, who could, upon all occasions, be seen in the thick of the fight valiantly and unostentatiously doing their holy duty.

It was not long before the name of our chaplain became well known among all classes of men and many who before had been prejudiced against a Catholic now gave them their full need of praise and respect.

Among all the chaplains of the army the Catholic priest stood highest for bravery, devotion, character and every other element of worth.

The onerous duties of a priest upon the Peninsula could not be otherwise than extremely distressing. A lack of any kind of decent accommodations, continually moving about from here to there, marching and fighting, and almost all the time without shelter in a rainy season, it is little wonder that even the indomitable Father Scully would succumb. He fell very sick and leave was granted to him to return to Boston to recruit. The Rev. Father reluctantly took leave of his brave boys and for a short time sojourned in Boston; upon arriving there, being bearded like a *Pard*,[2] he was mistaken for an oriental priest when he said Mass in one of the city churches. When it was learned by the public that it was Father Scully of the 9th—there was a *furore* to see him; he became the rage.[3]

After a short visit to Boston, Father Scully returned to his regiment, very much against the advice of his physician, and, finding them at Gaines Mills, resumed his arduous labors. These labors now became far heavier than ever before for he performed services in *two* divisions, no other chaplain being at hand. He might be seen continually going among the hospitals, hearing confession, consoling the wounded and, in a hundred ways, assisting the boys to make themselves comfortable in camp. The enthusiasm of Father Scully in his holy work often led him into danger; this was especially the case at Gaines Mills where the Rev. Gentleman was taken prisoner by the Confederates. Father Scully, however, was not the man to remain with them longer than he could help, so, [with] darkness coming on, he put his wits to work and soon found an opportunity. The night had fallen and it was a dreary and cheerless one indeed. Scarcely a star twinkled in the sky, and taking advantage of the drowsiness of his guard, the brave priest, crept away under the cover of the darkness in the direction of Chickahominy swamp. Soon he found himself floundering about in that awful bog, desperately striving to make his way in the direction of the Union lines. It was terrible work, rendered still more difficult by the fact that he lost his boots in the swamp; and, if he lost his way, he might feel pretty sure at least of being recaptured.

Several shots were fired after him by the guard upon discovering his escape, but none succeed[ed] in hitting him. At last towards morning, hungry, sick, and half dead, to his own joy and the unbounded delight of his men he reached camp where, after detailing his adventures, he partook of refreshments and then retired for the rest he greatly needed.

At Malvern Hill, Father Tom was again unfortunate enough to fall into the hands of the enemy, owing to his earnest desire to be with his boys in the thick of the fight.[4] This time he was captured by South Carolina soldiers. The colonel of these men was a big brawny brute of a Huguenot (or rather a descendent of that fiercely bigoted race).[5]

When this fellow learned that Father Scully was a Catholic priest and in the Union Army, his rage knew no bounds! He abused the young clergyman in the foulest manner! Being unable to upset his patience, he drew his revolver and (will the reader believe it) the cowardly brute placed it at the brow of this unarmed follower of God and threatened to blow out his brains! Were this act done to a miserable prisoner of the lowest grade it would have been cowardly. To a man of peace, a follower of Christ, whose standard was the Cross, it was a thousand times worse than cowardice. Even his own soldiers were horrified at his act and probably that was the reason he refrained from executing his murderous and fiendish threat! This *manly* officer, not satisfied with thus abusing Father Tom, turned the vials of his wrath upon the honored name of Archbishop Hughes, cursing him roundly and cursing the Irish who were helping the "black hearted nutmeg peddling Yankees!"

While a prisoner with this man's command our priest was visited by a sergeant of the Confederates, who beseeched him to hear his confession. This the priest consented to do [with] the man confessing to Father Scully standing in the attitude of conversation to avoid notice. Upon arriving at "Savage's Station,"[6] Father Scully was treated very kindly by him—his sister being a convert to Catholicity. This officer on his departure gave him a letter to Colonel [John H.] Winder, provost marshal at Richmond, asking for our clergyman every indulgence. This Winder reluctantly granted giving Father Scully permission to confine himself to the pastor's residence in Richmond, the mission of the Rev. Father [John] Teeling,[7] who had been a chaplain with the Confederates at Bull Run.

Here Father Tom remained. Saying Mass one Sunday, and thereby giving great offence to the Southern Catholics, [who][8] sent a petition to Jefferson Davis, who forwarded it to Bishop [John] McGill,[9] of Richmond, who in referring to it from the pulpit the following Sunday, took occasion to gravely excoriate these meddlers, telling that it was not for laymen to interfere with the affairs of the Church which were the affairs of God and warning them in future against such a course.

This reprimand doubtless had a good effect, as Father Scully had no further cause of mortification. In due time however, Father Tom was released from his uncomfortable situation and was once again among the lads he loved so well.

Hundreds of times on the march and in the saddle has Father Scully heard confessions, not only from his own men but from scores who only knew him as the soldier priest. It would be impossible to enumerate the nature of the various duties this young, energetic, and cool headed priest assumed from writing letters for the men to kneeling beside the wounded and dying on the field.

Strange as it may appear he passed unscathed through his innumerable dangers as if protected, especially for this holy work, by God himself!

Men have fallen dead beside him whilst he was engaged in tendering the consolation of our holy religion to some dying son of the Church. Cannon balls have plunged into the ground, covering him with earth. But he faltered not, his bearing was an example and encouragement to the men and the gallant fellows profited by it. Hundreds of dying men have often said to him on the field of battle after he had listened to their confession, "Ah, Father Scully I can die happy now—pray for me—don't get killed yourself!" And scores of other such expressions which showed how truly his invaluable services were appreciated.

Our chaplain would visit the hospitals upon every possible occasion, for there, generally, he would find somebody who needed his offices. The men found great consolation in these visits, and always, no matter how much they suffered, greeted him with a smile of welcome.

Upon one occasion, he visited a hospital in Virginia filled with negro soldiers.[10] Upon opening the door he said to the inmates, pleasantly, "Good morning; any Catholics here?"

"No Sar!" exclaimed one of them, "we is all from virginny!"

Pay day in the 9th Regiment was always a responsible as well as troublesome day for Father Scully—as he was entrusted with the money to deliver it at Adams Express. We recall one of these occasions which was attended with considerable danger. The road to Fort Monroe at that time was a very bad one to travel—Father Scully had in his possession $22,000 of the soldiers' money, for the express. Shortly after his departure from camp, the attention of the priest was directed to the suspicious conduct of three brawny villainous looking men who had been following him for some time. They were moving on in such a way that he was in a manner surrounded. In an instant Father Scully surmised their purpose—pulling forth his revolver he cocked it, saying calmly, "My men I am going ahead; if one of you attempts to follow or molest me, I'll drive a bullet through his head!"

The men hesitated a moment and then concluded probably, that Catholic priests are about like other brave men when in trouble. Had Father Scully been robbed at that time, there is not the slightest doubt but that he would have been murdered, too; his body flung into the woods to become food for the hungry half wild hogs which infested them. In fact all traces of him would have been lost. What, let our readers conjecture, would the world have said in view of such a fact? When Father Scully assumed the responsibility of taking that $22,000 to Fort Monroe he knew the danger he would encounter, but he never shirked a duty and he knew his men had unbounded faith in him.

Father Scully was not satisfied with keeping the men up to what we call the "mark"[11] in their morals and social duties; he went far beyond that, his aim being to make the men better than he found them and to send them to their homes, such of them as lived, with a higher appreciation of the duties of life and better guarded by the rules of their religion than when they first donned their soldier garb. For this purpose he was at work early and late to do away with that curse of a soldier's life, gambling. In a great measure he succeeded in this work but the boys would sometimes evade him for a while and manage to play out their "little game."

We remember upon one occasion, a number of the 9th gathered together in a wall tent at Gaines Mills, and pegged it down tightly on all sides, so that it was impossible for a person to get a peep within, and then the cards were brought forth and quite a lively game began. Father Scully heard of what was going on and determined to take a hand in it himself; so, making his way to the tent, he quietly reconnoitred, finding that both egress and ingress must be made with a knife. He no sooner ascertained that fact than drawing his weapon from his pocket he drove it into the canvas, and ripped the whole concern to the ground!

The men leaped to their feet and disappeared, leaving quite a heavy stake behind them, together with their artillery in the shape of cards, all of which the *attacking* party confiscated for the behoof and benefit of the Church!

"Well, boys," said one of the men one day, after they had been so treated.

"He don't do no more than Cromwell did himself—he used to *conwhiscate* money from the Church in the same way, and now our priest is thryin the same aisy game on us!"

This kind of sport the boys rather liked than other wise, if it wasn't "tried on *too* often."

The labors of Father Scully for the suppression of gambling were so successful that the 9th Regiment was freer from this peculiar fault than any other in the army.

While in the anecdotal humor we may as well relate an incident which happened at one of the ferries on the Potomac and which illustrates alike the discipline of the men of the 9th Regiment and the high respect in which they held the reverend subject of our sketch.

Father Scully had been, as usual, going his various rounds among the soldiers visiting the hospitals, etc., and was preparing to return to camp and for that reason was riding towards the ferry above mentioned. Upon arriving there he learned to his great chagrin that the boat was crowded and there was no room for him and his horse. Now it happened that a member of his regiment was present in the person of one Hinckley,[12] said to be one of the strongest men in the army.

He was a curious fellow. When he enlisted in the regiment, his first inquiry was before signing the roll, "Now yer sure this air's goin' tew be an Irish regiment—for I don't want tew git into a yankee one though I'm a yank meself—I want tew git with the fitin' boys an' them boys air the Irishers!"

Upon being assured that the 9th was *the* regiment, he signed the roll with alacrity and proved himself one of the best fighting men among its members but to return. Hinckley happened to be on hand when Father Scully arrived, and heard the captain of the boat tell him that he was crowded. Our hero cast his eyes over the boat and ascertained that there was plenty of room for a few more. Turning to the clergyman he said in his peculiarly quiet way:—

"Neow I ain't no Cathlic, but the Irish 9th is my crowd an' my chaplain's got tew git aboard that air boat—so here goes!"

And Father Scully having by this time dismounted, Hinckley clasped his arms around the barrel of the horse and lifting him bodily from the ground he carried him aboard the ferry to the rage of the captain and the unbounded astonishment of the passengers. Of course,

Father Scully was compelled to follow his "natty nag" which he did with ill-concealed delight. Hinckley got aboard also to see that "that an' chaplain of his'n shouldn't be interfered with while *he* was 'round!"

After his wonderful exhibition of strength it is unnecessary to say that both himself and his chaplain were treated with the highest respect.

We might easily fill a volume with anecdotes and adventures of the subject of this sketch but the space allotted to our work peremptorily forbids our dwelling in *extenso* upon them. Indeed it is not necessary, our design being merely to present illustrations of the trials, sufferings, and patient endurance of the chaplain of the 9th Massachusetts Volunteers; of the faithful and energetic manner in which he performed his holy and responsible duties, which won for him a reputation outside the limits of the 9th Regiment which will live long in the military annals of the nation, and gave him a warm corner in the brave hearts of more than a thousand men, among the living of whom, his name today is as familiar as a household word. Few living priests have shrived as many gallant men as he; few have witnessed such heroic death scenes; few indeed have encountered so many dangers; met them so bravely and passed through them so triumphantly—until worn down at last by the burden he assumed—broken by marches, and much suffering in the field, to the regret of his gallant men he was at last compelled to leave them and return once more to Boston. In bidding farewell to the regiment the men were affected to tears. He carried home with him the blessings and good wishes of the weather-beaten and war-marked braves, and hundreds of kindly messages to the friends and relatives of the men he so reluctantly left behind him.

After a period of rest and quiet he returned to his pastorship and finally became permanently settled in his present large and important mission in Cambridgeport, Massachusetts, where in the midst of a loving and appreciative people he is laboring with his usual energy and assiduity.

EPILOGUE: After the war, Father Scully returned to Boston for pastoral ministry. He became pastor of Immaculate Conception Church in Malden, Massachusetts (1863–1867), until assigned to the young St. Mary Church in Cambridge where he would serve for thirty-five years as pastor. A strong temperance advocate, he was president of Boston's Catholic Total Abstinence Union. He was active in the veterans' organizations, including the Grand Army of the Republic, serving as Massachusetts state chaplain. He died in Cambridge on September 12, 1902, and is buried at Holy Cross Cemetery in Malden.

SOURCES: Frank J. Flynn, *"The Fighting Ninth" for Fifty Years and the Semi-Centennial Celebration* (MA: 1911), 92, 108; Daniel George Macnamara, *The History of the Ninth Regiment, Massachusetts Volunteer Infantry* (Boston: E. B. Stillings, 1899), 166–68, 429; Patrick R. Guiney, *Commanding Boston's Irish Ninth: The Civil War Letters of Colonel Patrick R. Guiney*, ed. Christian G. Samito (New York: Fordham University Press, 1998), esp. 30–31, 74, 87, 115–16, 151, 153.

Rev. Peter Tissot, S.J.

Chaplain 37th New York Volunteers

*The application to Archbishop Hughes for a chaplain to
the 37th—Father Tissot appointed—His zeal in the service
and obedience to orders—His narrow escape at Fair Oaks—
His capture—His duties in camp and services in the field—Raising
a new flag—Father Tissot's prayer and address—His exertions
to raise money to send to Ireland—How the soldiers loved
and reverenced him.*

INTRODUCTION: Father Peter Tissot, S.J. (1823–1875),
served the 37th New York Volunteer Infantry. Born on October 15, 1823, in Megève, Savoy, France, he began his education
at the Jesuit college in Melun and entered the Society of Jesus
at Avignon in 1842. At his request he was sent to the United
States in 1846. Arriving in New York, he continued his studies
for the priesthood at St. John's College (later Fordham University) in addition to serving as a tutor. He was ordained in 1853,
remaining at Fordham.

At the war's beginning, Tissot volunteered as a chaplain,
serving from June 26, 1861, until June 22, 1863, when the 37th
New York Infantry Regiment, known as the "Irish Rifles," mustered out of service in New York City. In this short chapter,

Conyngham portrays Father Tissot as a humble, likeable chaplain who never strayed from his regiment. A deleted note at the end reveals that the chapter was written by Dr. William O'Meagher, the regiment's surgeon.

❁   ❁   ❁

Long before the complete organization of the 37th New York Vol., formerly known as the 75th Regiment of state militia, or "Irish Rifles," when, as yet, no commissions had been issued to the officers and the men were kept in barracks at Broadway Park, Bloomingdale Road, it was suggested by Adjutant Cornelius Murphy [of the 82nd New York] and Dr. [William] O'Meagher that a deputation should wait on Archbishop Hughes requesting him to appoint a chaplain for the regiment. Accordingly, a committee of the officers waited on his grace, to represent the general wish of all, at the same time requesting the appointment of Rev. M[ichael] Meagher, S.J.,[1] who had previously, when asked by the doctor, expressed his willingness to accompany the regiment provided he could be spared from his college duties and authorized by his superiors. But other important work had been assigned this reverend gentleman, who was subsequently sent on a mission to Quebec, and the Rev. Peter Tissot of the same order was at once appointed. Father Tissot was then professor in St. John's College, Fordham, New York, but, at the call of duty like a true soldier of the cross, with all the ardor of his illustrious order, he abandoned his books, his classes, and collegiate quiet for the din of arms, the field of battle, the hardships and privations of a soldier's life, for all of which, surely, there is no one so well adapted, as well by tradition as by profound knowledge of human nature, and the military discipline reserved by the followers of [St. Ignatius] Loyola, the soldier saint.[2] The regiment received him with the utmost respect and he forthwith set to work at his sacred calling.

Father Tissot was born a subject of the King of Sardinia in the year 1823, in the ancient Duchy of Savoy, since ceded to France to which it originally belonged by right as well as by its kindred population which is chiefly French. That his early life gave promise of more than ordinary grace and goodness, no one who has had the happiness of even a casual acquaintance with him could fail to perceive in later years. His preliminary studies were completed at the Jesuit college of Milan, within shadow of the grand old cathedral of St. Charles Borromeo, where no doubt he distinguished himself by studious habits, devotion to learning, piety, absorbing zeal, and patient perseverance, all which qualities he afterwards exhibited in their greatest perfection, and practical application, to the salvation of his fellow men, for whose spiritual welfare he always evinces the most affectionate solicitude, never wavering in his efforts to bring back stray sheep by gentle persuasion to the peaceful pasture and the security of the fold. His classical attainments were of the highest order.

From the almost monastic seclusion of the College of Milan, he was sent to the United States, where he arrived in the year 1846, and immediately commenced his theological studies in St. John's College, preparatory to ordination for the American mission. At the conclusion of this course he was ordained by Archbishop [Gaetano] Bedini, when that distinguished prelate visited the United States, in the capacity of Papal Nuncio.[3]

When Father Tissot first joined the 37th, his health was so much impaired by constant study and close attention to the routine duties of a college professorship, to which his priestly functions were superadded, that some apprehensions were felt and expressed by anxious friends as to his physical ability to endure the hardships of campaign life. But these fears were speedily dissipated, for before the regiment had been long in camp, a gradual and steady improvement taking the place of extreme debility, the flush of health soon irradiating his pale and wasted cheeks, and emaciation resulting from ascetic habits, studious and prayerful visits giving way to a state of physical health to which he had long been a stranger.

He soon adapted himself, with the well-known facility of his illustrious order, to the strictest discipline of a soldier's life, being always one of the first to obey orders, and among the earliest "to pack his knapsack" and fall into line, ready to move even at the most unseasonable hours, observing a most enviable coolness and self-possession in the midst of the most bewildering hustle and confusion, hurry and excitement incident to sudden military movements caused by the near approach or presence of danger. On such occasions it was an impressive and memorable sight to see the good father's quarters crowded by a throng of eager penitents, who not only committed to him their spiritual burthens, but fairly loaded him down with deposits of money, watches, jewelry, letters, testamentary deeds, and any conceivable article which it was desirable to preserve for absent relations. The good souls thought that he at least would be secure and sacred from molestation, but with all this, his burning zeal and devotion to duty often urged him into the thickest of the fight, and on more than one occasion his life was in imminent danger, for at Fair Oaks his horse was shot under him, and again he was taken prisoner and carried to Richmond whither he was obliged to go on foot, the enemy having appropriated his horse.

When the orders to move admitted of no delay, and the men could not leave their ranks, he was constantly among them, encouraging, advising, listening to hasty communications, and when immediate action was imminent, and there was no time for even a hurried prayer, he would pronounce a general benediction which all received with bared heads, reverently bowed. After such an inspiration even a coward learns to be a soldier and the brave man is invincible.

During an engagement he was hovering around the field of battle, riding hither and thither, wherever the indications were that the fight was hottest, ready to succor all, without exception, physically and spiritually. And to the wounded soldier no face was more familiar than that of the chaplain of the 37th. Everyone knew and loved him, from the general in chief down to the lowest camp follower.

After the battle, then his labors accumulated to such an extent, and his activity became so energetic, that, for a delicate frame, his physical endurance seemed superhuman. It was sustained only by the most intense interest and zeal he manifested for the service of his Master.

In camp his duties were equally engrossing. Before his own quarters could be rendered tolerably comfortable, his chapel claimed the first attention. Mass was celebrated every morning, and after that confessions were heard, letters written and received, visitors flocking from all parts of the army to avail themselves of the good father's services.

Among these it was quite common to see officers of every grade from the Major General to the second lieutenant, kneeling devoutly in the little chapel preparatory to confession and Communion. The French princes De Joinville and Chartres[4] were frequent visitors both at Sunday Mass and on other occasions. Numberless converts were received and instructed, among whom were three major generals and their families and such was the respect entertained for Father Tissot that crowds attended his services from all the neighboring regiments in preference to those of their own chaplains, and so universal was the feeling of reverence for his character that Protestant chaplains yielded him the palm with an easy grace. But his modesty and humility were such as to disarm even jealousy, and his great tolerance and love for all endeared him to even the hardened and depraved who to please the good man would feign a virtue they could not feel.

With all his intense zeal and absorbing interest in the work of his master, he was never morose, dull or forbidding in general society. On the contrary, he was quietly gay, and playful as a boy interesting himself in the conversation whatever it might be, chatty, social, unassuming, full of charity for the great and little foibles of poor humanity, so gentle in reproof that the heart was touched at once and humbled without an effort. A splendid scholar in ancient and modern literature, he rarely showed his great learning, except to a bookworm like himself, and his delight was to puzzle his companion, not so much by a display of knowledge, as by asking for information which he alone could impart. Extremely temperate in eating and drinking, he would be naturally a great restraint on the freedom and indulgence of a military mess-table, but he had the happiest knack of seeming to ignore the little excesses or improprieties of those with whom he associated, so that the fault was corrected and atoned for, spontaneously, as it were, but in reality because of the silent influence of his presence. Thus without seeming to do so he gave tone to his associates who learned, apparently without an effort, to adapt themselves to the good man's example and the officers' mess was always a model of quiet rational employment.

He took a deep interest in everything connected with the regiment, its good name, the temporal as well as spiritual welfare of all its members. For all these purposes he kept a roster of the entire regiment which included not only their names, but their addresses at home and the names of their nearest relatives. This he kept with such perfect system that he was frequently referred to for information which could not be obtained from the proper officers.

Into all the patriotic celebrations of the turn he entered with the heartiest concurrence, and in this way nothing was ever attempted without his cooperation and approval. Thus, while the regiment was encamped near Alexandria in the early part of January 1862, on the occasion of raising a new national flag, the ceremonial was marked by a most impressive religious ceremonial. An altar was erected at the foot of the flag staff, and after Mass at which the whole brigade assisted, including General [Israel] Richardson and wife,[5] Father Tissot pronounced a fervent prayer,

> begging God to defend the cause of the right and unity against rebellion, war and dissension of every kind. He prayed that peace with its countless blessings would again pervade the land, from the snow clad hills of Canada to the Gulf of Mexico, and east and west from ocean to ocean. For more than three quarters of a century the Stars and Stripes had been the emblem of a united people; had floated proudly amid the boundless wealth of commerce, in every sea and mart, in every quarter of the globe, respected and feared by despots, but to peoples who longed and yearned for liberty, it was a beacon light, girding them westward to liberty and empire, "no pent up Ithaca," but a boundless wealth of continents. He hoped his hearers of the 37th would bring back the flag without a stain of dishonor imprinted on its sacred folds. He exhorted them to behave like men and good Christians, and thereby merit honor and reward not alone from earthly superiors, but from God, the Lord and ruler of all. In conclusion, he begged them to persevere in the same line of good conduct for which they were so far remarkable and for this end most desirable he would not cease to offer up his most fervent supplications to the throne of grace. The good father then blessed the flag in the most solemn manner, every head in the large assembly bared, and

bowed in reverence, and the flag was hauled up, a gentle breeze unfolding its ample proportions, amid such an outburst of enthusiasm as the hills of Fairfax had never before witnessed. Colonel [Samuel B.] Hayman was greatly delighted and said he felt deeply moved to behold such an impressive sight. The flag of his country was never before so dear as now when the blessing of God was asked for it by the good and beloved chaplain. After the ceremony, the officers present were invited to the colonel's quarters where a collation had been prepared. The invitations included Generals Richardson, Thomas Francis Meagher,[6] Colonels O. M. Poe of the 2nd Michigan,[7] [Robert] Nugent of the 69th [New York] together with several others of Richardson's Brigade. And the chaplain of course was there to say grace, and by his presence give the entertainment additional honor.[8]

Again when a subscription for the relief of their kindred in Ireland was started in the regiment, Father Tissot took charge of it and sent quite a handsome sum to archbishop, afterwards Cardinal [Paul] Cullen[9] which was publicly acknowledged with thanks and blessings to the subscribers.

Occasionally the good priest would be inveigled into an impromptu race either by the colonel or some other mounted officer especially if there happened to be any question of his horse's speed or endurance. And, though not a good horseman, he made it a point not to be beaten too often or too much. He thus acquired considerable skill in riding and it served him well in the prosecution of his sacred functions throughout the army and also in regaining his health and keeping it up to the standard required to sustain his incessant labors.

With these soldiers of Loyola the devotion is so profoundly intense and absorbing, that earth and hell combined cannot crush it. Even martyrdom serves only to inflame it more and make it triumphant in the end. The Jesuit's knowledge of mankind is so extensive that he is never at a loss, though his mission may be in the most widely separated regions of earth in the full blaze of civilized intelligence, or the lowest stratum of human existence, when the soul seems to be a mere animal instinct, and the only gleam of intelligence that illumines the dense darkness of the brutal savage is the agent of cruelty and destruction.

Good bye, dear Father Tissot! May you have long to bless mankind and guide the rising generations, who sadly need your example and teaching. And, O, remember your poor "Irish Rifles" in your holy prayers. And when sin and temptation shall assail us, your sweet sad pitying face will rise up before our mortal sight and beckon us once more into the right way and be our guiding star to heaven.[10]

❀   ❀   ❀

EPILOGUE: After the war, Father Tissot continued to serve St. John's College (Fordham) as president and later treasurer. His last few years of ministry were spent preaching parish missions. He died July 19, 1875, at the College of St. Francis Xavier in New York. He is buried in West Park, New York.

SOURCES: Letters and other records of Tissot's chaplaincy are held at the University Archives and Special Collections of Georgetown University.

"A Year with the Army of the Potomac: Diary of the Reverend Father Tissot, S.J.," *Historical Records and Studies* 3, no. 1 (January 1903): 42–87; "Biographical Supplement: Fr. Peter Tissot," *Woodstock Letters* 19, no. 3 (1890): 407–8; "Chaplains in the Civil War: Father Peter Tissot, S.J.," *Fordham Monthly* 14, no. 7 (April 1896): 103–5; T. S. King, S.J., "Letters of Civil War Chaplains: Peter Tissot, S.J.," *Woodstock Letters* 43, no. 2 (1914): 168–80; Thomas J. Shelley, *Fordham, a History of the Jesuit University of New York, 1841–2003* (New York: Fordham University Press, 2016), 94–95; Thomas Gaffney Taaffe, "Rev. Peter Tissot, S.J.," *Historical Records and Studies* 3, no. 1 (January 1903): 38–41.

Chaplains and officers of the Irish Brigade, Harrison's Landing, Virginia, July 1862. Sitting: Captain J. J. McCormick, Father James Dillon, C.S.C., and Father William Corby, C.S.C. Standing: Father Patrick Dillon, C.S.C., and Dr. Philip O'Hanlon. (Library of Congress Prints and Photographs Division, Washington, DC)

David Power Conyngham, August 1863, on staff of the Irish Brigade, Bealeton, Virginia. (Library of Congress Prints and Photographs Division, Washington, DC)

(top left)
Father Jeremiah F. Trecy, photographed in Nashville, Tennessee, during the war.
(John J. Trecy and Elizabeth McLaughlin Trecy Estate/Carolyn Casady Trimble)

(bottom left)
Father Joseph C. Carrier, C.S.C., chaplain to the 6th Missouri Cavalry. (University
of Notre Dame Archives)

(above)
Father Paul Gillen, C.S.C., chaplain to the 170th New York. (University of Notre
Dame Archives)

Father Thomas Scully, photographed in 1861 with the 9th Massachusetts, celebrating Mass at Fort Cass, Arlington, Virginia. (Library of Congress Prints and Photographs Division, Washington, DC)

Father Peter Paul
Cooney, C.S.C., chaplain
to the 35th Indiana.
(University of
Notre Dame Archives)

Father James Sheeran, C.Ss.R.,
chaplain to the 14th Louisiana.
(Louisiana Historical Association
collection, Louisiana Research
Collection, Tulane University,
New Orleans)

Mother Teresa Barry, founding member of the Sisters of Our Lady of Mercy, Charleston, South Carolina, coordinated her community's care for soldiers on southern battlefields and in hospitals. (Sisters of Charity of Our Lady of Mercy, Charleston, South Carolina)

Sister Anthony O'Connell, a Sister of Charity of Cincinnati known as the "Angel of the Battlefield" for service at Shiloh, Tennessee. (Sisters of Charity, Cincinnati, Ohio)

Sister Mary Gertrude Ledwith, a Sister of Mercy of New York who served at Hammond Hospital, Beaufort, North Carolina. (Mathew Brady Photographs/National Archives and Records Administration, Washington, DC)

Mother Angela (Mary of St. Angela) Gillespie, the Holy Cross sister who oversaw the wartime service of her community. (University of Notre Dame Archives)

CHAPTER XII

Rev. Thomas Willett, S.J.

Chaplain 69th New York Volunteers

His reception by the officers and men—How he cheered the
men on board the transport—Mass at Alexandria, Virginia—
Solemnity of the scene—His raids against gambling, cursing,
and drinking—Sending the soldiers' money home—
Father Willett in the field—Preparing the men before battle—
His services under Foster—A high compliment—He returns
to the 69th again—His zeal and services—Leaves the army
at the close of the war.

INTRODUCTION: Father Thomas Ouellet (often angli-
cized to Willett) (1819–1894), a French Canadian Jesuit priest,
served as chaplain to the 69th New York Volunteer Infantry
Regiment for much of the war. Born in Joliette, Canada, in
1819, Ouellet entered the Society of Jesus and studied at New
York's St. John's College (Fordham) prior to his ordination in
1848. He was afterward employed for teaching and discipline
at Fordham. He left the post in 1854, perhaps in part due to
concern about the severity of his discipline, yet his rigor would
serve him well during his time in the army. He next taught in
Montreal, but eventually relocated to France, where he took
his final vows for the Society of Jesus. After teaching history

in France for a time, he travelled to Poland where he taught French. He returned to the United States at the outbreak of the war, and either volunteered or was assigned to act as chaplain for the 69th New York.

His enlistment began in November 1861 and continued through April 1863. Thereafter he served as chaplain to the hospital at Newbern, North Carolina. When the 69th New York was reorganized in February 1864, he resumed his role as chaplain, serving until the regiment was mustered out in June 1865. During the war, he brought his sense of discipline and counsel to this regiment, which earned him high praise and faithfulness from the men. The narrative relates Father Ouelett's attempts to rid his regiment of the vices of gambling and profanity and provide his men with the means of practicing their religion by supplying prayer books, rosaries, scapulars, and copies of the Gospels. The priest's simple, down-to-earth style is credited with attracting converts to the Church and helping to curb anti-Catholic prejudice among Protestants.

In the introduction to his work, Conyngham names two sources with ties to the 69th New York: Dr. William O'Meagher, the regiment's surgeon, and James E. McGee, captain and later lieutenant colonel. It is likely they provided the source material for this chapter on Father Ouellet.

❀   ❀   ❀

When the 69th New York Vols., the pioneer regiment of the now celebrated Irish Brigade, left New York for the city of Washington on the 18th of November 1861 it consisted not only of a full complement of picked men, but was officered by soldiers, many of whom had already seen service in this country and Europe, and all, field, staff and line, possessing the unlimited confidence of the men to whom they were destined to govern and lead through many stormy scenes of warfare and hardship. Of these latter, one of the most valuable though at the time least conspicuous was the Rev. Thomas Willett (called in his own language Ouellet[1]) the chaplain. He was a native of lower Canada of French descent and speech, and his small wiry physique and quick, brilliant eye denoting at once great physical endurance and perpetual watchfulness, bespoke equally his Norman descent and his capacity to perform the arduous duties imposed on him by his calling and by the stern rules of the illustrious order which claimed him as a member. Modest in dress and demeanor, courteous, even winning in speech yet unflinching in the performance of the sacred duties of his office, he easily won the love and respect of all classes.

His entire control over the men of the regiment was first conspicuous in the occasion of their departure from New York in the steamboat for Perth Amboy,[2] when filled with reports natural to men leaving families and homes to meet many and uncertain dangers, they gave way for the time to all the impulses of their varied natures, recklessness, grief, simulated hilarity, and in a few cases, very few indeed, to profanity. It was then seen how salutary an effect can be produced by the presence of a Catholic priest on a large mass of men so moved to excitement as to be almost beyond the control of their officers. All night long in the deck of the government transport, flitting to and fro might be seen the small lithe form of the chaplain and his voice be heard, reproving in low but emphatic accents the unreasonably boisterous or consoling in tender words those whose softer natures had overcome them for the moment. So efficacious indeed was his ministration during this their first trial that when the morning sun dawned on the regiment as it marched through the streets of Philadelphia, a more steady, contented and even cheerful body of men could not have been seen under any circumstances or any portion of the continent.

The 69th proceeded, via Baltimore, to the national capital and encamped at Meridian Hill for some days, where a temporary chapel was quickly constructed and the following Sunday the Divine Sacrifice of the Mass was attended by the regiment and a large number of officers and men from the neighboring camps. On the last day of November the regiment was ordered to the front and, crossing the Long Bridge, bivouacked for the night near Alexandria, Virginia. The night was cold and rainy, but the morning, Sunday, broke with all the glorious radiance of a southern autumn. The field on which the men had courted sleep was quickly alive with groups of soldiers hastily preparing breakfast or adjusting their accouterments previous to marching, when just as the sun's rays brightened Fort Ellsworth,[3] the silvery voice of a little bell was heard to resound on the clear air, and laying aside all occupation the soldiers hastened reverentially to a particular part of the field, where but a few minutes before had sprung up as if by magic, a simple wall tent containing an altar, tabernacle, and lighted candles. Here also was Father Willett robed in appropriate vestments prepared to celebrate his first Mass in Virginia, in the presence of the uncovered troops who knelt silently on the damp ground of a state which was destined to prove the last resting place of too many of their number. Few who were present on that occasion will forget the solemnity of the scene, intensified as it was by a general source of dangers and perhaps sudden death before them, nor was there one of that armed host that did not eagerly and deeply drink in the words of warning, hope, and encouragement which for more than an hour flowed from the good father's lips. The perverse were softened, the dejected comforted, and all resumed their military labors with better feelings.

Being soon joined by the other regiments of the brigade the 69th remained in Camp California, four miles from Alexandria, until April of the following year, with the exception of a short time spent in the neighborhood of Manassas and Warrington Junction previous to its departure for the Peninsula. While thus in winter quarters a rude but spacious canvas church was constructed, which was crowded every Sunday by worshipers, a large percentage of whom were usually communicants, for the chaplain was not content with his ordinary duties at the altar but devoted his evenings to hearing confessions and personally visiting the quarters of the men. Indeed, his zeal was untiring for day and night he might be found among the tents, comforting the sick, repressing turbulence and occasionally joining in the pleasant conversation of the camp fire groups. Gambling and profanity—the two besetting sins of the soldiers—though generally discouraged in the Irish Brigade, were not unknown, and against them as well as intemperance, the heaviest force of his eloquence and logic was directed with an efficiency that almost eradicated these vices from the camp of the 69th.

During this time also the regiment received its first installment of pay and by the assistance and under the direction of the chaplain thousands of dollars were sent home to wives and children that otherwise would have been squandered at the gaming table or what was nearly as bad in the sutler's canteen. In fact, throughout the whole time of his connection with the army, Father Willett paid special attention and devoted much of his time to the transmission of the hard earned wages of the too heedless soldiers, not a dollar of which failed to reach its proper destination, and to his unfaltering efforts many a household in New York and elsewhere were indebted for those periodical supplies of money, which if they did not compensate for the absence of the beloved father or husband, lightened their sorrows and showed that amid the din of battles, home and its comforts were not forgotten.

Father Willett accompanied his regiment in all its battles from Yorktown to Antietam, with the same religious fervor which at first distinguished him. His powers of enduring the fatigues of the march and the bivouac, the pangs of hunger and the inclemency of a climate proverbially destructive of animal life, even such as very frequently to elicit the astonishment and the envy of the most robust soldier, while his disregard of personal danger on the battle field, often excited the apprehension of his devoted flock for his safety. In anticipation of each recurring engagement, it was his custom to bend every energy of his mind to prepare by confession and Communion the soldiers under his spiritual command to face the coming danger, and then when the hour of actual combat had arrived, and a very few moments might see them in eternity, the good Soldier of the Cross unheeding the bullets that fell around him would solemnly pass through the kneeling ranks and administer to the postulants a conditional absolution. This done he took up his position near the scene of action, as the rules of the service would permit, ready to administer the last rites of the Church to the wounded and dying as they were borne from the field. But his labors did not even end here. The field hospital with its thousands of maimed and groaning victims, was his next sphere of action, and it is well attested that on many occasions after a great battle he would spend days

and nights continuously among the wounded without food or rest, assisting the surgeons and nursing the sufferers, very often administering
medicine and washing their scars with his own hands.

Death and disease having reduced the Irish Brigade to a mere
handful, and there being two other chaplains[4] attached to it, Father
Willett, in the winter of 1862–3, left the 69th with the regrets and good
wishes not only of his own regiment, but of every officer and man in
the entire division—for he was known to all—and departed for North
Carolina to be attached to General [John G.] Foster's command. Some
years afterwards, a member of the 69th happening to be in Washington in conversation with an officer, a Protestant who had held a high
rank in the army, enquiries were being made for old friends and particularly for Father Willett, when the general turning to a group of
brother officers said, "In fact, Gentlemen, the only real chaplains we
had in the army were Catholic priests and the Rev. Mr. Willett was the
best I ever saw."

Father Willett remained several months in the South, still laboring indefatigably among all classes, military, naval and civil, and being
the only priest in that [. . .][5] department at the time, he had sometimes to travel sixty miles to say Mass for some isolated group of poor
Catholics. His health beginning to give way he was ordered back to
New York where he resumed the ordinary exercise of his functions at
St. Francis Xavier's College in 16th Street. Meanwhile the 69th, at length
reduced to about a hundred effective men, was sent home on recruiting
service and was reorganized by the addition of eight new companies
under the command of some of the most efficient officers of the old
brigade who had previously been honorably mustered out of service
for want of commands. These gentlemen seconded by the enlisted men
were naturally anxious to have a chaplain return with them to the front
and of course preferred Father Willett whose valuable services in the
past were the subject of general admiration. At their unanimous request, Lt. Colonel [James E.] McGee, then at the head of the regiment,
applied to the superior of the Jesuits in New York to have their old
chaplain restored to them and that distinguished ecclesiastic replied favorably but left the choice of going or remaining in the more tranquil
scenes of cloister life to the Rev. Father himself. Though long familiar

with the dangers and hardships of camp life the zealous father did not hesitate a moment in his choice. He could not withstand the entreaties of the remnant of that flock, so endeared to him by many ties of affection and common suffering, and the regiment feeling safe under his ministration returned to the battle field with renewed ardor.

Before their departure, however, the returned veterans were to receive a bounty of three hundred dollars each, and Father Willett entered in his duties by providing himself with paper and envelopes, and might be seen each successive day in the paymaster's office hard at work writing and directing letters for the men, in which were enclosed to their relations a very large proportion, in some cases the entire of the bounty money. Considering the temptations to spend money recklessly presented by a large city like New York to men recently returned after years of active service, the results of his presence and advice in this can hardly be overestimated, and it is a fact highly honorable to the veterans and their officers that within four hours after the issuance of the order for their departure, and though scattered in New York and the cities in the vicinity, they were promptly at the place of rendezvous ready for embarkation, every man answering the roll call, and not one showing signs of the least dissipation, so much to be apprehended from a month's residence in the metropolis.

The devoted chaplain, of course, accompanied the regiment on its return and remained with it till the close of the war. His second term of service presented the same succession of indefatigable labors as the first. His ardor in the cause of religion knew no bounds. Finding that tracts, newspapers and other publications of a deleterious character were being circulated among the men by sectarian organizations, he wrote to friends in New York for a supply of Catholic books to edify the soldier in his hours of leisure on the field or console him on his sick bed in hospitals. The request was quickly complied with and books, scapulars, gospels, and rosaries in great quantities were forwarded to him by many pious men and women who had never enjoyed the pleasure of his acquaintance.

The war over, the worthy servant of God quietly returned to his original sphere of usefulness and to the companionship of the members of that order which though justly proud of the long list of its distinguished children, can hardly count among them many men excelling, at least in zeal and devotedness, the subject of this sketch. And it was not alone for his regiment or for the Catholic soldiers of the army that he labored and preached. The example of his immediate congregation assembled every Sunday before the rude altar, and his own sermons which were replete with sound maxims and delivered in plain and touching language, first excited the curiosity of soldiers of other denominations, who having lived in remote parts of the country seldom saw a priest and perhaps never were within [a] Catholic church. The curiosity was generally followed by respectful attendance, many conversions was the result, and those who did not have that good fortune found their early anti-Catholic prejudices corrected and their asperities soften in their intercourse with their Catholic comrades.

Though we have not had the happiness of meeting Father Willett of later years we are glad to learn that he is still in good health and laboring with his wonted assiduity and singleness of purpose; and if the wishes of the surviving soldiers to whom he administered in the hour of peril and suffering, and the prayers of the widows and orphans, for whose comfort and well-being he was solicitous, are of avail, he will yet live a long life of usefulness and his death shall be like that of the just.

EPILOGUE: Following the end of the war in 1865, Father Ouellet returned to New York and ministered at St. Francis Xavier Church before moving on to another post in Jersey City. Eventually, he returned to the land of his birth and settled in Montreal and Guelph, Ontario. He was later called to mission work with Native American communities near Sault Sainte Marie, Ontario, to whom he ministered from 1879 to 1893. In that year, his health began to fail, and he was sent to the College of the Immaculate Conception in Montreal. On November 26, 1894, a few months after celebrating his golden jubilee in religious life, Ouellet died at the age of seventy-six.

SOURCES: William Corby, C.S.C., *Memoirs of Chaplain Life: Three Years with the Irish Brigade in the Army of the Potomac* (Notre Dame, IN: "Scholastic" Press, 1893; reprinted and edited by Lawrence Frederick Kohl, New York: Fordham University Press, 1992), Patrick Joseph Dooley, S.J., *Fifty Years in Yorkville; Or, Annals of the Parish of St. Ignatius Loyola and St. Lawrence O'Toole* (New York: Frank Meany Co., Printers, Inc., 1917), 26–29; "Chaplains During the Civil War: Father Thomas Ouellet, S.J.," *Fordham Monthly* 14, no. 6 (March 1896): 85–86; "Father Thomas Ouellet: A Sketch," *Woodstock Letters* 24 (1895): 375–80; Aidan H. Germain, "Catholic Military and Naval Chaplains, 1776–1917" (PhD diss., Catholic University of America, 1929), 58, 104–7; Thomas J. Shelley, *Fordham, A History of the Jesuit University of New York* (New York: Fordham University Press, 2016), 94.

CHAPTER XIII

Rev. C. L. Egan, O.P.

Chaplain 9th Massachusetts Volunteers

His mission to the army—Prepares men under sentence of death—He is appointed chaplain—His school of logic—He visits the 5th Corps and exhorts the men to attend to their duty— Father Egan at the Wilderness—The 9th suffered dreadful loss— The soldier priest at his post—Mustered out with the regiment.

INTRODUCTION: Father Constantine L. Egan, O.P. (1828–1899), served as chaplain in various capacities during the war. He was born near Toomevara, County Tipperary, Ireland, to Michael and Honora (Meagher) Egan. He immigrated to the United States and settled in Kentucky, working as a schoolteacher. He briefly discerned life as a Trappist monk at the Abbey of Gethsemani in central Kentucky before entering the St. Joseph Province of Dominicans. He made his profession as a Dominican on June 17, 1855. After studies in Sinsinawa, Wisconsin, he was ordained on September 23, 1860. His first assignment was to the Dominican college at Sinsinawa.

In 1862, he was transferred to St. Dominic Church in Washington, DC. Here he heeded the call for priests to serve in the army. Beginning his service at the war's midpoint, Father Egan became chaplain to the 9th Massachusetts in September 1863 owing to the vacancy brought about by the resignation of

Father Thomas Scully because of ill health. Father Egan continued with the regiment until June 1864 when it was disbanded, the soldiers having fulfilled their three-year enlistment. Afterwards, Father Egan continued as hospital chaplain at City Point, Virginia, and as field chaplain with service to General Charles Griffin's 5th Army Corps.

Like the sketch of Father Scully's chaplaincy, the information on Father Egan was likely procured by Conyngham from Michael H. MacNamara, an officer in the 9th Massachusetts. Conyngham began his narrative with the unusual context for Father Egan's recruitment into the military: two condemned soldiers who needed a priest to hear their confessions. Father Egan ministered to them in the hours before their executions by firing squad, but because of the great need remained as a chaplain thereafter. In addition to spiritual counsel and sacramental duties, Conyngham provides the unusual detail that Father Egan convened a group of officers to study logic, described by the author as "one of the most interesting features of camp life."

On the 25th of August 1863, a messenger from the War Department called on Father Egan at St. Dominic's Church, Washington, handing him a note from Colonel James Hardie,[1] requesting him to call at the Secretary of War's office. Accordingly, he went up in the afternoon of the same day. Colonel Hardie handed him the following dispatch which he [had received][2] from General [Seth] Williams, Adjutant General of the Army of the Potomac.

United States Military Telegraph
Dated August 25th 1863
To Col. J. [A].[3] Hardie, A. A. G.
   Two of the five soldiers of the [5]th Corps[4] sentenced to be shot tomorrow, but the execution of whose sentence has been

suspended until Saturday next are Roman Catholics; and are exceedingly anxious to have the services of a priest. So far as I can learn there is no Roman Catholic priest with this army at the present. Cannot you ask one of the priests of your acquaintance in Washington to come down and see these unfortunate men and prepare them as far as may be for the solemn event that awaits them? I am sure the visit would be one of mercy. If the priest comes please let him telegraph the time of his departure from Washington to Reverend W[illia]m O'Neill,[5] chaplain, who will meet him at Rappahannock station to which place he should proceed on the cars. The trains leave Alexandria at 8 and 11 A.M. and 2 and 4 P.M. and are about four hours in reaching Rappahannock station. You would have to provide the pass in Washington.
   Please answer.

S. Williams
A. A. G.

After reading the above dispatch, Father Egan told the messenger that he would very willingly go on that mission so he procured a pass and started on the next morning, and arrived in the afternoon in the camp of the 118th Pennsylvania Vol. The colonel introduced him to the prisoners who were under guard and handcuffed in a tent. The prisoners under sentence of death were two Italians (Catholics) and three Germans, two of whom were Protestants and one a Jew. On being introduced to the prisoners, one of the Catholics shaking him by the hand very affectionately remarked that now he was not afraid to die since he had a priest with him. A tent was put up for him within the enclosure of the guard so that he could be free to talk to the two unfortunate men. After exhorting them to go about the work of their salvation, that there was no hope for them but to turn their thoughts to another world, and make their peace with God. The poor fellows complied with his exhortation, made their confessions, and went to Holy Communion on the morning of the day of their execution in the tent where he celebrated Mass for them. These five men were shot on the 28th of August 1863.
   The crime of which they were accused was desertion from the regiment.[6]

Immediately after the execution Father Egan was requested by Colonel [Patrick] Guiney[7] to visit the camp of the 9th Regiment at Beverly Ford to hear confessions, etc., having had no regular chaplain since the final departure of Father Scully. The Rev. Father joyfully complied with the request and remained with the regiment about a week, when he remarked to the colonel and other officers that he liked camp life better than the easier, but desultory life of a friar, and intimated that he would become chaplain of the regiment if he could get the appointment. Colonel Guiney was overjoyed at the offer, and forwarded the nomination to the war department, and, in due time, Father Egan was installed as chaplain. He soon won the respect and affection of the officers and men by his zeal and interest in their behalf.

He organized a school of logic for such officers who were not versed in that branch of study and in a short time made his school one of the most interesting features of camp life. Father Egan was peculiarly fitted for the career he had so strangely adopted; genial and confiding in disposition, dignified yet familiar with officers and men, possessing a fund of anecdotes and inexhaustible good humor, it would be strange indeed if our boys did not reverence and love him.

The winter of '63 and the spring of '64 found the regiment at Bealton, Virginia, at which place Father Egan[8] visited all the regiments of the 5th Corps, exhorting all the members of the Catholic faith, and showing them the necessity of attending to their religious duties, and begging of them to visit the camp of the 9th [Massachusetts] at any and all times, more particularly on Sundays as the regiment had erected a large log house for the purposes of religious services. The effects of his labors in this direction were shortly afterwards seen, for crowds of soldiers of other regiments thronged the chapel Sunday after Sunday, and to his efforts in a great degree was due the excellent discipline of the 5th Corps.

From this camp the regiment moved in May to take part in the campaign which culminated so far as the 9th was concerned in the memorable Battle of the Wilderness. In this battle nearly thirty of the officers of the 9th were placed *hors de combat* [out of action due to injury]— and a great number of our gallant men. This was the more to be deplored as the 9th had but about half [a] dozen more days to serve out the full term of their enlistment [of] three years.

In those bloody days Father Egan proved a ministering angel on the field and off the field, amid the hiss of bullets and the crack of shells, [and] amid the groans of the wounded and the sighs of the dying. Calm, cool, and consoling, he performed the duty of the soldier priest! He remained to the last with the regiment and on Boston Common was mustered out with it.

Father Egan arrived in Kentucky from Ireland a poor boy and was taken in by the Dominican Friars and educated in the institution at that place; after five years study he was prepared for college and finally ordained a priest. A branch of the same institution was established in Washington during the war to which place Father Egan was transferred and from which place he happily came to the 9th Regiment.

The soldiers of the old 9th hold his name and kindly deeds in the most affectionate remembrance. We wish that space would allow us to dwell more at length upon the life works of this truly good man, but wherever he may be, the warmest wishes of those he served so well will be ever with him!

EPILOGUE: After the war, Father Egan served twice as prior of the Dominican House at Springfield, Kentucky. From 1879 to 1881, he was chaplain to the Sisters of St. Mary's of the Springs in Columbus, Ohio. He also served as pastor of St. Thomas Aquinas Church in Zanesville, Ohio, and St. Peter's Church in Mendota, Minnesota, among other assignments. His final years were spent at St. Louis Bertrand Church in Louisville, Kentucky, where he died on July 7, 1899. He is buried in the Dominican cemetery at St. Rose near Springfield, Kentucky.

SOURCES: William Corby, C.S.C., *Memoirs of Chaplain Life: Three Years with the Irish Brigade in the Army of the Potomac* (Notre Dame, IN: "Scholastic" Press, 1893; reprinted and edited by Lawrence Frederick Kohl, New York: Fordham University Press, 1992), 312–49; Aidan H. Germain, "Catholic Military and

Naval Chaplains, 1776–1917" (PhD diss., Catholic University of America, 1929), 55, 68; Daniel George Macnamara, *The History of the Ninth Regiment, Massachusetts Volunteer Infantry* (Boston: E. B. Stillings, 1899), 343, 429; Andrew Newman, O.P., "A Blackfriar in Northern Blue," *Dominicana* 41, no. 2 (June 1956): 130–35; Victor Francis O'Daniel, O.P., *The Dominican Province of Saint Joseph: Historico-Biographical Studies* (New York: Holy Name Society, 1942), 269–71; John Vidmar, O.P., *Fr. Fenwick's "Little American Province": 200 Years of the Dominican Friars in the United States* (New York: Dominican Province of St. Joseph, 2005), 41–42.

Rev. Paul E. Gillen, C.S.C.

Chaplain 170th New York Volunteers

*He joins the army at the commencement of the war—
His services in and around Washington—His services in the
field—His attention to the sick and wounded—Mass in camp—
The 42nd [New York] Tammany [Regiment]—The Corcoran
Legion—Dr. Dwyer's sketches of Fathers Gillen, Dillon,
and Mooney—Chaplain's life in camp —Heroic endurance
and forbearance.*

INTRODUCTION: Father Paul E. Gillen, C.S.C. (1810–
1882), was one of seven Holy Cross priests from the University
of Notre Dame to serve as chaplains in the war. Born in
County Donegal, Ireland, Gillen arrived in the United States in
1840. He worked as a door-to-door salesman of religious goods
and an agent for the popular Catholic newspaper, the *Boston Pilot*. According to one legend, while Gillen was selling
books at West Point, a young William S. Rosecrans purchased
from him a copy of John Milner's *The End of Religious Controversy*, leading to the famous Civil War general's conversion in
the mid-1840s. In 1856, Gillen entered the Congregation of
Holy Cross at Notre Dame, Indiana. After his ordination, he
became the pastor of Immaculate Conception Church in
Michigan City, Indiana.

When the war commenced, Father Gillen was the first Holy Cross priest to volunteer. Asked to serve as a chaplain while in New York "on community business," he served a number of different regiments beginning in July 1861, enjoying the freedom of ministering to those most in need of his priestly services. During this time, Gillen was most closely attached to the 15th New York Engineer Regiment and its friendly colonel, McLeod Murphy. When his ministry became limited due to his unofficial status, he took an official commission as chaplain to the 170th New York Volunteer Infantry on October 19, 1862.

Conyngham's description of Father Gillen's service focuses on his itinerant ministry, traveling from regiment to regiment to offer confession and Mass. Bereft of government pay, Father Gillen pleaded for a means of transportation. The last part of the chapter was penned by Dr. John Dwyer, former surgeon of the 182nd New York Infantry Regiment (69th New York National Guard), who provided Conyngham with biographical sketches of Fathers Paul E. Gillen, James M. Dillon, C.S.C., and Thomas H. Mooney.

Father Gillen has probably seen more service than any other chaplain in the army of the Potomac, being the oldest chaplain in the army, and the longest attending to the field and hospitals. He served with the army from July 21st, 1861—the memorable day of the first Bull Run battle—until the mustering out of the Corcoran Legion after the close of the war in the end of July 1865.

Rev. Paul E. Gillen is a native of the parish of Moville Imishown, County Donegal, Ireland. Having studied his classical course in his native country, he came to the United States in 1840. After many vicissitudes in the United States and Canada, he finally settled at Notre Dame, Indiana, and became a member of the Congregation of the Holy

Cross, where he renewed and continued his studies and was ordained a priest of the order.

Shortly after the breaking out of the war, he chanced to be visiting New York, Philadelphia, and Baltimore, on business, and hearing that Catholic chaplains were so scarce in the army, and knowing that numbers of souls would be launched into eternity without the opportunity of a reconciliation with their offended God, he resolved to offer his services. Having obtained permission from his superior, he determined to visit the army and obtain faculties from Archbishop [Francis P.] Kenrick[1] for the dioceses of Baltimore, Richmond, and Wheeling. He proceeded to Washington where he arrived on Saturday July 20th the eve of [the] Bull Run battle, and visited Fort Corcoran, but the gallant 69th had gone towards Bull Run except a few left to keep garrison. He also visited the 9th Massachusetts, Revd. Father Scully had just returned from Centreville where he had been assisting Revd. Father Bernard O'Reilly[2] to hear confessions under the trees near Bull Run. Next day (Sunday) he celebrated a morning Mass with the Sisters of the Holy Cross who had charge of St. Joseph's male orphan asylum in Washington.

So after dinner, a Mr. McGuire (who was a red hot secessionist but a very charitable gentleman) took him in his buggy out to where the 22nd Regiment New York Vols. was encamped, and there Father Paul commenced to hear confessions in the army. Crowds of them[3] attended the confessional until about 7 P.M. when the news of the disaster at Bull Run had reached Washington, and the danger of the Rebels following the retreat into that city.

The roll was beat in all the camps and the regiment was under arms in ten minutes. Numbers of those who had been crowding the confessional came to Father Paul saying, "O Father, we have been waiting to go to confession and now we must be off, what will we do?" "Kneel down my brave boys, and make an act of contrition from your hearts for all the sins of your life, with the intention of coming to confession if you come back, or as soon as you can, and I will give you absolution." The men obeyed immediately, and, in a few minutes, regiment after regiment was marching down to Washington.

The 9th Regiment Massachusetts (Irish) with their green flag also got under way playing "The Girl I Left Behind Me." On arriving at

Washington, their march was stopped and all returned to their camps. The 9th Massachusetts playing on its return the very appropriate tune "Jenny put the Kettle on for a Cup of Tea." On returning the boys came to confession, with grateful hearts, and all came to Holy Communion at Mass in the little tent next morning. Father Paul's next visit was to the 33rd Regiment New York about half a mile off, especially to Captain McGraw and his Irish Company, from Seneca Falls, New York.[4] Then to the 34th New York stationed about a mile still further on, where a large number came to confession.

After the battle of Bull Run, the greater part of the army was encamped on the west, or Virginia side, of the Potomac. In the whole army of the Potomac there was at that time no Catholic chaplain, but Father Paul and Reverend Father Scully of the 9th Massachusetts. Father Paul could have got many regiments that would be glad to have him as their chaplain, but seeing the great scarcity of Catholic chaplains in the army, and knowing if he got mustered in with any regiment, he must remain with it except by permission, he therefore preferred not to take a commission so that he could attend to either field or hospital without restraint where he saw the greatest need.

He next crossed the river and commenced his labors on the sacred soil of Virginia, beginning at Fort Corcoran, with the Jackson Guards, an Irish Company, 2nd Maine Regiment. He next visited the 14th Brooklyn, which had been in the battle of Bull Run, and was encamped beside the Arlington house. He then went among the various regiments from there to Alexandria on that side of the Potomac. Having met with some of the 15th New York under McLeod Murphy[5] he was invited to visit them where they lay at that time in Fairfax seminary, four miles outside of Alexandria.

Colonel Murphy was highly pleased to have the father visit his regiment and made a bed for him on the floor, just beside his own, but they had scarce gone to rest when the roll was beat in all the regiments on that side of the river and all hands were called to arms. "Now Father," said the colonel, "it was God I hope [who] sent you here this night. I will go to confession before I go out, and you will go with us and give a blessing to our dear boys." The confession being over the whole regiment was under arms. Father Paul had no horse at the time. "Now Father," said the colonel, "as you have no horse, get on the horse's back be-hind me, boys lift his leg, get on, and hold on by me," and off the colo-nel dashed with the priest behind him until they came to where the men were in line of battle with rifles in hand, bayonets fixed, and all lying flat on the ground. "Now Father," said the colonel, "we may dis-mount." The colonel having given his horse to an orderly, proceeded with Father Gillen through the regiment and called out thus, "Co. A stand up, and all of you who are Catholics kneel down and receive the father's blessing." But Protestants were on their knees as quick as Catho-lics. After proceeding over all the companies and continuing until the break of day, the Rebels did not attack. "By dad myself was a little afraid getting into the line of battle before day, for the first time, but when I saw the priest riding behind the colonel my heart got up, and I would fight as many Rebels as would stand before me," said an Irishman.

After stopping some days with the 15th New York, Father Gillen returned to Washington, where new regiments were pouring in rapidly every day from the North. These he attended going from one regi-ment to another. A large number of these raw recruits had been some length of time from confession, and after enlisting had no more oppor-tunity offered them, but were marched off to Washington and thence to their encampments, and were most anxious for a priest by whom they would be reconciled with their offended God before the day of battle arrived. Hearing that the 24th New York (many of whom had been with him at confession some time before) were now on the out-side lines next to the enemy, four miles west of Washington, he got a Mr. Talty to bring him with his buggy out to them, and when Mr. Talty wanted to return home, he had no pass. So Father Paul was obliged to convey his friend back the whole way, and over the Long Bridge (with his general pass) into Washington.

On returning, Father Paul was fortunate in meeting with Mr. Gib-son's boy going home with a wagon to the next house to where the 24th New York was stationed where he had left his satchels and altar affairs. Mr. Gibson was a convert, and hearing that the stranger was a priest, he called out to his Irish servant, "Hallo Bridget, you'll not need go to Washington to Mass tomorrow, here is a priest." "A priest!" exclaimed Bridget running out, "Arrah, goodness where is he?"

"O, you are welcome Father, and will you be hearing confession tomorrow?" "O, certainly, but I will come over and hear your confession at home, and then you can go to Mass at 10 o'clock and Holy Communion with the soldiers."

A large number attended the confessional that evening. Next day he visited Colonel Kerrigan's[6] regiment and both regiments attended Mass at a deserted brick church, which Father Paul used as a Catholic chapel. Father Paul continued hearing confessions during the afternoon and in the evening there came on a tremendous rain storm, until the countersign was out, and he was obliged to remain in the church alone all night, having nothing but his boots for a pillow, the floor for his bed, and the roof his only covering.

The next Sunday he was with General [Darius] Couch's[7] brigade, at Brightwoods, five miles north of Washington, consisting of four regiments: 36th New York, 2nd Rhode Island, 7th and 10th of Massachusetts. General Couch was highly pleased to see the father visit his brigade, and sent an orderly to notify all his regiment to be at Catholic worship at the headquarters of the 36th New York Vols. [The] next day,[8] large bodies of Irish soldiers came from each of the regiments, making a splendid congregation under the green trees.

In consequence of the army being scattered so far apart, Father Paul had some difficulty in having his altar affairs carried from place to place in the hot season of August and September, and wrote a petition to Major General McClellan describing his situation, namely that he was a priest of the Holy Cross, from Notre Dame University, Indiana, and was serving those of his religion without any government pay, that if he had a horse and vehicle to carry such necessaries as a Catholic priest requires it would enable him to continue his services throughout the various camps and hospitals of his armies and wound up by saying this would give so much satisfaction to those noble hearted soldiers who had left behind them parents, brothers, sisters, wives and families, in order to fight for the flag and Constitution of their country—seeing so much done for their priest—[that] their hearts would glow with gratitude and thanks.

Before presenting it, he showed it to Major Garesché, Assistant Adjutant General. That excellent Catholic officer enlarged it, stating that the greater portion of the rank and file was composed of Catholics; that Catholic chaplains in the army were so scarce that were it not for the exertions of the Reverend Father Gillen and a few other zealous missioners, this want could not be supplied, and without some mode of conveyance, he would not be able to exercise these acts of charity, so much wanted in the army at that time. General McClellan granted the request immediately, reporting it by General [Stewart] Van [Vliet],[9] quartermaster general, who sent it to Captain [James Jackson] Dana,[10] who gave Father Paul a horse and ambulance.[11] He also invented a light altar with springs that could be folded up which he could erect or take down in one minute.

He also got a spring bed which he could double up and spread out at once and a tent. Thus having got his necessary equipments of altar, bed, tent satchels, bedclothes, [and] provisions for man and horse, he proceeded on with excellent success among the different camps in the vicinity of Washington, on both sides of the Potomac. After getting along for some weeks among these, he proceeded up the Potomac to where General Banks, with a large portion of the army, was encamped. After visiting these regiments he proceeded up to Poolville about forty miles from Washington, where General [Charles P.] Stone,[12] that excellent Catholic, was encamped with three brigades, or twelve regiments.

He was overjoyed to have Father Paul visit his command, for there was no other Catholic chaplain from there to Washington. Among his troops were the 42nd Regiment New York Vol. (Tammany Regiment), principally Irish. Three miles further up was the 69th Pennsylvania Vols., an Irish regiment under Colonel [Joshua T.] Owen;[13] both these he had attended in the vicinity of Washington before their coming up. On Sundays he celebrated two Masses frequently from three to ten miles apart. There on Sundays he celebrated first Mass with the 69th Pennsylvania, and last Mass at 10 o'clock with the 42nd Tammany, which was attended by men from eight regiments, among them was General [Willis A.] Gorman's 1st Minnesota Vol. On Sunday October 20th, Father Paul, in order to have a grand turnout, visited all the regiments the day previous notifying them that the second Mass would be at the Tammany [Regiment]. Colonel [Charles] Devens[14] of the 15th Massachusetts was highly pleased and gave orders for the captains of Irish companies to have their men attend Divine service at 10 A.M. at the Tammany Regiment headquarters. But the colonel of the 20th Massachusetts[15] would not let a man leave his camp, although many Irishmen in his ranks were anxious to go. "What is the objection," said Father Paul. "They will get whiskey," said the colonel. "There is not a house between this and the Tammany Regiment," said Father Paul. "It will come out of the woods to them," said the colonel with a sneer.

On coming from the 69th Pennsylvania to the Tammany Regiment, he met with Captain [Michael] Garretty,[16] and after him Captain [Timothy] O'Meara[17] with their companies going to the river on picket duty, who felt very sorry that they could not stop for Mass, but they had to obey orders.

A large number attended Mass, among others General Stone. In the afternoon, the troops had orders to prepare for crossing the Potomac River next day at Ball's Bluff. Some companies of the Tammany Regiment were on picket along the river, and Father Paul stopped with them that night, hearing confessions, and sleeping in a small log cabin that had been riddled by the bullets days before. He celebrated Mass there on Monday morning (a large number went to confession and Communion), and after Mass he resolved on visiting Washington on business, when the cannon opened on Ball's Bluff, on the other side of the river. The troops commenced crossing in a rather tedious manner; they had one boat which they ran to an island in the river, and another between the island and the Virginia shore. This was a tedious operation as the men could not get over quick enough to relieve their companions. Father Paul could not get his horse and carriage over, but determined to cross the river himself. Before crossing, each company of the Tammany Regiment received absolution and benediction from Father Paul. The 69th Pennsylvania, [under] Colonel Owen, were overjoyed to see Father P[aul] waiting for them; each company knelt down to receive his absolution and benediction. Having attended to the spiritual wants of all, he got a man detailed to take charge of his horse and wagon, and taking his oilstock, ritual, and stole, he determined crossing to the other side, where the sound of artillery and musketry were swelling into a grand chorus. As he was advancing to the scow ferry boat an officer called him to stop, saying the battle is over and we are beaten, but don't tell that to the boys. [He] also [said] that the boat was sunk on the other side of the island and no one could cross. "There is the lifeless body of Colonel [Edward D.] Baker coming over," he said, pointing to a stretcher. All returned to their camp. Had Father Paul gone over the river, he would most likely [have] be[en] either shot or a prisoner, or have [had] to swim the river. Next day he had business enough on hand, attending to the wounded and dying, no other Catholic chaplain being within forty miles of him.

At the battle of Ball's Bluff, Captain O'Meara with his company fought valiantly against a powerful force of the enemy until there was no hope of succeeding; he then withdrew down the steep bluff to the river edge, and the boat being sunk, got a skiff and came to the island in order to get the other boat hauled across the island, but could not get this effected, and the noble O'Meara (who would not desert his company in this crisis) went back to them; when all were taken prisoners, and marched off for Richmond, where he shared the hospitality of Libby Prison with his esteemed friend General Corcoran, who had been there some months before him. By the way, the same Captain O'Meara had a green flag with stars, stripes and shamrocks blessed by Father Paul the Sunday before, which he kept close buttoned under his clothes, safe from view during his year's imprisonment, and showed it to Father Paul safe after his liberation from prison. This same noble officer (it may be recollected) by General Corcoran's recommendation became colonel of an Irish regiment in Chicago, [the] 92nd Illinois (I think), and fell mortally wounded fighting at the head of his command on Lookout Mountain. Colonel Devens of the 15th Massachusetts (who sent his Irish soldiers to Mass) swam the river with his horse, and the colonel of the 20th Massachusetts (who would not let his men [go] to Mass) was taken prisoner and marched off to Libby Prison.

After the battle of Ball's Bluff, the Reverend Father [Michael F.] Martin[18] of Philadelphia became chaplain to the 69th Pennsylvania and continued with them until after the battle of Fair Oaks the June following. He attended to the soldiers in the vicinity of Poolville, and Father Paul came to Washington, where he met his old friend Colonel McLeod

Murphy and the 15th New York, just then joined to the engineer corps, and then encamped beside the Navy Yard Bridge on the east side of the Potomac. Here the colonel got Father Paul to make his headquarters with his regiment giving him a tent, cared[19] [for] his horse, and detailed a private to attend to him.

[Father Paul] made the 15th New York his home during the winter. [He] celebrated two Masses every Sunday, the first at the 15th New York and the second at either Couch's brigade at Brightwoods or Graham's brigade beyond the Soldier's Home. Both [of] these were stationed about seven miles from the 15th New York which in deep muddy roads made it very fatiguing. Also he attended the various hospitals on the Washington side of the Potomac.

There were a few days dry weather in December. Father Paul, taking advantage of them, crossed the river to see some of his old friends; after visiting a number of them, he learned that the Bucktails[20] and the Pennsylvania reserves under General [George A.] McCall[21] had no Catholic chaplain among them. He started off, and to get to these he went some miles beyond the Union lines along the Leesburg Turnpike until he was stopped by the Union pickets, but he presented his pass and said he wanted to visit the regiments there. "There is no regiment here," said the guard. "Yes there is," said Father Paul, "The Bucktails." "You are right," said the officer of the day, [who] let him go down to the "Bucktails." This regiment was from the mountainous regions of Pennsylvania and each man had his cap surmounted with a Buck's tail. They were one of the noblest and best fighting in the army and were commanded by Colonel [Thomas L.] Kane.

After visiting a number of regiments, he fixed his station in Colonel [Patrick] McDonough's tent of the 2nd Pennsylvania reserves as the most convenient for [the] Bucktails and all the regiments,[22] and never had he a greater crowd of colonels, majors, captains, lieutenants, etc., to say nothing of the privates at confession.

Next morning he had Mass very early and a large number of communicants, but immediately the drums were beat to arms, and many of them had scarce time to have any breakfast when they were off for the Battle of Dranesville.[23] Father Paul was off immediately, but the Bucktails and Pennsylvania reserves swept all before them, taking a number of prisoners, horses, wagons, artillery, etc. On returning after the battle,

Father Paul came on briskly ahead of the expedition, and meeting with General [John F.] Reynolds and his staff with some cavalry, [they] stopped him, taking him for a rebel, he being some miles beyond the Union lines. But, seeing his pass and learning he had been with the boys in the field and was a priest, [they] asked if he was not afraid of being captured, being in the rebel lines. "Not in the least," said Father Paul. "I have [a] strong force at my back of cavalry, artillery and infantry." "Go ahead," said the general, adding after his departure to his staff, "That is one of the d——dest venturesome old clergymen I ever saw."

He next proceeded to Washington and intended visiting the boys again when the roads would be hardened by frost, but there was no day during that winter that the mud was hard enough to carry a horse or wagon.

On Christmas day, he celebrated his first Mass at 7 o'clock with the 15th New York, at 9 on Meridian Hill with four brigades, and at half past 10 with the Pennsylvania artillery in a beautiful camp between Couch and Graham's Brigades, near the Soldier's Home, five miles from Washington. At the last Mass, he hunted up some who could sing and had a High Mass, probably the only High Mass in the army of the Potomac on that day. He spent the evening with Captains Flood and Brady, who entertained the father to a most elegant dinner.

The writer of this work failed in collecting the necessary materials and details to write an elaborate or extended sketch of Father Gillen, who served faithfully and zealously unto the close of the war. Dr. John Dwyer, who was brigade surgeon to the Corcoran Legion has furnished the following short sketch of the chaplains of the brigade.

The doctor says[24]—

As you are aware the "Corcoran Irish Legion" was so designated in contradistinction to "Meagher's Irish Brigade," both organizations being in service at the same time and for the same object, equaling each other in their noble deeds and reflecting equal credit on the land of their birth as on the land of their adoption.

The Corcoran Irish Legion (to which I had the honor to belong as surgeon of the celebrated "Sixty Ninth") consisted of the 69th,[25] 155th, 164th, and 170th New York regiments.

There were two chaplains connected with the Legion, the Reverend Ja[me]s Dillon,[26] chaplain of the 69th, and the Reverend Paul Gillen, chaplain of the 170th. Father Dillon was for some time our only chaplain and resided at headquarters where his usefulness was well known and where he established the custom of [at] night reciting the Rosary in which General Corcoran and his staff joined. How salutary this example was proved by the [con]sequence of one of the staff, an intelligent and leading American Protestant, afterwards being received into the Catholic Church, and giving as his principal reason for thinking of this step, that [of] the earnestness and unity of the little Catholic family at headquarters as well as the good conduct of the whole command made a great impression on him.

Father Dillon was a young impulsive able priest and a ready practical preacher. His sermons were extempore and fitted to his audience and the occasion and the chapel tent was always full on Sundays.

Father Dillon was always ready to take part in a skirmish or a ride thru the enemy's country and there is a story (which I believe) that on one occasion while attached to General Meagher's brigade that, all the officers of a certain regiment being *hors de combat* [outside the fight] while in action at [Malvern Hill],[27] the priest was seen to rally the men and lead them until a more fitting officer relieved him and then the priest saw for the first time that he had outstepped the line of his proper duty.

Father Dillon was a great favorite with the Legion but exposure while in the service superinduced a disease of his lungs which compelled me to advise him to resign in August 1864. Since then he travelled seeking for health which did not come and he died in [1868],[28] I think at the University of Notre Dame, Indiana.[29]

Father Paul Gillen was chaplain of the 170th and when Father Dillon left the Legion, Father Paul had all the duty devolving on himself. This duty he religiously and faithfully performed—early and late at his post I don't remember that he even had one day's leave of absence.

My first interview with Father Paul was at Newport News in December 1863. A tall thin spared old gentleman of clerical appearance asked me the way to headquarters and introduced himself as Father Gillen of the 170th. While Father Dillon always rode on horseback, Father Paul Gillen always rode in his carriage— and such a carriage! and such a horse! as he had. Don Quixote's Rosinante was a Dexter[30] in comparison. But Father Paul loved this horse nevertheless for by some peculiar construction Father Paul's horse and carriage was a combination of a Plimpton bedstead, a cathedral, and a restaurant all combined. In the twinkling of an eye his establishment was converted into a chapel and he was never at a loss for a covering or place for his altar wherever he travelled. If a large barn or building was to be had well and good or if the large chapel tent was up with the quartermaster's stores he used it but if not no matter whether we were on a march or a scout the Holy Sacrifice of the Mass was always offered every morning at Father Paul's establishment.

At Suffolk, Father Paul was accommodated with a room at hospital headquarters and to my own knowledge that room was morning noon and night besieged with soldiers from every regiment in the division who eagerly took advantage of the opportunities afforded them by the untiring chaplain of the Irish Legion.

Father Paul came to us from Colonel McLeod Murphy's regiment of New York Engineers the 15th (I think) and so was already an old campaigner and looked upon as an authority in military as well as religious matters and I am indebted to him for good advice on at least one occasion.

The Legion being engaged at the Battle of Deserted House near Suffolk which commenced while it was yet quite dark on the morning of January 30, 1863 and the wounded being brought to the rear the surgeons had to operate by candle light.[31] Our duties being of a serious nature, we devoted our entire attention to the wounded and did not notice either the approach of day light nor the fact that by the change of troops our position was becoming dangerous until Father Paul coming up gently advised us to go further to the rear and reminded us that the candles were not needed now. Father Paul had just walked over the whole field exposed to a crossfire and had given conditional absolution to an immense mass of kneeling soldiers who were counselled by him to this act on the battle field.

Father Paul served faithfully and laboriously all thru the war and was mustered out with the regiment. I have known many instances of his kindness of heart and he was the medium of correspondence with the families of many of the soldiers, cheering them with his advice and friendship.

Father [Thomas H.] Mooney[32] of St. Bridget's [in New York City] was also the well-known chaplain of the 69th in the early Bull Run days and on one occasion at Suffolk paid a visit to his old regiment and offered up Mass and preached a stirring sermon to us. The large chapel tent was full to overflowing for Father Mooney was familiar as a household word with all.

I only happened to meet the Sisters of Charity on one occasion while with the regiment and that was when Lieutenant Trecy of the staff was compelled thru sickness to accept their kindness at the sisters' hospital at Norfolk and I well remember the air of holiness and quiet which abounded there and which made the hospital seem to me at the time the beau ideal of a sick man's paradise and the self-sacrificing sisters ministering angels.

Sincerely Yours
John Dwyer M.D.
Late Brigade Surgeon Corcoran Irish Legion

[The following two newspaper articles were pasted at the beginning of the chapter. They contain reminiscences of Gillen's chaplaincy and life.]

THE REV. PAUL GILLEN AS AN ARMY CHAPLAIN

New York, November 20, 1882.
My Dear Mr. O'Reilly:[33]—I read the announcement a little while ago of the death of Rev. Paul Gillen and I think it appropriate to mention something of his great services in the army. He served as chaplain

of the 15th New York Volunteer Engineering Regiment under Colonel John McLeod Murphy who was afterwards in command of the Gunboat *Carond[e]let*. The old gentleman at his death was upwards of eighty years old and his devotion to his men while in the field was most remarkable. During the heat of battle, he would frequently expose himself to great danger in order to administer the [rites] of the Church to the dying men and at last his commanding officer was obliged to order him to the rear as he was constantly in danger of death from the fire of the enemy. He gained the greatest love and respect of the men of his regiment both Catholic and Protestant, for his sincere devotion to them on the battle field and in the hospital.

I well[34] remember the dear good old priest when the Army of the Potomac lay camped before Richmond on the Chickahominy[35] River going around among his men ringing his little bell to summon them to their evening devotions which he held every night in his tent where his neat little Altar was fitted up and where he celebrated the Holy Sacrifice of the Mass every morning. He was latterly stationed at Notre Dame, Indiana and was frequently in New York and he never failed to call on me when in the city and was frequently a welcome guest at my house in Brooklyn. He would take great delight in talking over reminiscences of the war which were so interesting. He was a good and holy man and has now gone to his reward.

CHARLES J. MURPHY[36]

REV. PAUL E. GILLEN, C.S.C.

Far from his college home, the beloved Notre Dame, Indiana, the Rev. Paul E. Gillen, C.S.C., died at the residence of his nephew [on] Degraw Street, Brooklyn, Friday evening, October 20th, at an advanced age.

Father Gillen was known in all parts of the country, and wherever he went he made innumerable friends, who ever looked up to him as a true friend and guide, and who, now that he is no more in the land of the living, cannot help repeating: "May the God whom he served so long and so well deign to receive his soul into everlasting peace! Amen."

Father Gillen was more than an ordinary priest. The priesthood was his highest ambition, was his soul's desire from the tender age of childhood, and in that sacred calling his labors were so grand, that now that he has been gathered to his fathers, we can say, without hurting the tender soul of "Father Paul," that he was an extraordinary priest.

He was born in the North of Ireland about the beginning of this century, and came to this country when young. After years of trials and difficulties, during which time he never misplaced confidence in his Heavenly Father, he was at last raised to the sacerdotal state, and soon he offered the Adorable Victim of Calvary's merit as a Father of the Holy Cross at Indiana. Before he was raised to the dignity of the priesthood, Father Paul was a missionary in the world, and if space would permit, numerous anecdotes could be told of his adventures in that direction. But if he gained souls to Christ while in the world, in religion his success was much greater.

When the late Civil War broke out he entered as a chaplain, and continued during the whole time of the rebellion, having a portable altar erected in an ambulance wagon, which could be moved as the regiments advanced. His story of life among the soldiers was as interesting as it was instructive, and the good that he achieved was very great. Among his greatest friends of those stormy times—and they continued their friendship till his death—were Generals whose names were renowned for valor and bravery, and who, when they met the priest, thought nothing too good for the old friend and companion of eventful days. And to none will the sad news of Father Gillen's death bring more genuine sorrow than to those brave warriors who were witnesses of the good wrought by this devoted man.

When the war was ended, Father Gillen returned to his home, and continued in the ministrations of his sacred calling, bringing back hardened souls to make peace with God, solacing the weak and the infirm, and rendering assistance wherever needed. Of late years, old age began to tell on the venerable priest, and, though unfitted for all the hardships of the sacred ministry, still he persevered, with a zeal worthy of him, in the discharge of his duties; and when death came to him he died, to use a familiar expression, "in the harness."

Father Paul's life was so beautiful, such grand lessons could be learned from it, that repeatedly was he asked to write it, but he would not hear of such a thing. Perhaps, now that he has gone to receive his reward, some good soul who knows will tell of the work of Father Paul—of how he labored in the Master's vineyard, in season and out of season; of the many trials and disappointments which he met during his eventful career; of his services in the late civil war; of the grand work he achieved for his beloved Notre Dame and St. Mary's Academy.

Father Gillen was not feeling well last summer, and though he wished to come to Brooklyn on business, his health would not permit it. He gained strength later on in the season, and obtained permission to visit his friends in New York. Whenever he came to Brooklyn he usually celebrated Mass for the Daughters of Mary, in charge of the deaf mutes, and it was on that errand of mercy that the aged priest of God was bent when his death-sickness seized him. He was borne to his nephew's residence, where all that could be thought of was done for the poor sufferer. Father [Thomas E.] Walsh[37] administered the last Sacraments, and, oh! it was a spectacle worthy of the occasion to see the old priest receive his Lord for the last time. He tried to robe himself, feeble through he was, in his cassock, as in days gone by, to receive the Divine object of his love, and the effort nearly cost him his life.

The Sisters of St. Joseph, the Poor of St. Francis, and the Daughters of Mary were constant in their attendance upon the dying priest; and Dr. Freel, Father Drumgoole, Father Walsh, and Brothers Paschal and Jarlath, of Notre Dame, were his companions. All that love could do was done by Mrs. McGuinness, and the consecrated hands of the dying priest were raised in benediction in behalf of this most estimable lady.

The end came on Friday morning, October 20th, just at the time when it was his wont to celebrate the Divine Mysteries.—*James McKenna, in the Sunday Democrat.*

❀   ❀   ❀

EPILOGUE: After the war, Father Gillen returned to Notre Dame. He also served as the superior of a new church named Holy Cross in Benton County, Iowa, from 1866 to 1880, when he retired from that post due to ill health. He died in Brooklyn, New York, on October 20, 1882. He is buried in Holy Cross Cemetery at Notre Dame.

SOURCES: Papers and records related to Gillen's chaplaincy and career as a Holy Cross priest are held at the University of Notre Dame Archives and the Congregation of Holy Cross United States Province Archives Center in Notre Dame, Indiana.

William Corby, C.S.C., *Memoirs of Chaplain Life: Three Years with the Irish Brigade in the Army of the Potomac* (Notre Dame, IN: "Scholastic" Press, 1893; reprinted and edited by Lawrence Frederick Kohl, New York: Fordham University Press, 1992), 307–11; Aidan H. Germain, "Catholic Military and Naval Chaplains, 1776–1917" (PhD diss., Catholic University of America, 1929), 69–70; John William Cavanaugh, C.S.C., *Daniel E. Hudson, C.S.C.: A Memoir* (Notre Dame, IN: Ave Maria Press, 1934; reprint, 1960), 14–15; Arthur J. Hope, C.S.C., *Notre Dame: One Hundred Years* (Notre Dame, IN: University of Notre Dame Press, 1943), 124–26; Edward Sorin, C.S.C., *The Chronicles of Notre Dame du Lac*, ed. James T. Connelly (Notre Dame, IN: University of Notre Dame Press, 1992), 209, 276, 304; Joseph M. White, *Worthy of the Gospel of Christ: A History of the Catholic Diocese of Fort Wayne–South Bend* (Fort Wayne, IN: Diocese of Fort Wayne–South Bend, 2007), 70; James M. Schmidt, *Notre Dame and the Civil War: Marching Onward to Victory* (Charleston, SC: The History Press, 2010), 31–33.

CHAPTER XV

Rev. Innocent A. Bergrath

Born in Prussia—His parents emigrate to America—His early
career—His desire to go as a chaplain opposed by his bishop—
His mission among the Federal and Confederate soldiers—He is
cut off from communication with his bishop—The celebration
of Mass in the little church of S.S. Peter and Paul in Chattanooga
the morning of battle—His services given to Federals
and Confederates alike.

INTRODUCTION: Though Father Innocent A. Bergrath
(1836–1881) was never commissioned as a chaplain for either
side, he was pastor of Catholic congregations in eastern Tennessee and during wartime was permitted to minister to soldiers in that region. The son of Theodore and Anne Marie
(Heinrichs) Bergrath, he was born in Hönningen, Kreis Ahr-
weiler, in Germany's Rhineland-Palatinate region. In 1842, the
family immigrated to the United States, first to a town near
Fremont, Ohio, and then Westphalia, Michigan, in 1848.
He began studies at St. Vincent's College and Seminary in Latrobe, Pennsylvania, before studying for the priesthood at Vincennes, Indiana. Just prior to ordination, he became affiliated
with the Diocese of Nashville, Tennessee. He was ordained in
Scranton, Pennsylvania, on April 2, 1860. After ordination, his
first assignment was to the Church of the Assumption of the

Blessed Virgin Mary, a German congregation in Nashville. During the war he was headquartered in Knoxville with care of outlying missions, placing him in close proximity to the hostilities.

❀   ❀   ❀

Revd. Innocent A. Bergrath was born at Hoeningen, a little village in Rhenish Prussia on November 24, 1836. In 1842 his parents emigrated to America where they located themselves for a time near the present town of Fremont in Ohio. In 1848 however they concluded to remove to Michigan, where they purchased a homestead on the outskirts of the village of Westphalia, Clinton County. From here the subject of our sketch was sent in 1852 to St. Vincent's College,[1] Westmoreland Co., Pennsylvania where he finished his classical studies with distinction, in 1858. His health having suffered in the mean while he was obliged to return home to recruit it,[2] after which he attached himself to the diocese of Vincennes and entered the seminary of the Rt. Revd. Bishop de St. Palais[3] at Vincennes in the fall of the same year. At this seminary he remained for one year devoting himself to the study of theology, and other kindred studies. At the end of the year however his health made it again necessary for him to go further south. Having acquaintances in Nashville, Tennessee, he went thither, and was adopted into the diocese by Rt. Rev. Bishop Miles,[4] and continued his studies under private teachers, chiefly the Very Revd. Father Birmingham, V.G.[5] of the diocese, and was ordained [a] priest on Palm Sunday of 1860. For the first eight months, he was assigned pastor of the German Church of the Assumption in the city of Nashville. Towards the close of the year he was sent to East Tennessee to take charge of the congregation at Knoxville together with the extensive missions attached to the same.

When the war had broken out and hearing that the Catholic volunteer regiments from Tennessee required chaplains, he begged repeatedly of his bishop[6] to be permitted to go with them but was refused on the ground that he could not be spared from his parish and missions, the more so as already out of the very small number of clergy in the state some had been sent out with the army.

The bishop therefore charged him to remain at his post; but at the same time to perform the duties of a chaplain towards any regiment or army that might pass through or be stationed within his district, and who had no priest with them. The importance of this charge was a serious one, as the entire country, lying between Chattanooga and Bristol, Virginia, and extending from Kentucky, on the north, to Georgia and Carolina on the South, were comprised in his mission.

At first, and before East Tennessee was seriously threatened by the enemy,[7] it was easy enough, for the camps of instruction were confined to the principal plains along the railroads, and were all easily accessible. But when the invading armies began to draw near the borders, and it became necessary for the Confederate States government to station its troops along the distant mountain passes on the border, in most cases, many miles from any railroad, father had a hard time of it. Generally he would start out on Mondays and after traveling on horseback or otherwise, for a day or so, would reach the camps. Here he would remain for two or three days as the case seemed to require, saying Mass, hearing confessions, preaching or cheering the "boys" up amidst their many privations, and then he would return again in time to reach home for Saturday where he had the same routine of duties to perform again for the members of his congregation. His duties were still yet more increased when the extensive army hospitals began to be established in and around Knoxville principally after the retreat of General Bragg from Kentucky. These hospitals it was necessary to visit almost every day—a day's work in itself. After Father Nealis, the pastor of Chattanooga, was shot and disabled, Father Bergrath's duties became still more arduous, for then he had not only his own mission to attend to but also those of Chattanooga which reached as far as Bridgeport, Alabama. Thus far there had been, at least, a constant means of communication between himself and his bishop in Nashville. But when the latter place fell into the hands of the Federals he was even deprived of this consolation. From this time forward he had to be his own bishop in a measure, until the Federals succeeded one and a half years afterwards in occupying East Tennessee. From this time forward he had to perform the same duties towards the U.S. armies camped, doing duty, or lying sick within his district, as he was ordered to do towards the Confederates previously.

Having occasion, and with the permission of the Confederate States government, to cross the lines a little before the surrender of East Tennessee, for the purpose of consulting with his bishop on certain points of importance, he returned by way of Chattanooga and reached that place just a few days before the memorable battle fought there by General Rosecrans. At the request of the general he remained for the battle, and said Mass—the general attending in the little Church of SS. Peter and Paul on the morning of the battle.[8]

Having at last reached home again he passed through the siege of Knoxville under General Burnside, and was finally relieved at his own request—his health having given away again—of his difficult charge just one day before the fall of Richmond.

He was a good and zealous priest and worked equally in his attendance to the spiritual and temporal wants of the Federals as he had done previously for the Confederate soldiers.

Like a true Soldier of Christ he believed that his mission was not of the sword but of the Cross, and that he was bound to uphold this peaceful symbol of man's redemption, in the service of Federals and Confederates alike.

Their bloody conflict was to him only a source of grief; [the soldiers'] eternal salvation his only object and ambition.

EPILOGUE: After the war, Father Bergrath continued parish ministry. Deeply interested in literature and theology, he translated several works from German into English, including *Aner's Return; or, The Migrations of a Soul* (1867), *Ecclesiastical Celibacy* (1870), and *St. Helena, or The Finding of the Cross, a Drama for Girls* (1872). His later years of ministry were spent at St. Michael Church in Pensacola, Florida. He died there on September 25, 1881, and is buried in the parish cemetery.

SOURCES: Robert J. Miller, *Both Prayed to the Same God: Religion and Faith in the American Civil War* (Lanham, MD: Lexington Books, 2007), 110; Westphalia Historical Society, *Of Pilgrimage, Prayer and Promise: A Story of St. Mary's, Westphalia, 1836–1986* (Westphalia, MI: Westphalia Historical Society, 1986), 104.

CHAPTER XVI

Rev. Peter P. Cooney, C.S.C.

Chaplain 35th Indiana Volunteers

*His birth and early education—His connection with Notre Dame,
Indiana—The order of the Holy Cross—He joins the 35th
Indiana as chaplain—His popularity with the troops—He saves
a man from being shot—His mission of mercy—Carrying
funds for the soldiers under difficulties—A perilous trip to
Nashville—Irish wit and humor—The march—Its trials, dangers,
and hardships—Gallant charge of the 35th Indiana—
Father Cooney's conduct in the camps, the hospital, and the field.*[1]

INTRODUCTION: Father Peter P. Cooney, C.S.C. (1822–
1905), was born in County Roscommon, Ireland, on June 20,
1822. His parents moved to Monroe, Michigan, when he was
about four or five years old. After graduating from Notre
Dame in 1854 and spending time as a teacher and a semi-
narian elsewhere, he returned to South Bend and was ordained
a Holy Cross priest on July 1, 1859. At the request of Indiana
Governor Oliver Morton and with the approval of President
Abraham Lincoln, he mustered into service as the 35th Indiana
Volunteer Infantry Regiment's chaplain on December 11, 1861.

The average length of service for a Civil War chaplain was
only eighteen months. Many found the work difficult and

211

unfulfilling. Cooney, however, served longer than most, remaining almost four years with his regiment. In his sketch of Father Cooney's life and service, Conyngham admitted in a footnote that he relied almost exclusively upon David Stevenson's *Indiana's Roll of Honor* (1864).[2] Here he highlights Cooney's efforts to prevent a wrongly condemned soldier from being executed, his ministry of conveying soldiers' pay to family and friends back home, and his temperance leadership among his soldiers. The author also provides detail on the career of the 35th Indiana prior to General Rosecrans assuming command in late 1862.

Among the many Catholic chaplains who had distinguished themselves by their zeal and devotion in the discharge of their duties during the war, few more loyally distinguished themselves than the subject of this sketch. He was cool and brave and never intimidated by fear or danger from the faithful discharge of his duties to the sick, the dying, and the wounded.

Father Cooney was born in the County Roscommon,[3]

Ireland, in the year 18[2]2.[4] He emigrated, with his parents, to this country at the early age of four years. His parents settled near Monroe, Michigan. This place was the scene of Father Cooney's school boy days. Here it was he prepared to enter college; and in the beginning of 1851, he matriculated at the University of Notre Dame, near the town of South Bend, Indiana. In this institution he remained three years, prosecuting his studies vigorously. At the end of these three years, he sought the shadows of the theological seminary of St. Mary's Baltimore, Maryland, where he remained and completed his literary and theological studies, returning to Notre Dame, Indiana, in 1859. He was ordained a priest on July first, 1859, and at once joined the order of the Holy Cross. Immediately after his ordination, he was sent to Chicago, where he filled the honorable and important position of Vice-President of the University of St. Mary's of the Lake.[5] He continued for two years in this position, when, on learning that an Irish regiment was being organized in Indiana, and of Governor Morton's[6] application for a priest as chaplain, Father Cooney tendered his services to the country, and was commissioned as chaplain of the Irish regiment on the fourth of October, 1861.

The work from which we quote says:

> Notwithstanding he left his native land at an early age, he loves and cherishes with affection the memories of Ireland. The flutter of the "Green Flag," or the sweet strains of "Patrick's Day," or "Garryow[e]n" arouses his Irish blood, and for a moment he forgets he is a priest, and thinks himself a soldier. United to a kind heart, he has a deep fund of wit and humor, and many an hour is pleasantly passed in listening to his native wit and risible anecdotes. He knows human nature thoroughly, looks leniently upon the frailties of mankind, mildly censuring the misconduct of the men, and zealously urging them to a faithful performance of their duty to God and country. To say that he is much respected

by the men of the regiment is saying too little; he is loved by them. To illustrate this we will relate an incident.

Around a blazing campfire sat a few comrades smoking their dhudeens (short pipes) and discussing strategy with all the intensity of controversialists. Father Cooney came hurriedly along, evidently bent on a visit to some sick soldier. The little squad instantly rose to their feet with the hand to the cap. "Good evening boys," said the father with one of his pleasant smiles, as he hurried towards the hospital. "There he goes," said one of the group, "he's always where he does good and never idle. The likes of him, God bless him, is not to be found betwixt here and the Giant's Causeway."[7] "Thrue for you, Tim, by gorra; his match couldn't be found if ye traveled from Dan to Barsheeba,"[8] said his comrade. "He'll be saying his beades among the stars, when many of his callin will be huntin a dhrop of water in a very hot climate." This last remark was received with a hearty acquiescence by the entire group. Rough and witty as it was, it expressed the feelings of the soldier for the chaplain.

In the discharge of his duties, Father Cooney does not confine himself to his own regiment. Wherever and whenever his services are required then and there are they freely bestowed. This gives him a reputation co-extensive with the Army of the Cumberland, and makes his friends of the 35th Indiana that much the more proud of him. A short time after the battle of Stones River,[9] while the regiment was at Murfreesboro; an incident occurred, which showed the kind heart of the chaplain.

Michael Nash,[10] a private in the 65th Regiment Ohio Volunteers, was sentenced to be shot to death at Nashville on the fifteenth of June 1863. The sentence was to take effect between the hours of two and four P.M. Father Cooney, hearing of the affair, started for Nashville to be present at the execution, and administer the rites of his Church to the condemned man. Having prepared the unfortunate soldier for his final march, the chaplain made enquiries respecting his case. The facts were these: on the morning of the thirty first of December, when [Richard W.] Johnson's[11] division[12]

was surprised, and [Alexander M.] McCook[13] hurled from his position by a superior force, the 65th was thrown into momentary confusion. Nash, being separated from his command, fell into the tide of fugitives who were retreating towards Nashville. By the irresistible current of panic-stricken soldiers, he was carried back to Lavergne.[14] Here he was arrested. From the evidence it appeared that Nash did not intend to desert. He might have been brave as those, who stood the galling fire; but having been caught by the rushing current of a panic, he was swept from the field. It was now half past twelve, P.M. If the unfortunate man be saved, no time must be lost in communicating with the general. Without making known his intentions to any one, Father Cooney telegraphed to General Rosecrans, at Murfreesboro, the facts of the case, and the circumstances supporting them, and concluded by saying:

Were I under the impression that he intentionally deserted, I would not say a word in his behalf; the good of the service would require his death. But I am convinced of the contrary. I respectfully beg, therefore, for him some other punishment than death.
Signed,

P. P. Cooney,
Chaplain 35th Indiana Vols.

Two o'clock arrived, but brought no answer to the dispatch. The detail to fire upon Nash assembled; their guns were loaded; the ground for his execution was selected, and about three thousand persons were assembled to witness the tragedy. The open coffin awaited its victim, and an artisan unfastens the heavy shackles from the culprit's limbs, that he may take his last march on the great highway which leads from Time to Eternity. A messenger enters the cell and hands to the jailor one of those "yellow covered" communications. "His death warrant," whispered someone, and all was still as death. The jailor broke the seal and read aloud:

"Michael Nash, sentenced to be shot today, is reprieved.
By order of
Major General Rosecrans."

The prisoner, heretofore calm and collected, now became pale and agitated. Instantly those around him rushed forward and clasped his hands in hearty congratulation. The prisoner, looking intently on Father Cooney, knew the source of all his mercy. Tears of joy rolled down his manly cheeks. But another trouble. Nash under the direction of his confessor, had written a farewell letter to his mother, informing her of his sad fate and saying his last farewell. That letter had gone, carrying news which would break her heart. "Not a bit of it." Father Cooney, keeping his secret, had that letter in his pocket. Nothing now remained to complete the soldier's happiness; he walked from his prison a free man—thankful to God and the good father and grateful to his general, whom he now knew to be merciful as well as just and brave.

A chaplain has more than one duty to perform to the men of his regiment. Whilst the spiritual welfare of the men is of primary importance, he is not at liberty to neglect the soldiers' temporal comfort and happiness. To the duties of the priest, Father Cooney adds the kindness of father and friend. On every pay day he receives money from the soldiers and becomes banker without fee or discount. It is a difficult work faithfully and honestly to discharge the duties of banker to a regiment.

A certain amount is ordered to be sent to "the dear ones at home," a few dollars kept to be drawn at will for a "bit of tobaccy" or may be a "dhrop of the dhrink to warm the heart." Of this latter commodity the good chaplain is extremely jealous. He has often declared that this same "dhrop of dhrink" is the curse of Irishmen, and in order to guard against its baleful influence, Father Cooney has organized a temperance society of which he is the president. This society does not embrace all the members of the regiment, nor are its members "life members." The pledge is generally taken for six months or a year, and to their credit be it said, it is rarely if ever violated.

Through the practice of temperance and economy, the Irish regiment on three different occasions has sent home by the hands of Father Cooney alone the round sum of forty[15]

thousand dollars. To be the custodian and messenger to carry such sums of money is at once a responsible and perilous position.

In November 1862, the regiment lay in camp at Silver Spring, eighteen miles from Nashville. It was after the severe campaign of Buell *versus* Bragg and Bragg *versus* Buell; when each in turn, to use the phrase of Emil Schalk, "had recourse to the offensive-defensive strategy."[16] During the repose at Silver Spring the paymaster visited the troops, and the 35th Indiana placed in the hands of Father Cooney the snug sum of twenty-three thousand dollars, to be carried home and distributed to their friends. The road between Silver Spring and Nashville was thronged with guerrillas, and many a blue jacket, unconscious or careless of the danger, was taken prisoner. Colonel [Bernard F.] Mullen[17] having business at Nashville—where General Rosecrans then had his headquarters—placed an ambulance at the disposal of Father Cooney to carry himself, companions, and treasure to Nashville. The party, consisting of Colonel Mullen, Father Cooney, the Colonel's orderly, and a Mr. Korbly, formerly sutler of the regiment, expecting to overtake General Crittenden and escort, boldly pushed forward. After going four miles it was ascertained that General Crittenden and escort were not on the road. Then came the question, "Shall we go back or go on?" "We'll go on," said the colonel. And away the party dashed, believing there was safety in speed. On the road were courier posts about three miles apart, but this gave no security to our travelers. Our party, with fresh caps on their pistols, moved forward. Duck River, hemmed in by bluffs, was to be crossed. The enemy had destroyed every bridge, and the party was compelled to "take water." They met and overcame every difficulty—for the stream had to be crossed many times on the route—until they arrived at the last ford. In crossing the river the ford was missed, and a steep bank presented itself. Jimmy Welch, the driver of the ambulance, was bold of heart and had unbounded confidence in his team. He "made a run on the bank"—"the bank broke,"— Jimmy and his team rolled gently back to the river; his horses, that "couldn't be matched either at Doncaster or a circus,"

wouldn't pull a pound. Night was fast approaching. What was to be done. "Arrah, give them their wind and, they'll come out o' that like a daisy," said the ever confident Jimmy. A few moments were allowed the beasts to rest; all put their shoulder to the wheels, but the off horse would not move. Jimmy applied the whip and the party yelled, but the "off horse" still refused. The sun was setting, the party had yet to travel eleven miles, and carry twenty three thousand dollars, which were locked up in Father Cooney's trunk.

"Halloa, gentlemen," said a courier, dashing up, "you must get out of here; there is a party of sixty or seventy guerrillas a short distance over here; and you'll go up." Just then a sharp rifle crack added to the persuasive speech of the dragoon. A council of war was called. "Father Cooney," said the colonel, "divide your money among us four, and we will run when we can and fight when we must." This did not meet with favor only as a last resort. Two or three other propositions were made, all in quite an unparliamentarily manner when the spattering picket firing in the rear and on the flank of the road suddenly broke up the council of war. Emergencies develop men's genius. A small mill being near, the long rope which had been used for the purpose of dragging logs from the river was pressed into service, likewise two yoke of oxen. One end of the long rope was fastened to the tongue of the ambulance; the oxen were hitched to the rope; up came the wagon and its treasure. Bang! Bang! again went the rifles of the guerrillas. "Come Jimmy, hurry now and let's be off." "Don't be hasty," said Jimmy, drawing his pipe out of his mouth and coolly throwing over his nose a column of smoke. "Go easy I'll take yees to Nashville inside an hour, or I'll not leave hide enough on the horses to make a pair of brogues for a tinker."

And Jimmy kept his word. Within the hour the party were safe inside the lines at Nashville. Was there really any danger? The post in the rear was attacked and driven in; the whole line was broken up, and the army moved and concentrated at Nashville. These sketches and incidents are given to show the reader what is necessary to make up, in detail, a campaign, and we[18]

take those of the Irish regiment because of its "peculiar institutions." With its

Fighting and marching,
Pipe-claying and starching.

The sorest trials and severest sufferings of the soldier are on the march. Toiling beneath a burning sun, dust shoe-mouth deep, water scarce, the soldier marches and suffers. A battle to him is a thousand times preferable to tramping and marching. Sometimes he presses through the choking dust, his lips and tongue being dry and parched and crisped. Again he struggles through the tenacious mud, with knapsack on his back, and forty rounds of ball cartridge in his box—"arms at will—route step." With all the fatigues of the march, there are many little occurrences which give life and spirit to the troops. The light hearted members of the Irish regiment will cheerfully respond to the enthusiastic calls for a song—a merry, rhyming, chiming lilt, that raises Irish blood to boiling heat—and the response is received, as usual, with a cheer.

"Come Dennis, ye sowl, give us a song."

"Oh, the bad luck to the one iv me can sing a bit. Shure me throat is as dhry as a magazine," was Dennis's reply, as he evidently wanted "coaxin."

"Can Dennis sing?" asked another. The question was propounded only to provoke discussion.

"Is it him? he sings like a Mavish; (Mavis) he has a voice that would brake[19] up a female boardin school or a nunnery," was the reply. This last superb compliment caused Dennis to clear his throat. After a few coughs, shifting his musket to the opposite shoulder, he gave to his comrades a history of Irish courtship in verse. At the end of every verse, there was loud applause, but when that which recounted the fair one's shyness and coquetry, as,

Arrah Paddy, says she, don't ye bother me,
Arrah Paddy, says she, don't ye taise me,
Arrah Paddy, says she, would ye smudther me;
Oh the divil go wid ye be aisy.

The applause was "tremendous," shaking the column from company A to the rear guard of the regiment. Such occurrences as the one narrated frequently occur. They lighten the heart and quicken the steps of the soldiers.

It is astonishing the number of miles traveled by Indiana regiments since the opening of the war. As an example the Irish regiment marched from January the twelfth to December first 1862 eleven hundred and forty-five miles. On the twenty second of May 1862, the 35th and 61st and 2nd Irish regiments were consolidated. Colonel Mullen of the 61st became lieutenant colonel of the 35th. Soon after the consolidation, Colonel [John C.] Walker[20] resigned and was succeeded by Lieutenant Colonel Mullen.

The march from McMinnville, Tennessee, to Louisville, Kentucky, was the most severe the regiment ever experienced. The weather was extremely hot; no water could be obtained, save from stagnant pools. The men were on half rations. Officers and men exhibited great stamina and heroic endurance.

At Franklin, Tennessee, the enemy appeared on the flank, and frequent skirmishing was the result. As the "flanker" opened fire, the column came to a halt, ready to deploy into a line of battle. A few rattles of musketry, interspersed with the hoarse barking of a howitzer, settled the affair; and along the line was heard the soul stirring command "forward."

At Louisville the Irish regiment was in the brigade commanded by Colonel Stanley Matthews[21]—[Horatio P.] Vancleve's[22] division and Crittenden's corps. From Louisville to Wild Cat[23] the march of the army met with continued resistance. At Perryville the enemy gave battle.[24] The 35th was not seriously engaged.

On the morning of the eighth of October, heavy skirmishing on the left and front gave evidence that the enemy intended to stand. The occasional rattle of musketry was drowned by rapid battery explosions. All doubts were now removed.[25]

> The gallant Crittenden pushed his corps rapidly forward. Nearer and nearer sounded the rattling musketry and the heavy reporting howitzer. The men cheered and pushed forward.
>
> "Steady, boys, steady; you'll get enough of it directly," said the colonel.
>
> "Be the holy poker, thin, it'll take enough o' that same to go round the 35th," replied one of its members.
>
> "Where's Colonel Mullen?" asked a staff officer dashing up, his horse reeking with foam.

"Here he is, sir," replied the colonel.

"Colonel, you will occupy the extreme left of your brigade. There is the line on the crest of that hill"—pointing with his sword. "Now look out; the enemy is about turning McCook's right. Be ready to change front on tenth company," and away he dashed.

The men heard the orders, and were in the best possible spirits. Jokes passed freely among the dauntless, light-hearted Irishmen. "All were eager for the fray." A little incident here occurred which we must relate.

At Munfordville some of the men took "a dhrop too much;" and while the regiment was resting in column by companies, a difficulty occurred between the officer of the guard and those that had been drinking. The guard was about being overpowered—the mutineers cocked their rifles to fire. Colonel Mullen, seeing the guard in peril, and discipline violated, drew his sabre, and dashed into the midst of the mutineers. The guard fired, killing the ringleader, and wounding one of his followers. A mutineer, who aimed his musket at the colonel, was promptly arrested. This man (Daley) was tried by court-martial; but his sentence had to be approved—which led to the opinion that the sentence was death—before it could be made public. He was handcuffed, and ordered to march in the rear of the regiment. As the orders to get into the line of battle at Perryville were given, the Colonel rode from front to rear of his regiment. Daley was ironed and surrounded by the guard. "Lieutenant," said the colonel to the officer of the guard, "take those irons off the prisoner." The order was promptly obeyed. "How do

your wrists feel, my man?" asked the colonel. "Pretty well, sir," replied Daley. "Can you shoot with them?" "I think I could sir if I had a gun." "Orderly bring this man a musket and equipments, and forty rounds of cartridge."

"Now Daley," said the colonel, "you have been tried by a court martial for mutiny and attempting to take the life of your superior officer. I don't know what that sentence is; you can judge as well as I. Take that musket and on the field ahead of us, wipe out that sentence, and, by the blessing of God, I'll help you to do it." The poor fellow rushed forward, and seizing the hand of his officer, covered it with tears. "There, there, now go. You are a free man and a soldier once more." Daley has since proved himself, on more than one occasion, to be a soldier.

"Forward the 35th!" and away went the regiment to its position. The battle raged furiously. The line of the third brigade was formed and ready for the enemy, or for orders to go to him. From two o'clock until five P.M. the storm of battle raged. All our left w[as] engaged. Mc-Cook, [Charles C.] Gilbert, [James S.] Jackson, Rousseau, [William H.] Lytle, and the gallant [John C.] Starkweather, were there. Here comes a staff officer. "Send forward two companies of your regiment as skirmishers, and clear that underbrush, General [Thomas J.] Wood's division is coming up to occupy your left," said an officer of Colonel Matthew's staff. Co. D., under Lieutenant [Augustus Gabriel] Tassin,[26] and Co. B, under Lieutenant [Christopher H.] O'Brien, were ordered to that duty. Major [John P.] Dufficy[27] commanded this battalion of skirmishers. He kept his eye well to the front, and marched upon the enemy's deployed line. The enemy fell back, making but a feeble resistance. Wood approached in fine style, and entered the conflict; but it was too late. The sun had gone down, and hostilities ceased.

> Night threw her mantle o'er the earth
> And pinned it with a star.

The next morning the enemy fled, and were pursued by the victorious Union army, Crittenden in the advance. Nothing of importance occurred until the 35th approached the little town of Crab Orchard. Here it was reported the enemy would make a stand. It was three[28]

o'clock, A.M. The round, full moon made everything light as day. Vancleve's division is ordered to march and dislodge the enemy, who is said to be three miles ahead. Skirmishers are thrown out, and the column moves. "Bang, bang!" The enemy is found. The fire of the platoons in reserve is instantly answered by three rapid shots from the enemy's artillery, posted beyond a creek. The 7th Indiana battery, in the rear of the first line, replies, but their shot and shell whiz over the 35th and fall a few yards in advance. The contending batteries wax warm, and the road is literally plowed up.

"Did you see that?" said Father Cooney, as a shell burst immediately in front of him. "I think I did," replied the colonel. "This must be stopped," said the chaplain, referring to the Indiana battery's bad range. "That's what I am going to do," said the colonel, referring to the enemy; "if I can only get across that narrow bridge." Orders were received to cross the bridge, and take position. "Now, every mother's son of you keep your mouths shut until we cross the bridge, when you may yell till your hearts' content," said the colonel. "Fix bayonets and forward," and away they go. A short turn in the road saves the regiment, the enemy shelling the road. The 35th debouches to the left, until the creek is reached. Instantly they rush to the right for the bridge. The head of the column is over. "Double-quick," and with deafening yells the 35th, closely followed by the 51st Ohio, rush for the battery. The artillery fly at their approach, leaving two artillerymen, and a few infantry skirmishers, in the hands of the assailants. Not a man of the 35th was injured in this little affair.

From this time till General Rosecrans assumed command of the army, nothing of special interest occurred.

EPILOGUE: Although Conyngham's account of Cooney's service ends abruptly, the priest continued to serve under Generals Rosecrans, Stanley, and George H. Thomas until he was mustered out of service on June 16, 1865. He returned to pastoral and educational work, serving St. Patrick's Church in South Bend, Indiana; St. Bernard's Church in Watertown,

Wisconsin; and Our Lady of Lourdes in Vidalia, Louisiana. He spent many of his years after the war at the University of Notre Dame and served briefly as Provincial Superior of the Congregation of Holy Cross in the United States. He joined the university's Grand Army of the Republic (GAR) post #569 and served as its chaplain. On the fortieth anniversary of his priesthood, he had a special chalice made, commemorating his Civil War services, which can be found today at the Basilica of the Sacred Heart Museum. He died in 1905 at Notre Dame and is buried in the Holy Cross community cemetery.

SOURCES: Cooney's papers, including his wartime diary, are housed in the University of Notre Dame Archives. A portion of his letters was published by Notre Dame archivist Thomas T. McAvoy, C.S.C., in three parts as "The War Letters of Father Peter Paul Cooney of the Congregation of Holy Cross," *Records of the American Catholic Historical Society of Philadelphia* 44 (March, June, September 1933): 47–69; 151–69; 220–37. Additional records and papers related to Cooney's priesthood can be found at the Congregation of Holy Cross United States Province Archives Center in Notre Dame, Indiana.

See also Thomas T. McAvoy, "Peter Paul Cooney, Chaplain of Indiana's Irish Regiment," *Journal of the American-Irish Historical Society* 30 (1932): 97–102; Arthur J. Hope, C.S.C., *Notre Dame: One Hundred Years* (Notre Dame, IN: University of Notre Dame Press, 1943), 129–32; James M. Schmidt, *Notre Dame and the Civil War: Marching Onward to Victory* (Charleston, SC: The History Press, 2010), 37–39, 57–58, 103–6; Benedict R. Maryniak and John Wesley Brinsfield, Jr., *The Spirit Divided: Memoirs of Civil War Chaplains; The Union* (Macon, GA: Mercer University Press, 2007), 86–92; Kevin C. Murray, *The 1st Fighting Irish: The 35th Indiana Volunteer Infantry; Hoosier Hibernians in the War for the Union* (Bloomington, IN: AuthorHouse, 2013), 63–71.

CHAPTER XVII

Rev. Thomas Brady

Chaplain 15th Michigan Volunteers

At the request of a deputation from the regiment he becomes
their chaplain—His services in the field night and day—
A war of words—His services in Vicksburg and Chattanooga—
After the battle of Nashville his regiment proceeds to
North Carolina—His regiment disbanded at the close of the
war—Father Brady's death from disease contracted in the service.

INTRODUCTION: Father Thomas M. Brady (1824–1865)
served as chaplain to the 15th Michigan Volunteer Infantry
Regiment. Born in Ireland, likely in Galloon Parish in County
Fermanagh, to John and Bridget Brady, he immigrated to western New York along with several brothers. It appears that soon
after arrival he began teaching in Rochester, New York, at
which time he met Bishop John Timon. Brady was ordained
as a priest on April 9, 1854, for service in the Diocese of Buffalo. He resided with Bishop Timon in Buffalo and served as
a teacher and hospital chaplain. From 1855 to 1859 he served as
pastor of St. Patrick Church in Seneca Falls, and from 1859 to
1860 at St. Mary Church in Medina.

In New York he became associated with a community of Irish
religious, the Brigidine Sisters, who served briefly as school
teachers in Buffalo, Rochester, and Medina, New York, as well

as Kenosha, Wisconsin. Father Brady, along with the sisters, transferred to the Diocese of Detroit in 1860. In Michigan, Father Brady served at St. Andrew Church in Grand Rapids from July 1860 to January 1862. The sisters also located there to establish a girl's school. During his short time of ministry in Michigan, Brady ran afoul of the Brigidine superior, Mother Angela McKay, as well as the Detroit coadjutor bishop Peter Paul Lefevère. By January 1862, Brady was released by his bishop for military service. Father Brady was active as chaplain from March 13, 1862, to August 13, 1865. In addition to his service with the 15th Michigan, he also served as chaplain to the military hospitals in Memphis, Tennessee.

Conyngham's account of Father Brady's[1] service as chaplain is drawn from an undated, unattributed newspaper clipping with only a few minor changes. Given its style and knowledge of the details of Father Trecy's chaplaincy (see chapters 1, 2, and 3), the article was almost certainly written by Conyngham.

This good and zealous priest was a native of Ireland, which country he never ceased to love with all the yearning of a true patriot. He came to America in charge of a colony of Sisters of the Order of St. Bridget and was assigned to a mission at Grand Rapids, State of Michigan. Here, for several years previous to the breaking out of the rebellion, he labored faithfully, attending to the spiritual wants of his flock, and, by his piety and zeal, greatly tended to the advancement of Catholicity. The 15th Michigan was mainly an Irish and a Catholic regiment, and was among the foremost to respond to the national call for troops. A deputation from the regiment waited on Father Brady, requesting him to become their chaplain. He at once consented, provided the bishop[2] of the diocese gave his consent. This was soon obtained, and the patriotic priest at once prepared to encounter the numerous fatigues, dangers, and perils inseparable from the life of a Catholic chaplain in the field, in order to minister to the spiritual wants of his fellow Christians and countrymen. It was the soldier of the Cross following the example of his Divine Master, volunteering to embrace all kinds of hardships and perils, in order to alleviate the sufferings and pangs of the victims of the soldiers of the sword.

His first services in the field with his regiment was in Kentucky, where he labored night and day, both in the camp and in the hospitals, hearing confessions, nursing and consoling the sick and wounded, and cheering the last moments of the departing with the rites of his holy Church and the promise of a glorious resurrection. In the hospitals and on the field, he acted the Good Samaritan, and freely rendered assistance to all alike, regardless of religion or politics. From Kentucky, he removed with his regiment into Tennessee. At Memphis he met with considerable annoyance, even from members of his own Church whose devotion to the Confederate cause blinded them to the Christian duties of a Catholic chaplain. These extremists assailed him as a *Yankee* priest and a supporter of the Yankee invasion. The good Father bore all this with humility, and, by his acts and example, soon convinced them that he was the soldier of Christ, not of any earthly power. The regiment was next ordered to Vicksburg, and was accompanied by its devoted chaplain. Among the many camp incidents that varied the lives of chaplains, the following occurred to him:

An Irishman and a German, both wounded, occupied contiguous beds, near the door of the hospital. Father Brady, on entering, used the Christian salutation of "God bless you all." "Amen, and you, too!" said the Irishman. "Vat you mean?" asked the German. "I be in von hell now mid these pains, and me vants no other hell; mine vound is as much hell as I vant. I bees no d— —d Christian."

"Faith, in troth, you're a nice chap," said the Irishman. "I'm thinking the devil has a lease of you, anyway; but troth, you must be a Jew. Ar'nt you, Dutchman?"

"So I bees, and ish as good as you."

"Yiz, faith; but you never heard me grunting as you do, like an old woman with a toothache."

"Yoh, yoh, a tamp nice place mine tooth be, in mine back."

"Och, your back," said the other with contempt, "did you ever know a good sodger to get shot in the back?"

"Och, mine broder bees one fool!" exclaimed the other; at which there was a roar of laughter from the other beds.

Father Brady took advantage of this diversion to give some seasonable advice, which had its effect, not only upon the wordy combatants, but also upon the other patients.

After rendering good services at Vicksburg, and contributing towards its surrender, the 15th Michigan was dispatched, by General Grant, to reinforce the Army of the Cumberland under General Rosecrans. The regiment participated in that arduous march across the States of Alabama, Mississippi, and part of Tennessee, which General Logan's command, and others, had undertaken, in order to hurry to the support of Rosecrans, who was hard-pressed at Chattanooga. On arriving at Huntsville in northern Alabama, General Logan received orders in obedience to which the command rested for some time. As the Catholic inhabitants of the place had not the services of a priest for some time, for Father Trecy, the pastor, and missionary priest of northern Alabama, was serving in Chattanooga as chaplain to General Rosecrans, Father Brady extended his ministrations to the Catholic inhabitants. His offer was coldly received, particularly by the ladies, who seemed far more bitter[3] against the Northerners than the men in the field. Father Brady met this bitter hostility with mildness and firmness. To an Irish lady, who showed her ignorance by refusing to shake hands with a Yankee chaplain, he simply said, "My dear lady, it is not the duty of the chaplain, the minister of Christ, to take part with either side in this unnatural conflict. Out duty is to shrive the penitent and dying, to attend to the sick and wounded, and try and alleviate their sufferings—no matter whether they are Federals or Confederates." She commenced a virulent abuse of the Yanks, but was stopped by the chaplain who simply replied: "Madame; I do not want to argue politics with you; to me it is not a pleasant subject; and it ought to be much less so to a lady, if she has the feelings and instincts of a lady. Pray tell me, have ye a church here?" "No, Sir, Father Trecy commenced one here, but gave it up when the war broke out and is now chaplain to the Yankees." "Where then did Father Trecy celebrate Mass when he was here?" "In the upper part of the Callahan building, which he had temporarily fitted up as a church." Madame was a very bitter rebel, and did not attend Mass, because [it was] celebrated by a Northern priest—thus showing her Christian humility and obedience.

The regiment, accompanied by its chaplain, marched for Chattanooga, where a new and extensive field awaited him, though the Rev. Fathers Trecy, Cooney, Christie, O'Higgins, and Fousettees,[4] were [already] located in and around the town, with their commands, and rendering all the aid in their power. The hospitals were full of sufferers after the battle of Chickamauga and the engagements around Chattanooga. So that the chaplains found unceasing labors, night and day, in ministering to the spiritual and temporal wants of the inmates. Here rather an amusing incident occurred. Father Brady, on entering the hospital one morning, gave his usual salutation of "God bless all here!" "If he does," said one of the men, "I rather guess you'll come in for a fair share; for I never saw a preacher who had not the best furnished table, and come in for more than his share of all the good things." "Shut up!" cried out a sergeant of Minty's Regular Brigade, "shure, he is a priest and no preacher." This doubtful compliment reminds us of the officer; who, being addressed as Mr. soldier, haughty replied—"Sir, I am an officer." "Oh, I beg pardon, Mr. officer and no soldier," replied the other. Father Brady, without heeding the remark, quietly sat beside the cynical invalid and meekly asked him, "Where are you wounded, my friend?" "Under, the arm, sir," replied the other. "I got a bullet-hole there; but it's nothing worth talking of." The father entered into conversation with him and soon learned that he belonged to no religious denomination and had never been baptized. "Be gad!" exclaimed the sergeant, who had quietly listened to the conversation; "he is a pagant; d——l a bit of the grace of God about him. Lord deliver us!" The ardent sergeant was silenced by the priest; but occasionally he showed his contempt for the other's ignorance on religious matters, by a shake of the head and a wink to his companions. Father Brady talked for some time with the other on religious subjects; and so great an impression had his solemn advice and warning upon him and others, that, after a few days, they asked to be received into his Church, to the no small delight of the Pennsylvania sergeant who took upon himself the full credit of having discovered "the pagant." This is only one of the many instances of the good effected by this pious priest in the hospitals of Chattanooga; and many a man living today can date his awakening to the truths of religion, from his impressive discourses and Christian ministrations.

The 15th Michigan followed the fortunes of General Sherman in his grand campaign through the Southern States. Father Brady had been detailed to attend hospital duty in Chattanooga, and, therefore, did not participate in the Atlanta campaign. He again joined the regiment in front of Atlanta, but was again sent back to attend the hospitals in Chattanooga, which affected him sorely, as he had a kind of paternal affection for his own boys, as he called the men of the 15th Michigan.

General Sherman had now cut loose for the sea, and General Thomas had fallen back through Alabama to counteract the movements of General Hood upon Nashville. As General Hood, in his movements, threatened Chattanooga, a considerable force was concentrated there under command of the lamented General Thomas F. Meagher. Between Father Brady's attendance at the hospitals and his ministrations to the troops, he had a busy time of it in Chattanooga; indeed, so overpowering and laborious were his duties, night and day, that his health gave way; and he began to break down rapidly.

After the battle of Nashville, and discomfiture of General Hood's army, Father Brady accompanied the troops detached to Wilmington, North Carolina, to co-operate with Sherman. He rejoined his regiment at Raleigh; and the men were overjoyed to see their faithful chaplain once more. He marched with them from North Carolina to Washington, and had the satisfaction of seeing the gallant remnant of his old Celtic regiment proudly march in review before the president of the nation.[5] The regiment, having fulfilled its mission and earned for itself a high reputation, returned home, and was disbanded in the city of Detroit, Michigan.

Though the good father's health had been failing for some time, the excitement of active, hard duties and the pleasure of being again united with his favorite regiment, had sustained him. The reaction soon proved fatal; for in three days after the disbandment of the men, he sickened, and was removed to the sisters' hospital where he died in eight days afterwards.

Thus had the good priest fought the good fight, and worked untiringly in the vineyard of God, who now rewards, with a crown of everlasting glory, *His good and faithful servant!*

EPILOGUE: Father Brady mustered out with his regiment, then in Little Rock, Arkansas, in August 1865. The regiment returned to Detroit on September 1, 1865. His health quickly failed and he died a short time later on September 9, 1865. His burial place is unknown.

SOURCES: Some letters discussing Father Thomas Brady's ministry in Detroit can be found in the "Archdiocese of Detroit Collection" (CDET) at the University of Notre Dame Archives.

See also Aidan H. Germain, "Catholic Military and Naval Chaplains, 1776–1917" (PhD diss., Catholic University of America, 1929), 59–60; William B. Kurtz, *Excommunicated from the Union: How the Civil War Created a Separate Catholic America* (New York: Fordham University Press, 2016), 73; Margaret Haley Leonard, *History of Saint Patrick's, Seneca Falls, New York, 1831–1979* (Seneca Falls, NY: 1979), 29; "Rev. Thomas Brady," Find A Grave (website), last modified December 27, 2011, https://www.findagrave.com/, memorial ID # 82435751.

CHAPTER XVIII

Rev. William Corby, C.S.C.

Chaplain 88th New York Volunteers

His connection with the Irish Brigade—A rustic chapel in
the field—The service—How faithfully the men attended to
their spiritual duties—The priests as the soldiers' banker and
amanuensis—Father Corby at the battle of Fredericksburg—
The wounded chaplain—The officer's indignation at finding
Father Corby in the front of battle—His failing health—
He resigns and returns to his university in Indiana.

INTRODUCTION: Father William Corby (1833–1897)was
born in Detroit, Michigan, on October 2, 1833. His Irish-born
father made his fortune in real estate, but in 1853 William
chose to study to become a priest at Notre Dame in nearby
northern Indiana. Ordained in 1860, Corby was serving as pastor and helping to run Notre Dame's manual labor school
when the war broke out. Corby was one of seven Holy Cross
priests sent by Father Edward Sorin to serve as Union chaplains during the war.[1] Corby distinguished himself as one of
the small college's most zealous chaplains, serving from the fall
of 1861 through September 1864 when poor health forced him
to retire from his position as the 88th New York Volunteer Infantry's regimental chaplain. Corby said Mass, provided the
sacraments, and helped care for the wounded of the Irish

233

Brigade and other Catholic soldiers of the Union's Army of the Potomac. The brigade's only chaplain at the Battle of Gettysburg (July 1–3, 1863), Corby famously gave a battlefield absolution to his men on the fight's second day. Gettysburg's prominence postwar as the high tide of the Confederacy and the war's turning point helped to make Corby the most famous of all Catholic chaplains on either side of the conflict.

Although more is known about him than practically any other Catholic chaplain in the war thanks to his *Memoirs* published in 1893, Conyngham's chapter is frustratingly vague and short on specific details about Father Corby's service. In fact, the inclusion of a long excerpt from another book[2] praising Catholic chaplains compared to Protestant ones and the general nature of the story relayed in his chapter, which sometimes says as much about other Irish Brigade chaplains if not more than Corby, suggests the chapter was not originally meant to be about Father Corby at all, but about priests in the brigade more generally. Much of the chapter is apparently repurposed from Conyngham's own Irish Brigade book published shortly after the war's conclusion. However, this chapter is still valuable for its description of Catholic worship and the service of priests in the Army of the Potomac.

The Irish Brigade, which was almost entirely composed of Catholics, was indeed fortunate in the good and pious chaplains who accompanied it during the war. The Rev. Thomas J. Mooney was chaplain to Corcoran's 69th until after the battle of Bull Run, and the men of the new brigade found in the Rev. William Corby a worthy successor to him.[3] We know little of Father Corby's early career, except that he is a native of Michigan, but as soon as the war broke out, and when a demand was made for chaplains to accompany the Catholic soldiers to the field, he and several other members of the Congregation of the

Holy Cross, Notre Dame, Indiana, at once responded. The parent house at Indiana sent forth no less than six[4] of these Soldiers of the Cross to attend the sick and wounded and to cheer them by their presence and advice, and to console their last moments by administering to them the sacred rites of their holy religion.

Nothing could give the poor soldier greater pleasure than to find that the priest, who had always been his guide and friend, had even volunteered to partake with him all the hardships, dangers and privations of a soldier's life in time of war. It was to him a great consolation indeed to hear Mass in the rustic chapel, formed of a few tents and green boughs, and to know that even if he fell, he would be fortified by the sacraments and would most likely receive the final absolutions from the Minister of God as his spirit winged its flight to stand in judgment before its maker. A religion of ceremonies and no sacraments can never make such a solemn impression on the mind as one that combines both as the Roman Catholic religion does. On this account, we too often found in the army, that while Catholics paid reverential respect and obedience to their chaplains, soldiers of other denominations, in too many cases, treated theirs with discourtesy and indifference. It is not in any sense the writer's intention to attempt to disparage or undervalue the services of the chaplains of various other denominations, among whom were many truly pious and good men; but it did not tend to improve the morale of the men, nor to impress them with reverence or respect for their chaplains[5] to find, as was often the case, illiterate men, who professed to have a religious calling, stepping from the ranks into all the sanctity and dignity of army chaplains.

General Butler felt this when he said that the chaplains in the army were a nuisance and a pest except the Catholic chaplains, whom he always found attending to their duties, and ministering to the spiritual and temporal wants of the sick, the dying, and the wounded. From a work published in 1864 entitled "Battlefields of the South" written by an English officer[6] in the Confederate service, we take the following account of the services of the chaplains, not to reflect upon anyone, but simply to show the opinion entertained of their respective merits by an English Protestant.

Speaking of the chaplains, he says,[7]

Another class who patriotically rushed to Richmond and obtained salaries to which they were unaccustomed, was a race of
long-jawed, loud-mouthed ranters, termed for courtesy sake,
"ministers of the Gospel." With profound respect for a class
"called of heaven" for the administration of holy offices, I may
be allowed to observe that, taken as a whole, these long-bodied
individuals who were saddled on our regiments simply considered themselves "called" to receive one hundred and twenty
dollars per month, with the rank of captain, and the privilege
of eating good dinners wherever chance or Providence provided—to be terribly valiant in words, and offensively loquacious upon every topic of life, save men's salvation. Where they
all came from, none knew or cared to know, especially as but
little was seen or heard of them, save when some fortunate
"mess" had turkey or chickens, and then, of course, the minister was sure to put in his appearance, and fuss about until
invited to dine. Most of these gentlemen were particularly con-
descending in their small talk, could wink at "trifles" after a
few days' residence, and sometimes betrayed alarming profi-
ciency in handling cards at a social game of poker.

The sermons preached to us were decidedly original. On
one occasion I was almost petrified to hear one of the most
popular of these camp-preachers confess before an audience
of a thousand intelligent beings that "it has never yet been positively known whether Christ came down from heaven to save
the body or the soul of man!" I also remember having heard
such words of wisdom from the lips of some of these worthies
as the following: "It is certain that God is infinite, and therefore he requires some infinite habitation—therefore space is
infinite, and was possibly prior to God." Another quietly remarked to his hearers: "Man cannot fulfil the law—all you
have to do is to believe, trust to God for and in all things, and
as to the rest, you may do as you please." Again another said:
"If I disagree with my brother upon points of religion, it is not
much matter; he may believe in universal salvation; another
denies that Christ was God; one believes in infant baptism,

and another does not; but all these little things are not of much consequence, my brethren; all are trying to get to heaven as best they can, and all no doubt will finally reach there—at least, *we hope so!*"

It is hardly necessary to say that little or no good was effected in the army by these "gospel ministers," (as they termed themselves); their conduct was not as correct as it might be, and they seemed so eaten up with indolence that they were usually considered as bores and drones. They were seldom or never found administering to the sick or dying; service was offered occasionally, but in time of battle or in the hour of anguish at the hospital, they were looked for in vain. Little, however, could be expected from such a class of men. The majority had received calls to retire from blacksmithing or wood-chopping to preach the Gospel, and as they enjoyed but little celebrity or remuneration at home, they patriotically offered their services to the government, and were assigned duty among us. The proof of their "divine vocation" is seen in their subsequent conduct, for when government, in its calmer moments, reduced their salaries, these spiritual heroes for the most part resigned, alleging as reasons that eighty dollars per month and rations was insufficient *remuneration!*

Nevertheless, truth compels me to add, by way of exception to this general condemnation, that many good and true men were to be found, who, by their upright conduct, self-denial, and zeal, counterbalanced much of the evil here adverted to. Among others who were distinguished for their correct deportment, persevering industry, unaffected piety, restless activity, and sound moral instruction, I would mention the Episcopalians and Roman Catholic priests. The latter, especially, were remarkably zealous; their services were conducted every morning in tents set apart for the purpose; and on Sunday large crowds of the more Southern soldiery were regular in their attendance and devout in their behavior; and I have not unfrequently seen General Beauregard and other officers kneeling with scores of privates at the Holy Communion

238 THE FEDERAL CHAPLAINS

Table. Such an instance occurred on the morning of Manassas, and I could not help remarking it, as I rode past in the twilight on that eventful occasion.

The Jesuits were perfect soldiers in their demeanor; ever at the head of a column in the advance, ever the last in a retreat; and on the battlefield a black cassock, in a bending posture, would always betray the disciple of Loyola, ministering to the wounded or dying. No hospital could be found wherein was not a pale-faced, meek, and untiring man of this order. Soldierly in their education and bearing, they are ready for anything—to preach, prescribe for the sick, or offer a wise suggestion on military or social affairs. It is to the foresight and judgment of one of them that Beauregard and Johnston escaped death or capture at Manassas, for had they not met one of these missionaries during the heat of the conflict, and heeded his modest advice, one or other of these calamities must have inevitably ensued.

While the Irish Brigade lay encamped around Washington, previous to the Peninsula Campaign, the duties of the chaplains were pleasant enough, and consisted merely in celebrating Mass, hearing confessions and writing letters, for such of the men as were unable to write themselves, to their families. The chaplain was kept busy enough when the paymaster came round, for then he became the soldiers' adviser and banker. They consulted with him as to how much of their pay they should send home, and in all cases strictly followed the priest's advice. Being entrusted with remittances to the amount of several thousand dollars, the chaplain proceeded to Washington to forward it according to instructions. It is a fact that during the war hundreds of thousands of dollars were entrusted to the Catholic chaplains for remittances, and yet, we believe there is not a single instance on record, where a dollar of all this was either misappropriated or lost.

The Irish Brigade spent its first Christmas day in Camp California, near Alexandria. Though the officers and men enjoyed the holidays in as jovial and festive a manner as if they were in New York, they did not forget their religious duties, and commenced the day's celebrations by attending the Midnight Mass in camp. It may strike our readers as absurd to keep up this solemn ceremony of the Catholic Church in the tented field where there was no stately temple, nor cathedral dome to cover the pious worshippers.

But had they seen the rustic chapel that the piety of the Irish soldier raised to the worship of God, they would change their opinion. The chapel was a really picturesque structure in itself. A dense cluster of pine and cedar trees was selected for the site. The brush in the center was cleared away for the body of the house, many of the large trees were left standing, so that their thick foliage would answer as a roof and their trunks as pillars to support the huge branches that were piled overhead for a covering. A stockade, or wall of cedars, formed the sides of the house, while a large tent at the end answered for altar and priest.

Such was our chapel and though not a stately or grand one, there was something more solemnly simple and imposing in that Midnight Mass celebration under the shade of those old forest trees, than if it were the stateliest edifice ever raised by the hand of man to the worship of God. The Mass was celebrated by the three chaplains of the brigade, namely Fathers Corby, Willett, and Dillon, and as their voices rose in psalmody and hymn, and as the prostrate worshippers humbly bowed their heads in response and muttered their silent prayers, there was something wildly grand in the ceremony. The glare of the candles suspended from the trees, the flickering, feeble light barely making the gloom of the night visible, the sigh of the wind and the gentle pattering of the falling snow and sleet, the surpliced priests, the soft tinkling of the bell, and the low responses of the attendants and pious worshippers, all combined to add a solemn sanctity to the celebration that we have never experienced inside the walls of the most stately edifice. It reminded us of stories we had read about the white-robed Druids who collected their followers to join in midnight worship under the shade of some mighty oak trees.

Father Dillon read the beautiful gospel from Saint Luke, giving an account of the journeying of Mary and Joseph, and the birth of the infant Savior in the manger at Bethlehem, after which he delivered a short and telling address to his hearers, who, at the conclusion of the ceremony quietly retired to their tents.

Such was Christmas morning, 1861, in the camp of the Irish Brigade, and thus did these fearless soldiers of the sword bow in pious submission to the teaching of the cross, and in honor of this holy festival, which is leaden with the richest freight of human blessings and happy recollections. This first Christmas day in camp was spent pleasantly enough. The men and officers crowded into hospitable tents; the materials for toasting old friends and loved ones, absent but not forgotten, were plenty, and, in song and jest and story "Auld Lang Syne" was not forgotten, and the day and night were spent as happy and as merrily as they possibly could be under such circumstances.

The Irish Brigade formed a portion of the army corps commanded by General [Edwin V.] Sumner, an accomplished veteran of more than forty years' military experience. Their first experience of real service in the tented field was in the spring of 1862 when, after General McClellan taking command of the army of the Potomac, a reconnaissance took place towards Centreville and Manassas in order to develop the enemy's strength and position. The enemy fell back across the Rappahannock so that no engagement more serious than mere skirmishing took place. During this movement the chaplains of the brigade, in a very impressive ceremony, placed their regiment under the special protection of the Blessed Virgin and Saint Patrick.

The brigade took a prominent part in the Peninsula campaign, in its fighting as well as in all the hardships of the marches by night and day, and in the horrors of the retreat from before Richmond. While the army lay in front of Yorktown the brigade had provided itself with comfortable quarters and the men made an effort to celebrate May day, according to Catholic[8] custom, by decorating the rustic chapel in the most gorgeous manner with the wild flowers that grew in such luxuriance, even at that early period, and by attending divine service. The chaplains were kept busy for the confessional was crowded by pious worshippers—men who felt that for many of them this would be their last confession, for all the symptoms indicated that a bloody and fierce campaign was inaugurated.

The few days' rest the men enjoyed here were spent to good advantage making their peace with God, writing letters and sending little souvenirs to loved ones at home. While the brigade was encamped on

Tyler's farm the officers got up a race, which came off on the 31st of May, just the day on which the battle of Fair Oaks commenced. The amusement was broken up by an order to march in quick time for the battlefield. As the conflict was a fierce one, and as the brigade suffered severely in it, the chaplains soon found their hands full, and all their time was taken up in administering the [rites] of the church to the sick and wounded and oftentimes too, in acting the Good Samaritan in attending to the temporal wants of some poor fellow. While the brigade was lying in front of Richmond it was honored by a visit from General Prim and also by being specially complemented by General McClellan for its conduct at the battle of Fair Oaks.

After the battle of Gaines' Mill, in which the brigade gallantly participated, the army commenced to retreat toward Malvern Hill. This retreat was attended with all the worst horrors of war. The dying and wounded were neglected and abandoned. Brave men seemed to have lost all sympathy for their fellow creatures and to be solely absorbed in trying to secure their own safety. Perhaps, the doctors and Catholic chaplains were the only persons who did not forget their missions of charity, peace and love. Many of them refused to leave the sick and wounded but remained with them until captured by the enemy. We have seen the chaplains take on some poor wounded fellows, who had been left abandoned, behind them on their horses.

When the army commenced falling back to the James River, over one thousand wounded men were at Savage Station, and when these poor fellows found that they were to be abandoned to their fate, it had a terrible effect on them. Some of them, pale and emaciated, rose from their beds and hobbled on crutches after the retreating troops—poor fellows! They soon fell faint and wearied by the way side, but most of them were kindly cared for by the enemy. The sight of that long line of ambulances crowded with wounded men, and of these ghostly looking creatures hobbling after them, was heart-rending in the extreme.

The brigade suffered severely at Savage Station and White Oak, but it lost more men and officers at the battle of Malvern Hill, than during the other seven days fighting together. The sick and wounded were so numerous here that the chaplains found little time for recreation or even to take the necessary sleep or refreshments.[9]

Fathers Scully and Willett, who had remained to cheer and console the abandoned sick and wounded at Savage Station until captured by the Confederates, were kindly treated by the latter and were allowed to return to their command while encamped at Malvern Hill.

While among the Confederates an officer remarked to Father Scully, not knowing who he was, "What a fine lot of yanks we have got today!" On finding out his mistake he at once apologized in the most polite manner.

While the troops lay encamped at Malvern Hill, previous to their evacuation of the Peninsula, the men of the Irish Brigade, with their usual attention to religious matter, constructed a cozy rustic chapel in which Mass was daily celebrated and to[10] which the men from several other commands continually flocked. The paymaster too had come round, and the survivors of the campaign kept the chaplains busy remitting money to their friends and also in writing to the families of those killed in battle.

Between their duties of celebrating Mass, hearing confessions, visiting the sick and wounded, and writing letters, the chaplains were kept busy and had very little time to themselves. Even many of the men who could write themselves would not be satisfied unless the priest wrote, for they would say: "Shure, your reverence they will think a good deal more of the letter at home if you'd write it!" There was no resisting this and the kind good natured priest would sit down and write it for him.

While the brigade was encamped at Malvern Hill, General Meagher returned to New York to recruit its ranks. After the evacuation of the Peninsula, the brigade was sent to support General [John] Pope,[11] whose army of the Virginia was threatened with wholesale destruction by Lee and [Stonewall] Jackson.[12] The brigade was hastily marched about from place to place; so irregular and uncertain were the movements of Pope's demoralized army that no sooner did it reach Aquia Creek, than it was sent to Fredericksburg, thence to Alexandria, thence to Fairfax[13] and Bull Run. Things looked as if the movement was altogether without a head, and the troops [were] completely demoralized.

All this time our chaplains were kept continually on the march, and when the troops halted at night, instead of being allowed to snatch a few hurried hours of repose, they had to hear the confessions of some scrupulous poor fellows, who did not wish to go into battle the following day with their conscience burdened even with the most trivial sins.

When Washington was threatened and McClellan restored to command, the advance of the army to meet Lee, who was marching into Maryland and Pennsylvania, was rapid, so that the chaplains had just as hard a time of it as any officer or soldier.

The brigade suffered fearfully at Antietam, and the duties of the chaplains of its various regiments were proportionally severe. After the retreat of Lee, the brigade was encamped on Bolivar Heights. The country around was beautiful. The camp itself had a most lovely and picturesque appearance. There the Potomac and Shenandoah rivers formed a junction, while in front extended a panoramic view of surpassing grandeur. The Blue Ridge Mountains rose in front in all their majestic grandeur, while in the distance extended the rich Shenandoah Valley, the garden of Virginia.

In this lovely region, surrounded by all that could delight the imagination—a delightful country with unrivalled scenery, a sky of Italian Blue—the men soon forgot all their losses and hardships and began to enjoy themselves as only Irishmen know how.

The battle of Fredericksburg was perhaps the most disastrous one of the war to the soldiers of the Irish Brigade, and at the same time the most glorious for their military reputation and renown. The mad charge on Mary[e]'s Heights was never surpassed in fierce bravery and reckless daring nor in the wholesale slaughter of the assailants. Fully two-thirds of the officers and men of the Irish Brigade lay dead or dying on that bloody field on that cold winter's night. The cold snow of December fell silently on the battle field. Thousands lay along the valley and hill side extending from the town, to the enemy's entrenchments, whose oozing wounds were frozen and whose limbs were suffering by the sharp frost.

Masses of dead and dying were huddled together, some convulsed in the last death agonies, others—delirious—writhing in torture—gasping for water—tried to shelter themselves behind the dead bodies of their comrades. Cries, groans and shrieks arose from that battle field like the fearful wails of lost souls. No one could or dare relieve them, for the enemy ruthlessly continued to sweep that field with artillery, long after all opposition had ceased.

Some of the Catholic chaplains ventured forth armed only with their stoles upon their necks, and canteens of whiskey and water. They had to move cautiously and display no lights so as not to attract the attention of the enemy. In this way they saved many a poor penitent in the solemn silence of the night and cooled their parched lips.

But their mission was not without its danger for we are informed that while so engaged Father Corby received two bullets through his clothes from the fire of the enemy, while another Catholic chaplain received an ugly wound from a dying soldier who, mistaking him for one of those ghosts who prowl over battle fields to rob the dead, fired at him.

After the battle of Fredericksburg the brigade encamped near Falmouth, where it remained for the winter. There the men erected a pretty rustic chapel, where they attended service and where the chaplains celebrated Mass, heard confessions, and attended to the general wants of the men of their regiments. I recollect often seeing at early morning a crowd of men outside the priest's tent waiting to go to confession, and in the afternoon another crowd, some sending home money to their friends, others waiting to have him, "Just write a letter home."

In May 1863 the battle of Chancellorsville was fought and the brigade as usual took a prominent part in it. Nothing of unusual interest took place. A little incident occurred though which gives a good idea of the dangers incurred by the Catholic chaplains.

An officer going into battle gave his purse to Father Corby to keep it safe for him. While engaged he met the priest at the front preparing a dying man. The officer halted, looked at the chaplain and exclaimed, "Father Corby what brings you here?"

"My duty, Captain!"

"Well, Father, hand out my purse, it is safer with me than with you!"[14]

About this time General Meagher left the brigade. At Gettysburg it took an active part in the fierce assault made by the 2nd Corps. Before going into the desperate conflict the remnant of the brigade reverentially knelt down while Father Corby piously raised his hands over them and bestowed his benediction upon them. The scene was solemn and imposing and forcibly impressed the other commands with the piety of the Irish Catholic soldier.

In January 1864 the brigade returned to New York to be recruited. Father Corby accompanied his regiment, the 88th, and while the regiment was recruiting he paid a visit to the University of Notre Dame, where he was joyfully received. We next find the Irish Brigade partly recruited, serving under General Grant in the Wilderness and Spotsylvania, where they suffered severely. The Corcoran Legion also suffered heavy casualties in the above engagement. It is needless to follow the brigade through the various battles in which it participated. The chaplains were kept busy all the time attending to the sick and wounded and preparing them for death. Father Corby scarcely got a rest during the restless movements of the army. In fact, so zealous was he in the discharge of his duties and in his attendance, that his health rapidly failed and he was compelled to resign, which he did in the month of September 1864 to the great sorrow and regret of the remnant of the Irish Brigade.

He returned to his monastery in Indiana, and is at present superior of the Mission House at Watertown, Wisconsin.[15]

EPILOGUE: A combination of poor health and Sorin's request for him to return to South Bend led Corby to resign his commission in September 1864. Corby returned to Notre Dame and became the school's third president in 1866. After next serving as president of Sacred Heart College in Watertown, Wisconsin, from 1872 to 1877, he returned again to Notre Dame and again served as its president from 1877 to 1881. In 1886, he became the Congregation of Holy Cross's Provincial General for the United States. Late in his life, he dedicated himself to recording his wartime memories in *Memoirs of Chaplain Life* (1893), joining various veteran organizations including the GAR, and collecting Civil War flags, swords, and other items for a proposed military museum at Notre Dame. He died on December 28, 1897, and was buried with the ceremonies of the GAR and the Catholic Church.

SOURCES: Although very few letters exist from his time as a Civil War chaplain, Corby's service record and papers related to his priesthood can be found in Notre Dame, Indiana, at the Congregation of Holy Cross United States Province Archives Center and at the University of Notre Dame Archives. William Corby, C.S.C., *Memoirs of Chaplain Life: Three Years with the Irish Brigade in the Army of the Potomac* (Notre Dame, IN: "Scholastic" Press, 1893; reprinted and edited by Lawrence Frederick Kohl, New York: Fordham University Press, 1992), ix–xxv; Edward Sorin, C.S.C., *The Chronicles of Notre Dame du Lac*, ed. James T. Connelly (Notre Dame, IN: University of Notre Dame Press, 1992), 276–91.

See also David Power Conyngham, *The Irish Brigade and its Campaigns*, ed. Lawrence Frederick Kohl (New York: William McSorley, 1867; reprint, New York: Fordham University Press, 1994); Arthur J. Hope, C.S.C., *Notre Dame: One Hundred Years* (Notre Dame, IN: University of Notre Dame Press, 1943), 123–43; James M. Schmidt, *Notre Dame and the Civil War: Marching Onward to Victory* (Charleston, SC: The History Press, 2010), 39–40, 55–56, 74–77, 100–101, 111–17, 127–30.

THE CONFEDERATE CHAPLAINS

CHAPTER XIX

Rev. Louis-Hippolyte Gache, S.J.

Chaplain 10th Louisiana Volunteers

---

*His services in and around Richmond—He attends the Federal
prisoners—At the desire of Bishop Odin he joins the army
as chaplain of the 10th Louisiana—He visits the camps on the
Peninsula—His forbearance, meekness, and kindness subdue
his enemies—A grateful penitent—Father Gache's account of scenes
around Richmond—Interesting incidents and anecdotes—A soldier
anxious to be baptized in the "Sisters' religion"—His account of the
treatment of the Federal prisoners in Richmond and Lynchburg.*

INTRODUCTION: Father Louis-Hippolyte Gache, S.J.
(1817–1907),[1] served as chaplain to the 10th Louisiana Volunteer Regiment. He was born in Beaulieu near Ardèche in
France. He attended Jesuit-staffed schools before entering the
Lyons Province of the Society of Jesus on September 8, 1840.
He prepared for the priesthood at the Jesuit theologate in Vals,
France, where he was ordained on March 28, 1846. As the Jesuits of Lyons had been asked to assume responsibility for various ministries in the southern United States, it was decided
that the newly ordained Father Gache should be sent there.
Gache and five others left France on October 27, 1846, arriving
in the South in January 1847. He served first as prefect of studies at St. Charles College, Grand Coteau, Louisiana, for a year

before being assigned to Spring Hill College near Mobile, Alabama. Except for serving two years at Saints Peter and Paul College in Baton Rouge, Louisiana (1850–1852), he ministered in various capacities at Spring Hill from 1849 to 1861. With the outbreak of war, Gache agreed to an appointment as chaplain to the 10th Louisiana in July 1861. Gache remained with the regiment until August 1862 when he began serving as a chaplain to patients at military hospitals in Lynchburg, Danville, and Richmond, Virginia. Gache was effusive in his praise for Catholic sister nurses and the good work they did to heal the body and dispel prejudices among Protestant soldiers.

According to a deleted manuscript page, Gache sent Conyngham an overview of his services in June 1869. Conyngham used this account, as well as some of Gache's wartime correspondence, as the basis for this chapter. Fortunately for historians, seventeen surviving Civil War letters of Father Gache were translated from their original French and published.[2]

The Rev. Father Gache is a Frenchman by birth and was a most zealous and devoted attendant on the sick and wounded of the Confederate army in and around Richmond during the war. He also administered to the Federals' sick and wounded in prison and hospital and has had a trying and varied experience in the discharge of his duties as chaplain. He is at present pastor of the Church of the Holy Trinity, Georgetown. I am sorry that my sketch of him is not fuller, but from the limited notes and information I have received I could not make it more general.

On the 26th of July 1861, Father Gache, at the desire of his bishop, the Most Rev. Dr. Odin[3] of New Orleans, Louisiana, accepted a commission as chaplain in the Confederate service and was sent immediately with his regiment, the 10th Louisiana, to Richmond, Virginia. From Richmond the regiment was ordered to the Peninsula and was stationed near Williamsburg waiting the approach of McClellan. There he remained until the retreat from Williamsburg, which took place in April 1862. During this period his ministry was not very fruitful; however, he was able to keep the men alive to the sense of their religious duties and heard confessions, administered the sacraments, and celebrated Mass in the humble little chapel improvised for the purpose. The regiment was made up of men of all nationalities, comprising Americans, Irish, French, Germans, English and even Spaniards, Italians, and Greeks; the majority of whom were Catholics.[4] Father Gache, finding his services too restricted, got permission from General [John B.] Magruder[5] to visit all the camps of the Peninsula. He was then the only chaplain with the army,[6] and as there were several Catholics in all the regiments, he thought he could be of more service with a roving commission than of being tied down to one particular regiment. He next visited the different hospitals in Yorktown, Williamsburg and elsewhere. This visit was very welcome to the Catholic patients and he cheered many by his consoling words and by administering to them the sacraments. The poor fellows were glad to see him and to make their confessions and to use his own words—"for many that confession was a passport to heaven as they died soon after without having another chance of seeing a priest."

At first he found too many Protestants ready to mock and jeer at him, but after a time they learned to treat him with respect. In fact, his forbearance, meekness and kindness to all induced many of them to become converts, for it often happened that those that came to mock his ministry, knelt and prayed. I will give one interesting instance of this. One day Father Gache was visiting the Louisiana hospital, in Richmond, which was under the care of the good Sisters of Charity. One of the sisters said to Father Gache: "Father, you have a convert here who will be delighted to see you." "Why, Sister," replied the priest, "I was not aware that I had a convert here." She then told him that a young man had been sent there, very sick, a few months before. Some time after his arrival, he said to the sister in charge of his ward, "Sister, I would like very much to see Father Gache; could you send for him?" "Are you a Catholic?" asked the sister. "No, but I will tell you, I belong to the 10th Louisiana Regiment; and when I was sick on the Peninsula he used to come to see me very often. I was at first rather rude to him, but he did not abate his attention to me. His manner, forbearance and goodness have made such an impression on me, that I am convinced that his religion must be the true one; therefore, I'd like to see him to beg his pardon, and to be received into his Church." As Father Gache was not in Richmond then he consented to be baptized by another priest, but on his return there, he was overjoyed to see him. This young man became a good practical Catholic. He was a fine looking young man and had attracted Father Gache's attention by his general learning so superior to that of his comrades and he did all he could to make him as comfortable as circumstances would permit.

Father Gache devoted more of his time to ministering to the soldiers in the field than to those in hospital. He was always well received both by the officers and men. A large number of Catholics and even several Protestants availed themselves of his ministrations among them. The Catholics, from being indifferent, became zealous and attended Mass and went to confession regularly. Men exposed to all the dangers and vicissitudes of battle, must naturally turn their attention to God. Death is continually staring them in the face and the most hardened feels that they are liable every moment to be hurled into the presence of their Creator.

At first, those who attended their duties, were laughed and sneered at as cowards by their comrades; but when they found that these men were the bravest in action, a better feeling prevailed. He found himself unable to meet the demand for his spiritual services during and after a battle, for the hundreds of Catholics, that lay wounded, eagerly called on him to administer to them the last rites of the Church.

Under such circumstances he did the best he could, and by increasing labors, he was able to console the last moments of many a brave fellow. The very presence of a priest was an encouragement to them and reminded them of their duties. During the Seven Days fight around Richmond he was taxed to the utmost for both in the field and in the hospitals there was constant demand for his services. How often, after shriving poor penitents under the enemies' shot, had he to hurry to the field hospital in answer to the call of some dying soldier.

A young South Carolinian Protestant once said to him, "Father, you don't know me?" "No indeed." "Well, I thought so; but I know you, for during the Seven Days battle I have often watched you, on your black horse, riding from line to line attending to the wounded, cheering and consoling them. Do you know, Father, you made such an impression on me that I was often tempted to call on you and at least ask your blessing and benediction, but false pride prevented me, though I admired and revered you none the less." Oftentimes, while riding through the lines, soldiers would step forward, crying, "Father, we have no time to make confession, will you give us your blessing?"

From a private letter from Father Gache to a friend, I take the following extracts:

> *Speaking of the battle of Richmond, I had occasion to render a great service to a poor man of a Connecticut regiment who had fallen mortally wounded at Savage Station. He was left with many others on the battlefield, his breast and right arm were shattered by a piece of shell, and he was in such condition that I cannot understand how he was alive. I asked him if he was a Catholic. "No," he said, "but my wife and children are Catholics." "And you, would you not like to be a Catholic?" "Yes." "Well, if you wish to become a Catholic you have no time to lose, for you are very badly wounded, and I am afraid you will not live much longer. Have you ever been baptized?" "No, Sir, my parents were Baptist, they did not care to have me baptized when I was a child. And I never joined any church myself." "Therefore you wish to be baptized now." "Yes." "Very well, I will procure you that favor." Having ascertained by some questions put to him, that he was sufficiently interested, I baptized him with the water of his canteen. No doubt he lived a short time after, for he was very low, and his wound bleeding very much. But my duty would not allow me to stay any longer with him, and I never heard anything about him afterwards. I have thought very often of his poor widow and children, and I would have been very glad to be able to inform them of the blessing which Almighty God conferred upon him, perhaps in consideration of their prayers. That poor man was an Irishman by birth, but he had come very young to this country.*

I have said that the presence of a priest in the army was an encouragement to the soldiers; sometimes also it restrained them from evil. The next day after the fight of Malvern Hill, while riding from one camp to another, I saw a man, an Irishman too, who had alighted from his horse to go in to a garden and steal some cabbages. Just as he was getting over the fence, he saw me coming at some distance. Immediately he jumped out of the garden, and he came to me with a ten dollar note in his hand, saying: "Father, I want to give you this; you have prevented me from committing a sin. I was going to steal cabbages, when I saw you, and your presence made me overcome the temptation." I knew that the old dear man used to drink too much sometimes also, and in order to preserve him from the other sin, I took his note which I gave to St. Joseph's Orphan Asylum, Richmond, under the care of Sr. Blanche,[7] now in Washington City.

But it was in the hospitals that the largest amount of good was done. I was in charge of several military posts successively, and I had to take care of many hospitals during the last two years of the war. Of all the sick soldiers with whom I came in contact, and who died while I was with them, I remember only three who refused the service of my ministry at their last moments, and they were all free masons. All did not actually become Catholics, for a good number of them were, avoiding to all appearances, Protestants in good faith, too, but they listened with pleasure and attention to all my little exhortations; they requested with fervor all the acts and prayers which I recited for them such as the Lord's prayer, the Hail Mary, the Apostles Creed, the acts of faith, hope, charity and contrition. The larger number however had become Catholics and received, at least, the sacrament of baptism. But it was in the hospitals entrusted to the Sisters of Charity, or to the Sisters of Mercy,[8] that the most good was chiefly done, and it is to the influence of those good sisters that it was due. In fact, no body except those who have seen it, can imagine how efficient was the presence and the conduct of the sisters to soften those rough nature[s], and to cheer and console them during their attendance at the hospitals of Danville, Lynchburg, and Richmond, Virginia.[9]

A young Tennessee soldier, who knew very little about religion, and who had probably never attended any place of worship, was one day brought into a hospital under the charge of the Sisters of Mercy in Montgomery, White Sulphur Springs, Virginia. The sisters received him with their usual kindness and bestowed upon him all the attentions his condition required. While one of them was dressing his wound, he burst into tears. "Did I hurt you?" she asked.

"No, no," he replied.

"Then, why do you cry?"

"I cry," said the poor boy, "because for the last six months I have not had a kind word spoken to me."

Thus we see the salutary effects of kind attention and edifying behavior on the human mind. The kindness, meekness, and devotion of the sisters removed the prejudices of many and disposed them to become Catholics merely because it was the religion of the sisters. Father Gache, on one occasion, found a soldier very sick; according to custom he asked him if he were baptized and if he was aware that without baptism he could not be saved.

He said that he had never attended religious duties, but that he had heard that baptism was necessary to salvation and would therefore wish to be baptized. "I am a Catholic priest," replied the Father Gache; "Do you wish to be baptized in the Catholic Church?"

"Oh, no," he replied, "I don't want to be a Catholic."

"In what church then do you want to be baptized?"

"In the church of the sisters," was the immediate reply.

"But, my dear friend, the church of the sisters is the Catholic Church."

"Is that so?"

"Certainly, ask the sisters themselves."

Just then the sister in charge of the ward happened to pass by and turning to her he asked, "Sister, is it true that you are a Roman Catholic?"

"Most certainly!" she replied; "If I was not a Catholic, I would not be a Sister of Charity."

"I declare," said the young man, "I thought the Catholics were the worst people in the world. I never heard anybody speak well of them." This was enough to convince him. He was baptized soon after, and he died the following night. Once the brother of a Baptist preacher was in the hospital. As soon as it was evident that he would not live, the sister who nursed him, asked him if he would like to be baptized and become a Christian; she knew that he had never been baptized. He answered "Yes." As the Rev. brother had come to see him, and was present, the sister asked him if he wished to be baptized by his brother, or by her chaplain, that is by Father Gache. He answered that he preferred to be baptized by a priest. And he was. And I must say that his brother did not seem to be the least bit displeased at it.

But the greater good perhaps effected by the presence of the Catholic chaplains and Sisters of Charity or Mercy in the army, was the removal of sectarian prejudices from the minds of thousands who had never seen Catholics before, and knew nothing of them, but what they had heard from Protestant preachers, or read in Protestant books. The change effected in that respect among the Southern people is so great and so striking that it has been re-marked by everybody. Let me give some instances of it. One evening Father Gache was going from Lynchburg to Richmond, with a young lady who had become a Catholic under his direction, and who had requested him to take her to Richmond to be confirmed by Bishop [John] McGill. They were on the rail road cars and were talking in a tone of voice loud enough to be heard by their neighbors. The young lady asked Father Gache a number of questions on religion, which he tried to solve the best manner he could. After two or three hours of talking, they stopped to indulge in a little sleeping. Their neighbors, who seemed to have taken much interest in the conversation,[10] to which they had listened with attention without making a remark, but as soon as the priest and his companion appeared to be asleep, they commenced talking among themselves and to make their comments upon their conversation.

"Who are they?" asked one of his companions. "I really don't know, but then I am sure she is the gentleman's daughter for she called him Father," was the reply of another. "It is evident from their conversation that they are Catholics for they are all the time speaking of the Catholic Church as their Church and the true one," remarked another. "Well," said a weather beaten man with the learning of a veteran soldier, "I'm dog gone but I think they are right, before the war I was strongly prejudiced against Catholics. I looked upon them as little better than infidels and heathens; but since I have changed my opinion.

"During the war there were several Catholics in my regiment, and I had an opportunity of studying them and I must say, that I have found them more sincere and honest and affectionate to their families than those of any other denomination. Just think how the Sisters of Charity attended the poor fellows in hospitals. I tell you boys, but for them I would not be alive today. When laid up with wounds in hospital they cared [for] me as kindly as my own wife or sister would, and never asked what religion I belonged to. I ask, Could they do all the good they have done? Could they be what they are if their church was not the true church?"

"I agree with you," said another veteran, "I too have been in hospital and the kindness and attention of the sisters have made such an impression on me that I intend bringing up my family Catholic, for if there is any good in religion at all, it is in theirs."

From some private letters written by Father Gache and placed in the author's hand, I make the following extract in evidence of the efficiency of the sisters and the respect intended for them by the soldiers, Protestants as well as Catholics.[11]

I will tell you another instance of the efficiency of the Sisters of Charity in removing sectarian prejudices and favorably disposing men towards Catholicity. During the first year of the war, two or three sick soldiers belonging to a Company of Texans, were brought to the infirmary of St. Francis de Sales, in Richmond, which was under the care of the Sisters of Charity; Sister Juliana Chatard[12] being the superior. Those poor fellows had never seen any Catholic institution, and knew nothing of Catholicity, except the ridiculous charges brought against them by Protestants, found themselves in quite a new world. But, however strange things seemed to them, they soon discovered that everything was right and that it was good for them to be there. After a few weeks they returned to their command in good health, and so much pleased with everything they had seen at the infirmary that they determined to send to the same place every member of their company who would get sick. So they did, but in a short time, the applications came so numerous that [the] good sisters were unable to accommodate all the applicants. Seeing this, those brave Texans requested Sister Juliana to allow them to put up in her yard, at their expense, a temporary frame building exclusively for themselves. The request was granted, and as long as the Texan regiment remained within reach of Richmond, all its patients were sent there. It is needless to speak of their satisfaction or their admiration for the sisters. All I wish to say is this: One night some Texans were on picket duty on the Chic[k]ahominy, and while some were on guard, the others were making coffee, and as they were not commanded to silence, they were talking at the same time on different topics. The subject of religion was brought up and they commenced to abuse Catholics. One of the men on guard, hearing this, exclaimed, "Stop, stop, friends! I do not know what Catholics are. I know nothing of their creed, but from the time I have seen the Sisters of Charity, at St. Francis de Sales infirmary and been nursed by them, I have felt myself bound in duty not to allow anyone to speak against them or their religion. So I beg of you not to abuse the sisters or their church."[13]

Father Gache, writing of the treatment of the Federal prisoners, says:

I was in attendance on them as chaplain both in Lynchburg and Richmond. In both cases every faculty was afforded me by the Confederate officials to visit them and attend to their spiritual wants, and also to their temporal [needs] when I had it in my power to so do.

In Lynchburg a large number died from the effects of their wounds and all the Catholics, and even some Protestants, who desired my ministrations, were attended by me. That many suffered from the want of sufficient food and raiment I don't deny, but not one bit more than the Confederate sick and wounded. They were treated alike in hospital and it was not in the power of the Confederate authorities to do better for them. The army was short of clothing and provisions, in fact, on short rations; the hospitals and prisons were full of the sick, wounded, and prisoners of the Federal Army, and, under the circumstances, it was impossible to provide better for them. I do not enter into the right or wrong of the matter or whose fault it was that there was not an exchange of prisoners. I merely give a statement of things as they were. Out of many instances, coming under my own observations, of the kindness of Confederate soldiers toward their captured or wounded enemies, I will merely cite one.

Three days after the raid of General [David] Hunter,[14] Sister Rose,[15] the Superior of the hospitals in Lynchburg, informed me that she had just heard that a Federal soldier lay out in the woods wounded, and asked if there was a possibility of sending men to bring him in if alive. Two men were immediately dispatched to look for the poor fellow. It was then about six o'clock in the evening and about nine they returned with him. He was so exhausted from loss of blood and exposure that I saw he would not live through the night.

He was a Catholic and an Irishman, and after his wounds were dressed and cleaned, I prepared him for death. I can never forget the joy of the poor fellow at receiving the last rites of his church, and being attended by the sisters and a Catholic priest. He died soon after, but what a consolation that the poor fellow had not perished alone in the woods. The prisons of the South were not well cared [for] in a sanitary point of view and this told very much on the Federal prisoners. I had occasion to observe this particularly after the Battle of the Wilderness; but after a time, when the Federals found that the Confederates fared no better, they became reconciled to their lot, and bore their trials and sufferings more cheerfully.

I can never forget how my presence and consoling words seemed to cheer them, how warmly they shook hands with me and how humbly and gratefully they received my ministrations.

A young man from New York, after having made his confession and received communion, said, "Father, I am rich, after the war come to New York; you will see what a beautiful church I will build for you." I am sorry that I did not write down his name and direction.

In Richmond things were not quite as comfortable as in Lynchburg. The hospitals were more crowded, the regulations about them were more strict, though priests were always allowed to visit them; the accommodations not so good. The prisoners were less satisfied, and indeed numbers complained. I remember, once I met a poor Irishman, [who was] pretty sick. I asked him if he would not like to perform his religious duty (it was at Easter time). He answered in a rather rough manner: "No, Sir." "But, my dear friend," I said, "you are not aware that by neglecting your Easter duty, you commit a grievous sin." "Well, if I go to hell, I will not be much worse off than here," was the reply. "Oh, my dear, what do you say?" I replied. "Was there no other difference between this place and hell, but that of duration, it would be a dreadful one. I advise you not make the trial, you would be badly disappointed." The next day when I visited the same man, I thought that the best way to bring the poor man to a sense of his duty, would be not to notice him. I visited all the other patients around him, spoke to them, but did not say a word to him, nor even look at him. What I had anticipated really happened.[16]

The third day, when going my rounds, I did not mind him as usual. He sent the nurse to me to request that I would visit him as he desired to speak to me. I went to him and said, "Well, my friend, I am told you wish to speak to me. What's the matter?" "Pardon me, Father," he said, "for my rudeness to you the other day. Our privations here make us unreasonable." "I can understand that, my friend," I replied, "and make all allowances for it."

"Father," he said, after a pause, "you were right, though this place is bad, hell is a thousand times worse, and as one cannot know what may happen, I wish to make my confession." He made it and I was glad to hear that he was exchanged the following day.

A great deal of the privations and sufferings of the Federal prisoners was owing to the carelessness, negligence, and incapacity of the prison officials and nurses. As to the charges against the Confederate government in not providing them with better provisions and clothing, I again assert that they could not help it, for they were reduced to the last extremity themselves.

Their army was suffering from the want of supplies and there were so many thousands of Federal soldiers both in the prisons and hospitals that it overtaxed their already stinted means.

Had the Federal government regularly exchanged prisoners with the Confederate, much of this forced, but unnatural, cruelty might have been avoided.[17]

EPILOGUE: Following the war, Father Gache did not return to the Deep South but served in various ministry settings in Baltimore, Washington, DC, Philadelphia, and Worcester, Massachusetts, among others. His final assignment was as confessor to the Jesuit novices at St. Andrew-on-the-Hudson Seminary in upstate New York. He died on October 8, 1907, at age ninety near Montreal, Canada, at Longue-Pointe Sanitarium (St. Jean de Dieu Hospital).

SOURCES: Cornelius M. Buckley, ed., *A Frenchman, A Chaplain, A Rebel: The War Letters of Pere Louis-Hippolyte Gache, S.J.* (Chicago: Loyola University Press, 1981).

Rev. Charles P. Heuzé

*His mission in Vicksburg—The account of the siege and of
the suffering and hardships accompanying it—The horrors
at Vicksburg surpassing those at Sebastapol—A shell among the
worshippers at Mass—Heart rending scenes in the field and
hospitals—Sad picture of want and suffering.*

INTRODUCTION: Father Charles Heuzé (1833–1883) ministered to soldiers during the war but was not an officially appointed chaplain. Born in northwest France in the town of
Chelun, near Rennes, he studied for the priesthood first at the
minor seminary in Saint-Méen and then at the major seminary in Rennes. During his studies he sensed a call to become
a missionary in the United States. He was accepted by Bishop
William H. Elder of Natchez, Mississippi, who ordained him
in December 1860. He was assigned to St. Paul's Church in
Vicksburg, Mississippi, to assist the pastor, Father Francis
Xavier Leray. During the war both Heuzé and Leray ministered
to the soldiers in their vicinity. Related here is Heuzé's experience of the siege of Vicksburg from a letter he wrote to a friend
in February 1864.

❀   ❀   ❀

This gentleman was not a regularly appointed chaplain, but was pastor
of St. Paul's, Vicksburg. The following letter, bearing date February 7th,

1864, [and] giving a graphic account of the siege, was written by him to a friend, who has placed it in my hands for publication.

> An experienced pen could have written volumes on the subject that would have teemed with thrilling interest, as the French would say; and I can safely say that there is not a man in any city throughout this vast Republic, who has seen and suffered what we have. Sevastapol[1] itself could not have surpassed Vicksburg in horrors. There is not a priest throughout the North and South who has ever been in the situation of your friend, nor do I say this in the spirit of boastfulness. God has protected us and I fear we are not sufficiently thankful for his goodness.
>
> For forty-eight days was the city continually bombarded. I only speak of the last bombardment conducted by five iron-clads, mounting ten guns each five inches in diameter: seven mortars, thirteen inches bore; besides fifty siege guns, varying in bore from six to ten inches; at least 200 field pieces of all dimensions, such were the instruments of destruction. A hundred and twenty infantry regiments, among whom were many regiments of riflemen always on the alert with rifles carrying from a mile to a mile and a half. We were in the center of a circle of about a mile or a mile and a half in diameter.
>
> The bombs were continually passing over our heads and falling everywhere around us. The rifle balls also played an agreeable accompaniment to the discordant music of the Federals.[2] More than seven hundred cannons, sometimes playing altogether, may give some idea of the fabulous number of shells thrown at the old capital of Vicksburg. If it had been a city built on the European style, it would have been razed to the ground, but the houses being far apart did not suffer as much as they otherwise would have done. Visitors are surprised to see Vicksburg still the same city. I celebrate Mass every day—Sunday not excepted. The bell can be heard in the distance;[3] and soon a shell comes crashing through the church in the midst of the Mass.
>
> The disturbance frightens us a little but that's all. In the space of three hours three bombs passed through the church, and three

dropped in our little garden. The Sunday following,[4] a bomb pierced the door of the church and took off the arms of an old man, and another[5] passed through the window and struck before the altar of the Blessed Virgin. This good mother protected us. The splinters fell all around our people—at the side of women praying before the altar of Mary, but not an atom touches one of them.

People fly to the church. The same day another bomb comes towards the church. Too much to the left by near a foot. The house gets it all. We were four of us sitting together and not one of us wounded. The shell passed between my legs, cut the rungs of a chair, and a soldier, who was sitting on it at the time, suffered no injury whatever. The chair is now a relic.

The other evening I was eating a supper that had come from a restaurant when a shell, piercing the corner of the house, passed before me at the table, saluting me.[6] Well I think you would have done as I did. Of course I did not abandon my supper. Oh, no! It was too precious for that, especially as I had a mule steak dressed in oil and onions. For a whole week I didn't get anything else from the butcher, but mule steak. I discovered this on the second day and could not eat any more.

The meat is really delicious, which is all I can say for beef. The hard crackers and molasses were considered a fortune. We were gay and contented without being indifferent. But the poor soldiers! Their share was four ounces of bread a day!

Nine shells through the church have finished the work. It is still in the same condition.

I administered the holy Viaticum and Sacred Unction to a dying man in a rifle pit and while so doing two shells entered[7] and on returning two bullets flew by me, and three or four rifle balls whistled around my ears. I hastened my steps—a ball struck in front of me. A shell[8] fell some paces in front of me and turned up the earth and filled me with dust—That is all!

I was waiting on two officers while the two legs of one and the thigh of the other were being amputated. It was near the battle field. The shells respected us. Ah! my friend, do not think me romancing; no! It would take volumes to relate the horrors of that siege. But the worst terrible horror I ever saw happened in the case of a Louisianan.

His name was Hébert of Iberville, Louisiana, a young creole, and nephew of General Hébert.[9] Poor friend! The same shell that wounded seven of his comrades cut him in two just below the hips–how terrible! His legs and thighs were left on the battle field and the rest of his mutilated body was carried to the hospital. I arrived. Eight doctors and more than fifty persons were anxiously present.[10] The boy was stretched on a table. The blood flowed out almost in waves. The doctors declared it impossible to arrest it; all the arteries being broken. The flesh fell off in shreds and all the entrails were laid open. His first words were in Creole: "My Father, O, my father I am dying—I am passing away from all these anxious ones!" He then confessed with all the ardor and sincerity possible believing in his approaching death. Five minutes elapsed and he became as pale as death. I gave him absolution and administered Extreme Unction when he cried out, "Father I die, may God have pity on me! Jesus pardon me." I then commenced the prayers that follow Extreme Unction—He was no more. The last drop of his blood was spilt in remission of his sins as he himself publicly remarked before his death.

Three brothers, Babineau[11] of the Lafayette parish died here with all the rites of religion. Such examples may be cited by hundreds.

On going out to attend to young Hébert, I gave the holy Viaticum to two dying persons, attacked by the gangrene after amputation. In the case of one, the mortification went to the heart, and his breast became as black as a negro's. Poor friend! He was stretched out like a worm.

Consider now for a moment, without counting the dead during the siege, when the city surrendered we had 6,000 wounded or sick, many of them Catholics of Louisiana, and also those in the three or four large hospitals before the capture, and all this the result of 18 months. We have seen, alas! too much, I never wish you the same.[12]

It was terrible, dear friend, nothing but death, sorrow and desolation on all sides. War is a terrible scourge. We have had our share of it. May God pardon and pity us if we have sinned for we have suffered fearfully.

Yours etc.

Charles P. Heuzé[13]

❀   ❀   ❀

EPILOGUE: After the war, Father Heuzé left Vicksburg for New Orleans where he decided to enter the Society of Mary (Marists). After returning to France, he took his religious vows on April 29, 1866. He served briefly as a professor at the Catholic University preparatory school in Dublin, Ireland, and then served in parish ministry at the church of St. Anne in London, England. In 1869 he was called to Sydney, Australia, to help staff St. Patrick's Church. He would become the church's pastor, serving from 1874 until his death in 1883.

SOURCE: "Nécrologie: Le R. P. Charles Heuzé, S.M.," in *Les Missions Catholiques* 15 (January–December 1883) (Lyon: Bureaux des Missions Catholiques, 1883), 575.

CHAPTER XXI

Rev. James Sheeran, C.Ss.R.

Chapter 14th Louisiana Volunteers

His regiment joins Ewell's Corps—His reception—First appearances in Virginia battles—Stonewall Jackson—A night scene on a battle field—Jackson's marches—Sufferings and hardships of army life— Father Hubert—At Manassas—The Second battle of Bull Run— Scenes and incidents in Frederick City—How the Fathers of the Society of Jesus and the sisters acted—The battle of Antietam and its horrors.

INTRODUCTION: Father James Sheeran, C.Ss.R. (1817– 1881), was born in Temple Mehill (Templemichael), County Longford, Ireland. He likely immigrated to Canada at the age of twelve and then to New York City. He married his wife Margaret in 1842 and they had three children—Isabella, John, and Sylvester. Sylvester died young and Isabella and John eventually were boarded at Catholic institutions in Michigan and Pennsylvania. By 1845 the family moved to Monroe, Michigan, where Sheeran taught in a boys' school staffed by the Congregation of the Most Holy Redeemer (Redemptorists). After Margaret died, he joined the Redemptorists in 1855 and was ordained a priest in 1858. He was first assigned to the Redemptorist formation house in Cumberland, Maryland, and then to St. Alphonsus Church in New Orleans, Louisiana. In a short time, he became a Southerner in conviction if not by birth. When the war began he volunteered as a chaplain to the Confederate forces and was officially attached to the 14th Louisiana Volunteers beginning on October 2, 1861.

Related here is a greatly condensed version of Sheeran's wartime diary, which describes the events of his wartime ministry between August 1, 1862, and April 24, 1865. The five manuscript chapters contain numerous deletions and emendations as Conyngham tried to pare down Sheeran's detailed descriptions of camp life and battle to only the most interesting details. We have noted only a few of these changes, particularly in cases where he erased Sheeran's criticism of Protestants, Yankees, or his own men. Had Conyngham published his work before his death, it would have been the only publicly available version of the diary and thus a tremendously valuable addition to his larger work. The full diary consists of 1,656 manuscript pages and was recently published in its entirety. [1]

When the first tocsin of war sounded throughout the land, the 14th Louisiana volunteered for the front, and the Rev. James Sheeran of the Redemptorists accompanied them as their chaplain. The 14th participated in the first battle of Bull Run and almost[2] all the succeeding battles, which marked the deadly strife between North and the South. Up to the time of General Butler's entering New Orleans, the Revd. Father Sheeran transmitted to the Journals, then published in that city, a full account of the respective battles as each was fought and a general synopsis of all the incidents attendant on army life, occurring among the Confederate soldiers either while in the camp or on the march. But from the time General Butler got possession of New Orleans, no communications coming through a Confederate source were allowed publication, and from that time we will follow the father through his life of army adventure until General Lee surrendered.

Scarcely had the 14th Louisiana recovered from the fatigues of the terrible battles around Richmond, which were fought in July 1862, than it, along with the 5th Louisiana, was transferred to [Richard S.] Ewell's[3] division, then encamped near Gordonsville. On the 1st day of August the train conveying the transports left Richmond and on the following day reached Gordonsville. The two regiments immediately marched to where the 6th, 7th, and 8th Louisiana regiments were encamped, and with whom they were then brigaded. On arriving at the camp Father Sheeran, accompanied by Colonel [Zebulon] York,[4] Major [David] Zable,[5] and Dr. [Isaac] White,[6] reported to General Ewell who received them very courteously and at the same time introduced them to several prominent Confederate officers present, among them was General [Isaac R.] Trimble.[7] After the formality of an introduction had been gone through with, General Ewell expressed much pleasure in having a Catholic chaplain in his division and suggested that Father Sheeran's orderly should be mounted in order to give more effectual aid in time of an engagement.

When Father Sheeran was leaving Richmond he felt a little indisposed, and the want of rest in the cars caused from the crowding and suffocation, and the exposure to the dews of the night air the first night in camp aggravated his illness seriously. For a day or two all was quiet, and the good father having somewhat recovered heard a large number of confessions and celebrated Mass each morning. On the evening of the 6th, the brigade was ordered to Liberty Bridge, on the 7th crossed it, and on the 8th came up with some of the Federal cavalry and had a skirmish. Shortly after the skirmish, General [Stonewall] Jackson came riding along having crossed the Rapidan at the ford near a mill which had just been gutted by the Federal troops, and its contents thrown into the river. This was the first time Father Sheeran ever saw him and such was his plain attire that had the priest not been informed as to who he was, he would never have taken him for a commissioned officer. About an hour after the General's passing, the report of artillery was heard, and shortly after the news of a further retreat of the enemy. That evening Ewell crossed the Robinson River and encamped that night on a beautiful farm on the banks of that lovely stream. At 8 o'clock next morning orders were given to march instantly to Cedar Creek or

Mountain. The day was oppressively warm and as the march was very rapid, many of the soldiers got broken down and some were even sunstruck. At twelve o'clock the advance came in view of the Federal cavalry drawn up in line of battle on the north side of the creek, there was then a halt of two hours, during which time Jackson was engaged in surveying the position of the enemy. About 2 P.M. he commenced to place his men in line of battle and at 3 P.M. the deadly struggle began. It lasted until after dark and ended by the Federal troops retreating three miles from their first line of battle.

After the wounded of the division were brought to the hospital and properly cared for, Dr. White and Father Sheeran resolved to ride over the battle field to see if there were any overlooked. The moon was full and it seemed to envelope the noble dead with its softest and most refulgent light. Passing down from Cedar Mountain to the rich bottom lands beneath, nothing attracted their attention until they came to a cornfield through which runs the now celebrated stream after which this battle was called; here both killed and wounded lay all around. The father spoke kindly to the wounded and told them to have patience till daylight and he would have them cared for. One of them who expressed deep gratitude for this kindness attracted the attention of both priest and doctor, and they kindly inquired his name and nature of wound. The name he gave was Pat Sullivan[8] and the latter he told them was a fractured thigh from a musket ball. After the father remained some time attending to the religious comforts of the wounded men, he joined the doctor and then sought a hurried repose, having for his bed a grassy meadow, for his pillow a fence rail, and for covering the blue of heaven.

When he awoke in the morning the army was in motion, and the Federal artillery was commencing to shell part of the Confederate lines. Father Sheeran spent the whole afternoon of that day among the wounded attending to their spiritual welfare. On Monday, August 11th, Jackson fell back to Camp Wheat, the 14th Louisiana bringing up the rear. The 12th was a day of rest, but on the 13th a court of enquiry was held as a precursor to a court martial on all absentees from the late battle. On that afternoon Father Sheeran visited the camp of the 1st Louisiana and dined with Colonel [Michael] Nolan[9] and the Rev. Fa-

ther Hubert.[10] Returning that evening he visited the regiments composing the Louisiana Brigade and exhorted them to make use of the rest
they were then enjoying to attend to their religious duties. August 14th
Father Sheeran celebrated Mass in camp at which he had several communicants. He also delivered a short instruction which had the effect
of bringing numbers to confession. On Friday August 15th Mass was at
an early hour and there was a large congregation and many communicants. From the large number which attended Mass, Father Sheeran
cherished a hope that if a few days' rest were given he would have an
opportunity of preparing all the Catholic soldiers of the brigade to
which he was attached to meet their God. But these fond hopes were
not permitted to be realized for on the following morning orders were
given to prepare two days' rations and be ready to march at daylight.
The order was promptly obeyed. At Orange Court House, some fifteen
miles distant, they halted and encamped for the night.

The following morning it was expected that the march would be
pursued and an early breakfast was prepared. Father Sheeran, expecting
every moment to get the route, made no preparation to say Mass although the day was Sunday. About 2 P.M. word reached him that two
Virginian soldiers were about to be shot for desertion. Hastening to the
place of execution he found them surrounded by a crowd of soldiers
and accompanied by two Protestant chaplains. Inquiring of one of the
chaplains if either was a Catholic, Father Sheeran was informed in the
negative but was told that he might speak to the culprits. After a short
conversation with them he found that neither were baptized, but from
the necessary points of the doctrine explained to them by the father,
both expressed a willingness that they should [be baptized].[11]

On Monday August 20th, one of Stonewall's most famous marches
commenced. After wending his way some distance through the mountains he crossed the Rapidan at Sommerville, then crossed Cedar
Creek, then Dutch Creek, and passed through Stopperville to Mountain Creek, where there he encamped for the night. Next morning the
route was taken up and at eight o'clock the following morning Jackson
arrived at the Rappahannock. The Federal soldiers were in force and
occupied strong positions on the opposite bank; Jackson continued his
march along the Rappahannock. After a forced march of some ten

miles some of the men felt tired, and began to fall out of the ranks. It was not long before a large number of stragglers were all around. Father Sheeran who expected some work to do shortly waited the arrival of the Doctor and the ambulance corps. While doing so a cry was raised that "the Yanks were coming."

Finding that the alarm was too true and that a body of Federal troops were advancing on that spot. The enemy was advancing very cautiously through the woods, preparing to give their foe a sudden and warm attack, but General Trimble with his whole brigade anticipated their intent and received them with a hot fire.

After the enemy's retreat, [and] after riding some hours Father Sheeran overtook the doctor who had charge of the Mess Wagon. This was rather agreeable for the priest, as he had not broken his fast that day. After a dinner of corn bread and cheese taken on horseback, he pushed on at a rapid rate until he overtook his regiment resting by a road side. The march was resumed until a small ford crossing the Rappahannock was reached. Here Ewell crossed two of his brigades and retired to a wood not far distant and encamped. That night the soldiers had to sleep in pools of water and dry themselves next morning at the camp fires, Father Sheeran sharing the fate of the rest. For two days the men were without rations and were almost savage with hunger. Whilst a battery of artillery was occupying the attention of the Federal soldiers at Warrenton[12] bridge, General [J. E. B.] Stuart[13] made a raid into the heart of the enemy's camp and captured some of General Pope's private baggage and papers.

Jackson's corps resumed its march up the river unobserved by the enemy, and encamped for the night some two miles above a little town called Jefferson. The march was resumed next morning at daylight. The next morning the march was resumed for some fifteen miles to the town of Haymarket and here rested for some three hours. The march was resumed and at 5 o'clock the army arrived at where the Centreville and Manassas pikes join the Warrenton [turnpike]. Turning by a narrow path the army moved at a double quick for some distance after which the Louisiana brigade was moved to the front and then detached with Jackson at its head and went in a smart run to Bristoe[14] Station where it destroyed five trains bringing reserves and baggage to Pope.

The next morning General Ewell with the Louisiana Brigade and a few batteries were left at Bristoe Station to keep the enemy in check (for Jackson was then between Pope's Grand Army and Washington). Father Sheeran visited General Ewell that morning and conversed with him on many subjects. During the conversation the General bestowed some high encomiums on the Catholic soldiers composing the Louisiana Brigade. While General Ewell was at Bristoe, Jackson advanced to Manassas with his old division and that of A. P. Hill[15] and took possession of the commissary stores and other supplies at the station.

During the day Father Sheeran went among all the men he possibly could reach exhorting them to go prepare themselves to meet their God. Word was received that the Federal troops were advancing in force and orders were given to retreat on Manassas. On arriving there it was evident what Jackson's intention was in visiting the place. The sacking of the stores by Jackson's hungry and naked men was a scene that beggars description. The army became a perfect confused mob, and some of the officers believed that it would almost take a week to reorganize it again. However, they were agreeably surprised to find that when the order to fall in was given it was obeyed and carried out with the utmost promptness.

It was near sunset by this time and Father Sheeran felt anxious to learn the whereabouts of his regiment. For some time he watched the moving columns, hoping to get a glimpse of the riddled battle flag of the 14th, but without success. Whilst thus looking on, he received many a warm salutation from the 1st Louisiana brigade commanded by Colonel Nolan. Walking along with his regiment was the good Father Hubert. On seeing him Father Sheeran alighted and after a warm shake hands both retired for a few moments and settled their spiritual affairs as best they could.

Having been informed where his brigade was encamped, Father Sheeran rode over to it and found the men busily engaged cooking supper. Colonel York being the first he met made him dismount and partake of a splendid repast. After burning up all the stores which they could not carry off with them as well as the trains already loaded with commissaries, the Confederate Army started for Centreville, which place was reached shortly after sunrise the following morning.

The overwhelming force of General Pope was now threatening to fall on Jackson's seemingly doomed corps then scattered over the heights of Centreville, but the latter made a flank movement, got behind Pope and took up a position on the left flank of the enemy and disputed the position until after dark. It was here that General Ewell received the wound which necessitated the amputation of his leg.

Father Sheeran was informed that his regiment had been cut up in the battle. His first impulse was to go to the front. He mounted his horse and started for the scene of strife. In crossing Bull Run, the morning being dark, he saw something which he could not discern paddling in the water. Stopping to ascertain what it might be, he was surprised to learn that it was Father Hubert washing himself. He had been up all night at an adjacent hospital, and was covered with blood and dirt.

On reaching the field of strife Father Sheeran was agreeably surprised to find his regiment in good spirits and eating a hearty breakfast. They were not engaged the night before. All were glad to see the father but not more so than he was to see them. He breakfasted with Colonel York. A short time after breakfast and while conversing with the colonel a movement was perceptible along the lines. It was then hinted by the major that he, Father Sheeran, was in a hot place and should better retire. The latter felt no alarm, but rode over the battle field in front of the lines in order to see if he could recognize any of the dead or wounded. He was at that time in a dangerous position being only three quarters of a mile distant from the Federal lines. Soon however he rode up to one of the batteries in order to speak a few words of encouragement. As he did so a shell passed directly over his head burst some hundred yards in advance. Turning round he saw the Federal troops had a battery placed in position on an opposite hill from which they immediately sent another missile. He now looked upon a change of base as the most prudent strategy and with a speed [surpassing][16] even many of Stonewall's flank movements, he filed to the right and made for a wood some yards distant.

During that day until late in the afternoon, the battle waged rather hot for General Jackson and his men. At about 4 P.M. Longstreet formed a junction, and that evening and next day, a terrible battle raged. During each day and night of battle Father Sheeran was almost incessantly in attendance upon the wounded and did all in his power for them both spiritually and temporally. The great battle of the Second Manassas or Bull Run was now fought, and the hospitals were filled in every direction with the wounded of both sides. On Sunday, August 31st, the day following the last one of carnage, Father Sheeran felt inclined to rest, but was unable to do so as orders were given to remove all the wounded who could possibly bear the change to Aldie and Middlebury. This removal occupied nearly all the day, and [during] the part of it not taken so, the father devoted [himself] to visiting several hospitals and preparing some of the Catholic fellow soldiers for death. That night after a weary toil of three days and nights, he sought a needful repose under the shelter of a house not far distant from the scene of strife.

The next morning Father Sheeran visited the battle field in order to see if all the wounded Confederate soldiers were taken off, or if any of the enemy needed his services. The Confederate soldiers removed numbers of the wounded enemy to adjacent farm houses. These men were in a deplorable condition for want of food, drink, or medical assistance. Father Sheeran did whatever he could for them in every respect. He met with some Catholics and endeavored to prepare them to meet their God. Returning back to his quarters that evening Father Sheeran was informed that another battle was fought at Chantilly and started next morning. About 2 P.M. he reached Chantilly, sought out his regiment and heard from it the account of the battle. It was here General Phil Kearney was killed. Having ascertained where the dead and wounded were, the father had the former buried and the latter removed to hospitals. He spent the night, up to a late hour, ministering to their spiritual wants, and washing and dressing the wounds of those not yet forwarded to hospitals. On this occasion a Protestant gentleman went around among the wounded in order to discover who were Catholics so that he could tell Father Sheeran so that they might make peace with God. Having all the wounded cared for, Father Sheeran, accompanied by this gentleman, started about 10 o'clock for the hospital. As the night was dark and not knowing the way they lost the route, and seeing a light in the distance advanced towards it. On reaching it they

278 THE CONFEDERATE CHAPLAINS

found it to proceed from a house. Entering they prevailed on the proprietor to let them spread their blankets on the floor where they slept heartily all night. The next morning at daylight they started for the hospital. On reaching it they found only a few seriously wounded. Major [William] Monaghan[17] and Captain O'Connor were among the slightly wounded.

Having heard that the army was in motion in the direction of Blue Ridge he started off after it. Reaching the army Father Sheeran learned that his regiment was in advance and pressed forward in order to overtake it, and in passing along the columns received many kinds of salutations from numerous members of different regiments. A little before dark he came up with the old 14th Louisiana, whom he found encamped for the night near the town of Dranesville.[18] Friday morning, September 4th, 1862, the army moved toward the Potomac by way of Leesburg, crossed Nolan's ford next day, and went in double quick in the direction of Frederick City.

The following day about noon the army encamped within a few miles of Frederick City, and Father Sheeran, after refreshing himself at a farmhouse, resolved to visit Frederick City before going to camp. By some accident he lost his orderly and had to pursue his journey alone. As this road was often traversed by him before, during his college days, the contrast between both periods caused him many sad reflections. The first thing that occupied his attention after entering Frederick was the old barrack, then occupied as a hospital by the Federal soldiers. On riding into the yard he met with one of the Sisters of Charity[19] who had charge of the hospital. He dismounted in order to speak to her, but was surprised to find her very much embarrassed. He was, however, not long in discovering the cause, as he had on a Confederate uniform and several Federal officers and surgeons watched him from the gallery of the barracks. The poor sister feared that she might be accused of giving information to the enemy, or showing sympathy for the rebels. Perceiving this, Father Sheeran mounted his horse and left.

His next object was to find a Catholic Church. In riding through the streets he was kindly saluted by many of the citizens. He met also many acquaintances from various divisions of the army, all of whom showed him marked respect. The Louisiana boys came to him to know if he stood in need of anything but in fact the poor priest stood in need of everything, for he had not seen any of his baggage for three weeks, and a clean shirt, if nothing else, would be a boon. Entering a Jew's clothing store with some of the boys they supplied him with a white shirt, handkerchiefs, and other useful articles. When the proprietor discovered that he was a priest he invited him into a room and furnished him with water, soap, and towel wherewith he cleaned himself and then donned his newly purchased apparel. He then repaired to the house of the Jesuit fathers by whom he was kindly received. Here he had the pleasure of meeting Father Hubert for the first time in some days. He was, like himself, disguised in Confederate mud. They were soon introduced into the bathhouse whence they returned much cleansed, if not better looking. The good fathers made them change their clothes and then repair to the refectory where they did ample justice to all the good things with which the table was laden. In the meantime, Father Sheeran's horse had been taken to the stable and he was informed that he could return to camp that night. The next day being Sunday Father Sheeran had the consolation of offering up the holy sacrifice of the Mass for the first time in three weeks.

The next day was a gala day in the city. Ladies from the surrounding country came in to see the Southern soldiers and the latter crowded the city and showed off their equestrian skills before the ladies. The good Father [James A.] Ward, Master of the Novices, was busy as possible waiting on the poor soldiers and giving them refreshments. Father Sheeran had the pleasure of meeting here the Very Rev. Father [Provincial] of S.J. and the Rev. Father Maguire of Washington, who requested him to procure a passport for their return to Baltimore.[20] In company with the Rev. Father Maguire, he then visited the convent of the visitation, a splendid building directly opposite the novitiate. Here he found that numbers of soldiers had also refreshments.

When Father Sheeran was returning to the novitiate he met Father Ward with a dozen canteens strung around his neck, and said to him; "What on earth are you doing with all the canteens?" "Well," replied Father Ward, "when I was out on the street I met some of your boys inquiring for molasses to buy, and I thought them to be so jaded looking I took their canteens from them to fill them in my cellar."

Father Sheeran visited Generals Jackson and Lee on business and then returned to camp. Two days after viz. on Wednesday September 10th the army was again on the route and passed through Frederick and Middleton, and at four miles beyond the latter place encamped for the night. The next morning at 4 o'clock[21] the march was resumed by way of the junction of the Willlamsport and Hagerstown pike and Beaver Creek to Antietam. Here he met with an old lady who was a singular specimen of inquisitiveness. Among a host of questions which she asked she wanted to know had the priest a family? "Yes mam," was the reply, "and a large one too." "Ah indeed, and how many children have you?" "When I am at home I have over a thousand." "A thousand children!" she exclaimed at the same time surveying him from head to foot.

During the march that evening the army passed by a splendid mansion adjoining an extensive plantation owned by a gentleman named McGary.[22] This gentleman had a very interesting family of three accomplished daughters. As Jackson and his staff were passing by, some person informed the young ladies that there was old Stonewall. They immediately dispatched a messenger after the general and staff, requesting their presence on urgent business. Jackson obeyed the summons and old Mrs. McGary received him with true Irish hospitality. The ladies apologized for calling him back and two of them kept him in conversation whilst the third was making his coat-tail minus his buttons. Father Sheeran was invited to stay overnight, which invitation was accepted. After hearing the confessions of all the family, Father Sheeran retired to rest and next morning was off after the army, whom he overtook at [Hedgesville][23] in full march to Martinsburg. Father Sheeran visited Dr. [Thomas] Becker,[24] the Catholic pastor of the place, and was received kindly by him. He also met Father Hubert there. About noon next day, September 13th, the army arrived in view of Harpers Ferry and after part of three days' skirmishing that town was in the hands of the Confederates.

Father Sheeran now took a ride around to see were his services needed anywhere. In so doing he visited a cemetery where several Federal soldiers were burying their dead. Many of these men were Catholics and the poor fellows were greatly rejoiced when they found that Father Sheeran was a priest. Several were of the 12th New York and were very eager to have a chat with the priest and all paid great attention to his remarks. After spending about an hour with the prisoners, Father Sheeran returned to Harpers Ferry and repaired to the house of Dr. [Michael A.] Costello,[25] the Catholic pastor of the place, who treated him very kindly and asked him to remain as his guest as long as the army remained in Harpers Ferry. Dr. Costello introduced him to many Catholic families in the place, all of whom treated him kindly. He also showed him John Brown's monument and many other places of note. After dark the same evening, Father Sheeran visited General [Dixon S.] Miles who was wounded during the siege and found him unable to speak; on a third visit he was dead. About eight o'clock that night Dr. Costello and Father Sheeran visited General [A. P.] Hill in order to procure a pass for the former. General Hill was very kind and informed them that he would do anything in his powers for them. On the afternoon of the 16th the army moved towards Shepherdstown and crossed the Potomac.

The next morning Father Sheeran followed and arrived at the "Bluffs" of the Potomac near Shepherdstown, from which the bloody battle of Sharpsburg or Antietam was visible. He then repaired to the town to see after the wounded and started for the battle field. It being dark and having no one to show him the road, he returned to the town where he attended to both the spiritual and temporal wants of the wounded. Early in the morning he visited the field of battle and repaired to the temporary hospitals. The first visited was that of the 2nd Louisiana Brigade. Here Father Hubert was attending to the spiritual and physical wants of his many wounded children. Colonel Nolan, Captain [Patrick R.] O'Rorke,[26] and other officers of the first Louisiana were among them. Father Sheeran next visited the hospital of the brigade to which his regiment belonged, and found only a few of the members of the latter mortally wounded. The other regiments of the brigade however did not fare so well, and Father Sheeran worked hard all day in helping the Catholic portion of them to meet their God. During the night the wounded were being removed to Shepherdstown and the last batch but seventeen had gone when about midnight some stray cavalry called at the hospital and told them that the army was in motion across the river.

CHAPTER XXII

Rev. James Sheeran, C.Ss.R., Continued

Father Sheeran falls back with Lee's Army—His visit to Richmond—His return to the army—Gambling in the army—A surprise—His services in Winchester—En route to Fredericksburg—Caught in a snow storm—The battle of Fredericksburg—Scenes and sufferings in the field and hospital—A generous donation—A day of fasting and prayer—Easter days in camp—The piety of the poor soldiers—The slaughter pen of the Irish Brigade.

When Father Sheeran and the surgeons in attendance had heard that the Confederate army was falling back from Antietam they held a council of war and concluded to leave the two surgeons and a sufficient number of nurses to take care of the wounded and to leave the rest to follow the army. In the dead of the night they started off across fields and byways and finally reached the rear of the grand army before daylight. On the way Father Sheeran attended to the wounded who were still in the ambulances, consoling them, some spiritually and more physically. At Shepherdstown he met Colonel Nolan and Father Hubert at the house of a Mr. Shephard. Next morning, Sunday September 21st, Father Sheeran had the consolation of offering up the holy sacrifice of the Mass for the second time in five weeks, and he also on that day aided the pastor by hearing some confessions and performing other sacred duties.

On the following day Father Sheeran reached camp near Martinsburg and was there informed that the army would have time to rest for a few days. Believing such to be the case he resolved to take a trip to the Rapidan Station in search of his vestments and altar furniture left there by the quartermaster. That afternoon he was introduced to a General Hays who was then in command of the 1st Louisiana Brigade. Having business to Richmond he got a pass from the general and a limited leave of absence. That afternoon he returned to Martinsburg and spent the night with Dr. Becker. He heard confessions and said Mass next morning, and then started for Winchester. There he met Colonel Nolan, Majors Monaghan and [James] Nelligan,[1] Captain O'Rorke, and Major Zable, and found his orderly whom he lost some days before. The next morning he started for the Rapidan attended by his orderly. On the way they put up at the house of a gentleman named McCormick,[2] with whom they had dinner. After dinner they had some conversation during the course of which he requested Father Sheeran's creed and McCormick who was a Seven[th] Day Baptist[3] was astonished to find that his guest was a Catholic priest. He instantly retired and after a few minutes entered the room accompanied by his wife and daughter. They both were rather loquacious and instantly introduced religious subjects, but they got enough of the religious topic before an half hour passed, and for once they had formed a rather favorable impression of the Catholic faith. He next started for Paris, where he spent the night; there he met some of the wounded men of his regiment who appeared rejoiced to have to inform him that some of the invalided put to flight a whole regiment of Federal cavalry the night previous on the suburbs of the town. These brave fellows too were countrymen of his own.

The next day he reached Middleburg, visited the hospitals and prepared several Catholic soldiers for their long homes. That afternoon he started for Warrenton which he reached after dark and put up at the house of a Catholic gentleman named Pine. Here he met Father Smulders and Mrs. and Miss Semmes, the mother and sister of the Senator.[4] During the evening he was introduced to Dr. Fisher, who had charge of the hospital at Lynchburg. The next morning he started for Richmond where he arrived the same evening. After remaining in Richmond ten days he returned again to the army.

After two days' journey, by circuitous routes, he reached Front Royal on October 9th where he remained for the night. The next morning he visited General Trimble who was under the care of a surgeon at a private house. The general was glad to see him, [and] held a lengthy conversation with him. After wishing the general a good bye, he started for Winchester where he spent the night with Colonel Zable who was yet suffering from his wounds. Here he met with Captain Mitchel of the 1st Virginia and son of the Irish patriot John Mitchel.[5] Next morning, after breakfast, he started for his brigade which was stationed at Bunker[6] Hill, some twelve miles from Winchester. When he arrived there he found that his regiment had been transferred from the 1st to the 2nd Louisiana Brigades. The 1st Louisiana being now in his brigade, Father Sheeran took up his quarters with Colonel Nolan as there was no accommodation in his own regiment. The two following mornings he said Mass, and, notwithstanding the unfavorable weather, had a very large congregation. In the evening of the latter day on October 14th, Father Sheeran visited Winchester and received many pressing invitations from the Catholics to give them an opportunity of performing their religious duties. As he had promised the Marylanders of the brigade to be with them on the following day he could not grant this request. That evening he returned to camp and the next morning rose early, heard many confessions, celebrated Mass, gave Communion to those prepared, and delivered a short discourse to quite a large congregation. On the 16th Father Sheeran celebrated Mass in camp and heard numerous confessions. He visited Dr. Becker at Martinsburg, who pressed him to remain all night. The following morning he aided the Rev. Dr. in hearing confessions and said Mass. He then returned to camp. On the way he met General Stuart, who saluted him kindly smiling at the same time, remembering no doubt that he was once his prisoner by mistake. Early the following morning, marching orders were received and the army moved back through Martinsburg in the direction of Williamsport and encamped some two miles from the town.

After Mass on the morning of the 28th, the orderly informed him that Jackson's whole corps was in motion and that their divisions were moving to Berryville. It was late in the afternoon before Father Sheeran overtook his brigade. The army passed through Smithfield, crossed Harpers Ferry and Winchester railroad, advanced on the Berryville pike some three miles, where they encamped for the night in the woods. Here they remained until November 3rd when the army began to fall back. After a weary march, having no tent of his own, he spent that night with Colonel Nolan. The following day the army covered 7 miles in the direction of Winchester and encamped that night in an oak forest. Father Sheeran spent the night with a poor Catholic family about half a mile from the camp. Hearing that there were other Catholics living some three miles distant he sent them word that he would say Mass and hear confessions the next morning. The orderly brought back the news that Father Smulders was over in that neighborhood. This was the first Father Sheeran had heard of him since he left Warrenton.

Mass was celebrated every morning at which there were many communicants. The morning of the 9th of [November][7] marching orders were received, [but] in an hour afterwards were countermanded. The soldiers seeing that they were about to have the day to themselves they intended to spend it in their usual game of cards. Knowing that Father Sheeran had prohibited this vice in the camp, they usually retired to concealed places for the purpose of carrying on the games. This afternoon, knowing that he was absent, they played publicly and in some cases for stakes of 150 dollars. Anxious to know how things were going on he visited the camp late in the afternoon and saw a number of the boys surrounding some object that seemed to attract their attention. Unobserved he advanced to the crowd and looking over some of their shoulders beheld two of them with cards in their hands and countenances very serious. Between them was a pile of bills. By this time he was observed by all around but not by the card players who were too much engrossed in their stake to notice anything else. Slowly he bent forward until within reach of the money when by a well-directed grasp he secured some $60 of the stakes. The gamblers not knowing who was there made a very rough exclamation, but finding out who it was, took to their heels amid the shouts and laughter of the whole camp. This money he afterwards gave to the orphans of St. Joseph's in Richmond.

On the 10th the army got the route and on the 11th the division passed through Winchester in the direction of Bunker Hill. On the 12th Father Sheeran followed it, fearing that his services might be needed and overtook the brigade some eight miles below the town. As it was wet and cold and having no tent in camp he resolved to take up his quarters in town. He was also glad of an opportunity to remain about Winchester as there were Catholic families in the place who had no opportunity of attending to their duty for some time. And besides there were many Catholics of the Maryland line and Irish battalion then stationed around Winchester. He made his headquarters at the house of a Mr. Hassett,[8] who gave him his parlor for a chapel and who had vestments and all the altar furniture necessary for the celebration of Mass. On the following Sunday morning Father Sheeran said Mass in the church and preached a short sermon to a very large congregation, mostly soldiers. After Mass a large collection was made which was left for the repair of the church. During his stay in Winchester, the Maryland battery and several regiments, principally Louisianans, availed themselves of the opportunity offered to settle their peace with God.

On November 29th, being informed that the whole army was in front of the Federals[9] and that Burnside was marching towards Fredericksburg, Father Sheeran resolved to proceed to his regiment. On the morning of the 30th, several of the Maryland boys were at confession. December 1st was also spent in hearing confessions. On the morning of December 2nd, Father Sheeran bid adieu to Winchester and started for the army. During the day he passed through Kernstown, the only place wherever Jackson was defeated, and that too by the gallant Irish soldier General [James] Shields.[10] About 5 P.M. he arrived at Woodstock, a town some twenty nine miles from Winchester and put up for the night at a hotel, the proprietor of which was a Catholic. Here he met several Maryland refugees and Confederate officers, several of whom embraced the opportunity of attending to their religious duties.

The following morning the town was all in commotion. The postmaster of Winchester had arrived during the night with the contents of the post office. The Federals had advanced to within a few miles of Winchester and the Confederates were retreating. That morning Father Sheeran left Woodstock and passed though Edinburg, Mount Jackson, and New Market[11] and arrived in Harrisburg after dark and spent that night with a Catholic family named Scanlan. The next day he started for Gordonsville and after a terrible ride through the lonely paths of the Blue Ridge Mountains and in the midst of a terrible snow storm was obliged to put up at a farm house on a lonely hill. The next morning he resumed his journey and reached Gordonsville in the evening and spent that night at the only hotel in the place. Here he met Colonel Goodwin and Majors Brady, Nelligan, and Wilson on their way to join the army. The next morning all started off together. They stopped the following night at a splendid mansion, but all had to sleep in one room.

The next day about noon, feeling hungry, they repaired to another mansion where they were served with a splendid dinner, and where Father Sheeran was treated with highest honors, the host believing him to be the governor. This false impression Father Sheeran was several times about to remove, but feared if he did so he might betray some of his companions. That night they stopped at another mansion about twelve miles from Guinea's Station. Here the army was stationed and was only within eight miles of the afterward bloody field of Fredericksburg. After a little inquiry Father Sheeran found his regiment encamped some two miles from the station. That afternoon, December 10th, he received a letter calling him to Richmond and next morning after procuring a pass he started off.

He remained at Richmond till the morning of the 13th when hearing that a battle was likely to take place he started back for the army. He did not reach the old camp ground till the afternoon and then found that the terrible battle of Fredericksburg was raging. The next morning he said Mass at daylight and after borrowing a horse started for the scene of carnage. Approaching the battle field, he observed a hospital flag in the distance. In riding up to it he found it was the hospital of Father Smulders's brigade, but the father was at some of the other hospitals attending to the wounded after having first cared for his own. Father Sheeran found the hospital of his brigade some half mile distant, where he had plenty of work but not so much with his own men as with those of other commands. After attending to the spiritual wants of the Confederate soldiers he went around among the Federals and prepared several of them for death. Having attended to the spiritual wants of those who needed his services he rendered all the assistance in his power in helping to dress the wounds of the soldiers. That afternoon orders were given to have all the wounded transported to Richmond as soon as possible. Father Sheeran took charge of the ambulance train, and had those belonging to his own brigade transferred first. That whole afternoon he worked unmindful of blood and mud in relieving and transporting the poor fellows. After dark, he took his rounds of several hospitals and then fatigued and weary lay down to rest. The next day he took a ride over the battle field and then made his way to his regiment, the boys greeted him heartily on his appearance.

In the morning he proceeded to the hospitals and attended to the wounded incessantly for four days until the 22nd. This day he announced he would begin to hear Christmas confessions. The following two days he was busily engaged in hearing confessions preparatory to the great feast of the Savior's Nativity. On that day he said three Masses one after another and gave eloquent instructions at each, and after Mass the men of his command made up a splendid collection for the orphans of St. Joseph's Asylum in Richmond. The following paragraph taken from the Richmond papers at the time speaks for itself: "The sisters and children of St. Joseph's Female Orphan Asylum gratefully acknowledge the receipt of twelve hundred and six dollars from the esteemed chaplain of the 14th Louisiana regiment it being the Christmas gift of that noble and brave body of heroes."

Christmas day was spent with all the festivities of a New Orleans home. During the day Father Sheeran received visits from numerous Catholics of A. P. Hill's Division. The following five days' Masses were offered up every morning both by Father Sheeran and Father Hubert. On the 1st of January 1863 Father Sheeran procured a pass from Colonel Nolan, then in command of the brigade, and started for Richmond for some necessary articles. After arriving in Richmond, two of the clergymen there took sick, and the bishop requested him to remain till one of them would get better. Having left Father Hubert in the camp and knowing that he would attend to the spiritual wants of the soldiers till his return, Father Sheeran complied with the bishop's request, and remained in Richmond till the 26th of March, on which day he returned to the camp in order to give the soldiers of the brigade a chance to comply with their Easter duties. The following day was appointed by President Davis as one of fasting and prayer and an unusual[ly] large congregation attended Mass. From that day till Easter Sunday (April 5th) Fathers Sheeran and Hubert were as busy as possible hearing confessions, and on Easter Sunday morning, when they went to the camp to offer up the sacrifice of the Mass, the crowds of soldiers were standing knee deep in snow awaiting the celebration and almost every man of them received Communion. He visited the Washington Artillery, the Madison Artillery, and the Donaldsville Artillery, all Louisiana men and nearly all Catholics.

On the 17th he reached Father Smulders's camp and both priests visited the Irish battalion then acting as provost general to General Jackson. The members of this battalion were all of Irish birth and Catholics. They had done some very hard fighting up to this time and were the particular favorites of General Jackson, as he was entrusting to them the most important duties. As Father Smulders visited this battalion regularly, Father Sheeran's visit was one of friendship more than business. After spending a few pleasant hours with the officers and men of the battalion, they returned to camp. The next morning, wishing to visit the Wilcox Brigade among whom were a large number of Catholics, both priests rode over the bloody field of Fredericksburg. Although terrible were the imaginations of the priests as they rode over that field of slaughter, still no part of that bloody theatre presented such a melancholy spectacle as that known as the slaughter pen of the Irish Brigade. The boarded fence in front of the stonewall, behind which General [Howell] Cobb's Brigade were posted, could be compared to nothing but a sieve, so thickly perforated were the boards with musket balls. Here it was that Meagher's Irish Brigade made those desperate charges which have immortalized their name. Many of those brave heroes were buried on the spot where they fell, but a large number of them were thrown into an ice house a short distance in rear of the battle field. After giving the men of Wilcox Brigade a chance of complying with their Easter duty, Father Sheeran visited the 8th Alabama where he received Lieutenant R[obert] [R.] Scott[12] into the church. He afterwards visited Posey's Brigade, Mahone's Brigade, and on April the 25th he returned to Fredericksburg in order to give a mission there, but soon after had to join his command on account of the advance of the Federal army.

Rev. James Sheeran, C.Ss.R., Continued

*Father Sheeran's account of Stonewall Jackson's death—
The battle of Chancellorsville—Jackson's council adopted—
The attack on Hooker's right—Jackson wounded—The terrible
sufferings—His last orders on the field—"You must hold
your ground, General Pender."—Jackson's last words—
"Let us cross over the river and rest under the shade of the
trees!"—His death.*

EDITORS' NOTE: Conyngham was generally very careful in acknowledging the sources he relied upon in writing *Soldiers of the Cross* and his other works on the American Civil War and Ireland's history. In this chapter, Conyngham tried to give the best account yet of the wounding and death of the Confederacy's famous hero, General Stonewall Jackson. Given that so many "various and conflicting statements" had been written on the subject, Conyngham was eager to claim that his account was written by Father Sheeran himself in his diary. Given that Father Sheeran was part of Stonewall's command and thus "thoroughly conversant with the manner of his death," the author predicted it would "be read with deep interest."

Unfortunately, the manuscript's long and detailed account bears little resemblance to the one actually in Sheeran's diary. Sheeran was not present on the Chancellorsville battlefield when Jackson was wounded, and his description of the engagement relies on what others told him or what he read later about the battle. His full diary makes it clear that Sheeran was not present for any portion of Jackson's lingering illness.[1] In fact, the description of Chancellorsville and Jackson's demise that Conyngham planned to publish was almost word for word identical to a chapter titled "Jackson's Death-Wound" in John Esten Cooke's *Wearing of the Gray* (1867). Given that the manuscript chapter is not what it claimed to be, it has been omitted from this publication. Sheeran's reaction to Jackson's death is covered in the following chapter.

Rev. James Sheeran, C.Ss.R., Continued

Father Sheeran celebrates Mass in camp—March of the army—
He takes charge of the hospitals around Winchester—Father
Smulders—The march to Gettysburg—The battle—The retreat
and its hardships—Father Sheeran goes to Mobile—He visits Bragg's
army in Tennessee in order to attend to the Catholic soldiers there—
His visit to Savannah and Charleston—A terrible scene—Shells on
all sides—He returns to the Army of Virginia.

The battle of Chancellorsville ended after four days of heavy skirmishing and fighting by Hooker withdrawing his forces across the Rappahannock and falling back to his old camp ground. This was a trying
time for Father Sheeran. Night and day had he to labor, attending to
the temporal as well as the spiritual wants of the dying and wounded.
Besides attending to his own men he had also to minister to members
of the Federal wounded who had fallen into their hands. Among these
were several of the Irish Brigade to whom he gave special attention. He
also had members of the Federal prisoners paroled as nurses to attend
to their wounded companions.

On the 7th of May the army fell back to Hamilton crossing and
went into permanent camp. Three days after, viz., Sunday [the] 10th the
death of Jackson became generally known and there was universal sorrow throughout the camp. On the following day Father Sheeran offered

up the holy sacrifice of the Mass for the souls of the Catholics killed in the late and previous battles. Every day until [June] 5th the men gave themselves up to religious devotion. On that day, the army moved and continued the march till the 9th when the battle of Brandy Station was fought. The next morning the army moved up the valley in the direction of the Blue Ridge, and on the 13th arrived before Winchester, then in possession of the Federal General [Robert H.] Milroy. Next evening Winchester was in possession of the Confederates and Milroy was retreating to Harpers Ferry. The next day General Ewell asked Father Sheeran to take charge of the hospitals around Winchester. Believing Father Smulders to be a better nurse, he had him appointed in his stead.

After having assisted Father Smulders in setting things to right, he started after the army, then on its way to Maryland, and overtook it within two miles of Shepherdstown, and continued with it in its march to Plainfield, Pennsylvania, and back to Gettysburg, which place was reached on Wednesday, July 1st, and on that same day the famous battle of that place commenced. After three days' hard fighting, the Confederate forces were compelled to retire and the labors of Father Sheeran on this occasion were almost unendurable; for between his attendance of the wounded on the field and transporting of the ambulances on the retreat, he scarcely had an hour cessation from work during that time, or the following three days and nights.

On the morning of the 7th, the army reached Hagerstown and here Father Sheeran introduced the Rev. Father [Malachy] Moran,[1] the pastor of the place and a gentleman named McLeary to General Lee. During the conversation which passed between them, the general said he came on a visit to the enemy's country and showed them that he had the power to retaliate on them if he so desired, and lamented that he had always to throw his brave troops against overwhelming numbers of the enemy. Lee in his retreat determined to cross the Potomac, but that night when he reached it, there was a very high flood and so had to draw up his army in line of battle and prepare the pontoons. These were not ready till the 13th and during the time of preparation much skirmishing took place. On the morning of the 14th all were on the Virginia side of the Potomac. On the evening of the 15th the army encamped at Martinsburg and on the 22nd started for Winchester and on the following afternoon passed through the latter place in the direction of the Blue Ridge, which it crossed on the 27th. On the 29th Lee went into camp within four miles of Madison C[ourt] H[ouse]. The next morning Father Sheeran started for Richmond for altar breads and other necessary articles and returned on the 10th of August.[2]

On the 17th he commenced to visit all the Catholics of the army in order to give them a chance to make their peace with God before active operations would commence. During this mission he received many converts into the church, and was personally thanked by General Ewell and [Robert D.] Johnston[3] for his denunciation of vice. On the 14th September, the army was again in motion, but only proceeded a few miles from Orange C[ourt] H[ouse] where it again halted until the 19th when it would move towards Raccoon Ford right over the same road where Jackson went during his Maryland Campaign the year previous. Jackson's memory now rushed fresh to the mind of every man of the army and several of them actually shed tears. About noon this day the army diverged from the road leading to Raccoon Ford and by a circuitous route reached a place called Morton's Ford, where it encamped. Here Father Sheeran visited some battalions which he did not attend before, among other[s] a Maryland Cavalry regiment, the men of which had sent a special request for him to do so. While here also Father Sheeran washed his shirts and articles of apparel. This however was not his first time to do so. On October 8th orders to march were received and in less than an hour the boys were on the road and in a few hours were across the Rapidan. On the 12th they crossed the Rappahannock and during that night Father Sheeran's overcoat was stolen and he had to wear a blanket next day as the weather was getting cold. In this apparel he met General Ewell and staff. The general laughed heartily at the idea of the men commencing to steal from the priest.

Between Bristoe and Warrenton the troops had a brush with the enemy whom they succeeded in routing. As it was evident that the latter were making for Centreville, Lee resolved to follow them no further and ordered his wagon trains to be removed to Warrenton. Father Sheeran hearing that several Catholics were among the prisoners taken visited them. The next day Lee made a retrograde movement in the direction of the Rappahannock which he crossed and went into camp.

Father Sheeran now being informed that the army would remain in camp for some time, procured leave of absence for thirty days and started for Mobile for articles sent to him there from New Orleans. Some months previous he went by way of Richmond, Macon, Georgia, Montgomery and Selma, Alabama. Soldiers on furlough, refugees from New Orleans, or residents whose acquaintance he had previously formed greeted him at every place he stopped. On the 18th he arrived at Mobile and instantly prepared to visit the bishop[4] who was very glad to see him. Father Sheeran and the bishop talked over the scenes of the bloody drama of the war. The next morning after Mass, Father Sheeran in company with Father [William] Duncan[5] visited the infirmary and general hospital, which were under the care of the Sisters of Charity, the Visitation convent, the gunboat *Tennessee,* and several New Orleans refugees and Louisiana soldiers stationed there. Father Sheeran remained at Mobile until the 27th when at the request of the bishop he proceeded to Bragg's army in Tennessee, the Catholics of which, the bishop had learned, were in a sad state for want of priests. He went by way of Montgomery and Atlanta and arrived at the headquarters which was then near Dalton on December 7th.

All along the way he [was] met with the greatest respect and attention. At Atlanta he met General Cobb, who telegraphed to Colonel [George W.] Brent, Bragg's adjutant general, in order to announce that Father Sheeran was on his way to the camp as well as to procure a pass. On arriving at the headquarters he first met Colonel Brent who received him with many marks of friendship. Having handed him a letter of introduction from Bishop Quinlan the colonel said he was most glad to see him, and instantly provided him with a horse and orderly whilst he would stay. Father Sheeran then proceeded to the residence of a Mr. Tucker, a Catholic of the place, whose house he made his headquarters while he remained with the army of Tennessee. The following morning he first visited Captain Semmes, Colonel Ives, Colonel Brent, and several other officers for the purpose of getting information concerning the position or localities of the various commands in order to make arrangements for his intended visits. These were stationed from three to eight miles from Dalton. The following morning after procuring a horse and couriers, he visited the fifth company of the Washington Artillery, Fenner's Battery, and Adams Brigade, and met many an old acquaintance and many a familiar face among them. The next day he met with Father Bliemel,[6] a Benedictine father who had just arrived in camp, and both clergymen earnestly went to work. On the 12th they were joined by Father [Thomas] O'Reilly,[7] and never did three missionaries affect more in so short a space of time as did these three priests. They brought sinners to repentance who had not been to their duty for numbers of years, and were the means of checking numerous vices, not alone of the Catholic soldiers, but of numbers of others as well. Among the Kentuckians, Father Sheeran found many intelligent and well instructed Catholics. After having visited all the commands of the army and given missions to each and hearing that Father [Anthony] Carius[8] was coming to assist the good priests already at work, Father Sheeran thought that he now might leave and rejoin the army in Virginia. On the morning of the 21st he visited the "Tennessee Camp," a regiment composed entirely of Catholics, and introduced Father Bliemel to several Catholic officers of the army.

Next day he started for Macon and on the following afternoon arrived there. [On] Christmas Eve he assisted Father [William J.] Hamilton[9] in hearing confessions and preached a sermon at the Midnight Mass which was celebrated by Father Hamilton. On the 28th he left Macon for Fort Valley, and there visited a number of New Orleans refugees, among whom were a Mr. [Patrick] and Miss [Mary] Gleason,[10] formerly members of his congregation in the Crescent City. Miss Gleason being a young lady of rare accomplishments: religious, prepossessing, gentle, and talented. Father Sheeran thought best to place her under the care of the sisters in Richmond until events would permit her to return to her native city. On Tuesday, January 5th, 1864, accompanied by Mr. and Miss Gleason, Father Sheeran started back to Macon. Mr. Gleason there bid the worthy pair good bye and returned the same evening to Fort Valley.

On the following day Father Sheeran had all their baggage booked to Richmond and started with his charge via Savannah and Charleston. On the morning of January 8th they arrived at Savannah and drove straight to Bishop [Augustin] Verot's house.[11] After breakfast Miss Gleason was sent to the residence of a worthy lady named Prendergast, where she stayed while she remained in Savannah. During the day Father Sheeran met at the Bishop's house Fathers Dufort,[12] [Peter] Whelan,[13] [Jeremiah F.] O'Neill,[14] and [Charles C.] Prendergast.[15] Father Whelan was the chaplain who was captured by the Federals at the fall of Fort Hamilton and who was afterwards detained as a prisoner of war for six months. Father O'Neill was at that time the oldest missionary in the South and supposed to be the best mathematician in the country. As Father Sheeran wished to view the city, Father Prendergast acted as his chaperon. After visiting the barracks, the park, and other public places, they repaired to Mrs. Prendergast's residence where they spent the evening. This lady was a pious Catholic of Irish descent. Two of her sons joined the Southern army at the outbreak of the war, one of whom died in hospital from wounds received at one of the early battles. One of her daughters was a nun; and another son has since joined the priesthood. Such was the family with which Miss Gleason was sojourning. On the following morning, in company with Father Whelan, Father Sheeran visited the Convent of the Sisters of Mercy, the hospitals, and the residence of Mrs. Prendergast and the mother of his Revd. companion. That afternoon, he heard confessions at the request of the bishop and the next day (Sunday) preached the sermon at the principal Mass. After Mass, the bishop congratulated him but said he thought he had forgotten something. "When," he continued, "you commenced your sermon in the name of Jesus and Mary, I thought you would kneel down and say: *Ave Maria*. Yes, I thought you forgot that's the way we do in France." "But, Bishop, you know I am no Frenchman." "Yes, I know, but we do that way in France and I thought you forgot. But Father it was very good. Come now and let us have some dinner."

The next day Father Sheeran, in company with Father Prendergast and two other friends, visited almost all the places of note down the Savannah river, including Fort Jackson, Fort Lee, Battery Lawton or Naval battery, Lady's Gunboat, [the] *Savannah*, and Fort Barlow. In returning home that afternoon he made the acquaintance of several Confederate officers, among them General Anderson of Georgia. The following morning Father Prendergast took him to visit the Bonaventure Cemetery, the Thunderbolt battery, and the Catholic cemetery, where at the grave of Bishop [Francis X.] Garland[16] the party recited their prayers and then returned to prepare for their journey to Charleston on Wednesday January 15th.

Father Sheeran with his fair charge started for Charleston, where they arrived the same day and drove at once to the residence of Father [Leon] Fillion[17] of St. Joseph's Church. The Rev. Father received them in most agreeable manner and then domiciled Miss Gleason with a Catholic lady named Mrs. Cantwell. During the night the shells from the Federal men of war who were then bombarding the city could be distinctly heard over the lower part of the city. The next morning Father Sheeran accompanied by Father Fillion visited Bishop [Patrick N.] Lynch[18] who was still living near the ruins of his cathedral. The bishop gave him a cordial welcome to Charleston, but lamented that he could not invite him to stay with him during his sojourn as he (the bishop) was that day compelled to abandon his house on account of the proximity of the shells. Whilst they were conversing a large shell burst quite near the house. After remaining some time with the bishop, the two clergymen visited the scene of the great fire in [1861],[19] the bombarded part of the city, the breastworks and batteries on the wharves, and the splendid convent and academy erected by the Sisters of Mercy.[20] These latter, as well as the chapel thereto attached, had suffered from the dreadful missiles of war and were therefore reluctantly abandoned by the good sisters. The chapel was entirely destroyed with the exception of the altar and statue of the blessed Virgin, which miraculously escaped any injury. That afternoon the bishop spent some time with the two Rev. gentlemen at Father Fillion's house, and told Father Sheeran that whenever he came to the diocese he had all the faculties that he, the bishop, could give.

In the evening, the two fathers paid a visit to Mrs. Cantwell's residence to see that good lady and family as well as Miss Gleason. At the request of the bishop, on the following morning they, accompanied by Miss Gleason, met his Grace at the cupola from which could be seen the harbor and in fact the whole city. The bishop had with him a powerful glass and showed them the various islands, batteries, rivers, positions of the Federal fleet, as well as those of the Confederate forces on land. Whilst reviewing the harbor an engagement occurred between one of the batteries on the wharf and one of the Men of War outside the harbor. It lasted about an hour and a half, but the scene was truly grand to those in the cupola as they could see every shot fired. As Father Sheeran had been requested to preach on the following Sunday, he retired to his room after dinner to reflect on his sermon, but was not long in his meditation before he was disturbed by the whiz! whiz! whiz! of a shell coming close over the house and falling some fifty yards distant. As this was a quarter of a mile higher up than any other shell had yet reached it was evident that the Federals had opened a new battery and the whole neighborhood was in great alarm. Soon another shell came in the same direction, and then another and another, and continued in this way for nearly two hours.

Not caring, however, so much for his own safety as for that of his ward, he had her instantly removed out of danger under the care of the sisters who were then residing in the suburbs of the town and removed himself to new quarters. The shelling continued over the lower part of the city all night, which made Father Sheeran feel very uneasy for the good Father Fillion, who remained at his house, and in the morning early he repaired to see if he were yet living. He found him all right. As this day was Saturday, Father Fillion sent around word that Father Sheeran was to preach the following day. Father Fillion made the following announcement at the early Mass in his broken English, "My brethren the Rev. Gent. you see now at the altar is a Redemptorist Father and the chaplain of General Lee's army. He will preach for you today at last Mass and I know will tell you many good things. He has stood upon twenty battle fields and was not afraid. You must not then be afraid of the shells today, but come and hear the good father; and not only come yourselves but bring your neighbors." An immense concourse of people attended the 10 o'clock Mass, the celebration of which was ended before the sermon commenced in order that if any shelling took place the congregation could be dispersed at any time; all having got the full benefit of the holy sacrifice. The choir sang some of its most beautiful pieces. The sermon was on mortal sin and was listened to with the most profound attention for about half an hour, when suddenly comes a hundred pound parrot shell, whirring directly over the roof of the church and then ploughs right into the earth some fifty yards distant. Suddenly a wild cry was heard on the organ loft, and something tumbled down stairs. Some half dozen people ran to the door and most of the congregation jumped to their feet. For a second Father Sheeran himself felt panic stricken but soon overcame his feelings and addressed the congregation in an authoritative tone, commanding them to keep their places, asking, "What are you afraid of? Do you think God is not able to protect you from shells? Is he not able to protect you in the church as well as out of it? Keep still, there is not one bit of danger." Before giving the congregation any further time for reflection, he resumed his sermon and fused into it as much animation as possible. The congregation seemed to forget all about the shells, and not being disturbed by another, they listened during a full half hour with the most earnest attention. After Mass, Father Sheeran was visited by young [Neville] Soulé of General Beauregard's staff and the bishop dined that day with the two fathers and then took Father Sheeran out to view the fortifications around Charleston. Both returned to Father Fillion in the evening where after supper he bade the bishop good bye and returned to his quarters.

On the next morning, Monday, January 18th, after bidding Father Fillion goodbye, [Sheeran], with his charge, left for Wilmington, North Carolina, and at 6 o'clock on the morning of the 19th reached there. After spending a couple of very pleasant days with Dr. Corcoran, a resident pastor of the place, Father Sheeran took the cars for Petersburg, where he arrived on the morning of the 21st. At the request of Father [Thomas] Mulvey, pastor of Petersburg, Father Sheeran promised to stay over Sunday and preach for him. His ward was taken care of by the Miss Keilys, worthy young Catholic ladies of that place. During his short sojourn at Petersburg he was visited by many of the boys of the Washington Artillery who were then stationed around that city. On Sunday he preached according to promise and left the following afternoon for Richmond, where he arrived the same evening and instantly repaired to the asylum where the sisters received them with their usual kindness. The bishop, who happened to be at the asylum at the time, manifested pleasure at his return and treated his travelling companion with much kindness. Having partaken of some refreshments prepared by the good sisters, Father Sheeran, at the bishop's request, accompanied him home. After having settled Miss Gleason with the good sisters, Father Sheeran attended to some business in Richmond until February 5th and then started for his brigade, which was camped some seven miles from the Convent house on the Fredericksburg and Plank road. Here he was surrounded by swarms of soldiers who welcomed him back warmly and heartily shook his hands, many of them saying, "We missed you much." The same day the division received marching orders and was instantly on the road off for Morton's Ford.

On coming up with General Johnston, the Division Commander, he and Dr. Coleman and the other members of the general's staff welcomed him back saying, "Father, we have missed you!" The general then informed him that the Federals were crossing at Morton's Ford, which was nine miles ahead. When about a mile on the way, rain fell as if the flood gates of heaven opened. When within three miles of Morton's Ford the loud and frequent reports of artillery were heard. Soon, too, the sound of the distant musketry was also audible and the division now pressed forward, regardless of the mud and darkness, at a double quick to participate in the deadly strife. About 8 o'clock the Federal troops had crossed the Rapidan and all was quiet again. Campfires were soon lighted along the Southern lines and as this was a sure signal that no other advance of the enemy was expected that night, Father Sheeran began to look about where he would locate himself for the night. As he was wet, cold and hungry, and as the troops had taken neither tents nor blankets with them, he found himself in a rather unpleasant position. At the request of one of the drivers he slept in an ambulance, but what a night! It was cold and he was wet and without blankets.

Towards morning he fell into a slumber from which he was disturbed by the report of musketry in the direction of the river. He rode to the front and found the boys in good spirits enjoying themselves around the campfires. Hearing that there were some of his regiment wounded, he started for the hospital some four miles distant. Arriving there, he only found four wounded.

On the following morning the brigade returned to camp but on the next afternoon was ordered for picket duty for a week to Morton's Ford. Father Sheeran, of course, accompanied it. After remaining a week the brigade returned to camp. On the way back Father Sheeran visited, by request, General Ewell and lady.²¹ The latter, although respectful to Catholic dogmas, was very fond of discussing religious subjects. She opened on Father Sheeran and the response of the latter made the General laugh heartily and caused the lady to cut short her controversy. Having returned to camp on February 17th, a mission was opened for the brigade the following morning by Fathers Sheeran and Smulders. It ended on February 28th when Father Smulders went to Charleston to assist Father Fillion with the Easter confessions. During that time, almost every Catholic in the brigade went to confession and Communion and many converts were also made. On Wednesday 2nd March, orders were given to march in the direction of Chancellorsville. During that evening the battle of Mine Run²² was fought which ended in the retreat of the Federals across the Rapidan. From then until the 16th he heard the confessions each day in the camp of the Irish battalion and accordingly he started to the camp of Father Smulders's Brigade to give a mission there. That evening while walking through the camp in order to see what was going on, Father Sheeran was agreeably surprised to hear the sturdy voices of numbers of the Catholic soldiers in an adjacent tent united in reciting the rosary of the Blessed Virgin.

After spending four days with the brigade and with fruitful results he left for the Frazer battery composed principally of young men from Savannah, Georgia, many of whom were Catholics, but had not a priest to visit them since the beginning of the war. They were in camp at Somerville Ford, and on reaching there he was treated by the Captain (although an ex-preacher) with all possible marks of respect. During that afternoon he provided him with a comfortable tent and a good fire, where he heard confessions during the afternoon. The next morning he said Mass in an adjacent house and gave Communion to all the Catholics of the company but three, and had the reverend Captain as one of his audience during the sermon. After bidding the boys good bye he started for Posey's brigade but the members were so much scattered that he determined to visit his own camp that evening and return in a couple of days. The day previous, viz. March 23, two of the divisions, Johnston's and [Robert E.] Rodes's,²³ fought a regular scientific battle with snow balls, General [Reuben L.] Walker commanding

Johnston's and General [Stephen D.] Ramseur, Rodes's division. Johnston's men came off victorious. The two days after returning to camp he heard confessions preparatory for Easter Sunday. On Easter Sunday (March 27) Mass was said at 7 o'clock in the improvised chapel composed of tents and branches of trees at which a large congregation attended with many communicants. So large was the attendance that members had to kneel out on the cold slushy ground where they piously prayed with bowed uncovered heads and [chastised hearts?]. After Mass he left camp for Richmond intending to visit several of the other commands before returning. He arrived there the same day, and on the 31st he left Richmond and visited the Maryland line and the Irish battalion, the Maryland Brigade, and returned to camp on April 6th.

On April 8th Father Sheeran left camp again with the intention of giving a chance to the Catholic soldiers of other brigades to perform their Easter duties. He visited Posey's Brigade, the Wilcox, Alabama Brigade, the Florida Brigade and the Maryland Battery, the Irish battalion, the Donaldsville Artillery, the Montgomery Emerald Guards, the Confederate battalion, and then returned to his own camp.

Rev. James Sheeran, C.Ss.R., Continued

Father Sheeran's missionary labors continued—An important convert—An officious officer—The horrors of a battle field— A visit to the grave of Stonewall Jackson—The march toward Washington—Battle of Winchester—General Mulligan's death— Father Sheeran and Sheridan—His arrest and imprisonment— His release—He leaves the army and returns to Richmond and witnesses its surrender.

During Father Sheeran's mission he received many converts into the church, among whom was a Captain Cleaveland, son of a distinguished doctor of New Orleans.[1] Father Sheeran visited General Ewell, who gave him an orderly and a tent for his own use. The general on this occasion asked him if he would not have service at headquarters every other Sunday. Father told him that there were too many Catholics who needed his services but that he might preach for them occasionally.

Orders were given to strike tents and reduce baggage. As there was no provision made for the chaplain in the orders, an officious officer named Boardman, a captain on General Stafford's staff, thought to prevent Father Sheeran from bringing his tent along. Father, however, did not only do so, but General Lee offered him a place at his own headquarters. On April 30th, the army got the route in the direction of Morton's Ford. Father Sheeran then started for Richmond on business and returned in a few days.

Hearing that the Federal troops had crossed the Rapidan and Germania Ford, and that the whole Confederate army was in motion, the father pushed rapidly on after his command and the next morning about 8 A.M. came up with the brigade which was then drawn up in line of battle on the right of the Plank Road running from Culpepper to Fredericksburg. After about two hours the troops again advanced and in another hour the terrible contest known as the second battle of the Wilderness commenced. For two days this fearful battle raged and the Federal army suffered terribly. Their wounded were on this occasion principally attended to by the Confederate surgeons. Father Sheeran was kept busy among them; he baptized several and attended them in their last moments. The number of legs, arms, feet, and hands amputated was enormous.

On the morning of the 8th the army moved in the direction of Spotsylvania Court House, the father accompanying the medical surgeons and ambulances.

During this forenoon the advance [elements] of both armies met near Spotsylvania and had a sharp fight and that night the Southern army camped nearby. During the night much skirmishing took place between the pickets of both armies. This was continued all next day with occasional shelling. For the next four days severe fighting took place, during which Johnston's division was partly captured and scattered.

On the next day, Sunday May 15th, a change in flank was made and on the following two days' heavy skirmishing was kept up but no battle except a severe fight between Breckenridge and Siegel's brigade in which the latter was defeated.

During the afternoon of the 17th, Father Sheeran visited the Federal wounded. He found that many of them were several days without having their wounds dressed, some of which were complete masses of maggots. There were several Catholics among them who had belonged to the Irish Brigade. He heard their confessions, anointed some, called the attention of the surgeons and nurses to their wounds and aided in washing and dressing them. On the 18th, General Grant, being reinforced by Corcoran's Irish Legion, the troops from along the R. R. and from the heavy batteries around Washington, Baltimore, and other places, made a desperate attack on the Southern lines. That day's battle and a skirmish the next morning gave the surgeons, nurses, and chaplains of both armies work enough for several days. On the morning of the 21st, the army moved in the direction of Hanover Junction and arrived there the next day. During this march several of the best soldiers broke down—men who had never missed a battle or who were never absent an hour from post. The surgeons of the regiment had followed the brigade that morning so that there was no one left to see after the poor fellows but Father Sheeran himself. As there were a great many empty ambulances the good Father asked Dr. Stephens[2] to let these brave, but now tired, soldiers ride in them. The doctor replied that they might follow after and if they should break down, they might get in as best they could.

Father Sheeran thought this too hard treatment for men who were always at their post and insisted on the men being carried, but the sapient doctor paid no attention and rode off rapidly. The ambulances followed, leaving the poor soldiers to shift for themselves or fall into the hands of the enemy. Being pretty well broken down by the almost incessant labors of the previous three weeks, Father Sheeran was near giving out this night. A hundred times did he recover himself from falling off his horse, as sleep had overpowered him. Being no longer able to remain on his horse without exposing himself to a fall, he dismounted and led his old grey. This was no better for he soon fell asleep whilst walking and was in danger of being trampled by the horse or run over by some of the wagons.

Next evening he came up with his brigade camped in a field. The wagoners and hospital nurses had already commenced cooking supper, and although without food from early the morning before, he threw himself down on the ground and slept till daylight. On awakening his first thoughts were about those poor men left behind and he was satisfied that they fell into the hands of the enemy. Father Sheeran then reported Dr. [Stephens] to Colonel York and General Ewell. The latter settled the affair by telling the father to give tickets to such men to get into the ambulances and then to let him know who would refuse to carry them. On the morning of the 23rd, a line of battle was formed on the north Anna River, [the] left resting on Fredericksburg R. R., and the right extending in the direction of the Central. The cause of the rapid march to the junction from Spotsylvania was now evident. The enemy by a sudden movement thought to cross the North Anna and get possession of the junction. No sooner had they taken up the position than the Federals appeared in force on the opposite side of the river, and instantly the dogs of war were let loose. During the evening and night entrenchments were set up. From thence until the 27th heavy skirmishing and some sharp fighting took place, but no actual battle. On that forenoon General Grant moved down towards the Pamunkey River and immediately after the Southern army moved in the direction of Richmond. The next morning on reaching Catlett's Station the Federal army was seen moving toward Cold[3] Harbor and the Confederate wagon trains were then encamped near Yellow Tavern, within seven miles of Richmond. Fathers Sheeran and Smulders then held a consultation which resulted in Father Smulders remaining with the army while Father Sheeran proceeded to Richmond to say Mass the following day and procure some clean clothes.

On Monday May 30th, hearing that the Federal army had crossed the Pamunkey and were reaching toward Cold Harbor on the north side of the Chickahominy, and that the Southern army was occupying a line between them and the latter river with their right resting on Cold Harbor and their left some distance west of the Mechanicsville Road, Father Sheeran started in quest of his command, some four miles from Mechanicsville, and when he reached the hospital of his brigade, he found that his services were much needed.

During the forenoon a sharp fight had taken place between General Rodes's command and part of the Federal troops in which a large number on both sides were killed and wounded. All the wounded were brought to the Confederate hospital. Among them were many Catholics to whom Father Sheeran paid the utmost attention. Battles were now fought every day without any advance being made on either side but with terrible slaughter.[4]

On the morning of June 9th the hospital was removed to James farm, where Mass was offered up. On the night of the 13th a column under General [Jubal A.] Early[5] was ordered to Lynchburg where it arrived on the afternoon of the 19th and attacked General Hunter, then in front of Lynchburg. Hunter retreated in the direction of Liberty, and

Early pursued him next morning. On arriving at Lynchburg, Father Sheeran proceeded to the house of Father [O. A.] Sears, pastor of the place, where he remained till the morning of the 21st when he started after the army. On the afternoon of the following day he passed through Liberty, called at the hospital, and found a good many soldiers wounded, principally Federals. After attending to them, accompanied by his orderly, he again started after the army. That night both slept in the woods, and in the afternoon of the 23rd overtook Breckenridge's corps bringing up the rear of the column, and soon after came up with his brigade. That night the army camped near a beautiful stream, a tributary of the James River, and on the following morning got the route across the James River, via Buchanan. The next morning the army was in motion and marched to Lexington. On entering this town, orders were issued that all should visit the grave of Stonewall Jackson. Hence the army filed off to the right and entered the cemetery where lay the remains of the Confederates' greatest hero. It was a solemn scene as they marched past the grave, with uncovered heads, slow paces and sorrowful countenances, which bespoke souls that were deeply impressed. No doubt they remembered the many times the departed chief led them to victory and the long and arduous marches in which they followed him.

The next morning the march was resumed and the route lay through Fairfield, Greenville, Staunton, and Mount Sidney to the north branch of the Shenandoah River near Mount Crawford where they arrive[d] after two days, viz. on June 28th and encamp[ed] for the night. As Harrisonburg was only 7 miles distant, Father Sheeran started there and stopped over night with a Mr. Scanlon of that place. While here Father Sheeran met General Early standing in front of one of the hotels of the place and as usual had a shake hands. "Well, General," said the father, "I have a grave complaint to make for the manner in which you have treated me." "How is that, Father?" "Well, General, you took us out of the breastworks at Richmond and never told us where we were going, and the consequence is I left without money or clothes, only what I had on my back and since I have had to live on the charity of my friends." "I guess, Father, you are better off than I am. I brought with me but one pair of drawers and had to do without them whilst they were being washed. And my Adjutant-General had but one shirt, and he had to go to bed to get it washed. So I think there are people worse off than you, Father."

Father Sheeran came up with his brigade near Mount Jackson. The march was continued through Strasburg and on the following two days through Cedar Creek and Winchester to within about a mile and a half of Martinsburg, when the column halted and had a skirmish with some Federal cavalry, drawn up in line of battle.

The next day Father Sheeran visited several friends in Martinsburg and took dinner with General York, at Dr. McSherry's. On the following day about noon, the troops passed through Shepherdstown, crossed the Potomac, and marched in the direction of Sharpsburg. About half way between the Potomac and Sharpsburg the column turned to the right and made along the canal in the direction of Harpers Ferry, or South Mountain, and on the following morning, July 6th, crossed the Antietam River and moved along the base of the South Mountain, from where the Federal positions on the Maryland heights and around Harpers Ferry could be distinctly seen.

There was skirmishing that night and some cannonading. In the morning the column was drawn up in line of battle some two miles up the mountain. That day some skirmishing took place but no severe fight. At night the column retreated and many of the brave soldiers tired and weary lay down on the road side and fell asleep. But a squad of cavalry bringing up the rear soon aroused them from their slumbers. On the march a man ran out from the side of the road, caught Father Sheeran's horse by the bridle and said, "D—— n you, get off my horse!" "Do you know to whom you are talking, Sir?" responded the father. "I don't care," said he, "who you are. You must give up my horse." "Now my good friend," said the father, "let this horse go or I shall let you know who owns this." "It's my horse," responded the soldier, "and you took it while I was sleeping." One of the boys then whispered to him, "Do you know you are talking to Father Sheeran? That's his horse." The poor fellow got quite confused, asked the father's pardon, but said some rascal took his horse while he was sleeping and he thought that that was him.

At half past two the column went into camp pretty well tired and sleepy. The men had not much more than time to close their eyes when orders came to prepare for marching and at four they were on the road again. After a heavy march of nearly two days they reached the suburbs of Frederick City, turned off to the right and crossing some fields got out on the Baltimore pike where they halted. The medical train however entered the city and Father Sheeran accompanied it. After receiving many salutations from the citizens, and paying a short visit to the Jesuit Fathers, Father Sheeran went to the camp. In the afternoon, the Battle of the Monocacy was fought, and the wounded were brought into Frederick and cared for by the good Sisters of Charity.[6] Not knowing that the army intended moving soon, Father Sheeran returned to the house of the Jesuit Fathers in order to say Mass the next morning. During the day he made several unsuccessful efforts to purchase some articles of clothing, but however obtained a summer coat and pants from the Rev. Father O'Callaghan.[7]

The next day the army halted within 22 miles of Washington. On the following morning the army was again in motion and had advanced to within five miles of Washington. There was much skirmishing and sharpshooting during the remainder of the afternoon. The next morning the whole column was drawn up in line of battle. In the afternoon the Federals sent out several lines of skirmishers and the Confederates fell back in order to draw them from their works and then gave them battle, killing and wounding several and capturing some. Among the captured were several of the 6th Corps from Grant's army. This satisfied General Early that his mission to Washington was accomplished, viz. to draw the Federal forces from before Richmond. That afternoon Father Sheeran had the misfortune to lose his horse by the carelessness of his orderly who allowed both horses to straggle off. At dark the whole column was in motion and the father, mounting on an old carrier, joined the cavalcade. The route was taken by way of Rockville to the Potomac which was reached about 36 hours after leaving the heights before Washington. During the march Father Sheeran discovered his horse with an officer of the 5th Alabama who immediately gave it up on being claimed.

On crossing to the Virginia side of the Potomac the men were informed that they would rest for the day.[8] The following morning the column, again on its way, passed through Leesburg and Hamilton in the direction of Snicker's[9] Gap; when about half way up the "blue ridge" the Federal troops made their appearance and for three successive days attempted to dispute their return towards Richmond until the battle of Rockford on the Shenandoah fought on the third day compelled the Federal forces to retire. On the following night, July 19th, the column resumed its march.[10]

On July 24th a battle was fought at Winchester and Father Sheeran attended to both Confederate and Federal wounded when the day's carnage was over. Among the Federal wounded was the celebrated General [James A.] Mulligan.[11] His body was riddled with balls. Father Sheeran attended to him in his last moments and found him to be a sincere and fervent Christian. He lived but a short time after making his confession and two days after his body was handed over to his wife who went into the Confederate lines for that purpose.

The army continued its march via Martinsburg to Darksville, where it rested for a few days. During the rest, Father Sheeran remained principally at Winchester.[12] On the day of the route, he overtook the army camped near Shepherdstown and found most of the officers away in the town on a frolic. Father Sheeran having had his horse put away and feeling very tired spread his oilcloth[13] outside his tent and went to sleep for the night. About 10 P.M. the officers returned, some of them pretty tight and one of them shamefully drunk. He was no less than a colonel and rode a large horse. The father was at the time lying on his back and in a kind of slumber. He heard the noise of the horse approaching, but anticipated no harm as he was lying close to the tent. Suddenly the foot of the horse was pressed upon his left breast and the whole weight of the animal and his drunken rider pressed upon him. The father was brought into the tent and having received some stimulants became composed and went to sleep again. The next morning General York, seeing that he was much bruised, thought to send him into Winchester in an ambulance but the father, fearing that there might be an engagement and his services needed, thought [it] better to put up with some personal sufferings and remain with his command. The Colonel who was near being his murderer went over to Father Sheeran's quarters that morning, not knowing anything of what had happened. The father rebuked him for his intemperance, forgave him the bodily injury unintentionally inflicted but exhorted him to take better care of himself and give a better example to his men.

About an hour afterwards, the army was in motion and passed through Shepherdstown, crossed the Potomac, and had a sharp fight at Sharpsburg or Antietam; passed through Williamsport next day and across the Potomac to old Virginia. There was no hospital erected during this battle near Smithfield as it was a running fight so Father Sheeran had to go through the neighboring farm houses, and even into the town of Smithfield, looking for the wounded. The next day he accompanied the wounded of the brigade to Winchester, and attended to them punctually.

After remaining two days at Harrisonburg, Father Sheeran learned that General Early after his defeat at Winchester had turned off towards Port Republic and that the Federals were making towards Harrisonburg, thus cutting him off from his command. After a serious reflection he concluded to try an experiment, and ride into the Federal lines and ask Sheridan for a pass to go to Winchester to see after the wounded. The next morning, September 25th, he commenced his journey. Having travelled some seven miles, he met with three cavalrymen dressed in Confederate uniform but was shrewd enough to observe that they were Federals in disguise. One of them halted the father and proposed the following questions. "Do you belong to the Rebel Army?" "I belong to the Confederate Army." "Well, then get in here," pointing to where he should go. "No sir, I will not," replied the priest. Here the soldier drew his pistol. Seeing the object the father remarked, "You are perhaps mistaken in the opinion you have formed of me. I am a Catholic priest and wish you to bring me to General Sheridan. I am desirous of going to Winchester to look after our wounded and want a pass from your General." At this the soldier lowered his pistol saying, "I am a Catholic myself, sir, and am glad to meet with you."

They were conversing for a few minutes when another Federal soldier came up and, taking particular notice of the father's spurs, inquired if he belonged to the Rebel army. Meeting with the same response as his companion, he attempted to take the spurs, when the father informed the soldier who he was. The first young man brought him to General [Horatio G.] Wright, commanding the 6th Corps, then in advance, and gave him an introduction. Father Sheeran soon made known the object of his visit, and the general having examined his papers ordered his adjutant-general to write a pass for himself and horse. After the general thanked him for the kind manner in which the good father treated the Federal wounded at the battle of Kernstown, [he] bid him goodbye. Some three miles from the front [Sheeran] met General Sheridan and staff riding on the right of the road. In advancing towards him he was met by his adjutant who being apprised of the father's business said General Wright's pass was sufficient.

That night Father Sheeran stopped with a Mr. McFall, a very worthy Catholic gentleman of the place. During the evening and next morning he visited the hospitals and heard some confessions. After breakfast he started for Winchester and after calling at all the hospitals along the way, reached there safely. The following day the father visited all the Confederate hospitals and told the inmates that he came to stay with them for some time. The poor invalids were highly delighted when he made the announcement. At Mass the next morning there were several Federal soldiers present. During the service the father gave notice of the object of his visit to Winchester, namely that he came to see after the Confederate wounded, but was willing to extend his services to the wounded of the Federal hospital, and further that he would have Mass every Sunday morning and requested all Catholics to attend, and that he was ready to hear the confessions of all who came with proper dispositions. In conclusion he requested the Federal soldiers that if they knew of any of their companions sick or wounded who needed his services to let him know and he would attend to them. Having procured a pass to visit the Federal hospital at will the father made his rounds daily and repeatedly of both hospitals until October 12th and caused the invalids to be attended to in a becoming manner. On this day he received numerous visits from Catholics of the Federal army, all of whom were kind and respectful and promised to come to Mass on the following Sunday. During the afternoon the father was called to see a Captain [James] Brady of the 26th Massachusetts who was lying dangerously ill at the Logan house.[14] He had been wounded at the late battle of Winchester, had a leg amputated and two other wounds. He was very low when the father visited him but after receiving the sacraments he rapidly recovered and was soon able to be taken home by his brother who came from Boston to wait on him. The father attended him until the day he was removed.

From the 12th to the 19th, there was skirmishing between Early's division and the Federal troops around Winchester. On that morning a great battle was fought, in which part of the Federal army was taken by surprise and retreated to Winchester. The same morning Sheridan arrived from Washington and rallying the Federal troops advanced them against Early and forever routed and disorganized his army. For the following five days the wounded of both armies poured in to Winchester and the good father attended to them indiscriminately. During these days some of the Confederate wounded were transferred to Martinsburg. On the morning of the 27th after visiting the hospitals, a large wagon and ambulance train started for Martinsburg and General Duffié[15] and staff intended to[16] accompany it and then join their command of cavalry in front of Petersburg. About nine miles from Winchester, [John S.] Mosby[17] captured the party who were sent to Libby Prison.[18]

Every day until the 31st Father Sheeran visited the hospitals and attended to the wounded. On that day, as General Sheridan was in town and as nearly all of the Confederate soldiers were convalescent and numbers of them removed to Martinsburg, the father resolved to call on the general in order to know by what route he wished him to return home. Accompanied by Captain [Richard] Fitzgerald[19] of the 17th Pennsylvania Cavalry he proceeded to headquarters. The captain introduced him to the adjutant general of the post, viz. Captain [James W.] Latta of the 119th Pennsylvania Infantry, the same officer who had refused Father [Michael] Müller[20] and him the pass. The father told Captain Fitzgerald that he had a slight acquaintance with the adjutant and then asked him if he could see General Sheridan. The adjutant told him to take a seat and he would see. Captain Fitzgerald and the father then took a seat and in about ten minutes the adjutant returned with an armed guard and told him to "take that man," pointing to the father to the provost marshal's.[21]

Arriving there, crowds assembled to know the cause of his arrest but no information could be received. The marshal on reading a note handed to him by the guard called for an orderly whom he told to take the father to the military prison. That afternoon the father was visited by numbers of citizens and Catholic soldiers of the Federal army, all of whom deeply sympathized with him, while several of the latter vowed vengeance against the adjutant and those who had a hand in his arrest. The first three nights of his arrest he was allowed, through the interference of some Catholic officers, to sleep outside, but on the 4th the greatest strictness prevailed. On the following day, viz November 4th, the father with a large batch of prisoners was sent to Martinsburg. On driving there he introduced himself to the provost marshal and made known his case. That officer having examined the list of prisoners found no charge against Father Sheeran, and allowed him his parole for the night, which he gladly accepted and repaired to Dr. McSherry's where he was received very kindly. His parole extended to the following Tuesday by calling at the marshal's office every day.

During this time he said Mass daily and heard numerous confessions. On Tuesday he along with a number of other prisoners were transferred to Baltimore, which place they reached that evening and spent a most horrible night in prison along with a number of pickpockets and blasphemers, and sleeping on a floor reeking with vermin and filth. The next morning the father discovered that his present abode was the old slave pen. During the day he communicated twice with the father provincial[22] but the latter would not be permitted to respond. Towards evening one of the hard cases appeared to be very respectful to him. On talking to him, Father Sheeran found he was brought up a Catholic. He then called the whole party to an account for their conduct the previous night. They all expressed sorrow and promised not to repeat it again which promise they kept. On November 11th the prisoners were transferred to Fort McHenry,[23] where Father Sheeran was detained until December 5th and then released only on condition of not giving any information to the Confederate army. Thence until the 9th he remained around Baltimore and Annapolis, where the father provincial prevailed on him to sever his connection with the army and if necessary to take charge of a parish under the bishop of Richmond.

After the father provincial giving him the general orders and telling him to take whatever money he and Father Smulders stood in need of, Father Sheeran, in company with Father Müller and [Brother] Dennis

[Halpen],[24] started by the cars for Cumberland, and reached there the afternoon of the following day. He remained in Cumberland till the 19th when he left for Martinsburg. There the provost marshal told him he should go by way of Harpers Ferry to Winchester, as Mosby was about the Valley Pike Road. On the 21st he left Martinsburg for Harpers Ferry where he remained with Dr. [Michael] Costello, pastor of the place, until the 26th when he left for Winchester and arrived there the same day and repaired to the house of Mr. Hassett where he was received with every demonstration of kindness. Being sick, he remained inside of doors until the 28th when he repaired to the provost marshal's to have his pass extended, and to apply for another through the lines, in order to have everything ready (when his health would permit him) to start for Richmond. The former application the provost marshal granted, but the latter he referred to General Sheridan. After much fuss, Sheridan permitted him to go.[25] During his stay he was lionized not alone by the citizens but also by numbers of Catholics in the Federal army and even some Irish boys serving in the 18th Pennsylvania Cavalry attended to his horse while he was in prison, and had him in splendid condition. On January 3rd, the good father left Winchester for Richmond and took his route by way of Woodstock, Jackson, Harrisonburg, and Sta[u]nton, stopping with familiar friends in each place, and reached Richmond on the 10th where he remained under medical treatment until the fall of that city suffering much from his breast and eyes. A few days after the surrender of Richmond when matters had settled down, he obtained a pass and started for Baltimore in company with thirteen sisters. He then visited Philadelphia and Reading and New York, but finding his health again failing him he returned on May 6th to his own beloved Crescent City, New Orleans, but subsequently returned to New York.[26]

EPILOGUE: At the war's conclusion, Father Sheeran returned to St. Alphonsus Church in New Orleans, Louisiana. He remained there until 1868, when he was assigned briefly to

St. Alphonsus in St. Louis before taking up ministry at St. Alphonsus in New York City later that year. Following a dispute with his superior, he left the Redemptorists in February 1871 and was dispensed from his vows the next month. He then served as a priest in the Diocese of Newark, New Jersey, at the Church of the Assumption in Morristown. He died there on April 3, 1881. He is buried in Holy Rood Cemetery, the parish burial ground that he had established.

SOURCES: There are several extant manuscript versions of the journal, but the most complete according to Patrick J. Hayes is held at the Redemptorist Archives of the Baltimore Province. This version has been recently published by Hayes (editor) as *The Civil War Diary of Father James Sheeran: Confederate Chaplain and Redemptorist* (Washington, DC: Catholic University of America Press, 2016).

See also William H. Dodd, "A Confederate Chaplains' War Journal," *Historical Records and Studies* 32 (1941): 94–103; James B. Sheeran, C.Ss.R., *Confederate Chaplain: A War Journal*, ed. Joseph T. Durkin (Milwaukee: Bruce Publishing, 1960).

THE SISTERS

CHAPTER XXVI

The Sisters in the Army

How their services were at first received—All prejudices soon disappeared—True charity knows neither creed, station, or persons—The charity that teaches us to love our neighbor as ourselves—What the sisters have done and how gratefully their services have been appreciated.

INTRODUCTION: In his introduction to his chapters on Catholic women religious who nursed the wounded of both sides, Conyngham lavishly praises their work as an example of true Christianity and as a severe blow against the prevalent anti-Catholicism of nineteenth-century America. Historians have generally agreed, often citing the sister nurses as the most positive aspect of the Catholic Civil War experience. Recent research by sister archivists indicates that over seven hundred sisters nursed soldiers on the homefront, on the battlefield, or in dozens of hospitals in the East and West. Had Conyngham published *Soldiers of the Cross* during his lifetime, it would have been the first attempt to bring to light sister nurses' heroic deeds despite long-standing antebellum prejudices against the sisters.

Instead, George Barton's *Angels of the Battlefield* (1897) was the first important study of Civil War sister nurses, followed

quickly thereafter by the even more impressive work undertaken by Ellen Ryan Jolly, head of the Ladies' Auxiliary of the
Ancient Order of Hibernians. Jolly worked tirelessly throughout her life to compile records from female religious communities across the North and South, which she used to obtain
special government grave markers indicating that the deceased
sister had been a Civil War nurse. With Congressional approval, she also succeeded in funding a monument erected in
Washington, DC, in 1924 that serves as public memorial of
their service. Her work culminated in *Nuns of the Battlefield*
(1927), the first systematic study of Civil War sister nurses. Subsequent studies have built upon the work of Barton and Jolly,
most notably Sister Mary Denis Maher's *To Bind Up the
Wounds* (1989), serving to chronicle and analyze the work of
female religious during the conflict.

SOURCES: For more on Civil War sisters, please see George
Barton, *Angels of the Battlefield: A History of the Labors of the
Catholic Sisterhoods in the Late Civil War* (Philadelphia: Catho-
lic Art Publishing, 1897); Ellen Ryan Jolly, *Nuns of the Battlefield*
(Providence, RI: Providence Visitor Press, 1927); Mary Denis
Maher, *To Bind Up the Wounds: Catholic Sister Nurses in the
U.S. Civil War* (New York: Greenwood Press, 1989); and Wil-
liam B. Kurtz, *Excommunicated from the Union: How the Civil
War Created a Separate Catholic America* (New York: Fordham
University Press, 2016), 80–88, 170. For a thorough description
of Jolly's efforts to commemorate their wartime services, see
Kathleen Szpila, "Lest We Forget: Ellen Ryan Jolly and the
Nuns of the Battlefield Monument," *American Catholic Studies*
123, no. 4 (Winter 2012): 23–43.

If the services of the Catholic chaplains, in the field, exposed them to
all the dangers and hardships of a soldier's life, the devotion of the sisters, of the various Catholic orders, to their sacred duties as nurses and
attendants in the hospitals, brought them in contact with sickness, dis-

ease, and wounds of the most malignant kind, and with men of uncultured minds, who scoffed at religion as a sentiment, an idea, a kind of bugbear if you will, and at the good sisters, as the mere agents of priestly influence and[1] intrigue.

The scoffs, the sneers, and even the insults of such men did not deter them in the least from the faithful discharge of their duties, and hate and prejudice now gone by before the chastening influence of works of mercy and charity.

When the Protestant soldier found that the sister did as much to cool his aching wounds and to refresh him by delicacies and luxuries as she did for the Catholic patient who occupied the adjoining bed, he began to think that all his bigotry and prejudices were simply the result of his unchristian education, and that it was possible for one to be a Catholic and even a *sister*, and still to possess all the noble attributes of true Christianity.

Prejudices gave way to facts, and the most bigoted, when he found the sister to watch at his bedside with the devotion of a mother, to cool his fevered brow, to soothe his aching head, and to minister to his every hurt, began to realize the fact that true charity knew no distinction of religion or persons; and that the charity, which prompted these good souls to sacrifice all worldly goods for the services of Jesus Christ, was too noble, too pure, too heavenly, to be circumscribed by the narrow and selfish limits of country, creed or station.

It was the charity of Christ Himself when he looked with pity on Mary Magdalen and told her to go and sin no more. It was the charity of Christ when he praised the heartfelt contrition of the poor publican—it was more—it was the charity and humility of Christ when he washed the feet of his disciples. Let sceptics and atheists sneer as they smile at religion, how much purer, better and holier would this life be if we had among us more of that divine charity which teaches us to love our neighbors as ourselves. Instead of this noble, this divine doctrine of love towards your neighbor, hate, persecution and discord seem to be the controlling principles of the Christian ethics of today. We see all around us men hating one another for the love of God, and[2] robbing the poor to enrich themselves, yet they walk around with an air of sanctified purity.

The sisters labored hard to render all possible assistance as nurses, without regard to the religious opinions or doctrines of their patients. They were as attentive to a Protestant as to a Catholic, without interfering with his religious opinions or prejudices. In fact they knew no religion in the discharge of their duties, but Christianity, and pure charity; and they made no distinction, whatever, in their attendance but such as suffering humanity demanded.

If they removed prejudices from the minds of the soldiers of other denominations, it was because their good works impressed them with the conviction that their mission must have been from on high; and if they made converts it was by the force of example not by entreaty.

Though the paid and volunteer nurses rendered excellent assistance in the hospitals in Washington and elsewhere, we honestly ask did all these paid services reach the heart of the soldier, or make him feel that he was attended for some motive higher than the sordid consideration of dimes and dollars? Ask the soldier today, who had given some time in hospital, how he regards his nurses and attendant there, and ten to one, he will burst out into a fit of praise of the good sisters and their services to him.

When the war commenced, these sisters were quietly and modestly attending to their conventual duties and also to the wants of the suffering poor who want, and starve, and die, almost unknown in all large cities. Few could expect that the poor, modest, shrinking Sister of Charity would be the first to expose herself to all the hardships, privations, and rudeness of hospital life! Yet, so it was. She felt that there was her duty—there was her mission—there was where she could do the most good to relieve suffering humanity, and she cheerfully went forth on her errand of love and charity.

> She felt in her spirit the summons of grace,
> that called her to love for the suffering race;
> And, heedless of pleasure, of comforts, of home,
> rose quickly, like Mary, and answered, "I come."
> Unshrinking where pestilence scatters his breath,
> Like an angel she moves, 'mid the vapors of death;
> Where rings the loud musket, and flashes the sword,
> Unfearing she walks, for she follows the Lord![3]

Such was the humble religious. Whether Sister of Charity, Sister of Mercy, Sister of the Holy Cross, or sister of any other order, she cheerfully responded to the call of suffering humanity, and devoted her time, her services, her prayers, and in many cases her very life, to relieve the wants and sufferings of her fellow creatures.

Their good works have proclaimed the success of their mission, and thousands today, even of different denominations, bless the name and memory of the good, pious and faithful sisters. Though the writer has left nothing undone to collect materials for the sketches of the sisters and of their services in the field and hospitals, he must confess that he has not been as successful as he was in the case of the chaplains; for shrinking, modest, and retiring, the sisters on the whole declined to furnish much information, on the grounds that they labored for the glory and honor of God and not for the approbation of men. However, the following sketches will give the reader a good insight into what they have done and how gratefully their services were appreciated.

CHAPTER XXVII

The Sisters of Mercy, Charleston

*Their attendance on the Federal prisoners—Their best donors—
Their influence on the soldiers—Anecdotes and incidents
in hospital—The sisters provided with a general pass—Letters from
Federal officers and soldiers—Their generous testimony to their
services and kindness—Protestants and Catholics alike bear testimony
in their behalf—Their Christian charity and incessant labors.*

INTRODUCTION: The Sisters of Our Lady of Mercy were
first established in the Diocese of Charleston, South Carolina, by Bishop John England in 1829. Patterned after Mother
Seton's Sisters of Charity, the initial community was formed
by four women who came from Baltimore to Charleston and
made their professions in January 1831. Their earliest works included care for orphans and the education of young women.
From 1841 to 1861 the community's motherhouse served si-
multaneously as convent, girls' orphanage, and the Academy of
Our Lady of Mercy.

After running an academy in Columbia for many years, the
city's third bishop, Patrick N. Lynch, replaced them in August
1858 with a group of Ursulines from Ohio led by his sister,
Mother Baptista Lynch. The Sisters of Our Lady of Mercy then
took charge of a new boy's orphanage in Charleston, where
they remained until the outbreak of the Civil War. The sisters'

329

orphanage for boys, along with the cathedral and the offices of the city's Catholic newspaper, burned to the ground on December 11, 1861. Nevertheless, led by Mother Mary Teresa Barry, one of the community's founding members, the sisters cared for the wounded in their own convent and for Union prisoners at a nearby military hospital. Several of their number even journeyed north to White Sulphur Springs, Virginia, to run a Confederate military hospital at the request of John McGill, the bishop of Richmond.

Chronologically confused, the entire chapter consists of clippings from undated, unidentified newspaper articles. Given the style and language of the writer, it is likely that most of the anecdotal clippings were written by Conyngham himself, who, like in his later chapter on the Sisters of Mount St. Vincent, Cincinnati, reused previous articles he had written on the clergy and sisters in the Civil War for *Soldiers of the Cross*. The chapter is also full of letters of testimony written by former Union soldiers and prisoners of war in Charleston on behalf of the sisters who were seeking federal compensation for the destruction of their property by the Union bombardment. Conyngham took these letters from an 1870 petition put together by the state's legislature on the sisters' behalf.

The community at Charleston consisted of a superior and about nine sisters. Their charity and zeal in ministering to the wants, and affording material aid and consolation, to the Federal prisoners in the stockade and the sick and wounded in the hospitals, have been confirmed by the generous testimony of several officers and men, Protestants as well as Catholics. They made no distinction between Federals or Confederates in their attendance, and many an anxious parent, [in the] North, was indebted to the sisters for the information, privately conveyed, that their boys were living. In many cases they managed to send letters from prisoners, or portraits, to their friends in the North, or in other prisons.

About the time of the attack on Fort Fisher[1] great poverty, and in many cases actual want, prevailed in Charleston; still, the sisters, from their own scanty stores, and what they could get from the charitable, and Northern sympathizers, always managed to soften the hard fare of corn bread given to the Federals, by fresh bread and new milk. They often cheered and revived many a sick and wounded soldier with good nourishing diet, such as mincemeat, pies, soups and the like. Though the times pressed hard on themselves, they managed to keep all the time three cows, the milk of which went to the inmates of the prisons and hospitals. They collected all the clothes they could and when a ragged prisoner was brought in, they immediately clothed him from their store.

We must recollect that the sisters had neither public nor government funds at their disposal for the relief of prisoners. Their liberal supplies of bread, meats, wines, soups, clothing, and the like, were all supplied from their own limited stores, and from what they could collect from the Union sympathizers and charitable people of Charleston. Foremost among the liberal and charitable donors was an Irish Catholic family, Mr. John Kenny and his wife, of Queen Street. These almost exhausted their means in supplying the hospitals with soup, meats, and fresh bread, which was grateful to poor fellows whose allowance was only corn bread. When wounded prisoners came in, Mrs. Kenny tore up her own and her husband's linen to make lint and bandages, often stripping off the linen they had on for that purpose. Mrs. Kenny's brother, John Donahue, was equally charitable. A Mr. Johnson, a Protestant gentleman, was equally generous in furnishing clothing and soup for the prisoners on the race course.[2]

When their own supplies were exhausted, these and other charitable persons went around with the sisters to collect clothing and provisions, and as they well knew the parties to whom to apply, they were generally successful. Among those whose purse and heart were always open to the claims of the sisters, we should mention a Protestant gentleman, Mr. James McCarter, now living in

Newton, New Jersey. He liberally supplied with money both the sisters and Mrs. Eliza Potter, who was a daily visitor at the Queen Street Hospital for six or eight months after it was opened.

It is remarkable what influence the quiet, unobtrusive gentleness of woman has even upon the hardest natures. Men, who in camp could swear as hard as Uncle Toby's profanest soldier in Flanders,[3] soon become docile; and should an expression savoring of the profane escape them in presence of the sisters, they would humbly apologize. No child ever looked for the presence of his mother more earnestly than did the patients in hospital to the daily visits from the sisters; and gratefully and thankfully did they receive from them the cooling fruits and nourishing meats and broths which they helped them to. One of the soldiers went by the soubriquet of "Good for Me," from the fact that when a sister was feeding a sicker patient with anything nice, the fellow would whine out, "Wa-al, I reckon, sister, a little of that would be good for me." After the attack on Morris Island, the sergeant of a New York regiment, named Carrigan, was brought into hospital, badly wounded in the shoulder. He was attended by one of the sisters, a Southern lady, with strong sympathy for the cause of her people. While the wound was dressing he was insensible, but recovering consciousness, he looked up and exclaimed, "I tell you, we'll take that d——d island yet."

A fine strapping Michigan soldier named Francesco, greatly prejudiced against the Catholics, quietly watched the sisters day by day going around on their errands of mercy. One morning a sister was giving him some wine. Seeing the Rosary hanging by her side he said:

"Wa-al, I reckon you belong to some society?"

"Yes, to a religious order."

"Something like the Freemasons, I reckon?"

"Not exactly; our society is a Roman Catholic religious order."

"Wa-al, them Roman Catholics, are ba-ad people,—very bad people."

"What makes you think so, friend?"

"Wa-al, I have often heard so and I have read so in books, too."

"Most likely, but we are not to judge from all we hear and read, particularly from those prejudiced against the Catholics. Tell me, can you give an instance, yourself, of the wickedness of Catholics?"

"Not 'zactly, but there is a Catholic fellow in the next bed and he swears terribly."

"Now, you shut up!" said the fellow in the next bed, "I'm not a Catholic, but a North of Ireland Presbyterian."

"Wa-al! really, Sister—do hear that—there may be some Catholics like you, I'll not think so hard of them after your kindness, for you're re-ally good."

"Friend," mildly replied the sister, "do not judge harshly of those you know nothing about; there are some bad Catholics, no doubt, but many better than I am. Our holy religion teaches us love and charity to all. If we follow the teachings and precepts of that religion, we make no distinction between black or white, race or color, Protestant or Catholic, Jew or Gentile, but distribute our charity alike to all."

Another prisoner says, in a confidential whisper, to the attending sister:

"Sister, ain't you Union?"

"How do you know?"

"Well, you are so kind and good to us poor fellows, I know you must be Union, but, Sister," in a more confidential whisper, "you need not fear telling me, you know."

"Did I ever ask you, friend, whether you were a Catholic or Protestant?"

"Never!"

"Have you seen me, in my attendance on the prisoners, making any distinction on account of religion?"

"No, Sister, I am a Protestant, and am sure I would not be on my legs to-day, but for you, God bless you!"

"Well, my friend! What I have done for the Federal prisoners, I would do for the Confederate. Charity has neither politics nor religion. We try to alleviate the sufferings of the afflicted according to the teachings of our religion and Our Divine Master, and from Him alone we expect to reap our reward."

A fine young soldier named Markham, who was suffering from pulmonary disease, was removed from the stockade to the hospital; there was something so gentle and unobtrusive about him that the sisters took a special interest in him. He gradually sank and the racking cough increased to a painful degree, yet he never complained nor murmured. As the sister sat beside him to help him to his soup or medicine, he loved to converse about home, about his mother, brothers and sisters, until his large luminous eyes would become dim with tears. The doctor told the sister that his end was approaching, and that it might be well to break the news to him. So, going her rounds, she quietly sat beside him and taking his hand, asked,

"How do you feel to-day?"

"Oh, much better, Sister; the cough is nearly gone, and if I only get a little stronger I'll be all right."

"My dear friend," replied the sister, "symptoms are often deceitful, we should not be deceived by them, but prepare for a happier exchange, for this world is all vanity."

He raised himself gently in the bed and fixed his dark eyes on the sister, as he asked:

"Oh Sister! Are you trying to break the news to me that there is no hope? If so, do not be afraid to tell me, I can bear it—but then, I feel so well!"

"My dear, life and death are in the hands of God; you appear to be so good a young man, that I am sure you have no fear of meeting your Maker and Savior."

He lay still for a moment, with his hands clasped over his face, and the tears trickled through his fingers.

He aroused himself, as if ashamed of his weakness, and said:

"Excuse me, Sister! It is not the thought of death that thus unmans me, but it is so hard to die without seeing my dear mother and family." After a time he became quite reconciled, and talked freely of his approaching end.

"You ought to have a minister and make proper preparations, if you will tell me what minister you desire, I'll send for him."

"The truth is, Sister, I have been brought up in no denomination, and have never had any religious instruction, but, I would like to belong to your religion."

"My young friend, I am a Roman Catholic. A great many who do not understand our Holy Religion, are prejudiced against it."

"Was not the world prejudiced against Our Savior? I know your religion must be good, otherwise you could not be what you are."

The sister brought him the priest, who baptized and prepared him for death. A sister remained continually by him, joining in prayer and other acts of devotion, and in two days, he yielded his pure soul into the hands of his Maker.

The following letter from the Secretary of War, though not in chronological order here, will show that the services of the sisters were not limited by race or color. There were strong extenuating circumstances in favor of [Samuel J.] Benton. He committed the murder while in a state of intense excitement, caused by the murdered man and his friends. The sisters having learned the full particulars of the case, laid them, in a forcible manner, before Secretary Stanton, who favorably considered them, and granted a pardon to the prisoner.[4]

War Department
Adjutant-General's Office,
Washington, December 16, 186[5][5]

Mother M. Teresa,[6] Superior, and Sister M. Xavier,[7]
Convent of Our Lady of Mercy, Charleston, South Carolina

Ladies;—In reply to your communication of October 16th, 1865, addressed to Brevet Major General R. Saxton, Assistant Commissioner, regarding the pardon of Samuel J. Benton, colored, 54th Massachusetts Volunteers, imprisoned in Fort Delaware for the crime of murder, I have the honor to inform you that the release of Benton was ordered by letter from this office.

I am, very respectfully, your ob't serv't,

E. D. Townsend,
Ass't Ad.-Gen'l.

So great was the confidence in the sisters and so thoroughly did the Confederate officials appreciate their services, that they had a pass to go within the lines at all times and places.

The following is a copy of the pass given to the sisters at Charleston:

Headquarters, Department of
South Carolina, Georgia and Florida.
Charleston, South Carolina, October 1, 1864

The "Sisters of Mercy" have permission to visit the "Federal Prisoners of War" confined in this city, without distinction, until further orders.

By command of Major Lane Jones,

J. F. Lay
Major and Department Inspector

A French officer, being placed with some negroes, after arrest, felt very indignant and became very excited. He wrote to the sisters to come to his relief.

Charleston Jail

Sister M. Xavier, Convent of Mercy

Dear Sister:—I should be very glad if you would be kind enough to come to see me immediately in the jail.

Yours, very respectfully,

L. Duverge,[8]
Captain U.S.V.

The sister did go immediately, attended to his wants, got him better quarters, and finally succeeded in getting him out.

We make the following extracts from letters received from officers, who were prisoners in Charleston, to the sisters, after their release, thanking them for their care, attention and services.

These gentlemen are, I believe, all Protestants, and, therefore, their testimony to the kind charitable offices of the sisters, must have the more weight.

Sisters of Mercy, Charleston
Gen'l Post Office Department,
Washington, April 8th, 1869

Sister M. Xavier

Madam:—Having, by accident, been referred to a speech of Hon. F. A. Sawyers, in support of the appropriation for the Sisters of Mercy of Charleston, South Carolina, I have taken the liberty of penning a brief testimonial of my appreciation of the valuable services rendered by yourself and the sisters to our suffering and emaciated soldiers, who, like myself, were confined as prisoners of war, at Charleston, S. C., during the Summer and Fall of 1864.

On my arrival at Charleston, with the "immortal" six hundred,[9] who were placed under fire of the Union guns on Morris Island, I met you and your noble sisters in the hospitals and prisons, administering to the wants and comfort of my fellow prisoners, by furnishing them, not only with proper food and nourishment, etc., but even with clothing to those who were destitute. I also witnessed the noble sacrifices you made in nursing our sick during those dark days, when the yellow fever was carrying off our best officers and men—and when Confederate officers were too much alarmed to even furnish water for the sick and dying—and I know full well, that but for your untiring devotion to our helpless and unfortunate officers and soldiers, thousands to-day would have been sleeping the sleep that knows no waking.

Sincerely yours,

John E. Michener,
Late Captain 85th Pennsylvania Infantry[10]

Military Prison, Columbia, South Carolina
December 6, 1864

Sister M. Xavier

Dear Sister—I have been sick ever since my removal from Charleston to this place, and I now beg to remind you of your promise, to use your influence to get my name on the exchange list as I am told there will be an exchange of prisoners next week. I sincerely thank you for the money (dollars) which I received through Father McNeal. I assure you, it was very acceptable, and I hope, if I live, to repay you for all your kind favors.

Gratefully and respectfully yours,

John Dunn,

1st Lieutenant, Co. I, 164th Regt., New York Vols.

The writer of the following was a brave officer and worthy gentleman, and though a Protestant, bears honest testimony to the kind offices of the sisters.

New York, June 7th, 1867

I hereby certify that on the night of the 17th of June, 1864, I was captured by the enemy, in an attack upon their works, in front of Petersburg, Virginia, and, with many others, was soon after taken to Macon, Georgia, general rendezvous for officers, prisoners of war, from whence (in August) was taken to Charleston, South Carolina, and confined in Roper Hospital, on Queen St., and immediately under fire from our batteries. During my stay there, the building was several times perforated by shot and shell, and the Orphan's Asylum, standing on the opposite corner of the street, was almost demolished. Being very sick, I was taken to general hospital at Rikersville, near Charleston, which was filled with officers and men of our army and navy, the great majority of whom were dying for want of stimulating food and proper care. It was at this time that I met the Sisters of Mercy, from Charleston, who almost daily visited the hospital, not only cheering us with words of consolation, but substantially administering to our wants, by bringing us food and clothing, procured by them at their *own* expense, and furnished to us gratis. They saw that our letters were deposited in the proper channel, through which they would reach our friends at home, and attended to the delivery of letters and boxes which came from the North for us, and, in fact, exerted themselves in every conceivable way to render us comfortable and happy. I most cheerfully pay this tribute to the Holy Order of the *Sisters of Mercy* of Charleston, South Carolina, who were instrumental in many instances in saving the lives of our officers and men, and whose repeated acts of kindness were so grateful to us—as they were disinterested on the part of the sisters.

John S. Hammell,
Late Colonel of 66th Michigan Vols.
and Brvt. Brig. General U.S. Vols.

Grand Rapids, Michigan, July 12, 1865
Lady Superior.

Madam—Probably you do not remember seeing, last Summer, at the 1st South Carolina Hospital, a Federal officer, who told you "he had not spoken with a lady in two years." Doubtless, among so many poor, half-starved wretches, no particular one would be likely to make so much impression as to cause you to remember him; but, madam, I assure you, your kind looks and words sank deep into many a heart, and often have I heard both officers and men bless you and the good Sisters of your Order. I was twenty months a prisoner, and the only kindness I saw displayed towards us was at the hospital in Charleston, South Carolina. I was sent with the rest of the officers to Columbia, and from thence we became a sort of advance guard to Sherman, as we were run about from place to place as he advanced, till at length we were set at liberty on the 1st of March, 1865, at Wilmington, North Carolina, and once more stood under the protecting folds of our dear old flag. I immediately returned to my regiment, the 6th Michigan Cavalry, at Petersburg, Virginia, when I was mustered out of the service after serving with it until the 21st of June last, at Fort Leavenworth, Kansas, together with my whole company. I am now prosecuting my old profession (that of a lawyer) in this place. I beg you will pardon me for thus trespassing on your time, but I wished to testify my appreciation of your kindness to us in the hour of need. I am not of your Church, and have always been taught to believe it to be nothing but evil; however, actions speak louder than words, and I am free to admit, that if Christianity does exist on the earth, it has some of its closest followers among the Ladies of your Order. If not contrary to your rules, and if agreeable to yourself, I should be happy to receive an acknowledgment of the receipt of this.

Very respectfully your obd't. servant,

S. H. Ballard[11]

The first pass given to the Sisters of Mercy, Charleston, was from General Beauregard himself, dated June 18th, 1862, and granted them general permission to visit the Union prisoners without restriction.

This being lost, a new one was issued by Major Lay giving them similar privileges. Among those who contributed to the relief of the prisoners was General Thos. Jordan;[12] who gave the sisters fifty dollars and told them to call on him again should their funds get low, and requested them to report to him should they witness any bad treatment of the Union prisoners.

The Rev. Father Fillion and Rev. Dr. [John] Moore[13] were particularly kind and attentive to both the spiritual and temporal wants of the prisoners. Father Fillion, beside the stockade at Florence every Tuesday, remaining among the prisoners until Friday. In the zealous discharge of his duties there, he contracted camp fever on the 14th of February 186[5][14] and died a martyr to the cause of humanity and Christianity on the 21st, two days after the occupation of Charleston. The kind and charitable Rev. P[atrick] O'Neil,[15] who was an attendant at the Rikersville hospital and the race course, had died, like the Good Shepherd, tending the stricken flock of Christ, on the January previous. Not one of the then inmates, who read this, no matter what his creed or his politics may have been, can forget the kind, sympathetic priest, whose genial smile cheered him, whose advice and counsel consoled him, and whose timely aid relieved many a pressing want.[16]

We give the following among the many incidents occurring to the sisters during their ministrations to the sick and wounded.

One of the sisters brought peaches for one ward and grapes for another, not having a sufficiency of both for each ward.

She said to the men, while distributing the grapes, "Don't carry any of these into the next ward, as I have no more of them."

While distributing her pieces in the next room she found a poor Michigan invalid actually blubbering, and on looking around saw a one legged soldier from New York named McCarthy leaning on his crutch at the door, and tempting the poor fellow with the luscious fruit. "Ah," said the invalid, "if I could only get enough of them, how happy I'd be; I need not be drinking bad water."

A prisoner named Boyden from New York lost his right hand, and was very weak from loss of blood. As the sisters were going to the hospital, they met the bishop, who asked if they had seen Boyden, and told them to "give him stimulants and see that he did not get a chill, for if he did, he would certainly die." Previous to this warning, the sisters feared to give stimulants to wounded men. Afterwards, whenever the sisters came, Boyden would ask them if they had any of the "O be joyful." At first they were at a loss to know what he meant, but he explained by saying, "Have you not got a bottle in your basket?"

After a while Boyden learned to write with the left hand and the first note in his journal was about "the ladies in black," as he called the Sisters of Mercy.

A colored soldier was brought into the hospital wounded in the arm and knee. When the sisters came his wounds were still unwashed, and he said not a word, as none of the nurses noticed him. The sisters asked one of them why he was not attended to, and took cloths and water, commencing to wash and dress his wounds. After a while the poor fellow was made as comfortable as the case would admit. Asking him where he was from, he said, "Bermuda, Madame." "Why you are an English subject, how come you here?"

"Ah Madam, they gave me fifty dollars." "Why, I would not give that arm for five hundred," said the sister. "Madam," said he, "I would not give it for five thousand dollars." Poor fellow, both the leg and arm had to be taken off as there was no chance to save his life otherwise, and he got on apparently well for three weeks but afterwards died of jaundice. He was decidedly the most intelligent man in the room and a regular Othello in symmetry.

The mother superior gave a shirt to a prisoner who was in the hospital and the nurse could not imagine what caused his great uneasiness, when he allowed her to send it to the wash-kitchen; at last, he told her who had given it to him, and added "that it should be kept in his family while there was a shred of it together."

When the first shell fell near the Queen Street hospital, the men who were badly wounded begged the sister to ask the doctor to have them removed out of the range of the shells. She did so, and the doctor said he had already made a requisition to that effect. But when going through the ward he said, joking, "What, you Yanks, are you afraid of your own shells?" They were all in a great way to know who had asked the sister to beg the doctor, saying, "Now it will be in all the newspapers that we were afraid of our own shells?" Sister asked them if they did not think their own shells as hard as any others?

Two men were on one occasion brought to hospital from some stockade or prison, and they were so ill that they were laid in the piazza. While two of the sisters and one of the convalescents were trying to revive the two poor patients, a Confederate officer (Captain Simons)[17] wept over them, saying to the sisters, "I could meet these men in the field, but I cannot stand this." It was not a rare thing to see the officers, on guard at the race course, shed tears, while they accompanied the sisters in their rounds among the sick in the stockade.

An Irishman, named [William] Finton,[18] who lost a leg at Morris Island, and who was always very cheerful during his tedious imprisonment, was asked by one of the sisters, "What company do you belong to, Finton?" "Faith I'm ashamed to tell you, sister." "Why so?" "Because I belong to a mighty mean Regiment." "How is that, what have they done?" "Well, I'll tell you; I belong to the 9th Maine, who burned the Catholic Church in Jackson."[19] "How many Irish were among them?" "Nine or ten." "And why could not so many have saved the church? What were you all doing while they burned it?" "Oh! we tried to save it, but we were ordered to be put in irons and carried away, so we were locked up."

A colored prisoner, named Baltimore,[20] was asked, by one of the sisters, where he lost his arm. "On the *top* of *Battery Wagner*," was his reply. "Why did you go *there*," said the sister. "Because the fire was all around," said he, "there was no safety on any side, I had to go forward whether I liked it or not."

A young man from New Hampshire, named Wm. Merrill,[21] who lived sixteen days in the Queen St. Hospital, and died from the effects of a wound above the knee, asked, when near death, one of the nurses, to bring him the sisters' minister. He had never been baptized. Father Moore was called in, and the young man received all the Sacraments, and died blessing the sisters for their kindness to him and his comrades. He was only one out of hundreds who, of their own accord, made choice of the faith wherein they had found charity.

The following speaks volumes in behalf of the appeal of the Sisters of Mercy for the restoration of their asylum, destroyed during the bombardment of Charleston.

State of Connecticut,
County of New Haven, ss.

I hereby certify that I, F[rederick] R. Jackson (formerly a sergeant in company F, 7th Connecticut Volunteer Infantry), lost my left arm in battle, on James' Island, South Carolina, June 16th, 1862, and was then and there taken prisoner by the enemy. I was carried from the battlefield to Charleston, South Carolina, June 19th, 1862, and was then and there placed in a building known as "Mart Hospital" on King or Queen Street (I am uncertain which) in which were confined all of the prisoners taken June 16th, who were seriously wounded. Soon after our arrival in Charleston we were visited by Sister M. Xavier, accompanied by another Sister of Mercy, each bearing comforts for us, the wounded Union prisoners. Sister Xavier came to the hospital prison daily, accompanied each time by another sister, and each day went to all our number and gave fruit, corn bread, cake, meat, gruel, arrow root, and sometimes chicken and chicken broth. She brought me daily either a bottle of wine or of brandy—generally a bottle of old Malaga wine. There were eight wounded men confined in our cell, only one of whom, Captain Lawler,[22] was a Roman Catholic. All received the same attentions at the hands of Sister M. Xavier and [her] companion. The great majority of our number were of the Protestant faith, but there was no distinction made between us on account of religion or nationality. The sisters were, day and night, unremitting in their attentions to us. They provided for all of our wants, and made our prison life in Charleston a perfect heaven on earth, compared to what we experienced after leaving that place. Sister Xavier often brought interesting books of all kinds. Lint, medicines, and money were furnished by her to those in need, and nearly all, if not *all*, were daily supplied with wine, cordial, brandy, or some stimulating liquor. This kind treatment continued without intermission during the two months we were prisoners at Charleston. I have not the command of language wherewith to sufficiently attest the great benevolence and kindness of the Sisters of Mercy who were in Charleston, South Carolina, in 1862, ministering to the every want of our wounded Union prisoners, nearly all of whom, myself included, were Protestants.

F. R. Jackson,
Formerly Sergeant Co. F, 7th Connecticut Vols.

The next letter is from U.S. Consul at St. Thomas:

U.S. Consulate at St. Thomas
March 10th, 1869

To Sister M. Xavier, Washington.

I received your kind letters of January 18th, and February 3rd, and as per your request I enclose a letter to Congress which I hope will have some effect in your favor and which I recommend you to hand to the Hon. Joseph Fowler, member of the Senate, and the Hon. Isaac R. Hawkins, member of Congress, as coming from me, and I must say that I hope you will be able to succeed in your enterprise.

I must also embrace this opportunity to thank you for your kindness to me during my imprisonment in Charleston, which I shall ever remember.

I remain yours very truly,

John T. Robeson,[23]

U.S. Consul.

The following letters were received by the sisters from Federal officers, who had been under their care.

The first is an extract from a statement of Lieutenant Colonel L. S. Payne,[24] 100th New York Volunteers, now residing at Lockport, New York.

•   •   •

While acting under special orders of General Gillmore in the attempt to intercept the enem[y's][25] communication between Charleston City and Cummings' Point, on Morris Island, on the night of the third of August, 1863, I was attacked by a superior force, wounded and taken prisoner with nine of my men, four of whom were also wounded.

The wounded of my party were taken to Queen Street Hospital, Charleston, where there were a large number [of patients]. Several hundred of those had previously been at the bloody assault on Battery Wagner, and in other operations on Morris' Island, where they had been wounded, and had fallen into the hands of the enemy.

This hospital was assigned exclusively to wounded prisoners, and all citizens were forbidden permission to visit it.

The Sisters of Mercy, after much opposition, succeeded in obtaining permission to visit the hospital for the purpose of dispensing their truly Christian charity, and relieving the sufferings of the wounded and dying. I need not particularize, but I will state that the attention of these Angels of Mercy to our wounded soldiers were at this time incessant and unceasing, never failing to call daily and some one or more of them—for there seemed to be many of them—calling oftener, and administering to the severer cases. In their supplies of palatable food and changes of clothing furnished to those destitute, and in all their ministrations, they made no distinction between rank, color, or creed, but their relief was directed to all alike.

The excessively hot weather, the insufficient supplies of medicines and other necessaries, together with the little nursing help, induces me to believe that through the aid of these kind people the lives of many of our soldier-prisoners were saved.

After being transported from Charleston to Columbia, and since my return home, I have met with many of the officers and soldiers, who had been in Charleston as prisoners, and they all universally speak of the unbounded kindness and goodness of these 'Sisters of Mercy' of Charleston. The lives, occupation, and mission of these 'Sisters of Mercy' is truly one of mercy and charity indeed.

The following letter, dated Columbia, South Carolina, Prison, October 14th, 1864, by John Rourke, of Milbank City, Wisconsin, Captain of Battery L, 1st Illinois Artillery, was addressed to Mother Teresa, of Charleston. Captain Rourke and other officers had been removed from Charleston Prison to Columbia:

Revered Mother:—The officers, prisoners of war, who came from Charleston here are all well. We would prefer being prisoners in your city to any place in the Confederacy. I hope Confederate prisoners at the North are as favorably impressed with the kind attention of the sisters there. The night of the day we arrived here it rained very heavy, and as we had no shelter we had to stand up under it in torrents. It was not pleasant after leaving comparatively comfortable quarters in Charleston. However, it did not seem to impair the health of the officers. I think that two of them died here; one of them, it is said, of yellow fever. I hope the plague will soon subside in your city. I would like to know how Lieutenant Charles Trownsell is. You undoubtedly remember him; he roomed with me, and was taken sick the night before I left Charleston, and had to remain behind.

Please tender to Sister Xavier my sincere thanks and well wishes; also remember me to Dr. Moore.

Hoping to have an opportunity, some day, to prove my thanks, and liquidate the debt of gratitude to you and your co-workers, for your consoling and kind treatment to me, and also to all the sick prisoners of war in your city, I will conclude by wishing you all the happiness and joys of Heaven.

Colonel Henry sends his kind and grateful regards to you.

The next letter is from Adjutant Henry [T.] Kendall,[26] 50th Pennsylvania Volunteers, who was a prisoner in Columbia, South Carolina, inquiring after his brother, Lieutenant Joseph [V]. Kendall,[27] of the same regiment, who was a prisoner in Charleston. Sister Xavier managed to open a communication between them, which explains the subsequent letter from the brother.

Sister M. Xavier:

Your kind letter of the 13th, in answer to my request, and your recent efforts in brother's behalf, have again placed me under many obligations. I have succeeded in getting some articles of clothing, which will add to his comfort. My only regret is that I am unable, at present, to forward the money he needs. It gives me comfort to think that I will soon be able to supply his wants in this respect. I enclose a letter from brother. I will make application, this morning, to send the articles above mentioned to your care for him.

Camp of the 50th Regt., Pennsylvania Vol.
Near Georgetown, D.C.
June 17th, 1865

Sister M. Xavier, Convent of Mercy,
Charleston, South Carolina

Respected Friend:—I was paroled as a Union prisoner and sent into our lines from Richmond, just three days before it fell.

Your letter, written to brother Henry, was received while I was at home in Reading, and I at once mailed it to him at Philadelphia, where he is now at College. He is preparing himself for a civil engineer. I wrote to him at the time, telling him to send the letter to me, and I would reply to it, as I was very anxious to express my heartfelt gratitude for the many acts of kindness received by me, at your hands. I should have written much sooner, but I was then engaged in writing an account of my experience in the Confederacy, and I did not wish to write before I could enclose to you a copy of it. This embraces a short sketch of my eleven months' imprisonment, so I will not speak in my letter to you of my condition after leaving Charleston; it will be a greater satisfaction to you to read the full account.

I entered our lines on the 30th of March, and was taken to Parole Camp, Annapolis, Maryland, where I remained four days, to get cleaned up, paid, clothed, etc. I then started home on a furlough of 30 days. I was very much troubled on the way. During all my imprisonment, I had never heard one word from home, and numberless questions crowded themselves upon my mind. Would I find my mother alive—my aged grandmother—my dear sisters and brothers? I was also troubled about Henry. I knew he had entered our lines in December of 1864, for you wrote to me, stating that he had been exchanged at Charleston. I afterwards ascertained that he had made his escape before you were able to effect his exchange. I feared that he might have fallen in the late engagements before Petersburg, but, it appears that he was mustered out shortly after his return.

I did not write home from Annapolis, to apprise them of my coming. As I jumped from the cars at Reading, I did not expect to see any one I knew, but the first person I saw was Henry, dressed in citizens' clothing. His baggage was already on the cars—his ticket bought and he just going to start for Philadelphia, but my appearance changed his program, and he remained in Reading with me for two weeks, before going to College.

Our joy at meeting knew no bounds. For eleven months we had been separated; although, at times, we were so near to each other. At Charleston, we made repeated efforts to obtain an interview, all to no avail, and had it not been for your kind offices of mercy, I should not have known, until arriving at home, whether brother was alive or dead.

Indeed, I feel confident that had it not been for your efforts in my behalf, I could not have survived the winter in that terrible stockade at Florence. When I came to Charleston I was almost naked; so much so that when you came to the camp on the "Race Course" I was ashamed to make my appearance before you, but you noticed my condition and clothed me. Those clothes kept me from freezing at Florence. How anxiously I watched day by day for the arrival of that most welcome of ambulances with the good sisters, at the Race Course. It encouraged me to hope and keep up my drooping spirits.

At the depot I could scarcely muster courage to ask Henry, "How are all at home?" but when I found that they were all well and hearty, I made all haste in my power to embrace them. Oh! What a happy family we were that night! I had more questions put to me in half-an-hour than I could answer in a week.

There was no end to the kissing and shaking of hands, and Henry manifested his delight by turning summersaults on the floor. My three sisters clung to me at once, while mother laughed and cried alternately. It was the happiest moment of my life—but amidst all this rejoicing I did not forget my kind benefactress—she, to whom we owed this happy union, and all this rejoicing. I told them all about you and your kind ministrations on my behalf. We all feel that we are under everlasting obligations to you, and mother would give almost anything to see you herself to embrace you and thank you. Grateful hearts, that night, poured fervent prayers to heaven to reward and bless you, who, though of a different religion, have truly acted the good Samaritan.

They had heard of my second escape at home but after waiting seven weeks to hear from me, they had given me up as lost. At different times I have met soldiers who were prisoners at the Race Course, and it pleases me to hear them all speak in such high terms of the "Sisters of Mercy."

You can never know the amount of good you have accomplished, for it cannot be estimated.

I was very much grieved to hear of the death of Father Fillion. He looked so well the last time I saw him at Florence. I hope Father Moore is enjoying good health; please remember me to him, and tell him I often speak of him and the many favors he has done me.

Captain [William H.] Telford[28] of our regiment, who was a prisoner with my brother at the Roper Hospital, is now colonel of the regiment. He wishes to be kindly remembered to you. I remained home till the 19th of May when I returned to the regiment as 1st lieutenant of my company.

I hope our soldiers at Charleston are treating you with the respect due to your noble efforts in behalf of suffering humanity. I should feel bad to hear that they are not doing so. Henry wishes to be gratefully remembered to you. We have often talked together about how we could repay you for your kindness. We thought that you would not accept pecuniary compensation, and then we thought of other plans but could come to no conclusion. For the present, accept the gratitude of a happy, reunited family for your disinterested goodness and kindness, and may your labors be crowned with everlasting happiness.

Mother often speaks of you and wishes over and over that she could get a small photograph of one to whom she owes so much. Would it be improper to ask you for one for her; if not it would please her so much.

Of 110 of our regiment who were prisoners, but 40 have returned alive.

Will you please write to me?

Sincerely and gratefully, I am your respectful servant,

Joseph [V].[29] Kendall

1st Lieut, Co. H, 50 Pennsylvania Vol.

❀   ❀   ❀

EPILOGUE: Despite the devastation of their city and property during the war, the Charleston Sisters of Our Lady of Mercy continued to expand their teaching efforts beyond Charleston to Wilmington, North Carolina, during Reconstruction. They were also successful, with the help of the South Carolina Legislature and the testimony of many Union soldiers, in receiving $12,000 of a requested $20,000 in compensation from the federal government for the wartime destruction of their motherhouse, orphanage, and academy. With these funds, they bought an old mansion in 1870 for use as a convent and school. By the time of Mother Barry's death in 1900, the sisters had grown to sixty members and, in addition to their orphanage and schools, also administered a hospital and school of nursing.

SOURCES: South Carolina General Assembly, "The Petition of the Members of the Legislature of South Carolina to the Congress of the United States in Favor of the Sisters of Our Lady of Mercy, Charleston, S.C., for the Rebuilding of Their Orphan Asylum" (Charleston, SC: Edward Perry, 1870); Ellen Ryan Jolly, *Nuns of the Battlefield* (Providence, RI: Providence Visitor Press, 1927), 287–98; A Member of the Order, "A Southern Teaching Order: The Sisters of Mercy of Charleston, S.C., A.D. 1829–1904," *Records of the American Catholic Historical Society of Philadelphia*, vol. 15, no.3 (Philadelphia: American Catholic Historical Society, 1904): 249–65; M. Anne Francis Campbell, O.L.M., "Bishop England's Sisterhood, 1829–1929" (PhD diss., St. Louis University, 1968), 90–182; David C. R. Heisser and Stephen J. White, Sr., *Patrick N. Lynch, 1817–1882: Third Catholic Bishop of Charleston* (Columbia: University of South Carolina Press, 2015), 51–52, 155–56; Richard C. Madden, *Catholics in South Carolina: A Record* (New York: University Press of America, 1985), 168–69.

CHAPTER XXVIII

The Sisters of
Mount St. Vincent, Cincinnati

The sisters at Camp Dennison—Sister Sophia and her assistants—
With the Army of the Cumberland—Their services in Virginia—
Their devotion and attention to the Indiana soldiers—The sisters
fired upon—Their return to Cincinnati—They attend the wounded
after Shiloh and Pittsburg Landing—Honorable testimonials of
service—The sisters not subject to general orders issued to nurses etc.

INTRODUCTION: Conyngham curiously did not write a chapter about the Daughters of Charity, founded by Elizabeth Ann Seton in Emmitsburg, Maryland. This religious community provided over three hundred sister nurses to both the Union and Confederate armies, making them by far the largest single group of sisters to serve as nurses during the war. The Sisters of Charity of Cincinnati, Ohio, an offshoot of Seton's community, also proved to be valuable nurses on behalf of wounded Union soldiers. Following in the nursing tradition of Seton's original group, they operated a hospital in Cincinnati and thus were more experienced in nursing than most American women when the war began. Recent research suggests that about forty sisters left to nurse the Union wounded and sick in the eastern and western theatres of the war. In addition, the sisters' hospital in Cincinnati also cared for soldiers, meaning that well over half of the Cincinnati sisters nursed in some capacity.

The following chapter, with only minimal changes by Conyngham, is taken from an undated newspaper clipping from the most important Catholic newspaper of the nineteenth century, the *Boston Pilot*. It contains many letters of testimony on behalf of the devoted service of Sister Anthony O'Connell and her fellow sister nurses. The article was evidently written by Conyngham himself, for a note at its bottom asks others to send him more accounts of the chaplains and sisters for an upcoming work on their activities during the Civil War: "The author requests sketches, incidents, letters, and the like, from Chaplains, Sisters and others, for the above work. He will soon commence, in THE PILOT, a sketch of the services of the Rev. Father Scully while Chaplain of the gallant 9th Massachusetts. The Most Rev. Dr. Spalding encouragingly writes to the author:—'I applaud your noble undertaking, rescuing the history of our Chaplains and Sisters from obscurity, and shall render you all the assistance in my power.' Address 310 E. 18th street, New York."

The services and devoted zeal of the Catholic chaplains and sisters, in discharge of their Christian duties during the war, have evoked the admiration and praise of persons of all creeds and classes. In the field, in the hospital, they were ever foremost attending to the wants and sufferings of the sick and wounded. The same in the Confederate prisons and hospitals; they made no distinction between Federal or Confederate, Catholic or Protestant, but extended their charitable ministrations to all alike, regardless of their religious or political tendencies. Among the noble band of sisters who were to be found in every hospital, meekly and unostentatiously soothing the sick, comforting the dying, and ministering to the wants of all, the good sisters of the above community took a very prominent part.

The first year of the war, by request of Dr. [Richard R.] McMeens,[1] Medical Director, Sister Sophia, with six other sisters, went to Camp Den[n]ison[2] to attend the sick soldiers. While there they were quartered in a small Presbyterian Church, around which four soldiers were placed as sentries night and day. This church was used for the threefold purpose of chapel, dining-room and sleeping rooms. The sisters employed all their time in visiting the sick in the various tents within the camp grounds. When the regiments were ordered off to the battlefields, the sisters returned home. A short time after they were sent for by the Medical Director of the Cumberland, Dr. [George] Suckley.[3] Thither Sister Sophia and six sisters repaired, accompanied by Very Rev. Father [Edward] Collins of Cincinnati. The sisters boarded at a private house and visited the hospitals. They remained thus engaged about ten weeks. In compliance with the request of Dr. McMahon[4] they went to New Creek, Virginia; there they were lodged in tents on the camp grounds. There was a great number of sick and wounded. The hospitals here were most admirably adapted for the purpose intended. From here the soldiers were ordered to Strasburg. At times, the sisters were obliged to travel night and day in ambulances. The soldiers were encamped, for a short time, near Middletown. The doctors and sisters were hospitably entertained in the house of a worthy gentleman, Mr. Dingez, from whence they attended the sick and wounded in the camp.

One night an alarm was given that the enemy was going to attack the camp. Amid the greatest confusion and agitation, orders were given to depart. They proceeded to a town in Western Virginia, but were not allowed to remain long, fearing an attack from the enemy. In consequence of which the sisters, with the sick and wounded, were sent forward. After their departure, a severe battle took place. Again, at the request of Gov. Morton, of Indiana, the sisters went to Richmond, Kentucky, to attend the Indiana regiments. The soldiers here were terribly mangled, but had good medical attendance. A terrific battle had taken place a few days previous. The Confederates held the town and the roads leading to it, consequently the sisters had to pass through their lines with a flag of truce; but once, through mistake, they were fired upon.

The sisters' hospital in Cincinnati was given for the use of the sick and wounded soldiers, and even their chapel converted into a ward.

In compliance with the request of Mayor [George] Hatch, of Cincinnati, the sisters from the hospital went, on several occasions, down to the battlefields of Shiloh and Pittsburg Landing, to attend the sick and wounded who were being brought to the city in boats. They also went to Corinth for the same purpose, under the direction of Professor Blackman.

After the battle of Stone[s] River, the sisters went up to the field hospital to attend the sick and wounded, between which place and the Nashville hospitals there were some sixteen or eighteen sisters constantly occupied, and remained there about eighteen months. Finally, Dr. Stone, of Massachusetts,[5] requested the services of the sisters for the camp hospitals in Gallipolis.

Throughout their attendance on the sick and wounded soldiers, the sisters received, from both officers and privates, the utmost respect, courtesy and attention.

The following general order shows the high opinion held by officials of the services of the sisters; both the Federal and Confederate authorities exempted them from all restrictions.

War Department
Adjutant General's Office
Washington, October 29, 1863
The employment of women nurses in the U.S. General Hospitals will in the future be strictly governed by the following rules:—

1. Persons approved by Miss Dix, or her authorized agents, will receive from her, or them, "certificates of approval," which must be countersigned by medical directors upon their assignment to duty as nurses within their Departments.

2. Assignments of "women nurses" to duty in general hospitals will only be made upon application by the Surgeons in charge through Medical Directors, to Miss Dix or her agents, for the number they require, not exceeding one to every thirty beds.

3. No females, except Hospital Matrons, will be employed in general hospitals after December 31, 1863, borne upon the muster and payrolls without such certificate of approval and regular assignment, unless specially appointed by the Surgeon General.†

4. Women nurses, while on duty in General Hospitals, are under the exclusive control of the senior medical officer, who will direct their several duties, and may be discharged by him when considered supernumerary, or for incompetency, insubordination, or violation of his orders. Such discharge, with the reasons therefor, being endorsed upon the certificate, will be at once returned to Miss Dix.

By order of the Secretary of War:
OFFICIAL: E. D. Townsend
Assistant Adjutant General

†"Sisters of Charity" are not affected by this Order, nor are they included amongst the nurses subject to the order of Miss Dix.
By order of the Acting Surgeon General,
C[harles] H[enry] Crane, Surgeon, U.S.A.
Surgeon General's Office, Washington,
January 6, 1864

A Nashville paper, speaking of the services of the sisters there, says:

The negroes near Nashville were lately attacked with small-pox and would have perished, were it not for the Sisters of Charity who, under the direction of Sister Anthony,[6] visited them in their hovels and camps and saved many from perishing. We suppose the good Sisters will be called abolitionists, as we have been, for extending mercy to God's suffering creatures.

A communication in the *Nashville Times*, says:

The following extracts from a letter give the sentiments of many of "the boys" who have had the misfortune to need nursing at Nashville.

* * *

I am sorry to hear that the Sisters of Charity are to leave Nashville soon. All the hospitals are to be consolidated, and No. 14 goes with the rest into one of the two field hospitals. The building is to be made an exchange barracks. During the last year, next to getting well, a soldier desired to be sent to No. 14. If he got there he thought he was all right. The sisters are the best nurses in the world. They are so steady, so unremitting by night and day, in their attendance upon every want, that they make each patient look upon the hospital as his own private house.

The poor boys stretched upon their beds, when they found themselves nursed so tenderly, almost forgot that they were far from home, and that their mothers and sisters were not about them; for neither mother nor sister could do more for their comfort than the sisters do. Many a poor fellow has lived to bless them, who, but for their care, would now be under the sod of Tennessee; and many a one besides, has felt that under their care he almost got well too soon. Wherever Sister Anthony goes, she and her companions will carry with them the blessings and good wishes of thousands of soldiers, and you at home ought to thank them for us, when they come back among you. The people gave Old Rose[7] a good reception; the sisters deserve no less. They have worked as fearlessly, as untiringly, as devotedly for the country, as the bravest of the heroes in the Army of the Cumberland.

The following notice of the sisters' return from Nashville appeared in a Cincinnati paper:

THE SISTERS OF CHARITY AND THE SOLDIERS

Sister Anthony, the devoted hospital nurse, with her colony of six companions, returned from Nashville, after a year's absence, a few days ago. All the hospitals have been reduced to two—field ones—and, among the rest, No. 14, where so many sick and wounded soldiers had experienced the sisters' devoted care, was abolished.

These sisters have written as noble a record in the Civil War as the gallant men they nursed. They were employed at Camp Dennison until the hospitals there were systematized; then they went to New Creek, Virginia, and Cumberland, Maryland. During Pope's campaign they followed Sigel's corps in the ambulances. After the battle of Stone[s] River, they went to Nashville and took charge of Hospital 14, capable of accommodating 700 or 800. It was crowded during most of their stay. A correspondent furnishes us with copies of certain documents written on the occasion of their leaving Nashville, which will show the light in which they are regarded by the inmates of the hospital:

General Hospital, No. 14
Nashville, Tennessee, November, 1863
To the Lady Superior and Sisters of Charity
in attendance on said hospital:

The undersigned attachees and patients in said hospital, have learned with regret that you contemplate leaving your present post of labor, and the object of this is to express the hope that you may be induced to forego that intention, and kindly consent to remain with us.

During your stay in the hospital, you have been indeed sisters to the patients, and your uniform kindness to all has endeared you to all our hearts.

Should you leave us, we can only say that wherever you may go, you will bear with you the soldiers' gratitude; and our earnest prayer and hope is, that, in whatever field you may labor in the future, you may be as happy as you have been kind and charitable to us; and may Heaven's choicest blessings be showered upon you, for your kindness to the poor, sick, and wounded soldier.

This is signed by two hundred and thirty-six persons.

Private William H. Nelson, 19th Illinois Infantry, writes that he was passing through the ward getting signatures to the above petition, when "one poor fellow, who was lying on the bed almost dead, aroused himself and said: 'I want to sign that paper. I would sign it fifty times, if asked. For the sisters have been to me as my mother since I have been here and, I believe, had I been here before, I would have been well long ago. But if the sisters leave, I know I shall die.'"—and adds: "This is the feeling of every sick soldier now under their care."

On the same occasion, Dr. A[lbert] N. Reade,[8] Sanitary Inspector, under the impression that the sisters were about to leave to avoid coming into collision with the general superintendent of hospitals, addressed the following note to them:

> United States Sanitary Commission,
> Nashville, Tennessee, November 7, 1863
> Sister Anthony:—I learn with great sorrow that you and your associates are [thinking] about leaving our hospitals. I beg of you not to do it. I have long known of your faithful and efficient work, and have rejoiced at it.
>
> The commission you have received of Miss Dix only secures to you your pay; it in no way places you at her disposal.
>
> And I also take pleasure in assuring you that, with the approval of the surgeon in charge of every hospital, which you can easily obtain, we will freely issue to you any sanitary stores we have. I am, very truly, your friend,
> A. N. Reade, Sanitary Inspector.

There is no class of people employed in the nation's cause, more deserving of its thanks, than these self-sacrificing women. In the East and West, there have been many who labored faithfully; but there have been none more devoted than Sister Anthony and her associates.

EPILOGUE: Despite their concern about coming under Dorothea Dix's oversight, Sister Anthony O'Connell and many of the Sisters of Charity of Cincinnati continued to serve in hospitals until the war's end. Sister Anthony remained a popular figure with her fellow veterans and was buried with a Grand Army of the Republic honor guard in 1897. An outpouring of support and praise from Catholics and Protestants for Sister Anthony demonstrates that she and her sister nurses changed many hearts and minds prejudiced against Catholicism through their devoted service on behalf of the Union's hospitalized soldiers.

SOURCES: Archival materials related to the service of the Cincinnati Sisters of Charity are housed in the Sisters of Charity of Cincinnati Archives, Mount St. Joseph, Ohio.

See Judith Metz, S.C., *The Sisters of Charity of Cincinnati in the Civil War: The Love of Christ Urges Us* (Cincinnati: Sisters of Charity of Cincinnati, 2012), i–ii, 49–50; Judith Metz, S.C., "Sister Anthony O'Connell: Angel of the Orphan, the Sick, the Wounded, and the Outcast," *U.S. Catholic Historian* 35, no. 4 (Fall 2017): 53–78; Ellen Ryan Jolly, *Nuns of the Battlefield* (Providence, RI: Providence Visitor Press, 1927), 36–56.

See also the extensive history of the community: Agnes McCann, S.C., *The History of Mother Seton's Daughters: The Sisters of Charity of Cincinnati Ohio, 1809–1923*, 3 vols. (New York: Longmans, Green, 1917–1923).

CHAPTER XXIX

Mount St. Vincent,
St. Joseph's Military Hospital,
Central Park Grounds

*Resolution of Common Council—The services of Mother Jerome
and the Sisters of Charity accepted—Our sick and wounded
soldiers—E. M. Stanton on the sisters' services—The chaplains of
Mount St. Vincent—Dr. McGlynn's attention—Death and imposing
obsequies of Sister M. Prudentia Bradley—The benefactors of
the establishment—Thanksgiving day at the hospital—Feeling
letters to the sisters—The fruits of the good sisters' labor—
Mount St. Vincent of today.*

INTRODUCTION: Like the Sisters of Charity of Cincinnati, the Sisters of Charity of New York were derived from
Elizabeth Ann Seton's Emmitsburg community. Arriving in
New York in 1817, they quickly established a boy's orphanage
and then a hospital, giving them valuable experience in nursing not open to most American women. In 1847, they established a girls' academy in what later became Central Park. The
creation of the park led them to take up residence closer to the
Hudson River in Riverdale, New York. Here, with the generous
donation of land by Edwin Forrest, they converted his Font
Hill mansion into their new female academy.

The old site in Central Park, however, proved to be a good location for a military hospital and with the backing of local leaders and the federal government, the sisters reoccupied the newly renamed St. Joseph Military Hospital. Here the sisters cared for the Union wounded from late 1862 through the end of the war, assisted by Father Edward McGlynn, the hospital's Catholic chaplain. According to tradition handed down by the community, Sister Mary Ulrica O'Reilly was the hospital's great hero, entirely selfless in her care for the soldiers and even facing down rioters during the infamous New York Draft Riots in 1863.

This chapter, like previous ones, is based almost word for word on an undated, untitled newspaper clipping. It appears to be yet another one of Conyngham's postwar pieces written to celebrate and immortalize the activities of the Church during the war.

In a New York daily of May 17, 1862, we find the following preamble and resolutions as having been proposed in the Committee on National Affairs:

> Whereas, this Common Council has learned with sentiments of profound admiration and gratitude of the tender, voluntarily made by Mother Jerome,[1] Superioress of the Mount Saint Vincent Academy at Font Hill, of the invaluable services of herself and the Sisters of Charity in the community under her charge, in taking care and ministering to the wants of our sick and wounded soldiers; and whereas, in the tender of the services of the Sisters of Charity of the community, this Common Council also thanks Mother Jerome for the suggestion which resulted in obtaining from the Commissioners of the Central Park, the large, elegant, airy and commodious building for-

merly owned and occupied by the Sisters of Charity as a seminary, eligibly located on Harlem Heights, as a hospital and home for sick and wounded soldiers. We are confident that the wisdom and foresight which prompted the suggestion, with the active benevolence, Christian sympathy and charitable motives, which actuated the Mother Superioress in making the voluntary tender of the services of the sisters of the community, combined with their proverbial kindness, docility, meekness and perseverance in the work of caring for the afflicted, will be regarded as an earnest of the great good that will result to those of our soldiers who shall have lost their health, or been wounded while engaged in seconding the efforts of the General Government to suppress the present rebellion against its authority; be it, therefore:

Resolved, That this Common Council speaking in behalf of the gallant volunteers from this city, their families and friends, and, in fact, on behalf of the citizens of our city generally, gratefully accepts the offer of the services of Mother Jerome, and the Sisters of Charity under her charge, to nurse and care for the sick and wounded volunteers from this city; and we earnestly hope that the offer will be as gratefully accepted by the military authorities having cognizance of the matter; and be it further

Resolved, That the thanks of this Common Council are due, and we hereby tender them to the Commissioners of the Central Park, for placing at the disposal of the proper authorities, pursuant to the suggestion of Mother Jerome, the buildings in the Central Park, so admirably fitted for hospital purposes, and heretofore known as Mount St. Vincent.

Later, the following appeared under the heading,

Our Sick and Wounded Soldiers. — A preliminary meeting, or rather interview, took place yesterday morning, at the Roman Catholic Orphan Asylum in Prince street, between the Very Rev. Wm. Starrs[2] on behalf of the Sisters of Charity, Alderman [Terence] Farley and Councilman [William] Orton on behalf of the Common Council, and Colonel [George] Bliss on behalf of the U.S. Government, in order to consult on the arrangements to be made in regard to the charge of sick and wounded volunteers returning from the seat of war. The buildings formerly known as the Mount St. Vincent Academy, within the limits of the Central Park, will, we understand, be prepared within one or two weeks at the farthest, by which time, it is thought that the wounded and sick will begin to arrive. * * * Alderman Farley, Councilman Orton, and Colonel Bliss have been most assiduous in their efforts to forward the human task to which they have been entrusted, and are evidently determined that nothing shall be wanting on their part to render the services of the zealous and devoted sisters in every way successful.

The following are copies of letters written by Edwards Pierrepont, Esq.,[3] to the Secretary of War and of the response thereto on the subject:

16 Wall Street, New York
September 9th, 1862

Hon. E. M. Stanton,[4] Sec'y of War:

The Commissioners of the Central Park of this city have given a very large building for the reception of wounded soldiers. This building was formerly a Catholic School of high order. The point is this: We want the nurses of this hospital to be the *Sisters of Charity*,—the most faithful nurses in the world. Their *tenderness*,[5] their *knowledge*, and religious *convictions* of duty render them *by far* the best nurses around the sick bed *which have ever been found upon earth*. All that is asked is that they be permitted to be nurses under the direction of the War Department and its Physicians. Alderman Farley of this city will take this letter. I beg you to consider this matter and to do what is possible and you will truly oblige your numerous friends and especially,

Your friend ever truly,

Edwards Pierrepont

Surgeon General's Office,
Washington, D.C.
September 10, 1862

Sir,

The Commissioners of the Central Park having been given a large building lately occupied as a Catholic school, for hospital purposes, and having requested of the Secretary of War, through Edwards Pierrepont, that Sisters of Charity should be employed therein, the following copy of the Surgeon General's endorsement on Mr. Pierrepont's letter is sent for your information and guidance in the matter:

The building will be very gladly received and fitted up as a hospital. The Medical Director at New York will be at once instructed to receive it. No one can bear fuller or more willing testimony to the capability and devotion of the Sisters of Charity than myself. Several hundreds are now on duty as nurses under my charge. Those referred to within will also be accepted thankfully.

You will, therefore, take such steps in connection with the Quarter Master's Department as may be necessary to carry out the wishes of the Commissioners in regard to the building and of the Sisters of Charity.

By order of the Surgeon General.[6]

Very respectfully, your obedient servant,

James B. Smith,
Surgeon U.S.A.

Surgeon Chas. McDougall,[7] U.S.A.
Medical Director, 110 Grand St., New York

The band of sisters selected for the work and placed under the care of Sister M. Ulrica O'Reilly[8] were for months impatiently awaiting the completion of the necessary government arrangements which would enable them to enter on their sacred functions. Adverse circumstances prevented the realization of their wishes before the Feast of the Guardian Angels, October 2, 1862. For some months after their establishment the sisters were subjected to every possible inconvenience and annoyance, but they bore all with cheerfulness and exerted their utmost to serve the gallant suffering soldiers. Dr. [Frank H.] Hamilton[9] was for a few months in charge, but after a short time the government appointed John W. S. Gouley,[10] M.D., of the U.S. Army, surgeon in charge. Under his wise administration, the hospital flourished, and the sisters were able to do that good which they wished. The late Most Rev. Archbishop Hughes was deeply interested in the work. On Thanksgiving Day he visited all the wards of the hospital and spoke with paternal interest to the patients. Rev. Father Koeder[11] was the first chaplain appointed by him. The Rev. and excellent father was but a short time at the hospital. He was succeeded by the Rev. Dr. [Edward] Mc-Glynn,[12] whose amiable presence was very dear to the soldiers. His gentlemanly manners, his unobtrusive ways, his close and earnest attention to each and every one of his duties, his unwillingness to *force* the subject of religion on any one, his paternal, peaceful manner by the death-beds of such as sought his care, impressed all in the different wards, and the most profound respect was shown him on every occasion. During the three years of the existence of the hospital not more than one or two died unassisted by him. The sisters had the consolation of seeing that the dying soldiers not only deeply appreciated his and their kind services, but that they had learned to love the religion they professed, and to whose promptings those poor sufferers knew well they were indebted for the impartial care lavished upon them. The wards were twenty in number, some of them very large; one was about one hundred feet by eighty with lofty ceilings. This beautiful and spacious ward had been in former times the sisters' chapel, and the All-Seeing-Eye, on the stained glass window at the gable end, was at once an encouragement to the sisters and a consolation to the suffering. I need not dwell upon the pleasure and holy delight experienced by the sisters in being called back to the cradle of their religious life, to perform golden deeds of charity within precincts already so hallowed in their eyes. I cannot forbear making a quotation from the early records of the community in 1847 concerning this spot and its surroundings, whose location is thus described: "The property is situated on an eminence overlooking Harlem, Astoria, Manhattanville, and Yorkville, and it is marked on all state maps as 'McGowan's Pass.' The place is of some historic repute as the main building was occupied for a time as Washington's headquarters." A Franklin stove, which fell into the possession of the sisters, on the purchase of the edifice, is said to have been in the general's parlor. The premises had been held by the sisters as the seat of their central or mother house until 1856, when it was purchased from them by the Central Park commissioners.

In May 1864, a young member of the hospital corps of sisters died of disease contracted and developed during her service to the soldiers. All of the poor cripples, sharers of her care, and those of her sisters that were able, attended her Requiem Mass. The choir from Mount St. Vincent sang. The doctor and other officers of the government were also in attendance; military honors were paid to her as her funeral *cortege* passed out. Dr. McGlynn preached a beautiful discourse on this occasion. His sermons, simple, ungarnished, but replete with instruction and that unction which accompanies explanations of the Word of God when the interest of immortal souls is at heart, were always very effective.

The following notice of this sister is taken from the *New York Herald*:

On Monday, May 30, a High Mass of Requiem was offered in the Chapel of St. Joseph's United States Military Hospital, Central Park, for the repose of the soul of Sister M. Prudentia Bradley,[13] one of that devoted band of sisters which has been in constant attendance on the poor wounded soldiers since October 1862. We learned that deceased was in the bloom of life and health when she entered upon her self-sacrificing duties, filled with a noble emulation to be, in every deed, a ministering angel near the pillow of the suffering and dying. Her services were, no doubt, duly appreciated, since the gentlemen of the medical staff were present, and the chapel was crowded with soldiers. It was affecting to see the latter in their disabled state coming in to pay this last sad tribute of respect to departed worth. The services were conducted by the Reverend Dr. Mc-Glynn, the amiable and highly gifted chaplain of the hospital, assisted by Rev. J. B. Biretta,[14] of Fonthill. The Mass was sung with peculiar feeling by the sisters. The reverend doctor made some very appropriate remarks. He believed that all present were very deeply impressed, since so unusual a degree of interest had been manifested on the occasion. Deaths had occurred at the hospital before, yet he had never seen so large a number collected around the bier of a companion. It was evident a peculiar halo rested around the form of the deceased who was in life a member of the Community of the Sisters of Charity, one of those religious bodies or corporations, which had risen in the Church of God, as a necessary consequence, to fully carry out the views of the Savior of men. The deceased has been, then, one of those privileged beings who are called to give themselves unreservedly to God, having been chosen to serve Him in a stricter sense than Christians in general; for, although all are bound to observe the commandments of God and His Church, all are not called to the more perfect life to which the three distinct engagements of religious persons bind them, engagements which this sister had renewed and ratified on her deathbed, and had seemed, judging from her youthfulness and fervor, so well fitted to exemplify in a much longer life of usefulness. But Providence, he said, had had in view some wise end in thus calling her away, and no doubt it was to give him and them a lesson. This good sister had made no such excuses in the service of God as we read in the Gospel were given by men of the world wedded to earthly interests, and they might hope her soul was reaping the reward of its generous devotedness. Her career had been brief, it is true; yet Holy Scripture teaches us that honorable old age and gray hairs are not to be counted by length of years, in a spiritual sense; for a spotless life is old age, and the soul that is made perfect in a short space has fulfilled a long time before God. He added that she had in a manner consumed herself in their service for the love of God, having been filled, not only with a desire to relieve suffering, which is simply philanthropic, but nobler motives had mingled with her views a divine element. She had served the sick and dying through love of God and to please God alone; for they should know that these Sisters of Charity consecrated all their actions to God by prayer, rising in the morning before the generality of persons have left their places of repose to mediate on the Divine Goodness. They have their other hours of prayer, too, and even while serving others they strive to keep united to God by contemplation, etc., etc.

At the conclusion of the services, the remains were carried out to the hearse, the soldiers being filed off on both sides of the walk. The sisters sang the psalm "Miserere"[15] as the procession passed out to the carriages. We understand that the remains were conveyed to Calvary [Cemetery] for interment.

In May 1864, Sister Ulrica, who had devoted herself heart and soul to the interests of this Hospital, was sent by her superiors to lay another foundation of a good work and Sister M. Rosina Wightman[16] was named her successor. About this time the eminent and estimable Dr. Gouley[17] was removed to another field of professional labor. Dr. [Benjamin A.] Clements was his worthy successor. He continued in charge until within a few months of the closing of the hospital. In Dr. Gouley's[18] term of office, this hospital had been reported, by Government Inspectors, as the best appointed and managed of the U.S. Military Hospitals, and Dr. Clements gave it as high a tone. Dr. [John J.] Milhau, Jr.[19] succeeded him in January of the year in which the hospital finished its mission in behalf of poor suffering humanity. He was possessed of the desirable qualities of his predecessors, as surgeon and gentlemanly director of the hospital. Drs. [Charles A.] Phelps, [Sylvester] Teats, [George F.] Shrady, and [Louis] Fernandez of the Medical Staff, deserve particular notice for their skill and unwearied attention to the patients.

The sisters deem it but just to have the names of Mrs. Charles M. Connelly, Mrs. Kelly, Mrs. Johnson, Mrs. Martin, Mrs. Hagnet and Mrs. Chancey recorded as lady benefactors, untiring in their provision of delicacies, etc. etc., for the poor suffering soldiers. There are, no doubt, other names deserving of a like mention, which, however, cannot now be recalled,—but He who forgets not even a cup of cold water given in His name, bears them in His eternal memory. Another Military Hospital had been ceded to the Sisters of Charity on Fifty-First Street by the government, but owing to some chicanery of one or two self-interested individuals the sisters never took possession of it, although the official documents of authorization were held by them, as appears by the following:

Surgeon General's Office
Washington D.C., September 11, 1862

Sir—

The Surgeon General directs that the Sisters of Charity be selected for female nurses in the General Hospital, corner of Lexington Avenue and Fifty-First Street, and the building given by the Central Park Commissioners for Hospital purposes. The latter building, the Surgeon directs, you will immediately organize for a Hospital. By order of the Surgeon General.

Very respectfully, your obedient servant,

James B. Smith, Surgeon, U.S.A.
Surgeon Charles McDougall, U.S.A.
Medical Director, 110 Grand Street New York

It is but just to state, that the idea of establishing the Central Park Hospital and placing it under charge of the sisters is due to Mr. Charles Devlin.[20] He took a deep interest in it during its existence, and materially assisted it. Mr. Anthony Ellis gave his valuable services to the work; Mr. Charles Connolly, Mrs. Connolly, and Mrs. Daniel Devlin, collected several hundred dollars for the soldiers, among their friends.

The following account of Thanksgiving Day [1862][21] at the hospital is taken from a New York paper:

The wounded soldiers in this institution were provided by the sisters in charge, and by their friends throughout this city and vicinity, with the means of enjoying themselves on Thanksgiving Day. A splendid dinner, consisting of the choicest viands and delicacies, was prepared at the Old Mount, to which the soldiers and their friends sat down about one o'clock. The feast was heartily enjoyed, and after the physical man was satisfied, addresses were made by the Rev. Chaplain of the Hospital, Captain Tully,[22] Hon. Abraham Wakeman and others. Full justice was done to the edifying benevolence of the Sisters of Charity, here and everywhere and also to the excellent ladies who had aided in furnishing the banquet. Various toasts were given complimentary to the soldiers, the ladies of the institution, the lady and gentlemen contributors, and the interesting Orphan Band in attendance from the Catholic Asylum on Fifth Avenue. The dinner was presided over by Dr. Hamilton, the admirable surgeon of the institution whose lady was also in attendance on the soldiers. The hospital is conducted in a manner most creditable to Sister Ulrica and her assistant sisters and other assistants.

St. Joseph's Military Hospital is now an institution of the past. It was closed in 1865. Its old inmates however do not forget the kind sisters who ministered to their wants with such care. Happy in their homes and in the bosom of their families they bless the good sisters who cared and cheered them in their hours of sickness and affliction. Even the roughest and most depraved of the patients were softened by their gentle influence and we trust that they learned a lesson of charity, humility, and patience, which has made them ever since better men and worthier members of society. Though the sisters have received several grateful letters from their former patients, we take one as a specimen, written by a German, who had been fearfully wounded on the battlefield by a shot through the lower jaw. When he came to the hospital, he could take no nourishment except in liquid form through a tube inserted in his throat while in a recumbent posture. Hence for nearly three years he was literally fed by one of the sisters. By the skill and address of Dr. Gouley an artificial jaw was adjusted for him by means of which he was able to masticate certain food and his speech seemed more natural.

Hamburg, March 14th, 1868

Sisters of Charity, Ulrica, Mount St. Vincent.

My Dear Sister—

I thank you much for your kind letter. It was for me the most grateful surprise to receive your greetings across the ocean, and your praying wishes for my wife and child's welfare. May Heaven realize them!

My wife sends her hearty greeting and gratitude to you and all the sisters, who kept me alive for her. My little John is a source of pleasure to me; he is a sweet child, at least he appears to me.

I trust this letter will find you and your sisters in perfect health and happiness. Give them all my respectful greetings but a special handshaking to Mother Jerome, Sister Mary Teresa [McCloskey], and you, Sister Ulrica. Although it is an outsider who offers this tribute of affection to sisters of an order, it will, nevertheless, find the sanction of a high and holy God, who suffered death, not only for a creed but for all, yea, for his enemies. Your charity was the mother of my gratitude. I hear with regret of the loss of a letter which you wrote me. I never received any since you bade me "good-bye" in 1866, in which you answered me, offering me your assistance. Although sorry for the loss of anything you enclosed, I feel myself under the same obligations as if I had received it. Not the result, but the motive of the act, decided its worth. My hearty thanks for it.

How are Dr. Gouley and poor Dr. Clements? I should like very much to have the photographs of these two men—I owe them a heavy debt. At first I felt inclined to find fault with Dr. Gouley, but I owe him much in every respect, and am sensible of it. Please to tell him so, and beg him to give me his photograph as a personal favor. There are so many inquiries about this operation that I should be glad and proud for this and for my own sake, to have this remembrance of him. As for Dr. Clements, it was my intention to go and nurse him in his mental darkness, but was only prevented by receiving intelligence from my beloved wife. O! how I do pray that he may be well and happy long before this time.[23] If so, or if his sickness has intelligent moments, please tell him how deeply and honestly I sympathize with him, and how gratefully I feel indebted to him for all his kindness shown to me. Please to give Father McGlynn my grateful respects. How is that proud little orphan girl? Tell her to be good.

As for myself, I am doing well, considering circumstances. My health is feeble and will never improve I fear, but I have an object to live and work for, and my determination to do my duty vanishes the feeling of discouragement that sometimes arises from my bodily weakness. I work very hard, but I have a loving wife and child, whose smiles cheer me after my day's toil. My only serious drawback is my having to commence business without any capital, which is a hindrance to me at every step, and often painfully embarrasses me. But my will must make the way, and if I but remain well, in a few years I will overcome all, I hope. I have rented a nice little cottage half a mile from the city, and everything around me looks cheerful—there is no tinsel work and *firlefanz*,[24] but it is neat, plain, and comfortable, and if you or any of the sisters should ever cross the Atlantic, (and, certainly, none of your sisterhood would pass by), you will like it I trust.

Sister Mary Teresa has not yet written. What is the reason? I would be content with a few lines if she has not time to write more. Dear Sister Teresa, I esteem her so much. Often while I am sitting and thinking it all over, there is hardly one word or act that does not pass in review on the mental eye. It is for me a *fata morgana*,[25] and in every picture, true, honest, indefatigable Sister Teresa keeps the foreground, and after that, come to mind every little incident, and Sisters Columba [Lawrence], Genevino, Ann Scholastica,[26] Perpetua [Drumgoole], and at length there are so many around me that I feel quite at home once more until the Methodist preacher, with his sugar sweet face, and arms full of tracts, enters, and then I feel bitter for a moment.

Poor little "Louy" how is she?[27] Why are you no longer in New Haven? What has become of the St. Joseph Hospital?

Was there ever a picture taken of it? Is the cathedral on Fifth Avenue still going up, or is it already finished?

Adieu, my good Sister Ulrica. I shall not fail to inform you from time to time, how I am getting along, and remember that a letter from you will at all times be a welcome guest, from dear America. Sister Rosina Wightman was kind to me. Remember me to her.

God bless you, my dear sister, and all your sisters, and pray for me that He may bless me too.

With the most respectful friendship, I am very gratefully your obedient servant,

John Schiffler,[28] private Co. B.
1st New York Mounted Rifles

This poor soldier styles this country, "his dear America," but alas, after having bled for it, he has to go home to Germany in the steerage of the vessel, weak and feeble as he was; the letter enclosing thirty dollars to him, as a donation from persons whom Sister Ulrica had interested in him, never reached him. He was wounded at Indiantown, North Carolina, in July 1863. This letter is only one proof out of the many that could be adduced of the soldiers' gratitude to the Sisters of Charity.

In conclusion, we give the following extract from a letter received from one of the patients.[29]

Mother M. Jerome

Reverend Mother—It is time that I should write and return you, and all the sisters, thanks for their great and unwearied kindness to me.

I found the Hospitals in every respect, all that the most comfortable home could be. The doctors, particularly Drs. Gouley and Clements, gave me, not only the full benefit of their surgical skill, but in every respect treated me as a gentleman, aye, even as a friend.

As I was, to a certain extent, a free thinker, when I went to the hospital, I had strong prejudices against the principles of the

Catholic Sisters of Charity; but, the maternal care and self-sacrifices evinced by these sisters, their attention, relieving, as far as they could, my sufferings, their tenderness and anxiety in soothing my unsettled mind and dispelling the dark shadows of insanity that filled me with despair,[30] removed all my prejudices and make me look back to them with love and gratitude.

As long as I live I shall be a most grateful and determined champion of those good, indefatigable sisters against thoughtless, ranting fanatics, who try to cover their indolence and want for good works by noise and show, distributing tracts and singing hymns, but would turn away, in disgust, if called upon to do the least tiresome of the works performed by the Sisters of Charity. My mother, wife or sisters could have done no more for me. I cannot give sufficient proof of my appreciation of the thousand acts of kindness, by which the modest sister relieved my sufferings and soothed my weary mind.

The chaplain Father [Mc]Glyn[n] was also remarkably kind and attentive to me.

What a consoling moment and sunbeam of gladness was he to me in those dark hours of fearful suffering, when the present and the future were shrouded in darkness and despair. He sat by my bedside, gently soothed and advised me, never attempting to proselytize me, but by simple words of touching tenderness, he revived hope in my heart and saved my soul from the dark abyss.

"Every tree shall be known by its fruit." Your works of mercy, charity, and true Christian zeal to feed the hungry, clothe the naked, and console the afflicted, have produced good fruit, and have turned many a sinful, erring man from the paths that lead to destruction and eternal ruin, to the Joyous Road that leads to peace and happiness here and eternal blessings hereafter.[31]

God bless ye, dear sisters! and please accept the thanks and gratitude of

L. M.

Ten years have passed over since the good sisters ministered so kindly and tenderly to the poor sick and wounded entrusted to their care. God blessed their work, and the prayers of the grateful thousands

whom they relieved seemed to ascend to heaven, like grateful incense
and to bring down upon them and their glorious mission, blessings
unmeasurable.[32]

❀   ❀   ❀

EPILOGUE: The Sisters of Charity continued to care for soldiers at St. Joseph's Military Hospital until August 1865. They
then left their old home for the last time, moving once and for
all to their academy in Riverdale, which subsequently became
the College of Mount Saint Vincent in 1911. The sisters would
continue to help nurse sick New Yorkers during epidemics following the Spanish-American and First World Wars.

SOURCES: Letters and other primary sources related to the
Sisters of Charity of New York during the Civil War are available at their archives at Mount Saint Vincent College in New
York City. Marie de Lourdes Walsh, *The Sisters of Charity of
New York, 1809–1959* (New York: Fordham University Press,
1960), 166–75; Ellen Ryan Jolly, *Nuns of the Battlefield* (Providence, RI: Providence Visitor Press, 1927), 19–35.

CHAPTER XXX

The Sisters of Mercy, St. Louis

Their convent and school—The hospitals crowded with sick and wounded during the war—Prisoner and refugees—One priest baptized over five hundred prisoners—Liberality of the citizens— Instructing soldiers in the principles of religion—Soldiers asking to be baptized in the "sisters' religion"—How they supplied the soldiers with books—Physicians anxious to secure the services of the sisters—The soldiers' gratitude to the sisters—Their humility and obedience—An interesting patient.

INTRODUCTION: The Sisters of Mercy were originally founded in Dublin, Ireland, in 1831 by Mother Mary Catherine McAuley. At the request of a Missouri Jesuit, Father Arnold Damen, six sisters from a community of Sisters of Mercy at St. Catherine's convent in New York City were sent to establish a new convent in St. Louis. Led by Mother Mary de Pazzi Bentley, an Irish-born sister from the original Dublin community, they arrived in the city in June 1856. They quickly set about visiting the sick and prisons and establishing a school, orphanage, and House of Mercy for destitute girls. Their convent was legally established in 1857 as St. Joseph's Convent of Mercy.

When the war broke out, Mother Mary de Pazzi offered her convent as a hospital for wounded soldiers, but the city's archbishop, Peter Richard Kenrick, advised her against this, arguing that there were already many St. Louis hospitals able to take care of any wounded soldiers. Consequently, another group of Sisters of Mercy from Chicago, Illinois, took a more active nursing role in Missouri, taking charge of a hospital in Jefferson City and helping to care for wounded from the Battle of Shiloh being sent home on board *The Empress*. Nonetheless, the St. Louis Sisters of Mercy visited the city's hospitals and Confederate prisoners held at Gratiot Street Prison just as they had visited the sick and imprisoned before the war.

The Sisters of Mercy of St. Louis are a good example of a small female religious community who served during the Civil War with little recognition by contemporaries or subsequent historians. George Barton, Ellen Ryan Jolly, and even Mary Denis Maher's studies of sister nurses say nothing about this group of female religious. Conyngham's own account is brief and short on specifics, but it is by far the most important attempt to make known the Sisters of Mercy of St. Louis's selfless service on behalf of wounded and imprisoned soldiers. The chapter relies heavily on a letter, dated December 12, 1868, that he received from a Sister of Mercy that gives some general details of their service. In this letter, which was originally transcribed as part of this chapter before being deleted, the anonymous sister admitted, "I regret that we were unable in consequence of our multifarious duties to keep any regular journal or diary during the period in which we were employed in visiting the patients, prisoners, and refugees that crowded the city in war times."

There are several religious institutions in St. Louis, Missouri, and though we know that the sisters, in general, displayed a laudable and active zeal in visiting the hospitals, nursing the sick and wounded and dispensing to them the luxuries, in both food and clothing, procured by the liberal donations of the charitable and humane, the writer must confine himself, owing to the want of more general information, to the services of the Sisters of Mercy. The convent of this community numbers about twenty-five sisters, Sister M. Ignatius Walker,[1] superior, and has a school attended by about four hundred children. It also provided employment for about one thousand persons annually, and reforms and trains to useful employment a number of young women.

During the war, the hospitals of St. Louis were crowded with the sick and wounded, besides [which], the city was a great depot for Confederate prisoners and refugees. There was a wide field for the charity and Christian zeal of the sisters, and nobly did they fulfill their mission. It is impossible to give an exact account of the number and circumstances of these unfortunates who were attended by the sisters and priests. There was no regular chaplain appointed either to the hospitals or prisoners, but almost all the priests of the city attended daily without pay and did all in their power to console, aid, and render spiritual assistance to the unfortunates, who were brought there under such afflicting circumstances. One priest alone baptized over five hundred prisoners, and as priests were not always on the spot, the sisters baptized several hundred on urgent occasions. The benevolent citizens of St. Louis, forgetting party spirit, when human suffering called forth their charity, largely aided the sisters, by their generous bounty, to ameliorate, as much as possible, the dreary lot of the poor captives and patients, to whom the sisters, almost daily, distributed nutritious food, articles of clothing, and other little requests.

They made no distinction, but treated all alike irrespective of country, religion, or politics; the most distressed and suffering invariably calling forth their greatest sympathy. They found hundreds of soldiers, Federal and Confederate, ignorant of the simplest truths of religion, and when asked, they instructed them in the principles of religion, and if they demanded it, when the opportunity offered, they brought them chaplains of other denominations.

This, though, was seldom the case for the devotion of the sisters to their wants and their quiet unobtrusive manner made such impression upon them that invariably, when asked if they wished to be baptized they replied, "We wish to be instructed and baptized in your religion,

Sister; it must be the true religion, else, you who profess it would not be so good and kind to us, strangers to you."

In illness, the poor soldiers used to fancy that anything the sisters would give them would cure them. They were most grateful for whatever was done for them—if they gave them only a few spoonsful of preserves or a piece of cake, or something still more trifling, they would thank them warmly, never omitting to add, however, that their presence was more agreeable than anything else they could confer. "If you never have anything for us, Sister," they would say, "be sure you come see us; we like you to talk to us." It was heartrending for the good sisters to go among them sometimes. The poor fellows who were from time to time shot in retaliation were a most pitiable spectacle, crying and sobbing like children. Every one of them asked to be received into the Catholic Church, and thus received the only consolations remaining to them. Some of the Southerners showed great bigotry at first, but it always wore away in a few days, and these used to show most attachment to the sisters after. The St. Vincent de Paul Society[2] aided to keep the prisoners in reading matter—Mr. John [E.] Yore used to send over a hundred dollars' worth of books at a time. Mr. [Richard Francis] Barry, also an officer of the society, frequently has helped them in this way.[3] In fact all the books and catechisms they asked of these gentlemen of the Society were immediately sent them. They chose entertaining works, and books calculated to increase and foster brotherly love among them. For those who desired to become Catholics they had all the standard instruction books. These had the charm of novelty for most of them, and they were so delighted with the information imparted that they often asked to let them keep the book not only as a memento, but also that they might read them for their friends and families if ever they should reach home. The influence which Catholic priests and sisters had over them was quite wonderful. It was owing in a great measure to the fact that they came in the *name of religion*, and assisted the miserable, whether of North or South, Catholic or non-Catholic. You might see convalescents fall upon the neck of the priest on leaving the hospital, and weep most passionately. Often when an exchange of prisoners took place, men were in tears when they left. Sometimes strangers would watch to see whether the sisters were as attentive to secessionists as to unionists, to Catholics and to Protestants or infidels—not perceiving the slightest difference, they would question them, and when the sisters informed them that their religion commanded them to serve everyone to the utmost of their power regarding all as children of the same Father, and brothers in Jesus Christ, and refusing to look upon [any] human being as an enemy, some would ask to be further instructed, and others would say: "If ever I profess any religion, I'll go in for yours."

So far as I have been able to learn, all the non-Catholic ladies and ministers who endeavored to help the soldiers, required in them similarity of political platform, and that they would read such religious books or tracts as they supplied—some would not help a Northerner, others would not converse with a secessionist. One of the sisters, who spent four years in the military hospitals, chiefly in Mississippi, gives it as her experience, that Protestants of any denomination whatever had no influence on the soldiers. As nurses, the soldiers had no *confidence* in them, saying they connived at abuses, as they were generally paid by government or otherwise—when patients were neglected, when keepers of military stores neglected to forward necessaries, when physicians neglected their duty, when under-nurses became intemperate—and all these abuses frequently occurred—some paid officials remained silent for fear of losing their places—while sisters, and other Catholic ladies, who took no pay for their services, immediately made known to the authorities any serious break of discipline that came under their observation, and insisted that those under their charge should get what was allowed to them, and even some culpable officials were discharged on their representations.

On this account conscientious physicians were always anxious to procure the services of the sisters. Even one eminent Protestant physician of the city remarked to us that as a general rule the only volunteer nurses of any use were the sisters. Trained to habits of subordination and discipline, they always walked with unanimity and harmony. While, among the volunteer nurses of other denominations, desire to be considered the *head*, and other little petty jealousies often led to much insubordination and trouble. Nothing could exceed the gratitude of the soldiers for the sisters. In no instance that has come to my knowledge, did they commit the smallest depredation on their property throughout the country, for there was always among them, some men who remembered and were grateful for the kindness and services they had received at their hands, who were able to restrain their less scrupulous comrades. In Charleston, Columbia, and other places where their convents were destroyed, it was not through malice, but from the accidence of shells or burning houses. So fully sensible were the people of the South of this, that on the advance of the Federal army, they were accustomed to secret their valuables and daughters in the convents. When the war was at its height, the sisters were allowed to cross the lines and never were molested either by an official *letter de cache*[4] or by the most hardened soldier. As an instance, the Sisters of St. Augustine[5] had occasion to go to Columbus, the railroads were torn up, so, they had to make the journey as best they could.

The Federal soldiers escorted them through their lines, through forest and jungle, until they saw them safely within the Confederate lines while the latter escorted them to their destination. It was consoling on those occasions to find the horrors of war infused by such kindly acts and to witness the good feeling that existed between the rival soldiers when they met. They shook hands, inquired about old friends and acquaintances, and exchanged tobacco, coffee, and the like. Poor fellows! They seemed to trouble themselves little about the course of the great squabble, which was deluging the country with blood. Here they met as friends and brothers, though in a few days, they were arrayed against one another as inveterate enemies.

They vied with one another in showing respect and attention to the sisters, rendering them every possible little service in their power, and thus endeared themselves to the sisters who have been among them or attended them in hospitals, or in prison, as the Crimean soldiers did to the sisters and nurses who attended them during their weary and sickening campaign.

I will now add a few anecdotes to the information already given. One young man in hospital, dying of typhoid fever, was suffering intensely and seemed in wretchedly low spirits. Being asked whether he belonged to any particular church or had ever been baptized, he replied somewhat as follows: "No, Sister, I have been a bad man, but I would repent and be baptized if I thought it would be any use for me to do so, but it is now too late." The sister spoke to him thus of the sufferings and death of Our Lord, born for sinners, and the example of the penitent thief who was pardoned at the last hour—while she enlarged on these consoling truths, tears flowed down the poor patient's cheeks, and on receiving some instructions, he asked to be baptized, having previously made with her some short aspirations including acts of faith, hope, and charity. As his case admitted of no delay, the sister baptized him before she left, and he died that night in great sentiments of contrition.

Another young man who became a Catholic, and was for some time the only Catholic in the ward, on being asked by the sisters some days after his baptism whether there was any point on which he would like more information, or anything in the Catholic religion to which he was not quite reconciled, replied with great simplicity that only one thing troubled him, and that was his own pride. "I know," said he, "that it was wrong to be proud, but I cannot help being proud of my religion, I'm so glad to myself for becoming a Catholic." After his first Communion, for which he prepared most fervently, he left [the] hospital to join his regiment. As it was going to battle, he often said that he rejoiced, for he hoped he might be among the fallen, and thus get straight to heaven with his baptismal innocence. Another soldier, who was weak[6] from recent illness, was recommended by the sisters to say his prayers sitting or lying down, lest he should overtax his returning strength. But he insisted on kneeling down to pray morning and evening, and used daily to retire to a corner of the ward—he being the only Catholic in it—to pray and recite the rosary on his knees. An old man who had been baptized when apparently in danger of death, without receiving the whole of the usual instructions, lingered without any prospect of recovery for over three months, during which the sisters having taught him to say the Lord's Prayer and make the sign of the cross, he began to get better and was soon able to leave, fully impressed that it was on account of his acts of devotion and through the prayers of the sisters, [that] he recovered. Before being discharged he asked leave to take the Catechism with him that he might instruct his wife and children to become Catholics.

A young man under sentence of death for desertion was dying of consumption; he asked to be baptized and instructed in the religion of the sisters. He became very religious and frequently said that he hoped God in his mercy would take him to Himself by sickness and spare him the horrors of being shot like a traitor. He did not wish to take food from anyone but the sisters and the doctor kindly humored him and ordered the sisters to give him whatever he desired. The poor fellow's prayer was finally granted and he died in peace having first received the sacraments.

The sisters were allowed to transfer from the prison for women, to the convent asylum, two girls suffering from measles. One of them died having received baptism; the other was taught to read and expressed a great wish to become a Catholic.

The war being over her father came to collect his scattered family, but found this the only one alive. Though greatly attached to her father and overjoyed to see him, she would not go until he had to promise that he'd send her to the sisters' school, in the town in Arkansas where he lived. These are but a few of the hundred instances of the reverential attachment of patients towards the sisters. It was not confined to boys but strong men, who never quailed in the storm of battle, were as obedient and submissive as children in the presence of the sisters.

It is safe to say that thousands recovered, that would otherwise have died, owing to their soothing influence; and thousands, who knew not what religion was, died happy deaths owing to their pious ministrations.

❊   ❊   ❊

EPILOGUE: The Civil War was particularly fierce in the bitterly divided state of Missouri, devastated as it was by guerilla warfare waged by Confederates and Unionists alike. St. Catherine's orphanage, run by the Sisters of Mercy, took care of many children orphaned by the conflict. Despite the sisters' good deeds during the war, many of the state's radical Republicans were bent on punishing ex-Confederates and the Catholic

Church, resulting in the imprisonment of some priests who refused to take a loyalty oath mandated by state law. Nonetheless, the Sisters of Mercy of St. Louis continued to expand their charitable and educational efforts in the city.

SOURCES: Mary Isidore Lennon, *Milestones of Mercy: Story of the Sisters of Mercy in St. Louis, 1856-1956* (Milwaukee: Bruce Press, 1957), 1–23, 94–95, 107–9. On postwar anti-Catholicism in Missouri, see John T. McGreevy, *American Jesuits and the World: How an Embattled Religious Order Made Modern Catholicism Global* (Princeton, NJ: Princeton University Press, 2016), 84–97.

See also Mary Paulinus Oakes, *The Tapestry of Mercy: The History of the St. Louis Regional Community of the Sisters of Mercy of the Americas* (St. Louis: Sisters of Mercy, 2008).

CHAPTER XXXI

The Sisters of Mercy, New York

*The sisters of the Houston Street Convent in the hospitals—
Their services in New Bern—Sufferings of the patients before the
arrival of the sisters—Strong religious prejudices against them at
first—The sisters after landing—Strange surmises as to who and
what they were—Things soon changed—Touching instances of
love and confidence—The grief of the patients and Negroes
at the departure of the sisters.*

INTRODUCTION: Like the St. Louis community in the
previous chapter, the Sisters of Mercy of New York were an offshoot of the original group founded in Dublin, Ireland. During a trip to Europe in the mid-1840s, Bishop John Hughes
of New York personally pleaded with Mother Mary Agnes
O'Connor, the head of a group of Sisters of Mercy serving in
England, for sisters for his growing diocese. Hughes's request
was successful, and Mother Agnes and several nuns arrived
in New York in May 1846. In 1848, they purchased property for
a girls' academy and what would become the Convent of St.
Catherine of Siena in New York City.

When the war came, Archbishop Hughes was reluctant to
part with too many of his sisters, knowing their services were
badly needed in the diocese. While he was away in Europe, the
War Department petitioned the New York archdiocese's vicar
general, William Starrs, for nuns to superintend a new hospital at Beaufort, North Carolina, in June 1862. With Starrs's

389

permission, Mother Superior Madeleine Tobin quickly complied, sending fourteen nuns led by Sister Mary Augustine MacKenna and Father James Bruehl, a Hungarian-born Jesuit. They arrived in Beaufort in July at Hammond General Hospital, formerly a resort for wealthy southerners. But the sisters found very little relaxing in their new home, with debris, filth, and blood spread liberally throughout the hospital rooms and even their own quarters. They set to work immediately in the incredible challenge of turning their new home into a clean and healthy place for wounded Union soldiers. High tides and strong winds in late October forced the sisters and their patients to remove to nearby New Bern. There the sisters took over the home of Revolutionary War hero John Wright Stanley, turning it into their own private convent while they nursed wounded and sick men in nearby buildings.

Although much of Conyngham's narrative of the sisters in North Carolina is similar to Helen M. Sweeney's *The Golden Milestone* (1896), the addition of unpublished letters at the end makes this account extremely valuable. Like the chapter on the St. Louis Sisters of Mercy, the two chapters on the sisters from New York are written by the familiar hand of the rest of the manuscript with minor editing from Conyngham. The first chapter is primarily an account of the sisters' services in North Carolina, while the second reprints a number of related stories and letters written to the sisters by deceased soldiers' grieving relatives.

❀   ❀   ❀

The Sisters of Mercy were among the first to offer their services to attend the sick and wounded in the various hospitals during the late war. Trained up to visit the poor and afflicted, their minds were, in some measure, prepared for the sufferings endured by the victims of war. Their training and the precepts of charity and self-denial by their religious vows had prepared them for their mission, and, therefore, their attentions and ministrations to the sick and wounded were useful from the very start.

No one recognized this more readily than the doctors, of whom, it must be justly said that they allowed no religious prejudices to interfere with whatever tended most to the comfort of their patients. After a little time, when they had come to fully appreciate the devoted attention and nice care bestowed by the sisters on their charges, Protestant doctors were just as anxious to secure their services in the hospitals as the Catholic doctors themselves.

Among the houses that sent forth its inmates on their work of love and mercy was St. Catherine's Convent, Houston Street, New York, over which the grand and saintly Mother Augustine[1] presides. These sisters were welcomed by General [John G.] Foster[2] and the following order was issued by him.

> Headquarters, Department North Carolina
> New Bern,[3] July 22nd, 1862.
> **Special order No. 17**
> #5 Dr. Upham,[4] Post Surgeon at Beaufort will put the Sisters of Mercy, lately arrived from New York, in charge of the hospital at Beaufort under his supervision, and assign to them the sole charge of each department as he may deem necessary, and they will be obeyed and respected accordingly.
> By Command of Major General Foster
> Southard Hoffman, Asst. Adjt. General

Soon after the capitulation of Fort Macon to General Burnside and Foster, a large hotel on the mainland, opposite the island on which the fort stands, was converted into an hospital, but not until it had been completely rifled by its captors, and used, or rather abused, as their barracks. There, many of the survivors of that long damp watch at Roanoke came to linger out life's remnant in consumption or the chills; there the brave men who had besieged New Bern and taken it, came to await the healing of their wounds, some of them disabled for life by the super-human labor of dragging cannon into position after the horses had been shot down; there, in fine, came numbers of these young conscripts, who in the zeal of their patriotism, had abandoned the fascinations of college life, or had given up comforts of a happy, perhaps of a luxurious home, to endure the effects of marsh water, malaria, and hard tack.

These poor fellows were their own nurses, and were forced to improvise both means and methods of performing their functions as such.

The department was then[5] scarcely organized, and the necessary supplies so difficult to be obtained that those whose duty it was to make the requisitions were disgusted and discouraged.

The patients were almost to a man, thrifty New Englanders accustomed to order and comfort and so felt the more keenly the total absence of both. In July the heat became so intense that even the all sufficing sea was not enough to cool the atmosphere, and the filth so accumulated that the waves, which swept against the building on three sides, and even beneath it, were soiled and discolored.

Sickness was raging and misery had reached the extremist edge of endurance. Just at this time the noble hearted General Foster, in command of the department, visited the hospital and announced to its inmates that he had succeeded in inducing a band of religious from New York to take charge of it, and promised that everything necessary should be finished.

Notwithstanding all they were enduring, the men shrank from the idea of being relieved by Catholics, by nuns, creatures whose imperious lives and unimagined aims are so wildly misrepresented in that sort of literature in which many of them were well read.[6]

The most injurious opinions were formed with regard to the promised succor and every sort of suspicion whispered concerning them.

Very soon the religious arrived and it must be confessed that their first appearance was calculated to make impressions semi-tragical.

Imagine a diminutive steamer of southern build, exhibiting the most nonchalant absence of design and the most abstemious application of paint, approaching a low projecting wharf, in a dense rain. Negro and Yankee have united their efforts to secure it, a gangway of the simplest construction is laid down, and a band of inscrutable women make their appearance—Two, four, six—nay seven of those unfathomable veils.—What is hidden behind them? "Widows in search of the mortal remains of their husbands," answered the astounded "Nigger." "Chief mourners over the country's peace and happiness," said the unconsciously poetical ex-collegian. "Jesuits," sneered the bigots; "female Jesuits carrying all the craft and subtlety of their tribe under those ominous black surroundings."

Unaware of these and still more extravagant surmises the sisters made their way quietly over an unsafe causeway and entered the hospital.

Little preparation had been made to receive them and no welcome was afforded them.

The doctor, a man of refined sensibilities, felt so much his inability to afford them even the most ordinary hospitality that he kept out of sight and the honors were done by an old mulatto woman—good Aunt Clarissey.

I afterwards learned from some of the best men in the establishment, that they watched the new comers most narrowly expecting every day to make some wonderful discovery, to find them develop[ing] some scheme either of proselytism or of self-aggrandizement—some proof that they formed part and parcel of the very imp of iniquity itself.

When it is added that the place resounded every Wednesday night with Methodist canticles and Methodist manifestations delivered now by white and now by colored orators, the position of the "Sisters of Mercy" may be imagined. How did they fill it?

Simply by endeavoring to do their duty to minister to the comforts of the wretched sufferers around them with woman's adroitness and woman's tenderness as well as with the gravity and reserve of the religious; by keeping strictly within the enclosure of their rules and observances and no doubt by praying earnestly for the accomplishments of the design of Providence, both in themselves and in the poor suffering confided to their care. They preached no gospel, they questioned no un-Catholic conscience, they inaugurated no crusade against heresy or heretics.[7]

Immediately after the sisters arrived, a general order was issued by Major General Foster, placing the hospital under their charge. They very soon discovered that the poor officials were so wearied in their arduous and tiresome employment that they would be glad to cooperate with any one, willing to relieve them, and that quarter-masters, purveyors, and commissaries were ready enough to afford supplies when the order of the general in command backed the requisitions. In a little time, therefore, the whole place had undergone a thorough house cleaning and was furnished with what was really necessary.

The face of affairs brightened up, the first cargo of ice arrived, and the very heat was ameliorated. By degrees, the unacknowledged influence of the church, as represented by the humble and unpretending sisters, was seen and felt.

Disorderly conduct was given up, habits of cleanliness and even of politeness were restored, and at last, heretics of the truest blue began to consult the sisters about their little affairs, to confide to them their family sorrows, and to look to them for sympathy and consolation.

The following is a touching instance of that confidence. A sister entered one of the wards one morning and at once perceived that the hand of death was laid heavily on one of her patients; an elderly man, quiet and uncomplaining, a Bostonian, and of course not a Catholic. She took her place at his bed side and wiped the death drops from his brow; a grateful look of recognition passed over his face and making an expiring effort, he took an old pocket book from beneath his pillow and placed it in her hand, significantly yet silently, for his last word had been spoken. He was understood. She assured him it should be forwarded to his wife, and with it an account of his illness. He smiled gratefully, but she had hardly recommended his soul to God when he breathed his last. Another instance of this complete confidence was that of a poor young quartermaster, who had worn himself out in the discharge of his onerous duties. He was brought to the hospital he had helped to fit up, in fever, and sunk rapidly. He was a gentle, well-disposed, moral young man, although unbaptized and unbelieving, yet when death came nothing soothed him but prayers of the sisters and the sight of the crucifix.

He had in his possession a quantity of papers, which he said no mortal eye should ever see, not even his mother's and he entrusted them to the sister that she might destroy them. Poor boy, he died peacefully after a short busy life with the new grace of baptism whitening his soul.

There was one poor fellow home sick and sad hearted, who had no less than four likenesses of his wife under his pillow, and was constantly engaged in the contemplation of one or other of them. The doctors scolded him and his comrades laughed at him, so he flew for consolation to the sister in charge of his ward and flinging all his prejudices to the winds, he declared that she had raised his thoughts to better things, and that he would never say a word against a Catholic as long as he lived. This was prejudice overcome, and charity and good feeling took its place.

"Ah, Sister," said a poor young officer as he took his leave after a tedious convalescence. "I hate myself when I think of the false impressions with regard to religious women and of the way in which I shrank from you at first. But I know better now, and I believe that the religion that inspires such indiscriminate charity must come from God, no matter what men say."

But why multiply instances. The universal grief of the patients when the sisters were recalled to the mother house, some of them broke down completely, and one was actually even despaired of by the doctors—are the best proofs. The poor expatriated Catholics who were scattered here and there among the patients, and the converts recently baptized and full of their fervor did not seem to feel more than the honest Massachusetts men, who declared that they would respect the habit of a sister wherever they might see it, for sake of those who nursed them with so much care.

But I have left the poor Negroes out of my sketch. Who can forget their sorrow? Child-like and affectionate creatures, their whole hearts were taken captive by the kindness which so astonished them; they were ready to go with the sisters anywhere, and it seems [they] had a crude idea that they would surely be taken. It was sad to see the big tears rolling over those poor dusky faces and to know that they were likely to be succeeded by others more burning, more heart wrung.

The sisters left and so great was the respect and almost veneration paid to their very memory that the wing of the building they had occupied was left uninhabited for many months, because the men could not bear to see it filled with the sick and wounded. Hundreds of patients had passed through the hospital during the stay of the sisters, yet not one instance of any rudeness or want of respect could be recalled by any of them; not an angry word, not a curse, had ever been spoken in their presence. Time will produce the harvest that was then sown, it is to be hoped, by proving the better state of feeling, between "those who differ in religion," by checking the current of prejudice and by preserving Catholics from many of the insults it would have produced.

CHAPTER XXXII

The Sisters of Mercy, New York, Continued

A Unitarian minister's tribute to the sisters—The life of Christ exemplified—Writing letters for the soldiers—What a dying man wanted—Prejudice and religion at variance—Anecdote of the battle of Gettysburg—How Paddy buried the chaplain—A soldier's faith—How Mackey lost his leg—The story of a dead soldier— A father's gratitude—A wife's thanks—The grief of a loved one for her betrothed.

In the spring of 1863, a Unitarian minister was deputed by the City of Boston to inspect the military hospital[s] in North Carolina for the purpose of ascertaining their real condition and of discovering whether the supplies sent for the sick and wounded soldiers of the state of Massachusetts were honestly appropriated to their use. After having seen most of the other hospitals he came to that taken over by the Sisters of Mercy, and, having had no previous experience of their mode of managing matters of the kind, was more than usually suspicious.

He spent a great deal of time among the sick, and when his information with regard to them was complete, he called on the sisters and told them honestly that he had expected to find the men under their care, undergoing a sort of persecution for their faith, as very few of them were Catholics, and that he had been led to entertain the worst opinion of nuns in general. "But," he added, "I am disabused of my error and I must say that I never thought the life of Christ was so perfectly exemplified by any class of Christians as I have seen it by the

Sisters of Mercy, for they like our divine Master 'go about doing good.'"
He said that wherever he went he would endeavor to lessen the prejudice existing in the minds of non-Catholics against the sisters.

The gentleman in charge of the stores of the Sanitary Commission,
having been applied to by letter for supplies for the sisters' hospital,
replied that he would be most happy to furnish them knowing from
personal observation how they would be husbanded and how impar-
tially distributed. The hospital steward, who was a New Englander and
a Protestant of some denomination, told the sisters that when they first
came to Beaufort he watched them closely, even staying up till midnight for the purpose, as he had been led to entertain strange suspi-
cions of all nuns; but that after a time he gave up the practice having
found that the sisters went through an amount of labor and fatigue
that even the soldiers employed to nurse the sick would not undergo,
and in fact he became their most steadfast friend.

At first the patients who were for the most part Protestants and
New Englanders were very shy of the sisters, and took even refreshments from their hands in a stiff ungracious manner, but this so completely wore off that they used to apply to them in all their wants and
employ them to write their letters when unable to do so themselves
even when these concerned their most private family affairs.

One of these poor fellows having witnessed the death of a Catholic
soldier, who received the rites of the Catholic church with all the
solemnity that could be given to them under the circumstances, and by
whose bed the priest and the sisters kept constant watch during his
agony, called the sister to him next day and said, "Sister, I'd like to die
as P—— died." A long conversation ensued, and the result was that the
man resolved to send for the minister and enquire what preparation he
would recommend him to make for the death which he felt he was
surely approaching. This he did at the sister's suggestion. The minister,
a very eloquent and popular clergyman, came; the question was put to
him and he said, "Well my friend I shall read you a chapter of scripture." "Oh, thank you," said the man, "I can do that myself, and I do so
every day." "Then I shall pray with you." "Pray," said the dying soldier,
"why anyone can pray with me; [one]¹ does not need a minister to
pray. That is not what I want; I want you to prepare me for death."

"Now, I know how it is," said the minister, "is there something on your mind you would like me to write to your wife or to any of your friends? I see you are anxious about your affairs." "The Sister has done all that for me," answered the man, "and I believe she understands what I am anxious about better than you do," so he dismissed the minister without further parley. It may be inferred that he received the instructions of the sisters and became a Catholic. He did the former fully and freely but the latter if done at all was only an implicit act, for though he declared his willingness to embrace the Catholic faith at any cost, and made implicit acts of faith and explicit acts of hope and charity, yet he could not be convinced that the Catholic was the true religion, and could not overcome in his weak mind, suffering state, the long entrenched prejudices of his people and his associations. Yet he died in true sentiments and in contrition. "May he rest in peace."

The following anecdotes have been related to the author by a Sister of Mercy who was with the army:

ANECDOTE OF THE BATTLE OF GETTYSBURG[2]

As the Southern army was approaching the scene of conflict, one poor fellow seeking like many others, for food or clothing, went up to the house of a Catholic clergyman, and asked him to provide him with a coat and hat. The poor fellow was evidently [an] Irishman with a rich brogue still on his tongue. The father, who was of the same race and land, did his best to supply the many wants of his countryman and having nothing more military on hand, gave him a long clerical coat and a hat to suit; the poor fellow laughed at his own appearance as he walked off in his strange outfit. A few days after, that dreadful battle was fought and the priest almost exhausted his energy in ministering to the wounded and dying men.

Six days after the battle, he re-visited the scene and walking thoughtfully along was accosted by an Irish soldier belonging to one of the Northern regiments. "Your reverence," said he, "would you come and see where I buried the Confederate chaplain." "Why," said the priest, "there was no chaplain killed in the battle; I made inquiries and know there was not." "Fait[h], then there was your reverence," said the soldier, "and it is myself that buried him here below—come and see." The priest went with him and in answer to his enquiries found that the supposed Confederate chaplain had all the equipment of a Southern soldier, except that he wore a clerical coat and hat, and at once suspected that it was the poor fellow to whom he had given the venerated articles before the battle.

They came to a quiet spot, apart from the multitude of graves and there under a tree was the decent grave of the supposed priest with this inscription in black paint on a deal board: "Here lies his Reverence, the Confederate chaplain." The priest turned away with tears in his eyes, and had not the heart to undeceive the poor soldier, who made the coffin with his own hands, and painted the inscription in uncouth characters.

A SOLDIER'S FAITH

There was a tall County Meath man, named Mackey, in hospital, one of whose legs had been shot off above the knee, and when he began to recover, he gave the most graphic account of the way in which he met his loss. "In what battle did you lose your leg, Mackey?" asked a sister. "In no battle at all, Sister, dear, only in a bit of a scrimmage. Shure, I was on picket duty myself and two more of us, away out at the last post, and we had orders in case any suspicious persons came along, to arrest them, but if a body of men passed, to fire one volley as a signal to the next picket guard, and then protect ourselves as well as we could. Well in the dead of the night we heard the tramp of a body of men & began to discuss about what we should do. One man declared he would simply obey orders & after he had fired one shot, secure[d] his own safety by lying down behind the trunk of a tree which lay near our post—but myself and my comrade swore we would fire while we had a grain of powder and so we did. The Southerners came on five or six hundred of them and when they were pretty near, we all three fired. We, that is myself and Tim, did as we said—we fired and fired & they fired big volleys at us—soon we found our ammunition giving out and so we began to retreat firing back at them as often as we could get our guns ready; at last we got to the river's edge which is soft & marshy and after firing two good shots we rushed into the river hoping to swim to the other side, but before we got into deep water a shot struck poor Tim and he fell and rose no more. I heard him struggling in the water, and says I, "I'll let fly at them once more." I fired and the next minute a shot struck me above the knee, and that's how I lost my leg."

"But how did you save your life? And how did you escape a fate like poor Tim's?" "Well, Sister, shure I knew the Blessed Virgin would help me and I called on her." "How could you expect her to have pity on you when you were so bent on revenge and had just been committing sin." "Arrah shure I had the scapular and know she promised not to let anyone that has it die in mortal sin so I thought that the more sin was on my soul the more chance there was she wouldn't let me die without a priest. I stood out in the water with my arms supporting me till I was almost falling into it entirely when I heard a low whistle. I answered it & pretty soon our comrade who had lain down behind the tree waded out to where I was and helped me to the shore. He fixed up my shattered limb as well as he could & I lay there wrapped in a blanket till they came to relieve the guard and then they took me to the hospital and here I am." "Are you not sorry for firing so foolishly at those Southerners?" "Faith, I am not Sister; I'd be more ashamed if I lay down behind the old tree and I warrant you the Blessed Virgin will pray for me after all."

COPY OF A LETTER FOUND IN THE POCKET OF A DEAD SOLDIER AT NEW BERN, NORTH CAROLINA, STANLEY HOSPITAL 1862

About fourteen years ago the writer was but small in size but he went from his home to earn his own bread. The reason of this was because his father had left his mother without any property whatsoever. The writer will not at present relate the reason of the separation in knowing it to be enough that they did separate in about the year 1847, leaving my mother with three children of which I composed one of the number. After leaving home I went far away from my folks where I remained for several years not hearing from them but twice in the whole time. About the year 1860 I took it into my head to return to my mother but I found it a hard thing to do but I resolved to see my mother. I started on my journey, which was long and tedious, not seeing anyone I knew for a long time before I found my mother; she had got married and had two more children. I did not know her nor did she[3] know me, but we were not long together before we knew each other. Two sons which I knew nothing about appeared very handsome to me; the eldest one was about eight years old, his hair was nearly red; the other, was about six years old, his hair was nearly white or a silvery color, otherwise he resembled his brother very much. I had not been home long before an oldish man came in, perhaps he was seventy years old. I was introduced to him as his step-son. He took a seat and I did the same; he lit his pipe and began to smoke, when the youngest boy came running in, "John, you have not been gone long," said my mother, "have you seen Jane," speaking of my sister who was about a year older than myself. "Ya," said the boy, and Jane herself stepped into the door. She knew me not, but when being told, she grasped my hand, and shed tears of joy. She said that she did not expect that it was me, for she said that she heard that I was dead and then my mother went on to tell the whole history which I shall not stop or relate at present.

I remained at home for some time when I heard the dreadful news of the rebellion, of which I saw a good chance to serve my country by enlisting. I thought of course that it would not last long, and so did my new father, and he wished to have me stay with him to help him tend to his farm, for he said that he was getting old and he did not believe that the war was going to last long, two or three months at most. I told my folks that I must go for my country's sake, but they said that I was foolish for thinking so, but I told them that if everybody said the same what would our country come to in time of such a dreadful rebellion

as this was; but they said that there was men enough that could
be spared from their homes better than I could. I had got it into
my head that I must enlist, therefore I took leave of my new father and my mother, who was sure to give me some good advice
which I listened to with an anxious ear. My sister wept and so did
my poor old mother and my father told me that I would wish
myself home more than once before I could get back. This was
more than true, but I heeded it not. I started and crossed the lake
from Vermont into [New] York State. I found myself in Ticon-
deroga, a small village where I found an enlisting officer. I had
my name put down to go to the war. I stayed there for a couple of
weeks and then we started for Albany, which is a large town on
the Hudson River. The first day after we arrived when we left the
cars we marched back through the town or city as it is sometimes
called, for it being the capital of the state, back on a small hill
where there was some barracks built for the purpose of sheltering
the soldiers until they were prepared for going farther south. We
remained there for some time; nothing very interesting occurred
except that we had to learn a soldier's fare by sleeping on slats
about three inches apart and our meals were pretty hard for a
Northern soldier to tell about, but I have found out since that
I did not know anything about hardships, so you will soon
find out.

I had not remained there over three months and our company was not full, and there being another company in the barracks which was not full and our company was split up and put
into the other company, and then the two companies were called
the "Rocket Battalion." I was put into the second company, which
was called company B, our major's name was T[homas] W. Lion.[4]
After we consolidated, we started for Washington. On the road
we stopped in New-York overnight. The next day we started on
our journey and got as far as Philadelphia. At twelve o'clock that
night, we took supper at the Philadelphia Cooper Shop which
was a refreshment furnished by the Union ladies in that place. We
marched after our supper about four miles; after we ate we fired a

salute for the good people in that place, then got aboard of the cars and started once more. I will write more when I have time.

—Arthur M. P.[5]

LETTER FROM THE FATHER OF A YOUNG SOLDIER[6] WHO DIED IN THE STANLEY HOSPITAL, NEW BERN, NORTH CAROLINA

Lowell, March 19th, 1863

Sisters of Mercy

Dear friends,

Your letter of 27th February, bringing the sad yet not wholly un-expected intelligence of the death of my dear boy, came by regular mail—sad it is indeed that one so young should be taken just as it were in the bud of manhood we could bair without it otherwise but alas! it was so ordered and it behooves us to bow in meek submission to the decree of our al[l-]wise *Creator* who doeth all things well, and we would fain believe the Master had need of him and hath called him hence—

We followed him to his last resting place beside his mother, his battles of this world over, his race early run.

We sent you by last week's steamer four dozen one pound cans of condensed milk to be by you distributed to the sick under your charge (we were unable to obtain more as it was sold in advance to the medical department), directed to the Convent of Mercy, New Bern, North Carolina. There are but a few friends in this neighbor-hood who have sons in the 44th [Massachusetts Infantry Regiment], but to those I will instruct them in the wants of the sick in your care.

And with renewed assurance of very great respect and prayer for the choicest blessings to the noble Sisters of Mercy, who are always so ready at the post of duty to alleviate the pains of sickness and ease the couch of the dying.

I am with sincere thanks your faithful servant,

D[avid] Bradt

LETTER FROM A WOMAN ABOUT HER HUSBAND[7]

Harned[s]ville [Pennsylvania]
January 25th 1863

Dear friend, for so I must call you, for your kindness in writing to me the sad and sorrowful news about my dear husband. I thank you kindly for writing although it was bad news to me. My dear friends, you may imagine how I felt when I heard that my dear husband was dead. One of his company wrote to me after he was wounded but said that he was doing very well and in two months he would be at home with me again, and before I got that letter my dear husband was dead. It almost breaks my heart to think of it, but I will try and console myself with the thought that although his body lies far, in distant lands unknown to me, that his soul is in heaven and I will try to meet him there where war is not and where we will never part again.

Dear Sister of Mercy—allow me to ask you a few questions concerning my dead husband. Please let me know if he was sensible after he was taken to the hospital and if he suffered much; one thing in particular if he gave any signs of assurance that he was prepared to meet his God, and if he said anything about being willing to die, and also if he said anything about his children or wife that he would like to see us. I thank you very kindly for taking good care of him and I hope the good Lord will reward you for it. It is very hard to lose a husband at home, but it is much harder to think and hear that he had to die away so far from home, but if he was prepared to die he is a good dale better than to be in this troublesome world. I hope he was buried decent, O, how hard it is to think that I could not see my dear husband before he died! Please let me know all about him. I sent a letter to him and so did his brother and if there is any letters come in his name you can lift them and do as you please with them. I must now close hoping to meet you as a friend and my dear and kind husband in that glorious heaven. Answer this letter as soon as it comes to hand as my hear husband always lived a Christian life at home I would like to know how he died.

Nothing more but [to] offer to you my thanks and kindest sympathy.

Anna Pullin[8]

LETTER FROM THE BETROTHED OF A YOUNG OFFICER WHO DIED, UNDER THE SISTERS' CARE, OF HIS WOUNDS

Bridgeport, [Connecticut] August 30th 1862

Dear Madam,

It is with a sad and weary heart that I attempt to pen a few lines to you. I know it was my duty long since to thank you for your kindness to Lieutenant [Charles B.] Springer[9] and my-self. You said in your note to me that Captain [Samuel] Hufty promised to write me all the particulars but he has never written me one line that I know of yet. A gentleman friend of Charlie's wrote to him directly after his death, but he has never sent a line. I thought I could write to you better than the captain. So I ask of you to be kind enough to confer on me the favor of giving me every item that you know connected with his illness. You evi-dently know of the relation that existed between us and I need not feel any restraint in writing as I feel in this sad trial. There was a small gold book with my miniature which he always car-ried in his bosom. Could you tell me whether it was still with him when he was carried away or not? If it was buried with him I am perfectly satisfied, but if not I would like to have it myself as it is mine by rights. I heard of his death the fifth of August, it was indeed, a heavy stroke. The note you wrote for him during his ill-ness did not reach me until the following Saturday, August 9th, and I was wholly unprepared—as the last letter I had received from him but a few days previous was in the same buoyant and cheerful spirits as formerly. His parents received the word and forwarded it on to me. His loss is deeply felt by many as he was known and loved by a host of friends. But none can feel it and lament as bitterly as myself. God has afflicted me sorely and naught but time and submission to his divine will can sooth my grief. I have a pleasant home, kind parents, many dear relatives, and warm friends, but they fall far short of filling the vacancy. He was my idol and I fear I loved him too well—Loved the creature more than the Creator. He was truly noble and honorable as others will testify besides myself, and I trust his spirit now dwells with God and though we were not permitted to meet on earth we may greet each other in joys immortal, where parting is unknown and may the day be not far distant—life to me has changed; it is dark and dreary. You thought I was imprudent and not reserved enough. But I have no regret that I wrote to him as I did. I am well assured that my devotion and anxiety was fully appreciated by him and a shield to him in the hour of temptation. We were fondly attached and perfectly understood each other. But I am left to weep but not alone. This cruel rebellion is causing thousands of hearts to wail in sadness for their loved ones.

Yours sorrowing,

R. C. A.[10]

EPILOGUE: According to Sister Augustine's diary, four of the Sisters of Mercy died while serving the wounded at Beaufort. She herself took ill and suffered painfully for the rest of her life. Nonetheless, this Irish-born sister became the community's Mother Superior in 1868 and even founded another branch of the Sisters of Mercy in Balmville, New York. Retiring from leadership in 1877, she finally died in 1883. The Sisters of Mercy continued to visit hospitals and serve the many Catholic orphans of New York for the rest of the nineteenth century.

SOURCES: Helen Sweeney, *The Golden Milestone, 1846-1896: Fifty Years of Loving Labor among the Poor and Suffering by the Sisters of Mercy of New York City* (New York: Benziger Brothers, 1896), 6–22, 69–100, 134–80; Ellen Ryan Jolly, *Nuns of the Battlefield* (Providence, RI: Providence Visitor Press, 1927), 206–22.

CHAPTER XXXIII

The Sisters of the Holy Cross

Their response to the call of suffering humanity—Their devotion, their services, and their sacrifices—Governor Morton of Indiana gratefully accepts the offer of the sisters' services—The sisters under charge of Mother Mary Angela in care of the hospitals at Paducah—Their zeal not abated by their hardships—Scenes and sufferings in the hospitals—The sisters' trials and triumphs— How they conquered prejudice by meekness, charity, and good works—Touching incidents—Mother Angela at Mound City.[1]

INTRODUCTION: The Sisters of the Holy Cross were first established in France in 1841 as a female religious community attached to Father Basil Moreau's Congregation of Holy Cross. Two years later, the first sisters arrived in New York and made their way to Notre Dame, Indiana, where their help was needed in making Father Edward Sorin's dream of a Catholic college in the rural Midwest a reality. Although many of the first sisters were from France, perhaps the most important was an Ohioan who entered the community in 1853. Eliza Maria Gillespie (1824–1887) followed her brother, Father Neal Henry Gillespie, to Notre Dame, and became Sister Mary of St. Angela. After studying in France, she returned to Notre Dame and became Mother Angela.

Heeding a call for sister nurses from Governor Oliver Morton of Indiana delivered on October 21, 1861, Mother Angela led a group of sisters to care for wounded Union soldiers that would eventually total sixty-three sister nurses by the end of the war. Her education and family connections to the Ewing and Sherman families of Ohio proved useful during the Civil War, helping to secure the aid of General Ulysses S. Grant in getting positions for her sisters in hospitals despite occasional opposition from army doctors or female Protestant nurses.

Conyngham's handwritten manuscript contains five chapters on the Sisters of the Holy Cross. The first three are a complete first draft narrative of the Sisters of the Holy Cross during the war, with a note stating: "This has been corrected by the sisters themselves." These first three chapters are much longer and more detailed than the last two, which are essentially an abridged second draft. Because Conyngham's final table of contents refers to only two chapters, whose subheadings perfectly match the last two chapters in the draft manuscript, only the shorter version of the Sisters of the Holy Cross's Civil War story is included in this edited edition.

❀   ❀   ❀

Through the good and charitable works, performed by the sisters of the various orders, during the war, in their attendance on the sick and wounded, though they have made a grateful impression on the public mind, and have done much to remove groundless prejudices against both their order and holy religion, still, owing to the untiring disposition of the sisters, they have not been given due publicity, while trifling but more ostentatious services have been made the themes of poets and historians. Meek, humble, and retiring, laboring alone for the glory of God and expecting no earthly reward for their services, it is no wonder that they shrank from parading their Christian labors and good works before the eyes of the world.

On this account we have had much difficulty in collecting the materials, relative to the sisters, for our work. Through the aid and influence of kind friends we have succeeded in rescuing from oblivion enough regarding their gentle ministrations to the sick and wounded in the hospitals, and of that sweetness and meekness which conquered prejudice and error, to make our work not only interesting, but also, to leave in history a record, that will live as a shame and a reproach to the maligners of the pious sisters and their holy religion. We know that it is a very different thing to perform good and charitable works and quite another to give to posterity an accurate and faithfully written account of them.

The very qualities of mind and heart which enter into the life of a religious make the most sublime acts of heroism, self-denial and charity, appear to her as simple acts of duty. She regards not what the world says about her; if she is but conscious that she has fulfilled her mission and done the work allotted to her by her divine Master she is fully satisfied. She courts not the vain approbation of mortals; if conscious that she has done her duty she finds her reward in that inward peace and grace which are the fruits of good and pious action.

Of these humble sisters but faithful Soldiers of the Cross, it might be justly said in the words of Gerald Griffin:

Unshrinking where pestilence scatters his breath.
Like an angel she moves, 'mid the vapors of death;
Where rings the loud musket, and flashes the sword,
Unfearing she walks, for she follows the Lord.
How sweetly she bends o'er each plague-tainted face
With looks that are lighted with holiest grace.
How kindly she dresses each suffering limb,
For she sees in the wounded the image of Him.[2]

Among the numerous religious houses whose members went freely forth to encounter hardships, dangers, privations, and disease in order to alleviate the suffering of their fellow creatures, the house of Holy Cross, Notre Dame, Indiana, stands eminent for the number of sisters it sent to attend the sick and wounded.

In the early part of the war, in fact at its breaking out, the ecclesiastical superior of the mother house of St. Mary's, Notre Dame, namely, the Very Rev. Father Sorin, offered the services of the sisters under his charge to Governor Morton as nurses in the hospitals, which offer was gladly accepted.[3] In October 1861 the three military hospitals at Paducah, Kentucky, were in charge of a corps of sisters under Mother Mary of St. Angela.[4] When they took charge of these hospitals the patients were suffering from camp dysentery and measles, which diseases were much accelerated by the lack of proper attendance and nourishments. The sisters soon effected a total change for the better and the disease rapidly declined after they had taken charge of the hospitals. So great were the labors of the sisters that two of them died from disease brought on by exposure and fatigue while several of them had to return to St. Mary's in broken health. But their places were soon filled by fresh volunteers, who immediately filled up the depleted ranks, and no less than seventy-five[5] Sisters of [the] Holy Cross were actively engaged during the war as nurses in the military hospitals of Cairo, Mound City, Louisville, and the naval hospitals.

In November 1861 Mother Angela, at the request of the medical director of General Grant's staff,[6] sent some sisters to Mound City to attend to the wounded who had been carried there from the battlefield of Belmont.[7] The hospitals were a lot of improvised huts and store rooms, in which no fewer than seven hundred wounded soldiers were crowded without bed or covering. Their wounds, too, had become, from their long exposure on the battlefield, corrupted and full of creeping maggots, so that the sisters had an unpleasant task to perform to clean and wash them.

The hospital was in charge of Dr. E[dward] C. Franklin,[8] who, with the aid of the sisters, soon had all their wounds dressed and the poor fellows made as comfortable as circumstances would permit. This was made a general hospital for the wounded from the surrounding camps, so the Rev. Mother had to telegraph to St. Mary's for eighteen more sisters. The men too were poorly supplied with nourishing food, which was necessary to strengthen them, but through the exertions of the sisters supplies soon came in, and to the honor of William H. Osborn, Esq.,[9] President of the Illinois Central [Railroad], be it said that he authorized Rev. Mother Angela to draw upon him for whatever she needed, which generosity she liberally used for the benefit of the sick and wounded soldiers. During the month of December 1861 the numbers of the sick and wounded in the Mound City and Cairo hospitals were so great that more sisters had to be sent for to the hospital at Paducah.

Good old Sister M. De La P——,[10] one of the most efficient nurses was among those called on, and as she was on the steamboat about to leave for her destination some of the Protestant army chaplains seeing her, came forward to express their regret at her departure and to thank her for the untiring care she had bestowed upon the sick. "I'm at a loss," said one of the chaplains, addressing his companion, "to know where this good old Sister ever took any rest. I have gone to the hospital at daybreak to look to some of our sick boys and there was the Sister engaged in her work of mercy. I have been there at noon and she was still at her post, and I have sometimes gone late at night and found her there still consoling the last moments of some dying soldier." "It is a mystery to me," he continued, "how those Sisters can stand at their post without ever giving up." Addressing Sister P——, he said, "How do you account for it?" But she simply smiled and pointed to the beads hanging at her side. This pantomime answer only seemed to confuse him and the sister noticing his mystified look said to Mother Angela, "I not speak good English; please you tell the gentleman." "Sister means," said Mother Angela in her office of interpreter, "that our strength is sustained and ever increased in the daily discharge of hospital labors by our frequent meditations on the life and suffering of our Lord. When our minds dwell upon the love he manifested for us in his sacred humanity it is the most natural thing in the world for us to find strength and joy in relieving for his sake the sufferings of some of these for whom he died. Now the beads we carry at our side are to us replete with an eloquence of our Lord's life in his sacred humanity from the moment that the archangel declared to the Immaculate Virgin of Judea that she should be the Mother of God, to the morning of his glorious resurrection and ascension."

Then in as brief but forcible and touching a manner as possible Mother Angela passed before him the mysteries attached to the different decades. "Now," said she, "you can understand what Sister P—— means, which is that when worn out with fatigue she passes a decade through her fingers, meditates upon the agony in the garden, or the painful fall in the streets of Jerusalem, she feels a new strength and a new courage to perform her duties. When the details of the sick bed are calculated to disgust us, our beads help us to recall the bitter portion of vinegar and gall (the draught for that poor sufferer, as well as for us). When our own heads throb with the weariness and the excitement attending such terrible scenes, the mere touch of our beads reminds us of the agony endured by the crowning with sharp thorns, and this does a great deal towards soothing our own pain or making us indifferent to it." The chaplain listened attentively and then exclaimed, "Well now that is indeed Christianity; I used to think the Papist beads were great mummery, now I'll always regard them with respect. They remind me of what I myself often do. When I am at home and am going down the street my wife tells me to bring something for the family. Although I think a great deal of what she says, yet to keep it in mind, in the midst of other affairs that may attract my attention, I always tie a cotton string around my finger." "Yes," he continues, "I am convinced that there is a good deal of Christianity in those beads." The chaplain then left and the boat started with its freight, and the sisters on their way to their work of mercy.

When the news of the battle of Fort Donelson[11] arrived at the Mound City hospital, all the sick who could be removed from the latter place were transferred to St. Louis in order to make room for the wounded in the late bloody battle. Throughout the whole day and late at night the good angelic nurses were busy for their fresh work of mercy, which was to commence again that night. After midnight several boats came in literally packed with cargoes of wounded men. After the sufferers were placed in the hospital, one of the wards in particular presented a scene more than usually appalling. It was filled by the wounded of a certain command that had been placed in ambush during a part of the battle with instructions to be flat on the ground until the firing ceased. The order to rise unfortunately was given too soon, and as the men raised their heads they received a volley which almost placed the whole of them *hors de combat*.[12] The wounds being all received in the head, face, and neck, the sufferings of those men were dreadful. Some had to endure additionally the pangs of starvation, not being able to swallow, while one or two others frantically pulled the tongues from their mouths and threw them on the ground. The good sisters went to work with their usual attention and alacrity and from their humane treatment of the sufferers the gratitude of the latter knew no bounds.

The very name of "Sisters" rendered the services of the angelic women, the more welcome to the sick, for the latter would say, "When we call you Sisters we feel as if we could ask you for anything we need without fearing that you will be impatient or tired of us." Even in writing to their friends the whole of their secrets and family history would be placed in the sisters' trustworthy keeping. Letters from friends of the dead would be also received by the sisters inquiring for information concerning the last sickness, last words, and dying dispositions of the departed, and it was invariably touching to read their admissions of grief for the beloved dead as well as their gratitude to the sisters for the services rendered to them in their last hours.

Throughout the hospital the sisters were everywhere greeted with, "God bless you, ladies!" "Oh, Sisters, what good you are doing here!" "How happy we are to see you here among our poor fellows," would be the exclamations of the officers and surgeons while the poor patients would say, "I don't know what we boys would do if it were not for the Sisters!" The Protestant ministers always expressed a hearty good will towards them and the soldiers engaged in the different departments, always showed them great respect and evidently felt that the sisters' presence was necessary if only to keep the soldiers to their strict line of duty in attending to the interests of the sick. In the midst of all their sufferings, the wounded exhibited the brightest [traits][13] of patience and resignation.

The sentiments of courage which had inspired them upon the battlefield was in beautiful contrast to their meekness and nobleness in the hospital. Their preparation for death could not have been made with better disposition even if dying quietly at home. Often and often would a soldier say to a sister while ministering to his physical sufferings, "Sister, I know I must die. Do tell us what is necessary to believe and do by way of preparation, for I am sure what you tell us must be true." Then again with all of manhood's earnestness and childhood simplicity they would emphatically say, "Teach us what to believe and we will believe." And as such scenes were almost universal throughout the hospital, few, very few, breathed their last without a spirit of lively faith, a firm hope, and sincere contrition. In less than eleven months, fully nine hundred of those who died were baptized and well prepared for death, and this preparation for a happy death continued through the whole course of the war, in those hospitals of which the sisters had charge.

There were full fifteen hundred wounded under the charge of the sisters at Mound City hospital alone, and although their labors were unceasing still they never wearied in doing good. In addition to the nursing and caring for the physical wants and tending to the spiritual welfare of the soldiers, the sisters had another task devolved upon them, which was as praiseworthy and perhaps as laborious as either of the other two.

Many and many an affectionate brother, loving son, and faithful husband wished to transmit a note to the loved ones at home, bidding a last adieu in this land of misery and toil. It was here again that the good sisters' kindness struck deep into the gratitude of the wounded soldier's heart. Several of the most rapid writers were appointed to pass from one ward into another making it their special charge to go to those on whom the shadows of death were falling fastest, giving to them all the consolations which that supreme hour required, or at least all in their power to bestow, consoling alike the Federal and Confederates, by writing to their loved ones far away in the North or South, their last dying words, their farewell to parents, wives, and children. And when the agony was over and the face of the dead soldier settled in to the repose of death, before the camp blanket was drawn over it, the sister in attendance took care to enclose in the letter a lock of his hair as a last memorial of one so dear, who would be deeply mourned by the loved ones at home. The lock was severed by a scissors which always hung at her side with her "seven dolor beads,"[14] on which beads a few moments previously her hand [had] lingered in his call through his passage across the cold valley of death.

Three days after the battle of Pittsburg Landing,[15] additional wounded to the number of two thousand were brought to Mound City Hospital. At the same time several eastern surgeons arrived to assist the regular corps in charge. Among these was a young physician—Dr. M. who attracted attention by his great devotedness to the sufferers confided to his care. After a few weeks he was missed from his wards and was supposed to have been removed to another post. One afternoon however an attendant informed the mother superior that Dr. M. was quite sick and wished to see her. She went immediately to the suite of rooms assigned to the surgeons where she found him in bed and surrounded by several of his brother physicians. On beholding her he exclaimed in an excited voice, "Oh Mother, how glad I am to see you, I am going to die, tell me do you think I shall be saved?"

"Of course you will, M.," soothingly replied one of the physicians.

"Ah Doctor," said the sick man, "I did not ask you that question! Keep to your pill shops [for] there you are at home; but I fear you know very little about the next world." Judging from his manner that he was under the excitement of fever and not wishing to make the subject of religion a matter of comment for those present, the sister quietly endeavored to soothe him, and as she left the room she called aside the surgeon-in-chief to ask if Dr. M. was really in danger. He replied that it was impossible for him to live, that he had fallen a victim to his devotedness to others. On hearing this all the sisters in the hospital assembled in their little chapel in the presence of the Blessed Sacrament and offered up their prayers with the greatest fervor for his conversion.

At every leisure moment each sister's beads passed through her hands while her heart invoked the Mother of Mercy to be with him at the hour of death.

In the meantime the mother superior returned to his bed side when he again exclaimed, "Sister, I have never been baptized; my parents are both Unitarians. I have never really thought of the next world, but I came to the West full of high ambitious dreams of winning fame and renown in the surgical ranks. The devotedness of the Sisters to the suffering and the dying attracted my attention from the first, and now, when I am dying myself, I turn to you for some consolation." He then listened with the docility of a child to her instructions, and whenever she left the room he would say to the other sister in attendance, "Sister, continue to repeat those little prayers, so that they will not pass from my mind." There being no priest in the village a letter was written for the one at Cairo, but did not reach him in time; and as the clamming hand of death was settling on the brow of the sick man, the same sister, who had instructed him, then baptized him.

After death the countenance of the dead physician bore a beautiful and heavenly expression, and all who saw him were deeply affected by it, and the sisters whispered low to each other, "How could he look otherwise, when the Blessed Mother Virgin Mary heard their requests and obtained for him the grace of a happy death!"

Among the patients in the hospital at Mound City was young W. who had been brought up the river with some twenty or thirty of his regiment all sick with typhoid fever. From the moment of their arrival it was easy to see what a general favorite he was in his company, for all his comrades appeared as much concerned in his recovery as they were in their own. The soldiers who had been detailed from the regiment to assist in nursing them were so attentive to W. that a stranger would suppose him to be a relation to all of them, but in spite of all the kindness and attention shown to him, he grew weaker and weaker every day. Seeing this, the sister in attendance (as usual when any of the patients would be in danger) slipped a medal under his pillow, and, at evening prayer, beads were said in common for his conversion. W. had never been baptized and when the sisters spoke to him of his danger and the value of his immortal soul, he listened with the docility of a child who had never wil[l]fully done wrong; and with an earnestness that delighted and edified all who heard him, he would frequently say, "Sisters, I want to believe just as you do, I know you will teach me what is right, only tell me what I must believe and what I must do to be saved, and I will gladly believe and do it." As if inspired, nothing seemed more easy or more natural to him than to love the Blessed Virgin Mary. There being no priest near, the sisters had not only to instruct him but to baptize him. His death was affecting in the extreme.

At his earnest request two of the sisters said the prayers for the dying while all his companions in arms, who were able to leave their beds, were either kneeling or standing around him. Those who could not rise were propped up to take a last look at their beloved companion who was partially supported in the arms of two soldiers so that he would be seen by all. So long as his strength lasted he joined in the prayers, and he seemed to have more than ordinary strength at that supreme hour for he exhorted his companions to embrace the true faith and thereby find in life and in death the consolations he then felt. He died invoking the names of Jesus and Mary; and his death touched many among his comrades, leading them to think seriously and effectually of their own eternal salvation.

In addition to the labors which the good sisters had to undergo in the sick wards of the hospital, their duties in the kitchen attached thereto would to some persons be almost increditable. Dr. E.C. Rogers[16] who was sent down from Chicago to inspect the hospital complained of the [want?] of accommodation for cooking provided for by the sisters. When the doctor asked how they could cook with such implements, the lady superior exclaimed laughingly, "If you find fault with our cooking stove, Doctor, what will you say to our washing machines?" and held up her little fists with their ten digits raw from work at the soldiers' wash tubs. "This was too much for civilized humanity[," Rogers said, "]We could only beat a retreat, with a tearful assurance to the laughing Sisters, that we would never rest until we knew they were provided with everything necessary for carrying forward their sublime work of charity and self-denial."

In April 1862, the Mississippi and Ohio rivers had a grand overflow and Mound City as well as other places were affected by the swell— even the hospital came in for its share of the deluge. After several days' watching with anxiety from the sisters, physicians, and employees, the water began to ooze through the floors. This caused great inconvenience and occasioned many comical expressions of vexation. The officials exclaiming that they were writing with their feet in their desks and their coat-tails in the water, while the nurses would declare that they were wading to the dining rooms and rowing themselves through the kitchen. The good Dr. Franklin, whose energy always exceeded his patience, was beset on all sides with difficulties and questions, and one day was so annoyed that he declared he could not run an institution under water unless he was himself a fish and his patients oysters. "I don't mind," said he, "but these people—why they must think I can turn back the Ohio—doctors, stewards, clerks, cooks, ward masters, nurses, and washerwomen beset me on every side." Mother Angela at once tried to pacify him by reminding him how necessary it was for one of his energy and experience to have command during this trying and perplexing affair, but the good doctor went off reiterating his resolution of giving up his commission if the Ohio did not back down first. On Low Sunday,[17] the water being an inch above the level of the first floor, it was decided that the sick should be removed to St. Louis.

Accordingly Dr. Thomas was appointed officer of the day and to superintend the landing of the hospital boat and transfer of the wounded men. It was a sad sight to see the poor fellows, who though so very weak and racked with pains, had to be carried on stretchers down the stairs and then lifted into the boat and thence again to the steamer while others were limping on crutches or supported by attendants as they hobbled towards the boat.

CHAPTER XXXIV

The Sisters of the Holy Cross, Continued

Removing from the hospital—Gratitude to the sisters—Incidents and scenes—Fort Charles and the Mound City affair—The men in hospital going to kill Colonel Fry—The sisters interfere—Colonel Fry vindicated—Captain Kilty fully exonerates Colonel Fry from any blame relative to the firing on the men blown up with the Mound City—Close of the hospital labors of the Sisters of the Holy Cross.[1]

The nurses worked faithfully and showed great patience in assisting the poor sufferers from the hospital to the boat. Some of the slightly wounded presented a very grotesque appearance and the property room was so beset with applicants for clothes it was impossible for each individual to find his own uniform and therefore he had to take the first to hand, and many were obliged to leave in full hospital uniform. As the poor fellows left the hospital, many an expression of gratitude was tendered to the sisters for the services tendered them during their sickness and as a last good-bye was given, many a bitter tear coursed down a rugged but manly cheek. Those who were very feeble appealed so very powerfully to the sisters' sympathy that it was decided that twelve of them should accompany them. The patients left in the hospital numbered about one hundred and fifty. They were either in a dying condition or wounded in such a manner as to make removal dangerous. After these were all cared for, Mother Angela began to make arrangements for the comforts of the sisters. She had the apartments lately occupied by them vacated as they were in fear of being deluged by the rising water, nor was she any too soon in her providential care, for the water began to ooze through the floors and the rats having been floated out of the cellar took refuge in the vacated apartments and even ventured to the next floor.

While the water was yet below the first floor, the sisters in the hospital in Cairo left by advice of the surgeon who feared that the land would give way and the whole town be inundated. They flocked to Mound City and the only place there that could be afforded them was the floor of the little sitting room next to the chapel. One morning one of the refugee sisters was missing from prayer. Fearing she was sick from the effect of her damp lodging Mother Angela went to see about her. She found her sitting on a bunk in a most lugubrious state of countenance and thus addressed her, "What is the matter with you Sister?" "Why, Mother!" was the response, "the rats have nearly eaten my cape, here is all that is left of it," and she held up a fragment of cloth which was certainly only a very small part of a cape. Mother Angela smiled and went and borrowed another for the poor sister and thus released her from her awkward dilemma. At breakfast that morning, nearly everyone had some ridiculous adventure to relate, and as they ate their frugal meal some had their feet in the water and others had drawn them on to their chairs to see, if possible, to keep them dry, and all this was borne in a spirt of perfect resignation and even with jocularity.

The water at one time had risen so high that a person looking from the windows of the hospital would imagine himself in a great boat becalmed on a large lake; the chapel and apartments on the second floor became submerged, and only two of the sisters, who were provided with long boats, were allowed to go below. The damp hospital dwelling was, as may be imagined, injurious to its inhabitants, and among the victims to its effects was the good amiable and faithful Sister Fidelis [Lawler],[2] who was one of the first sisters [who] volunteered to nurse the wounded. On the 18th of April, [1862,] when the flood was at its highest mark, the soul of that dear and loving sister went forth to meet its Maker. What a contrast in the surroundings of her death bed to the peaceful one she had no doubt anticipated among the beautiful scenes and the spiritual privileges of St. Mary's. While lying in the shadow of death in that island hospital, the pace of the military guards echoing through the long halls, the beat of the military reveille taking the place of the holy Angelus bell. The half-submerged little chapel of St. Raphael, on that Good Friday morning, contrasted strongly with the Chapel of Loretto[3] where sweetly warbled the birds on the trees under which she had so often lingered to say an extra decade on her rosary or her "seven dolor beads." How solemnly too the wooden clapper of Holy week was striking the quarter and half hours. All this passed through the imaginations of the sisters around the dying bed of dear Sister Fidelis, and passed too, no doubt, in some mystical and pathetic way, through the mind of the dying sister herself, but she made no complaint.

At the call of her Master she had gone forth to gather in a harvest of souls to His honor, and to glean here and there some grace for a dying soldier; now her turn had come and to her the voice of the bridegroom was one neither strange nor unwelcome. He had come a little sooner than she expected but was not this a mark of love. He had come and found his spouse willing and ready, for she was the bride of heaven.

It was not till January 1862 that the Sisters of the Holy Cross commenced their labors in the hospitals at Louisville, Kentucky. This was in consequence of a fanatical opposition. Dr. Spalding[4] proffered their services at the beginning of the war, but not until Dr. Weed[5] was appointed head surgeon would the fanatics in charge hear of the sisters being there. And even after Dr. Weed had given notice that the sisters were coming no place was prepared for them and the beds on which they were compelled to rest after their arrival were miserable excuses; still they never murmured. It was not long before the good people of Louisville were aroused in behalf of the sisters, and means and supplies, which had been cut off from the sufferers, poured in to an abundant extent, and folks who had hitherto been in opposition soon came forward with the most friendly feelings and, confessing their previous prejudices, pledged themselves to make ample amends. Even the prejudice which existed against the Catholic priests vanished to such an extent that if a Catholic soldier stood in need of the services of a priest, a Protestant lady would go and tell the priest or sister about it. And this was all brought about by the meekness of the sisters, by their attention to the sick, and their undoubted sincere charity.

The following incident is worthy of notice. One of the patients at the Cairo hospital was made happy by the arrival of his good mother who spent three weeks at his bedside before she could take him home. A few days before his departure, she addressed the sisters as follows: "How often have I heard the Catholic Church, its priest[s] and nuns, injuriously spoken of in my own house. I blush to remember it, but I promise that so long as I live such conversation shall be henceforth banished from my house. You and I have not talked much, Sisters, but my eyes and a mother's heart have told me all I need to know to refute utterly the calumnies I have heard from childhood."

Sister Elise [O'Brien][6] having fallen sick at Mound City hospital thought to recruit her health by returning to Notre Dame. She was only able to reach Cairo when she grew worse, sank rapidly and alas there breathed her last.[7]

As an instance of the prejudices the sisters had to overcome and the difficulties they had to encounter, we give the following copy of a letter written by a sister in the hospital at Memphis to the Rev. Mother [Angela].

Dear Mother—I must tell you something that will please you. Dr. —— was speaking in my presence to a newly appointed medical director, Dr. [John] Holston,[8] telling him that the sisters had succeeded in overcoming some very strong prejudice in the mind of one of the surgeons, who, when he found them installed in the hospital, had declared his real antipathy to the *nuns* and aversion to having them around. Of this aversion I was wholly ignorant for though I saw that he was somewhat morose in his manner, I took for granted that it was *his way*, and gave myself no further trouble on the subject. But it seemed that it was the sight of *myself* that vexed him.

Well, it happened this same cross surgeon, with several others, held a council over a poor unknown dying man who had been stabbed in a street fight. The patient was past all hope so the surgeons left him. Sr. M. and I remained with the dying man for we hoped to get some word from him and felt that at least we might pray for him and suggest acts of faith, hope, love and contrition for if sensible these might cause him to raise his soul to

God in this terrible moment. Then again the poor man was covered with mud and blood and his hair all matted so we had to try
to make him look decent like, and as we were working with him
the blood was trickling from the wound in his side and this made
the resemblance to Our Dearest Lord so striking that we found
nothing repulsive in any duties, but rather a most touching tenderness, for the poor unknown. This little act of mercy brought a
quick reward, for our cross surgeon had from a distance been
overlooking the scene and knowing that we were ignorant of his
presence, he immediately made the reparation that just and honest men always make when they find they have wrongly judged.
He declared to the other surgeons that his prejudices were removed for he believed the sisters were working from a truly high
and supernatural motive.

In July 1862 the Federals under the command of Colonel [Gra-
ham N.] Fitch of Indiana attacked Fort Charles on the White River.[9]
Colonel Fitch was supported by the gun-boats of the Western flotilla,
which bombarded the fort from the front, while the land troops acted
in the rear. After a sharp contest, the commander of the fort, Colonel
[Joseph] Fry,[10] being severely wounded, the Confederate forces surrendered. During this engagement occurred one of the most distressing
aggravations of the horrors of war, with which the sisters came in contact while in the hospital.

Colonel Fry, seeing that the naval forces from some of the iron-
clads were attempting to land in small boats, gave orders to fire upon
them.

At this moment the boilers of the gun-boat, Mound City, exploded,
severely scalding the commander, Captain [Augustus H.] Kilty,[11] and
about fifty of his men; most of whom, in the frantic agony of their sufferings, sprang into the river, and received through their par-boiled
bodies the shots fired from the forts. With almost superhuman energy
on the part of the crews of other boats, nearly all of these poor sufferers
were rescued from the water.

As soon as the news of this disaster reached Commander [Char-
les H.] Davis at Cairo, he telegraphed to the sisters at Mound City,
to send if possible, some sisters on the hospital boat to the scene of

the disaster. There it was that the following touching incident took place.

A Federal officer of high rank discovered in the wounded commander of the Confederate forces, Colonel Fry, one whom he had known well in by-gone days. And at such moments all the best feelings of the human heart display themselves. Seated by the wounded man, he forgot the foe and remembered only his friend; in tones of the most earnest sympathy he asked what he could do for his relief. In that quick hurried utterance that ever tells how the ball has touched the lungs, he answered, "I shall be most grateful if you shall write a line to my wife, informing her of my situation."

The Federal officer beckoned to an orderly to bring writing materials, and the Confederate officer continued: "Tell her that the medal she placed around my neck, when I bade her good bye, has saved my life. The surgeon says that it rested on my left lung and turned aside the bullet, which glanced from it, inflicting a serious but not mortal wound."

"Ah!" interrupted his amanuensis, "that must be I am sure, the medal of the Virgin! I fully believe in its wonderful effects. I wear one constantly myself, and would not go without it." And as the wounded man with trembling hand drew forth the medal to prove what he had said, by the dent on its surface, so did the Federal officer reverently draw forth from the bosom of his military coat, which was decorated with all the insignia of his official rank and bravery, his also. The bright rays of the summer sun shone on those two miraculous medals of the Immaculate Conception, which in the midst of sufferings, and carnage of war, gleamed like a sign from Heaven! Both officers, non-Catholics as they were[12] and deadly foes on the battlefield, at that moment cordially united in one feeling, namely that the medals of the Virgin given to one by a Catholic wife, to the other by a Catholic friend, were their powerful protection amid the horrors and dangers of war.

But one summer afternoon, all this was changed. A report had spread that the brave Captain Kilty was dying from the effects of his severe scalds; and as a mistaken opinion had got abroad among the gunboat men, the employees of the hospital, and a company of soldiers stationed at Mound City, to the effect that Colonel Fry had ordered his soldiers to fire upon the scalded men, when in their frenzy they were sure to jump into the water, all the men around the hospital were roused to a fearful fury against the commander of Fort Charles. The rumor was not true, but it was firmly believed at the time, and in their belief without any further reasoning on the subject, all assembled in front of the hospital, declaring in loud angry voices, "The moment Captain Kilty breathes his last, that moment we shoot Colonel Fry as he lies in his bed!"

The sister in charge of him was ordered to leave his room, and the door was locked. Several sisters were in Captain Kilty's room, expecting every moment to see him draw that last sigh which was to seal the fate of another immortal soul.

Sister J[osephine Reilly] who was in charge of Colonel Fry came to the other sisters all in tears to report what had happened.

Not a moment was to be lost. Leaving Captain Kilty in the care of sisters fully equal to the emergency in that quarter, several others hastened to the doctor in charge and asked for the key to Colonel Fry's room.

"It will be at the risk of your lives, to approach, much less to enter that room," said the surgeon with an expression on his face which made the sisters feel that he spoke what he knew, as well as feared, to be true.

"Then," they replied, "we must all without delay leave the hospital. Ours is a mission of mercy and of charity. We know neither North nor South, nor can we remain where the spirit of revenge is the ruling spirit, even for one hour. Give us the key and we remain. Refuse it and we leave instantly!"

"Then," replied the perplexed surgeon, "Then all the danger you incur rests upon yourselves. If I give you the key I do not feel certain of your lives for a single moment. These men are terribly roused, for they are honest in the belief that all the rules of honorable warfare have been violated by Colonel Fry, and we have no force at hand to prevent their acting up to the full measure of this conviction at any moment."

But every word uttered by the kind hearted doctor only convinced the sisters of immediate action. Having secured the key they at once entered Colonel Fry's room. The sick [man] listened to the terrible threats that they would kill him in case of Captain Kilty's death. He listened to them call for blood, his powerful chest, heaving under the terrible excitement, the large eyes almost starting from their emaciated sockets, the perspiration which he was too feeble to dry from his face starting out in great drops all over him. The fierce threats and angry curses from the crowd in the yard below made the sisters feel the solemn responsibility of the moment. The savage cries for Colonel Fry's death were fierce and loud and the sisters trembled at the thought that the dreadful crime of murder would desecrate the hospital. The sisters knelt and prayed for Captain Kilty's recovery, and it pleased God that he did recover thus sparing them from witnessing the horrors of a cruel murder.

As soon as Captain Kilty was strong enough to be informed of what had taken place, he expressed great regret that Colonel Fry should be exposed to such dangers, grounded as they had been upon charges without a particle of foundation. Captain Kilty publicly declared that Colonel Fry was perfectly innocent of any blame in the matter, for the fort had opened fire just as the drum of the boiler had burst and the men were flung into the water and ceased as soon as the explosion was noticed. He further stated that he had known Colonel Fry in the United States Service, and felt confident that he was too brave and humane an officer to be guilty of anything of the kind. He also had the report contradicted in Cairo and elsewhere, and to show with what contempt he viewed it he treated Colonel Fry as a personal friend while they remained in the hospital.

From the time the sisters took charge of the Mound City hospital, Dr. [Francis N.] Burke,[13] head surgeon of the military hospital at Cairo, was anxious to secure their services. This hospital had been in care of a matron and assistants, but things not going on satisfactorily, repeated applications had been made for the sisters. In the early part of December 1861, Mother Angela had obtained additional sisters for Mound City, and on the journey thither they stopped at Cairo. As she had even then too few sisters to answer fully to the needs of Mound City hospital, she had no idea of leaving any at Cairo. When they called at the hospital they received a hearty welcome from Dr. Burke who supposed they had at last acceded to his request. On finding the hospital in such readiness for them, even to the apartments for their special use, Mother

Angela found it impossible to refuse the assistance so much coveted and certainly so much needed.

After passing through the whole building, which had four floors, all of which were crowded with the wounded from Belmont, and as the sisters thought they were about leaving the hospital, Mother Angela turned to Sister A[ugusta][14] and said, "You will remain, and you, and you," pointing to two young sisters in the party.

"Remain, Mother?" "Yes!" "But what shall we do?" "Go straight to work," and with a smile at their perplexity she took her departure for Mound City. The decision was so sudden and the sisters having been without sleep for three nights they were for a moment confused; but this feeling passed off quickly and to work they went at once. As soon as the change could possibly be made Mother Angela sent to Sister Augusta three sisters of experience in place of the two young sisters she left with her, so that there was one sister for each floor. Sister A[ugusta] and her faithful and efficient coadjutors continued in this hospital, whatever might be the changes going on with surgeons and officials; and to the end of the war the Marine hospital remained in charge of the Sisters of the Holy Cross.

The surrender of Memphis [on] June 6th [1862][15] gave another opportunity to the Sisters of the Holy Cross to pursue their work of mercy and at the suggestion of General [William K.] Strong the commander at Cairo this opportunity was immediately improved. The Overton hotel had been occupied by the Confederates as a hospital and before leaving it they took everything portable away with them. When Mother Angela and the sisters arrived at Memphis, they found everything was in a scene of direct confusion. It was not even safe to walk the streets, and in consequence they were obliged to remain on the hospital boat until some order was restored.

When they took possession of the Overton house it was in a most desolate condition, its walls, floors and ceilings were bare, and the suffering soldier had merely his knapsack for a pillow and his blanket for a mattress, but order and comfort were restored under the hands of the good sisters. At the same time that the Overton Hospital was a home for the sick and wounded in the southern campaigns, the Pinckney Navy Hospital at Memphis and the hospital boat running between

Memphis and New Orleans were put under the care of the Sisters of the Holy Cross.[16]

When Mother Angela returned to St. Mary's to obtain sisters for Memphis, a young and accomplished young lady from Baltimore, a Miss H. Sumner, was spending the warm months there. On finding out the object of the mother's mission, Miss Sumner volunteered her services in company with fifteen sisters who were to accompany the mother. The noble intellectual young lady, during the few months she remained at Memphis, shared every duty with the sisters in the same spirit as if she were one of themselves until her impaired health made it an imperative duty to return North.

One evening in the summer of 1862, while the full tide of hospital duty was in progress at Memphis, the sisters' frugal supper being over, the religious were holding a little cheerful conversation together before returning to the different wards; conversation which told how sincerely each one was interested in the sufferers under her charge. The happy face of Sister M—— however bore an expression of sadness altogether unusual, and she began to tell what had saddened her heart even more than her face. It seems that a large number of wounded had been brought to her ward, among them one in a very dangerous condition. The surgeon said he must die, but the poor fellow was determined not to believe it, although most grateful for every attention paid to him. When the sister heard his name, she exclaimed, "Oh, [that is a good] Catholic name in the old country." ["Well," said he, very impa]tiently, "what if it is? That is [no reason of my being a Catholic."] There was some[thing in his tone, and even in his] words, which con[vinced the Sister that this man had] been educated a Ca[tholic, but the least mention of] a preparation for [death excited his anger.][17]

Despite all his professions, when he found death approaching, he became penitent, confessed that he was brought up a Catholic, and died a good penitent after receiving all the rites of the Catholic Church.

Quite a large proportion of the patients were New Englanders and among them was one who at first continually passed sharp witticisms at the expense of the sisters. Near him lay another New Englander who rebuked him sharply for his conduct. The sister in charge finding out what was going on said to the man of gratitude to not mind him, but let him proceed as he wished and he would soon drop it when unnoticed. Soon the malady of the former obtained a dangerous character and extra attention had to be given him and during this attention the kindness he received from the sisters not only saved his life but won his heart, and he vowed ever after, to be a sincere friend of the Sisters of the Holy Cross.

Several of the Sisters of [the] Holy Cross were assigned duty in the hospital at Washington, which continued only one year under their charge.[18] At the end of that time great irregularities appeared with regard to the class of patients sent to the hospital and great irregularities as to discipline. It was no longer a strictly military hospital under military rule and the superior telegraphed to the sisters to return to St. Mary's. During all the first year it was a most edifying work of charity, and the little chapel bore witness to the desire of the patients to make some return to the sisters for their assiduous attendance. In consequence, an offering was made by the soldiers of a small sum sufficient to furnish this humble chapel, which act of courtesy the sisters have never forgotten.

EPILOGUE: During the war, two Sisters of the Holy Cross, Elise O'Brien and Fidelis Lawler, died from exposure to disease during their work as nurses, and many others carried illnesses with them back to Notre Dame. Nonetheless, the community determined to continue its work in nursing in addition to resuming its prewar labors in the education of young women. A number of sisters served as nurses during the Spanish American War and the community built a network of hospitals across the United States. In addition to founding other schools in America, Saint Mary's Academy in South Bend became a college in 1908. Relics of their Civil War service, two

Confederate cannons captured from Island No. 10 on the Mississippi River, were proudly stationed near the school's entrance until 1942 when they were finally donated to a scrap metal drive during the Second World War. Nonetheless, the college remains very proud of its Civil War nurses who served in so many hospitals across the North during the conflict. Not only do special government markers at St. Mary's mark the graves of those who were wartime nurses, but one of the college's main buildings, Bertrand Hall, was paid for in part by the money Holy Cross Sisters earned for their wartime nursing services.

SOURCES: The Sisters of the Holy Cross Archives at St. Mary's College, Notre Dame, Indiana, has many relevant sources including letters, recollections, the community's annals, and a good collection of secondary sources related to their community's Civil War service. Edward Sorin, C.S.C., *The Chronicles of Notre Dame du Lac*, ed. James T. Connelly (Notre Dame, IN: University of Notre Dame Press, 1992), 276–91; M. Georgia Costin, *Priceless Spirit: A History of the Sisters of the Holy Cross, 1841–1893* (Notre Dame, IN: University of Notre Dame Press, 1994), 7–18, 72–74, 179–94; Barbra M. Wall, "Grace Under Pressure: The Nursing Sisters of the Holy Cross, 1861–1865," *Nursing History Review* 1 (1993): 71–87; Ellen Ryan Jolly, *Nuns of the Battlefield* (Providence, RI: Providence Visitor Press, 1927), 124–57; Cindy Intravartolo, "St. Mary's Goes to War: The Sisters of the Holy Cross as Civil War Nurses," *Journal of the Illinois State Historical Society* 107, no. 3–4 (Fall/Winter 2014): 370–91.

See also: Sisters of the Holy Cross, *A Story of Fifty Years: From the Annals of the Congregation of the Sisters of the Holy Cross, 1855–1905* (Notre Dame, IN: Ave Maria, [1905?]); Sisters of the Holy Cross, *Our Mother House: Centenary Chronicles of the Sisters of the Holy Cross* (Notre Dame, IN: Saint Mary's of the Immaculate Conception, 1941); Barbra Mann Wall, *Unlikely Entrepreneurs: Catholic Sisters and the Hospital Marketplace,*

1865–1925 (Columbus: Ohio State University Press, 2005); James M. Schmidt, *Notre Dame and the Civil War: Marching Onward to Victory* (Charleston, SC: The History Press, 2010), 41–50, 121–23.

Notes

EDITORS' INTRODUCTION

1. Significant studies of Catholic chaplains in the war include Aidan H. Germain, "Catholic Military and Naval Chaplains, 1776–1917" (PhD diss., Catholic University of America, 1929), 42–134; Benjamin J. Blied, *Catholics and the Civil War* (Milwaukee: St. Francis Seminary Press, 1945), 108–23; Robert J. Miller, *Both Prayed to the Same God: Religion and Faith In the American Civil War* (Lanham, MD: Lexington Books, 2007), 109–19; and Sean Fabun, "Catholic Chaplains in the Civil War," *Catholic Historical Review* 99, no. 4 (October 2013): 675–702.

Works detailing Civil War sister nurses include George Barton, *Angels of the Battlefield: A History of the Labors of the Catholic Sisterhoods in the Late Civil War* (Philadelphia: Catholic Art Publishing, 1897); Ellen Ryan Jolly, *Nuns of the Battlefield* (Providence, RI: Providence Visitor Press, 1927); and Mary Denis Maher, *To Bind Up the Wounds: Catholic Sister Nurses in the U.S. Civil War* (New York: Greenwood Press, 1989).

2. Catholic chaplains and sister nurses are completely absent, for instance, from James McPherson's monumental *Battle Cry of Freedom* (1988) and even major studies of wartime religion such as Stephen Woodworth's *While God Is Marching On* (2001). Sister nurses are also ignored by most major works on women in the war including Mary E. Massey's *Women in the Civil War* (1966), Drew Faust's *Mothers of Invention: Women of the Slaveholding South in the American Civil War* (1996), and Judith Giesberg's *Army at Home: Women and the Civil War on the Northern Home Front* (2009). There are a few important exceptions to this general neglect of Catholics by nonspecialists, including Jane Schultz's *Women at the Front: Hospital Workers in*

Civil War America (2004) and George Rable's *God's Almost Chosen Peoples: A Religious History of the American Civil War* (2010).

3. Conyngham capitalized the word "Federal," and he used it to refer to the armies and soldiers of the North in the Civil War. In our added introductions, footnotes, and other explanatory material, we have also capitalized "Federal" when the word is used in this context.

4. See Randall M. Miller, "Catholic Religion, Irish Ethnicity, and the Civil War," in *Religion and the American Civil War*, eds. Randall M. Miller, Harry S. Stout, and Charles Reagan Wilson (New York: Oxford University Press, 1998), 265–66; and William B. Kurtz, *Excommunicated from the Union: How the Civil War Created a Separate Catholic America* (New York: Fordham University Press, 2016), 68.

5. Warren B. Armstrong, *For Courageous Fighting and Confident Dying: Union Chaplains in the Civil War* (Lawrence, KS: University Press of Kansas, 1998), 2–42; Germain, "Catholic Military and Naval Chaplains," 42–55; John W. Brinsfield, William C. Davis, Benedict Maryniak, and James I. Robertson, Jr., eds., *Faith in the Fight: Civil War Chaplains* (Mechanicsburg, PA: Stackpole Books, 2003), ix, 3–13, 54–73; Gardiner H. Shattuck, Jr., "Holy Joes: The Experience of Clergy in the Armies," in *A Shield and Hiding Place: The Religious Life of the Civil War Armies* (Macon, GA: Mercer University Press, 1987), 51–72.

6. Maher, *To Bind Up the Wounds*, 69–71, 120; Kurtz, *Excommunicated from the Union*, 81–82, 170.

7. Jane E. Schultz, *Women at the Front: Hospital Workers in Civil War America* (Chapel Hill: University of North Carolina Press, 2004), 15–141; Maher, *To Bind Up the Wounds*, 27–64.

8. For more on Corby's career and his place in Civil War memory, see William Corby, C.S.C., *Memoirs of Chaplain Life: Three Years with the Irish Brigade in the Army of the Potomac* (Notre Dame, IN: "Scholastic" Press, 1893; reprinted and edited by Lawrence Frederick Kohl, New York: Fordham University Press, 1992), ix–xxv, 393–400.

9. See James B. Sheeran, C.Ss.R., *Confederate Chaplain: A War Journal*, ed. Joseph T. Durkin (Milwaukee: Bruce Publishing, 1960); Patrick J. Hayes, ed., *The Civil War Diary of Father James Sheeran: Confederate Chaplain and Redemptorist* (Washington, DC: Catholic University of America Press, 2016).

10. Hayes, *Civil War Diary of Father James Sheeran*; David J. Endres, "'With a Father's Affection': Chaplain William T. O'Higgins and the Tenth Ohio Volunteer Infantry," *U.S. Catholic Historian* 31, no. 1 (Winter 2013): 97–

127; Betty Ann McNeil, D.C., *Balm of Hope: Charity Afire Impels Daughters of Charity to Civil War Nursing* (Chicago: DePaul University Vincentian Studies Institute, 2015); Judith Metz, S.C., ed., *Sisters of Charity of Cincinnati in the Civil War: The Love of Christ Urges Us* (Cincinnati: Sisters of Charity of Cincinnati, 2012); Judith Metz, S.C., "Sister Anthony O'Connell: Angel of the Orphan, the Sick, the Wounded, and the Outcast," *U.S. Catholic Historian* 35, no. 4 (Fall 2017): 53–78; Barbara J. Howe and Margaret A. Brennan, "The Sisters of St. Joseph in Wheeling, West Virginia, During the Civil War," *U.S. Catholic Historian* 31, no. 1 (Winter 2013): 21–49.

11. David Power Conyngham, *The Irish Brigade and its Campaigns*, ed. Lawrence Frederick Kohl (New York: William McSorley, 1867; reprint, New York: Fordham University Press, 1994), xviii–xix; "David P. Cunningham" file, *Letters Received by the Commission Branch of the Adjutant Generals Office, 1866*, Record Group 94, National Archives and Records Administration, Washington, DC; "David P. Conyngham," *Soundex Index to Petitions for Naturalizations Filed in Federal, State, and Local Courts in New York City, 1792–1906* (NARA microfilm publication M1674, roll 44), Records of District Courts of the United States, National Archives and Records Administration, Washington, DC.

12. Although a few sources claim Conyngham published a book titled *The Sisters of Charity on Southern Battlefields*, it is not listed among works he authored on the title page of *Soldiers of the Cross*. A thorough search of the WorldCat online library catalog and sources such as the *Nineteenth Century Short Title Catalogue* turned up no trace of this volume. Since the Daughters of Charity in Emmitsburg, Maryland, provided the largest number of sister nurses during the war, it seems unusual that they are not mentioned in *Soldiers of the Cross,* but this omission may be explained by the likelihood that Conyngham contemplated (or perhaps even drafted) a separate work on their wartime role.

For more on Conyngham, see editor Lawrence Kohl's introduction to Conyngham, *The Irish Brigade and its Campaigns*, ix–xxx; and Michael Fitzgerald, "From Ballingarry to Fredericksburg: David Power Conyngham (1825–1883)," *Tipperary Historical Journal* (1988): 192–200.

13. Many important studies of Catholics or religion during the Civil War cite the manuscript version of *Soldiers of the Cross*, including Maher, *To Bind Up the Wounds*; Miller, *Both Prayed to the Same God*; Kurtz, *Excommunicated from the Union*; Randall M. Miller, Harry S. Stout, and Charles Reagan Wilson, eds., *Religion and the American Civil War* (New York: Oxford University Press, 1998); Armstrong, *For Courageous Fighting and Confident*

Dying, George C. Rable, *God's Almost Chosen Peoples: A Religious History of the American Civil War* (Chapel Hill: University of North Carolina Press, 2010); and James M. Schmidt, *Notre Dame and the Civil War: Marching Onward to Victory* (Charleston, SC: The History Press, 2010).

14. Miller, "Catholic Religion, Irish Ethnicity, and the Civil War," 282–83; John T. McGreevy, *Catholicism and American Freedom: A History* (New York: W. W. Norton & Company, 2003), 71–76, 91–118; Susannah Ural Bruce, *The Harp and the Eagle: Irish-American Volunteers and the Union Army, 1861–1865* (New York: New York University Press, 2006), 176–85, 229–32, 246–56; Kurtz, *Excommunicated from the Union*, 129–43.

15. Patrick W. Carey, *Catholics in America: A History* (Westport: Praeger, 2004), 44–46; James Hennesey, S.J., *American Catholics: A History of the Roman Catholic Community in the United States* (New York: Oxford University Press, 1981), 155; James T. Fisher, *Communion of Immigrants: A History of Catholics in America* (New York: Oxford University Press, 2002), 57; Fabun, "Catholic Chaplains in the Civil War," 700–701; Kurtz, *Excommunicated from the Union*, 79–87; Maher, *To Bind up the Wounds*, 148–49.

16. Benjamin Butler, "Testimony Before the Joint Committee on the Conduct of the War, January 15, 1862," *Report of the Joint Committee on the Conduct of the War* (Washington, DC: Government Printing Office, 1863), 290; Mary Livermore, *What Shall We Tell Our Daughters: Superfluous Women and Other Lectures* (Boston: Lee and Shepard, 1883), 177–78.

17. The one exception is Conyngham's third chapter on Father Sheeran, which purports to be the priest's personal experience of Stonewall Jackson's mortal wounding at the Battle of Chancellorsville in May 1863 and his subsequent death. This chapter is almost word for word taken from an account titled "Jackson's Death-Wound" in John Esten Cooke, *Wearing of the Gray* (New York: E. B. Treat, 1867). The chapter remains in the table of contents and as a placeholder in the text with an explanation of its removal from this volume. In his full diary, Father Sheeran admitted he was not present for the beginning of the battle, and his account clearly relies on other authorities for its detailed depiction of this famous engagement (Hayes, *Civil War Diary of Father Sheeran*, 157–61).

18. Michael Kerwick to Father Daniel Hudson, January 4, 1897 and (1898?), Daniel E. Hudson Papers (CHUD), University of Notre Dame Archives, Notre Dame, Indiana (UNDA); Alex J. Wall to Father Thomas McAvoy, January 29, 1932, David Power Conyngham Papers (CCYN), UNDA; Ellen Ryan Jolly to McAvoy, February 13, 1932, CCYN, UNDA; and Thomas F. Meehan to McAvoy, February 14, 1932, CCYN, UNDA.

19. Digitized versions of Conyngham's draft manuscript of *Soldiers of the Cross* and the twentieth-century typescript are available on the University of Notre Dame Archives' website: http://archives.nd.edu/conyngham/index.html.

20. The original draft had three chapters on the Sisters of the Holy Cross, but a condensed and later draft only had two chapters. The latter draft was utilized in this edited volume as both extant versions of the table of contents only referred to two chapters about the Sisters of the Holy Cross. Of the two extant versions of the table of contents, we judged the first version's subheadings to match more closely those found at the beginning of each chapter. When there were discrepancies, we generally deferred to the way the subheadings were presented in the table of contents. As with the rest of the text, we made occasional edits to the subheadings for clarity or to add in missing punctuation.

21. Biographical and specialized reference works included, among others, Germain, "Catholic Military and Naval Chaplains," 42–134; Brinsfield, Davis, Maryniak, and Robertson, eds., *Faith in the Fight; The Metropolitan Catholic Almanac and Laity's Directory* (Baltimore: Fielding Lucas, John Murphy, etc., various years, 1850–1861); *Sadlier's Catholic Directory, Almanac, and Ordo* (New York: D. J. Sadlier, various years, 1864–1896); Ezra J. Warner, *Generals in Gray: Lives of the Confederate Commanders* (Baton Rouge: Louisiana State University Press, 2013); Ezra J. Warner, *Generals in Blue: Lives of the Union Commanders* (Baton Rouge: Louisiana State University Press, 2013). Access to military records was obtained through the "Civil War (1861–1865) Military Records" database on the Ancestry.com website, accessed May 1, 2018, https://www.ancestry.com/cs/civilwarrecords; the "Civil War Soldiers and Sailors System" database on the National Park Service website, accessed May 1, 2018, https://www.nps.gov/civilwar/soldiers-and-sailors-database.htm; the "Civil War Records" database on the Fold3 by Ancestry website, accessed May 1, 2018, https://www.fold3.com/browse/249/; and the American Civil War Research Database, by Historical Data Systems, accessed May 1, 2018, http://www.civilwardata.com/. The Hierarchy of the Catholic Church database by David M. Cheney, accessed May 1, 2018, http://www.catholic-hierarchy.org/, helped identify and provided more information about priests and bishops mentioned in the text, and the "Union Civil War Surgeons" database, accessed May 1, 2018,http://www.biblioserver.com/19centurydocs/index.php, hosted by the Ruth Lilly Medical Library at the Indiana University School of Medicine, helped identify many of the surgeons mentioned throughout the text.

INTRODUCTION

1. The typescript claims the word "back" comes here, but the manuscript is damaged and whatever word was here ("balm" makes more sense) is lost.

2. Martin J. Spalding (1810–1872), one of the leading ecclesiastics of his day, served as archbishop of Baltimore (1864–1872).

3. Spalding attended the First Vatican Council in Rome. In late 1871 he went to New York to attend a meeting of bishops. He became ill while returning to Baltimore and died on February 7, 1872.

4. "Huntsville" was replaced by "Bayou le [*sic*] Batre."

5. The phrase "superior of the mission at Watertown, Wisconsin" was replaced by "at Notre Dame, Ind."

6. The phrase "superior of the house of studies, Notre Dame, Indiana, and professor of chemistry, physics, and science in the University" was replaced by "professor at St. Laurents College, Montreal."

7. "Missouri" was replaced by "deceased."

8. "Missouri" was replaced by "Watertown, Wisconsin."

9. Father Zepherin Lévêque, C.S.C., also served briefly as a chaplain from Notre Dame before his death in early 1862.

10. Tissot was actually chaplain of the 37th New York Infantry, the "Irish Rifles." See chapter 11.

11. The phrase "is at present professor at Fordham College" was replaced by "deceased."

12. The 6th New York Infantry was also known as Billy Wilson's Zouaves after General William Wilson.

13. "Montreal" was replaced by "Troy, N.Y."

14. Francis McAtee, S.J. (d. 1904), was chaplain of the 31st New York Infantry. Conyngham misspelled his name as "J. McAtte."

15. There was no Father Brown in the Union army, but Conyngham might have in mind Father Henry V. Brown, a convert from Presbyterianism, who was a Confederate chaplain in the 10th Tennessee Infantry. See Aidan H. Germain, "Catholic Military and Naval Chaplains, 1776–1917" (PhD diss., Catholic University of America, 1929), 112.

16. William T. O'Higgins (1829–1874). See David J. Endres, "'With a Father's Affection': Chaplain William T. O'Higgins and the Tenth Ohio Volunteer Infantry," *U.S. Catholic Historian* 31, no. 1 (Winter 2013): 97–127.

17. Father Egidius (Aegidius) "Giles" Smulders, C.Ss.R. (1815–1900).

18. Father Prachenski served the 3rd Alabama Infantry. See Germain, "Catholic Military and Naval Chaplains," 129–30; Raymond H. Schmandt

and Josephine H. Schulte, "Civil War Chaplains—A Document From A Jesuit Community," *Records of the American Catholic Historical Society of Philadelphia* 73, nos. 1–2 (March/June 1962): 59.

19. Conyngham appears to spell the name as "Corrette." Father Cornette was a Jesuit assigned to Spring Hill College in Mobile, Alabama. See Schmandt and Schulte, "Civil War Chaplains—A Document From A Jesuit Community," 58–64.

20. Father Charles Boglioli, C.M. (1814–1882). See Warren Dicharry, C.M., "The Leper Priest of Louisiana," *Vincentian Heritage Journal* 11, no. 2 (Fall 1990): 171–82.

21. Francis Xavier Leray (1825–1887) also served as a hospital chaplain in Oxford, Mississippi. See Germain, "Catholic Military and Naval Chaplains," 123.

22. Father Anthony Carius (1821–1893) served the 1st Louisiana Infantry. See Germain, "Catholic Military and Naval Chaplains," 112–13.

23. Father Francois Isidore Turgis (1813–1868) served the 30th Louisiana Infantry.

24. Father Emmeran M. Bliemel, O.S.B. (1831–1864), was chaplain to the 10th Tennessee Infantry (after Father Henry Brown's departure). Conyngham spelled the name "Bliemmel."

25. Father Francis Nachon, S.J. (1820–1867), died in Washington, Louisiana, of yellow fever. Conyngham spelled the name "Machon" or "Machor."

26. Father Anthony de Chaignon, S.J., was chaplain to the 18th Louisiana. See Germain, "Catholic Military and Naval Chaplains," 115; C. M. Widman, S.J., "Grand Coteau College in War Times 1860–1865," *Woodstock Letters* 30 (1901): 38. Conyngham spelled the name as "Chignon."

27. Here, in an unknown hand, is a notation reading "(Sisters?)." Conyngham's introduction to their services can be found in chapter 26.

28. Major General George B. McClellan (1826–1885) was the former commander of the Army of the Potomac and General in Chief of the Union forces.

29. Ambrose Burnside (1824–1881) was commander of the Army of the Potomac after McClellan.

30. Joseph E. Hooker (1814–1879) was commander of the Army of the Potomac after Burnside.

31. George G. Meade (1815–1872) was commander of the Army of the Potomac after Hooker. Conyngham had mistakenly given his middle initial as "P."

32. Major General William S. Rosecrans (1819–1898), a convert to Catholicism, commanded the Army of the Cumberland.

33. Philip H. Sheridan (1831–1888), a Catholic, commanded the Army of the Shenandoah.

34. Irvin McDowell (1818–1885) was a Union commander at First Bull Run.

35. Winfield S. Hancock (1824–1886) commanded the 2nd Corps of the Army of the Potomac.

36. John M. Schofield (1831–1906) commanded the Army of the Ohio during William T. Sherman's 1864 Atlanta campaign.

37. William F. Barry (1818–1879) served as chief of artillery under Mc-Clellan and Sherman.

38. Lorenzo Thomas (1804–1875) was adjutant general of the U.S. Army.

39. Horatio G. Wright (1820–1899) commanded the 6th Corps of the Army of the Potomac.

40. Christopher C. Augur (1821–1898) commanded the 22nd Corps, which garrisoned Washington, DC, during the last half of the war.

41. Benjamin F. Butler (1818–1893), a Massachusetts politician turned Union general, gained public fame for declaring runaway slaves "contraband of war" and treating the women of occupied New Orleans harshly while in command there. In early 1862, he gave testimony about his experience with Union chaplains, stating "a good chaplain is a very good thing, but a poor chaplain is as much worse than none at all." He continued, "I am bound to say that I have never seen a Catholic chaplain that did not do his duty, because he was responsible to another power than that of the military. I would not ask for more than one chaplain to a brigade, except in the case of Roman Catholic regiments. In that case I think there should be a chaplain to a regiment, for they have a great many duties to perform, to write all the letters, etc. They have always been faithful, so far as my experience goes. They are able men, appointed by the bishop, and are responsible to the bishop for the proper discharge of their duties. That is not always the case with other chaplains" (Benjamin Butler, "Testimony Before the Joint Committee on the Conduct of the War, January 15, 1862," *Report of the Joint Committee on the Conduct of the War* [Washington, DC: Government Printing Office, 1863], 290–301).

42. Generals Leroy A. Stafford (1822–1864) and Harry T. Hays (1820–1876) both commanded brigades in the Army of Northern Virginia.

43. Born in Philadelphia, John McGill (1809–1872) served as Richmond's bishop from 1850 until his death.

44. Robert E. Lee (1807–1870) commanded the Confederate Army of Northern Virginia.

45. Pierre G. T. Beauregard (1818–1893), a Catholic, commanded the Confederate attack on Fort Sumter. Conyngham spelled his name as "Bouregard."

46. George Whitfield Pepper (1833–1899) served in the 80th Ohio.

47. "And then" was deleted in the text, but the sentence does not make sense without these words, so they were restored.

48. John J. Hughes (1797–1864), New York's first archbishop, played an important role in securing priests and sisters for the army. He was an enthusiastic supporter of the Union cause, serving as an unofficial envoy in Europe in the winter of 1861–1862.

49. William A. Hammond (1828–1900) served as the U.S. Army's surgeon general from 1862 to 1864.

50. Samuel Grandin Johnston De Camp (1788–1871) was an army medical director in St. Louis at the war's beginning.

51. "Sisters of Charity" was often utilized as a general term referring to all nuns or sister nurses, not just members of the religious congregations known as Sisters of Charity.

52. This spot in the text is marked with a handwritten "?"; some word is missing here in the handwritten draft.

53. Here and in the order below, Conyngham had mistakenly abbreviated Dr. De Camp's middle name with a "Q."

54. The words "he had before their arrival" were deleted from the end of the sentence.

55. "Ward's Island" was crossed out after his name. Dr. John Dwyer, former surgeon of the 182nd New York (69th New York National Guard), provided Conyngham with biographical sketches of Fathers Paul E. Gillen, James M. Dillon, and Thomas H. Mooney.

56. Dr. Gillespie (1820–1907) helped recruit the members of the 78th Pennsylvania Infantry, serving as captain in Company F. He provided information on the chaplaincy of Father Richard C. Christy.

57. Dr. William O'Meagher (1829–1896), a surgeon with the 37th and 69th New York Infantry regiments, wrote the chapter covering the career of Father Peter Tissot, S.J.

58. James E. McGee (c. 1830–1880) served in the 69th New York. Like Conyngham, McGee authored a variety of works on Irish and Irish-American history after the war: *Sketches of Irish Soldiers in Every Land* (1873); *Lives of Irishmen's Sons and their Descendants* (1874); *Glories of Ireland* (1877); and *Priests and Poets of Ireland* (1881).

59. Incorrectly spelled as "MacNamarre" in the manuscript, Michael H. MacNamara (c. 1838–1897) was an officer in the 9th Massachusetts Infantry

Regiment who later wrote a book about his unit called *The Irish Ninth in Bivouac and Battle* (Boston: Lee and Shepard, 1867).

CHAPTER I

1. A note below the chapter title in the manuscript reads "(Now pastor at Bayou La Batre, Alabama)."

2. The chapter originally began with an anecdote about an Irishman giving Father Trecy his wallet before a battle. Later, finding the priest at the front "under the heaviest fire preparing a dying man," the soldier took back his purse, declaring "it is much safer with me than you!" This amusing story, later deleted, was meant to show that Trecy was "as fearless in danger as he was zealous and energetic in the discharge of his duties." It is very similar to a passage in Conyngham's chapter on Father William Corby (see chapter 18).

3. Father Jeremiah Trecy's surname was spelled throughout the manuscript as "Tracy," "Tracey," "Trecy," or abbreviated as "T." For consistency's sake, it has been spelled "Trecy."

4. Bishop John Mathias Pierre Loras (1792–1858), born in France, was the first bishop of Dubuque, Iowa.

5. "Yankton" was misspelled as "Yanktown."

6. The remainder of this sentence, "bound for the Rocky Mountains," was crossed out.

7. Fort Union was an important trading post on the present-day border between Montana and North Dakota.

8. Bishop John Quinlan (1826–1883), born in Ireland, was the second bishop of Mobile, Alabama.

9. Albert Sidney Johnston (1803–1862) was commander of Confederate forces in the Western theater until his death at the Battle of Shiloh.

10. Dr. David Wendel "D. W." Yandell (1826–1898). Conyngham had mistakenly written his name as "Gondel."

11. The manuscript originally read "Abolitionists."

12. Originally, the author had written "Boys in Blue" to describe the "Federal troops."

13. This was first written as "old nigger."

14. Ormsby M. Mitchel (1809–1862) was promoted to major general for capturing Huntsville on April 11, 1862. Conyngham misspelled his name as "Mitchell" throughout this chapter.

15. "Secesh" is a reference to a secessionist.

16. Braxton Bragg (1817–1876) was commander of the Confederate Army of the Tennessee.

17. This was first rendered as "damned hounds."

18. The wartime correspondent William Halpin identified this soldier as a man with the surname of Cobb from Georgia. Military records show that Thomas Cobb of Murray County, Georgia, enlisted as a private in the 39th Georgia Volunteer Infantry (Cumming's Brigade), Company A, on March 10, 1862. Cobb died in a hospital at Huntsville, Alabama, on May 21, 1862, the timing of which matches Halpin's report.

19. The soldier was identified by Halpin as Bernard McGinnis of the 15th Kentucky Volunteer Infantry (Union) who died May 26, 1862, at a hospital in Huntsville, Alabama.

20. Halpin often corresponded with the *Enquirer* under the name "Gulielmus." The article on the funerals appeared as Gulielmus, "Our Army Correspondence," June 5, 1862, *Cincinnati Enquirer.* Halpin's report was dated May 26, 1862, Camp Taylor, Huntsville, Alabama.

21. Don Carlos Buell (1818–1898) commanded the Army of the Ohio.

22. Robert C. Murphy (1827–1888) was of the 8th Wisconsin Infantry.

23. David Sloane Stanley (1828–1902), then a division commander in the Army of the Mississippi, later became the chief of cavalry of the Army of the Cumberland.

24. Cherokee, Alabama, is midway between Tuscumbia, Alabama, and Iuka, Mississippi. Conyngham spelled the town as "Chicakee" and "Chearikee."

CHAPTER II

1. General Rosecrans ordered him to be court-martialed for failing to destroy the supplies before they were taken by the Confederates. See Thomas P. Lowry, *Curmudgeons, Drunkards, and Outright Fools: Courts-Martial of Civil War Union Colonels* (Lincoln, NE: University of Nebraska Press, 2003), 176–81.

2. The original description of "bastardly one" was crossed out.

3. Major General Sterling Price (1809–1867), a former Missouri politician, commanded the Confederate forces at the Battle of Iuka.

4. What had followed "with" was "Sullivan's Brigade of Hamilton's Division," which subsequently was crossed out.

5. Father John Ireland (1838–1918), later archbishop of St. Paul, Minnesota, was chaplain to the 5th Minnesota Infantry.

6. William M. Wiles (1834–1880).

7. Philip Dale Roddey (1826–1897) commanded the 4th Alabama Cavalry and was later promoted to brigadier general.

8. This was originally "S" in the text.

9. The phrase "or was let away by an Irishman" followed, but was crossed out.

10. Major General Earl Van Dorn (1820–1863) was in overall command of Confederate forces at the Battle of Corinth.

11. Battery Robinett (named for its commander, Lt. Henry Robinett) was one of the defenses built to the south and west of Corinth to prevent a Confederate capture of the city. Robinett was the site of the fiercest fighting of the Battle of Corinth (October 3–4, 1862).

12. Here "lady" was crossed out before "friends."

13. The 14th Corps was soon to be renamed the Army of the Cumberland.

14. This was perhaps a reference to Dr. David C. Spalding (1834–1904), surgeon of the 10th Michigan Cavalry.

15. Julius P. Garesché (1821–1862), a Catholic, served as General Rosecrans's chief of staff. Garesché later died on the first day of the Battle of Stones River. Conyngham spelled the name in various ways: "Garrishy," "Gareschee," and "Garache."

16. The Confiteor is a traditional penitential prayer that acknowledges one's sins while seeking God's forgiveness.

17. Father Francis Fusseder (1825–1888) was a Milwaukee priest who served as chaplain to the Wisconsin 17th and 24th Infantries. Conyngham spelled his name as "Fusator."

18. He was later identified in the manuscript as "J. S. Ryan, late Captain 12th Louisiana Regiment." This officer may have been Corporal John Ryan of Co. F, 20th Louisiana Infantry, who was wounded at Stones River on December 31, 1862.

19. Although the 12th was not at Stones River, the 20th Louisiana Infantry, which had consolidated with the 13th in November 1862, was present according to the Confederate order of battle.

20. Author's note: "In the Annals of the Army of the Cumberland great praise is given to Father Trecy during his stay with the troops at Stones River and Murfreesboro."

21. Major General Patrick R. Cleburne (1828–1864) was the most successful Irish-born officer in the Confederate Army. Conyngham spelled the name as "Clayburn."

22. Major General Benjamin F. Cheatham (1820–1886) was a longtime commander in the Confederate Army of Tennessee. Conyngham misspelled the name as "Chethem" and "Chetam."

23. The phrase "by the d——d h——ll hounds, God and you forgive me father, but I can't help it" was crossed out.

24. Colonel Charles Ready (1802–1878) was a former Tennessee congressman, lawyer, and Murfreesboro resident. His daughter, Martha "Mattie" Ready, married Confederate General John H. Morgan in December 1862.

25. Martha (Strong) Ready (1807–1877).

26. John Baptist Purcell (1800–1883) of Cincinnati, one of the strongest Union supporters in the U.S. hierarchy.

27. These sisters were members of the Sisters of Charity of Cincinnati.

CHAPTER III

1. Calvin Goddard (1838–1892) served as aide and staff member to General Rosecrans from early 1862 through late 1863.

2. Conyngham probably meant Major General Lovell Rousseau (1818–1869), who commanded a division under General Alexander McCook in the Army of the Cumberland.

3. The 14th Michigan Infantry officially became a mounted regiment in September 1863. The captain may have been Thomas C. Fitzgibbon (1836–1865), who commanded the regiment's all-Irish Company B.

4. The phrase "or a Know-Nothing" was crossed out.

5. John Hunt Morgan (1826–1864) was best known for his effective cavalry raids on Union supply lines and railroads in Kentucky, Tennessee, Ohio, and Indiana.

6. Joseph Richard McCann (1828–1880) was captain (later major) of the 9th Tennessee Cavalry.

7. Originally the text read "Praise," but someone changed it to "Press."

8. Originally the text read "Praise," but someone changed it to "Press."

9. Originally the text read "enemies," but someone changed it to "friends."

10. Originally the text read "enemies," but someone changed it to "friends."

11. This was likely Father John Mary Jacquet (1817–1896), a French-born priest who served in the Archdiocese of Cincinnati beginning in 1855.

12. Dominican Father John T. Nealis died of his wounds on March 18, 1864. Conyngham had mistakenly abbreviated his religious order as "O.S.P." in the manuscript.

13. The word "them" was previously written in the text as "the vile wretches."

14. The phrase "head off" was previously written in the text as "Roman guts out."

15. The word "side" was originally "bowels" in the text.

16. Thomas L. Crittenden (1819–1893) was a corps commander in Rosecrans's Army of the Cumberland.

17. Although the Battle of Chickamauga took place on September 19–20, 1863, Rosecrans remained in command of Union forces in Chattanooga until October 19 when he was officially relieved of duty by General Grant.

18. George H. Thomas (1816–1870) succeeded Rosecrans as commander of the Army of the Cumberland after the latter was relieved in October 1863.

19. Major General William Tecumseh Sherman (1820–1891) was one of the most successful Union commanders of the entire war, serving primarily in the Western Theater.

20. Confederate General John Bell Hood (1831–1879) served in the Army of Northern Virginia until being transferred to the Western Theater before the Battle of Chickamauga. He eventually succeeded General Joseph E. Johnston as commander of the Army of Tennessee in July 1864.

21. In recounting this story in his diary, Father Cooney mentions that it was he who gave Stanley the scapular after the general received his first Communion the previous Easter (Diary entries for November 30 and December 1, 1864, Peter Paul Cooney Papers, University of Notre Dame Archives, Notre Dame, Indiana).

CHAPTER IV

1. There is disagreement about his birthdate, birthplace, and date of entry into the Congregation of Holy Cross. See Edward Sorin, C.S.C., *The Chronicles of Notre Dame du Lac*, ed. James T. Connelly (Notre Dame, IN: University of Notre Dame Press, 1992), 284. An 1851 entry date (as asserted in

The Chronicles of Notre Dame du Lac) into the Holy Cross community does not match source material from his ministry with the Brothers of the Holy Family in St. Paul, Minnesota.

2. The word "having" was originally deleted from the text but is restored here for clarity.

3. The phrase "of Prof. of Natural Sciences and Librarian and Curator of the Museums" was crossed out.

4. Ulysses S. Grant (1822–1885) was then in command of the Department of Tennessee. In March 1864 he became the general in chief of all Union forces.

5. John Henry Luers (1819–1871), born in Germany, was Fort Wayne's first bishop.

6. Father Julian P. Bourget, C.S.C., died June 12, 1862, at Mound City, Illinois. He had arrived the previous spring to provide for the spiritual needs of those in the hospital there, including the Holy Cross Sisters serving as nurses.

7. Dr. Newton R. Casey (1826–1887) was assistant surgeon at the Federal hospital in Mound City, Illinois.

8. "Haines's" was spelled "Hain's" by Conyngham.

9. Lowell is the name for a section of South Bend where St. Joseph Church is located. Father Carrier served in local parishes in addition to his work at the university.

10. Ellen Boyle Ewing Sherman (1824–1888) was a devout Catholic, ardent Unionist, and wife of General William T. Sherman. Although from Ohio, she resided for part of the war in South Bend as some of her children were being educated at St. Mary's College and Notre Dame.

11. Originally the text continued: "After it was finished, the Rev. Father Provincial asked who was ready to volunteer, but he received no answer."

12. Father Alexis Granger, C.S.C. (1817–1893).

13. Captain (later General) Charles Ewing (1835–1883) and General Hugh Ewing (1826–1905) were brothers. A third brother, General Thomas Ewing (1829–1896), also served the Union cause. General William T. Sherman was their foster brother who became their brother-in-law when he married their sister, Ellen. See Kenneth J. Heineman, *Civil War Dynasty: The Ewing Family of Ohio* (New York: New York University Press, 2013).

14. Father Louis A. Lambert (1835–1910) served as chaplain of the 18th Illinois.

15. Memphis's Overton Hotel at Main St. and Poplar Ave. had been converted into a hospital.

16. The text has "that" here.

17. Major General Stephen A. Hurlbut (1815–1882), commander of the 16th Corps then garrisoning Memphis, Tennessee.

18. Charles McMillan (1825–1890) was the medical director of Sherman's corps.

19. Father Joseph E. "Napoleon" Mignault (1826–1895) served as chaplain to the 17th Wisconsin.

20. James B. McPherson (1828–1864) commanded the 17th Corps during the Vicksburg Campaign.

21. Conyngham mistakenly wrote "Ewell" here.

22. Major General Francis Preston Blair, Jr. (1821–1875) was a former Republican congressman from Missouri.

CHAPTER V

1. Born in County Kildare, Ireland, General Michael Kelly Lawler (1814–1882) commanded a brigade in Grant's army besieging Vicksburg.

2. This is likely a reference to Florence M. Cornyn (1829–1863), a Catholic medical doctor from St. Louis, Missouri, who served in the 10th Missouri Cavalry.

3. Frederick Steele (1819–1868) commanded a division during the Vicksburg campaign.

4. Joseph E. Johnston (1807–1891), commander of the Confederacy's armies in the war's early battles in Virginia, was then in command of the Department of the West.

5. Conyngham had originally written the pass into the text here, only to delete it later, perhaps because it already appeared in chapter 4.

6. George Holmes Bixby (1837–1901) served as an assistant surgeon in the Union navy in the Western Theater.

7. Ninian Pinkney (1811–1877). Later in the war, a Holy Cross sister would write: "I have learned to know and esteem Dr. Pinkney as one of the best and most cherished of the noble corps comprising the Navy" ("Pinkney," *Dictionary of American Naval Fighting Ships* as published on the Naval History and Heritage Command website, accessed May 1, 2018, https://www.history.navy.mil/research/histories/ship-histories/danfs/p/pinkney.html).

8. Phrase inserted for clarity, replacing Conyngham's original word "who."

CHAPTER VI

1. This was probably Stephen Purcell Bonner (c. 1837–1874), son of an Irish immigrant, who served as the surgeon of the 2nd Kentucky Infantry and 47th Ohio Infantry regiments.

2. An extraneous "the" was deleted here.

3. Bishop William Henry Elder (1819–1904) was famously arrested in 1864 for refusing to say the traditional prayer for the president of the United States.

4. McKinney L. Cook and his wife, Jennette, owned a large plantation near Vicksburg. Victorious Union forces occupied the grounds of their estate after the Battle of Champion Hill (May 16, 1863).

5. This was originally "Bolls" in the manuscript. This and the following instance were corrected to the more common spelling of "Bolles."

CHAPTER VII

1. Changes to the draft called for the word "who" to be inserted after "soldiers," the "ly" in "previously" to be deleted, and the word "were" to be inserted after "previous." But these changes were nonsensical or only partly done, so the text is shown here as originally written.

2. Conyngham referred to him as "Henzi" or "Henze," but Carrier is referring to Father Charles Heuzé, a French-born priest residing in Vicksburg at the time of the siege whose story is covered in chapter 20.

3. Unclear word replaced for clarity.

4. Beginning with this paragraph, the rest of the letter, according to a deleted subheading, was written two days later on July 6, 1863, from the Big Black River.

5. Father John Bannon (1829–1913) was chaplain of the 1st Missouri Brigade and later served as an unofficial Confederate emissary in Rome and Ireland.

6. The following was deleted from the text ". . . in general, and everybody and everything that came from the north of 'Mason and Dixon's line' were Yankee [Yankists?]! So greatly intense were his feeling of sadness at seeing the church filled almost exclusively with our soldiers that he positively refused to sing Mass and would not preach, although he had promised the assistant pastor to do both." In the following sentence, the word "therefore" was deleted after "He."

7. An extraneous "I" was deleted.

8. General Peter J. Osterhaus (1823–1917) was a former German revolutionary who moved to Missouri before the war.

9. "*Corps de genie*" is French for "corps of engineers."

10. "*Ventre affamé n'a point d'oreilles*" is a French proverb that can be translated as: "A hungry stomach has no ears."

CHAPTER VIII

1. For the record of Christy's court martial for desertion, see "General Orders No. 180, April 25, 1864," in *Adjutant-General's Office, General Orders [January 1864 to April 1864]* (Washington, DC: Government Printing Office, 1864), 4, 6.

2. Prince Demetrius Augustine Gallitzin (1770–1840), a Russian aristocrat and Catholic priest, was known as the "Apostle to the Alleghenies." Conyngham mistakenly spelled the name as "Gallitzen."

3. Born in County Donegal, Ireland, Father Hugh Patrick Gallagher (1815–1882) was ordained in 1840.

4. Conyngham had originally written 1845. *The Pittsburgh Catholic* carried the news of Christy's ordination on September 2, 1854.

5. The word "war" was originally "Rebellion" in the text.

6. Dr. Gillespie helped recruit the members of the 78th Pennsylvania Infantry, serving as captain in company F.

7. William Graham Sirwell (1820–1885) commanded the 78th Pennsylvania Infantry.

8. *Foxe's Book of Martyrs*, first published in 1563, is a classic apologetic for the Protestant Reformation offering an anti-Catholic perspective on Christian history.

9. General James S. Negley (1826–1901), a Pittsburgh native, was head of the 7th Brigade of the Department of the Ohio.

10. Both camps were located in south central Kentucky.

11. Conyngham had written the fort name as "Donaldson."

12. Originally written as "Rousseau's," Conyngham crossed it out and wrote, "Rosecrans." Since Rousseau, not Rosecrans, was commanding a division at this time, the original text was restored.

13. William S. Rosecrans.

14. During the successful Tullahoma Campaign (June 23–July 3, 1863), Rosecrans brilliantly maneuvered the Confederates out of middle Tennessee.

15. A French phrase meaning "hell fire."

16. The original word is unclear, but most closely resembles "hands," which we changed to "hand" for clarity.

17. A misspelled Latin phrase meaning "to teach and entertain."

18. This word is missing because of a tear in the clipped newspaper article.

19. Perhaps realizing that such conduct was improper for a priest, Conyngham deleted the rest of the sentence: "and it was easy to see from the bearing and martial character of Father Christy that if the boys had 'pitched in' he would certainly have 'pitched in' likewise."

CHAPTER IX

1. For the history of anti-Catholicism in Massachusetts, see, for instance, Nancy Lusignan Schultz, *Fire and Roses: The Burning of the Charleston Convent, 1834* (New York: Free Press, 2000).

2. Conyngham is here referring to Joseph Hiss, the Massachusetts State Representative who as head of the state's "nunnery committee" carried out anti-Catholic "convent inspections" looking for signs of criminal and immoral behavior by nuns. Though no immoralities were found in convents, Hiss was removed from the legislature when it became known that he was involved with a mistress and was using the inspection trips to engage in his own immoralities at the state's expense. See John R. Mulkern, *The Know-Nothing Party in Massachusetts: The Rise and Fall of a People's Movement* (Boston: Northeastern University Press, 1990), 117–18.

3. This is a reference to a biblical figure of that name who was a metalworker (Genesis 4:22).

4. Born in Ireland, Thomas Cass (1821–1862) was a militia officer in the mostly Irish Columbian Artillery before the war (Patrick R. Guiney, *Commanding Boston's Irish Ninth: The Civil War Letters of Colonel Patrick R. Guiney*, ed. Christian G. Samito [New York: Fordham University Press, 1998], 3).

5. Massachusetts Governor John A. Andrew (1818–1867) was one of the most patriotic of the North's wartime governors, known for his support for the raising of Irish and later African American regiments.

6. Bishop John B. Fitzpatrick (1812–1866) served as coadjutor bishop of Boston from 1844 to 1846 and later as bishop from 1846 until his death. Author's footnote: "Bishop Fitzpatrick died on the 13th of February 1866."

7. Father John McElroy, S.J. (1782–1877), served as an army chaplain during the Mexican-American War (1846–1848).

8. Conyngham spelled the famous Italian Renaissance artist's name as "Michael Angelo."

9. Stoneman's Switch is located near Falmouth, Virginia.

10. See Daniel George Macnamara, *The History of the Ninth Regiment, Massachusetts Volunteer Infantry* (Boston: E. B. Stillings, 1899), 279. Mooney was injured on St. Patrick's Day and died in Washington, DC, about a week later on March 26, 1863.

11. The original word here is unclear, but "Church" makes the most sense in context.

12. The original word here is unclear, but it appears to be a misspelling of "energy."

13. Also the *Pembroke* (Macnamara, *The History of the Ninth Regiment*, 26).

14. The farm was located in the Washington suburbs. Conyngham misspelled it as "Emarts."

15. Brigadier General Michael Corcoran (1827–1863) was an ardent Irish nationalist and colonel of the 69th New York Infantry Regiment. Captured at the First Battle of Bull Run on July 21, 1861, he was finally exchanged the following year. Promoted to the rank of brigadier general, he organized and led the Corcoran Legion, composed mainly of Irish regiments raised in New York, from the fall of 1862 until his death in December 1863.

CHAPTER X

1. Sergeant Daniel J. Regan, a shoemaker from Marlborough, Massachusetts, was killed at the Battle of Hanover Court House, May 27, 1862.

2. "Bearded like a pard" is an old expression, meaning as "hairy as a leopard."

3. Here Conyngham deleted a long anecdote similar to that of the chaplain's council from chapter 9. In it, Father Scully was invited to Boston's Fremont Temple in order to encourage more of the city's Irishmen to volunteer. Scully turned the tables on his hosts, however, asking for "the non-fighting Americans" to do their part and enlist as the Irish had already done. The chastened "Americans" of Boston "let him severely alone" for the rest of his recuperation.

4. Other sources indicate Scully was captured at Savage's Station (David Power Conyngham, *The Irish Brigade and Its Campaigns*, ed. Law-

rence Frederick Kohl [New York: William McSorley, 1867], 111; Daniel George Macnamara, *The History of the Ninth Regiment, Massachusetts Volunteer Infantry* [Boston: E. B. Stillings, 1899], 167).

5. While it is difficult to identify the colonel described here, he was probably an officer in Confederate General Joseph B. Kershaw's brigade, composed of the 2nd, 3rd, 7th, and 8th South Carolina Infantry regiments.

6. Savage's Station was located in Henrico County, Virginia.

7. Father John Teeling was chaplain to the 1st Virginia Regiment. Conyngham spelled the name as "Tieling."

8. Conyngham originally wrote "who," and he later crossed it out and wrote "they." Since "who" fits the sentence better, the original text has been restored.

9. Author's note: "This learned prelate died on the 14th of January, 1872."

10. As no black Union soldiers served in the Virginia theater at this time, it is possible that Scully actually visited a hospital for runaway slaves, also known as contrabands or freedmen.

11. "The mark" is an old phrase for "required standard."

12. Conyngham spelled the name "Hinckly," but this is likely a reference to John Hinckley, who served in the 9th Massachusetts, Co. D, from 1861 to 1863.

CHAPTER XI

1. Father Michael Meagher, S.J., was a teacher at St. John's College, New York, at the war's beginning. Later he was assigned to the College of St. Francis Xavier, also in New York.

2. Saint Ignatius Loyola (1491–1556) was the founder of the Society of Jesus or Jesuits.

3. Named nuncio to Brazil, Italian Archbishop Gaetano Bedini (1806–1864) toured the United States in 1853–1854, eliciting a strong anti-Catholic reaction.

4. French naval officer François d'Orléans, Prince de Joinville (1818–1900), immigrated in 1861, offering his support to the Union. Prince Robert of Orléans, Duke of Chartres (1840–1910), also arrived in the war's first year, serving under General McClellan in the Army of the Potomac.

5. Major General Israel Richardson (1815–1862) was a brigade (and later division) commander in the Army of the Potomac. He married Fannie Travor in 1861.

6. Brigadier General Thomas Francis Meagher (1823–1867) was a famous Irish revolutionary and commander of the Army of the Potomac's Irish Brigade.

7. Colonel (later Brigadier General) Orlando Metcalfe Poe (1832–1895) later served successfully as chief engineer under General Sherman from 1864 to 1865.

8. Author's footnote: "*extract of a letter from camp."

9. Cardinal Paul Cullen (1803–1878) was archbishop of Dublin, Ireland, from 1852 to 1878.

10. This paragraph was crossed out in the manuscript.

CHAPTER XII

1. Conyngham spelled the name as "Ouellette."
2. Perth Amboy is a city in Middlesex County, New Jersey.
3. Fort Ellsworth was part of the defenses of Washington, DC, and was located west of Alexandria, Virginia.
4. Fathers William Corby (88th New York) and Laurence McMahon (28th Massachusetts).
5. This word is unclear in the manuscript.

CHAPTER XIII

1. James Allen Hardie (1823–1876) was a Catholic then serving as assistant adjutant general of the U.S. Army.
2. This was originally "was after receiving."
3. Conyngham had mistakenly written "D" here.
4. The condemned men were members of the 118th Pennsylvania Regiment, 5th Corps. Conyngham erroneously believed they were part of the 15th Corps.
5. Chaplain William J. O'Neill (1831–1887), a Methodist, was chaplain to the 118th Pennsylvania.
6. For descriptions of the executions, see Henry N. Blake, *Three Years in the Army of the Potomac* (Boston: Lee and Shepard, 1865), 238–40; and William H. Powell, *The Fifth Army Corps (Army of the Potomac): A Record of Operations during the Civil War in the United States of America, 1861–1865* (New York: G. P. Putnam's Sons, 1896), 571–73. The details that Blake and Powell

provide are slightly different. Neither match Conyngham nor each other as to the date of the executions or the exact religious affiliations of the five, though all acknowledge the condemned men were Catholic, Protestant, and Jewish.

7. Born in Ireland, Patrick R. Guiney (1835–1877) became the 9th Massachusetts's colonel after the death of its former commander, Thomas Cass, in July 1862.

8. This was originally misspelled as "Eagan" in the manuscript. This and subsequent misspellings have been corrected to "Egan."

CHAPTER XIV

1. Francis P. Kenrick (1797–1863) was archbishop of Baltimore and a leading figure in the American Catholic Church.

2. Father Bernard J. O'Reilly (1820–1907) served briefly as the second chaplain to the 69th New York.

3. "Them" was crossed out in the original manuscript, but it was restored here for clarity and meaning.

4. Born in Ireland, Captain Patrick McGraw (c. 1825–1885) commanded company K of the 33rd New York Infantry. Conyngham spelled the name as "McGrath."

5. John McLeod Murphy (1827–1871) was colonel of the 15th New York Regiment of Engineers.

6. Colonel James E. Kerrigan (1828–1899) commanded the 25th New York Infantry Regiment before resigning in 1862 to take a seat in Congress. After the war, he took part in the Irish nationalist movement known as Fenianism. Conyngham misspelled the name as "Carrigan."

7. Conyngham misspelled General Couch's name as "Couche."

8. The extraneous word "where" was deleted for clarity.

9. The surname here is illegible, but this is a clear reference to Major General Stewart Van Vliet (1815–1901), who was chief quartermaster of the Army of the Potomac from August 1861 to July 1862.

10. James Jackson Dana (1821–1898) was then serving as assistant quartermaster.

11. The following description of Gillen's eventual mode of transportation was deleted at this point in the manuscript: "with two wheels, the only sort of carriage in the army at that time. But the cover overhead being rather low, it was rather uncomfortable, and having got some money from the boys he bought a horse covered carry all (or carriage) himself and then he could

go independent." Surgeon John Dwyer gives a fuller, more colorful description of Gillen's second carriage later in this chapter.

12. General Charles P. Stone (1824–1887) commanded a division on the Upper Potomac at that time.

13. Conyngham spelled his name as "Owens."

14. Charles Devens, Jr. (1820–1891) was promoted to brigadier general in 1862, eventually leading a division in the Army of the Potomac. Conyngham spelled the name as "Devin" or "Devine."

15. Colonel (later General) William Raymond Lee (1807–1891) led the 20th Massachusetts Volunteers, which despite having many foreign-born enlisted men was known as the "Harvard Regiment" because many of the officers were graduates or students from that university.

16. Captain Michael Garretty (Gerety) (1815–1861). While leading Co. K of the 42nd New York, he was killed in action at Ball's Bluff, Virginia, on October 21, 1861. Conyngham spelled the name as "Garrity."

17. Captain Timothy O'Meara (1835–1863). After serving the 42nd New York, he was promoted to colonel of the 90th Illinois (Irish Legion) when it was formed in the autumn of 1862. Leading his soldiers into battle, he was killed on November 25, 1863, at Missionary Ridge, Tennessee. Conyngham spelled the name as "O'Mara."

18. Born in Ireland, Father Michael F. Martin (1819–1884) was honorably discharged for disability on June 19, 1862.

19. This was originally "fed" in the manuscript.

20. The "Bucktails" was the popular name of the 13th Pennsylvania Reserves, also known as the 42nd Pennsylvania Volunteer Infantry or Kane's Rifles.

21. Major General George A. McCall (1802–1868) was a division commander in the Army of the Potomac. Conyngham spelled his name "McCaul."

22. An extraneous "convenient" was deleted here.

23. This was originally misspelled as "Drainsville." The Battle of Dranesville took place in Loudon County in northern Virginia on December 20, 1861. Although just a minor engagement, Union forces succeeded in driving off a smaller force of Confederates on a foraging expedition.

24. According to a deleted portion of the manuscript, the remainder of this chapter was taken from a letter sent by Dr. John Dwyer, M.D., of Ward's Island Hospital, New York, to Conyngham. The letter, dated August 21, 1869, was in response to Conyngham's request for information on the chaplain of the Irish Legion.

25. In 1864, this regiment was redesignated the 182nd New York Infantry Regiment. A fifth regiment, the 175th New York, was also raised but never saw service with the rest of the Legion.

26. Before joining the Corcoran Legion, James M. Dillon, C.S.C. (1833–1868), had previously served in the Irish Brigade as the 63rd New York Infantry Regiment's chaplain from October 1861 to October 1862.

27. The location is missing from the manuscript, but according to an account by Dwyer found in William Corby's famous *Memoirs of Chaplain Life*, Dillon took temporary command of the regiment at the bloody Battle of Malvern Hill, part of the Seven Days Battles that took place near Richmond, Virginia, from June to July 1862 (William Corby, C.S.C., *Memoirs of Chaplain Life: Three Years with the Irish Brigade in the Army of the Potomac* [Notre Dame, IN: "Scholastic" Press, 1893; second printing, 1894], 287–90).

28. The text originally read "last year."

29. Although Father Dillon took trips to Europe and California seeking to improve his declining health, he never recovered from his wartime illness and died on December 15, 1868 (Edward Sorin, C.S.C., *The Chronicles of Notre Dame du Lac*, ed. James T. Connelly [Notre Dame, IN: University of Notre Dame Press, 1992], 292–93).

30. A famous racehorse born in New York state in 1858, Dexter broke the world record for trotters in 1867.

31. Also known as the Battle of Kelly's Store, the engagement was a minor one but the first experience of combat for many of the Legion's soldiers. Led by General Corcoran, the troops drove the Confederates from the field, earning their first victory of the war.

32. Father Thomas H. Mooney was the first chaplain to the 69th New York, serving from April to July 1863. His chaplaincy was cut short by his bishop, John Hughes of New York, who was angered by Mooney's decision to "baptize" a Union cannon (Germain, "Catholic Military and Naval Chaplains," 85–86; William B. Kurtz, *Excommunicated from the Union: How the Civil War Created a Separate Catholic America* (New York: Fordham University Press, 2016), 73).

33. This letter was probably published in the *Boston Pilot*, a leading Irish Catholic newspaper in the nineteenth century, as it was addressed to the paper's famous Irish nationalist editor, John Boyle O'Reilly (1844–1890).

34. This was originally "will" in the text, probably a typesetter error.

35. This was misspelled as "Chicohominy."

36. Charles J. Murphy (1832–1921) was a veteran of both the Mexican War and the American Civil War, earning a Medal of Honor for his bravery

at the First Battle of Bull Run. This letter is similar to the one published in his *Reminiscences of the War of the Rebellion: And of the Mexican War* (New York: F. J. Ficker, 1882), 53–54.

37. Thomas E. Walsh, C.S.C. (1853–1893), was then president of the University of Notre Dame.

CHAPTER XV

1. Located in Latrobe, Pennsylvania, St. Vincent's College was a seminary founded by the Bavarian Benedictine monk Boniface Wimmer (1809–1887) in 1846.

2. The words "while" and "it" were deleted from this sentence in the manuscript, but they were restored here for meaning.

3. Jacques-Maurice des Landes d'Aussac de Saint Palais (1811–1877) was the French-born bishop of Vincennes, Indiana.

4. Born in Maryland, Richard Pius Miles, O.P. (1791–1860), was the first bishop of Nashville, Tennessee.

5. It is not clear to whom Conyngham is referring here, as no priest by the name of Birmingham appears in the *Catholic Almanacs* for 1859 through 1861. The diocese's vicar general at this time was Father S. L. Montgomery, O.S.D.

6. James Whelan, O.P. (1823–1878), was the Irish-born bishop of Nashville serving during the beginning of the Civil War. He resigned from his diocese in September 1863, leaving the state without a bishop until after the war's end.

7. In this case, the enemy was the Union Army.

8. Although Bergrath may have said Mass for Rosecrans during the Chattanooga-Chickamauga campaign, he could not possibly have done this during the Battle of Chickamauga (September 19–20, 1863) at Saints Peter and Paul Church in Chattanooga. The general, who did attend Sunday Mass the morning of the 20th, was more than ten miles south of town with his army (William M. Lamers, *The Edge of Glory: A Biography of William S. Rosecrans, U.S.A.* [New York: Harcourt, Brace and World, 1961], 336).

CHAPTER XVI

1. Author note: "This sketch is mainly taken from a work entitled 'Indiana's Roll of Honor.'"

2. David Stevenson, *Indiana's Roll of Honor*, vol. 1 (Indianapolis: A. D. Streight, 1864), esp. 561–72.

3. Here Conyngham inserted, with minor editing, page 562 from Stevenson's *Indiana's Roll of Honor*, volume 1.

4. This was "1832" in the manuscript.

5. The University of St. Mary of the Lake, now popularly called Mundelein Seminary, was formed in 1844 as Chicago's first institution of higher learning. Forced to close in 1866, it was not reopened until 1921.

6. Oliver P. Morton (1823–1877) was the Republican governor of Indiana during the Civil War. In addition to securing Cooney's services, he successfully petitioned Father Sorin for a group of Sisters of the Holy Cross to staff military hospitals across the Midwest (see chapters 33 and 34).

7. The Giant's Causeway is a geological formation composed of columns of basalt. Located in County Antrim, Northern Ireland, the causeway was created by a volcanic eruption.

8. "From Dan to Beersheba" is a biblical phrase used in the Old Testament to denote the area settled by the tribes of Israel. See, for instance, 1 Samuel 3:20: "And all Israel from Dan to Beersheba recognized that Samuel was attested as a prophet of the Lord."

9. The Battle of Stones River, also known as the Battle of Murfreesboro, was fought in Tennessee on December 31, 1862, and January 2, 1863.

10. Michael Nash served in Co. G of the 65th Ohio Infantry Regiment.

11. Richard W. Johnson (1827–1897) was a division commander under General Rosecrans. Part of the army's right wing at Stones River, he was badly outflanked and his men suffered heavy casualties.

12. Here Conyngham inserted page 564 from Stevenson's *Indiana's Roll of Honor*, volume 1.

13. Alexander McDowell McCook (1831–1903) was a major general and corps commander in Rosecrans's Army of the Cumberland.

14. Lavergne, in Rutherford County, Tennessee, lies outside Nashville.

15. Here Conyngham inserted page 566 from Stevenson's *Indiana's Roll of Honor*, volume 1.

16. A German-born author, Emil Schalk, wrote two popular works: *Campaigns of 1862 and 1863, Illustrating the Principles of Strategy* (Philadelphia: J. B. Lippincott, 1863); and *Summary of the Art of War: Written Expressly for and Dedicated to the U. S. Volunteer Army* (Philadelphia: J. B. Lippincott, 1862). Stevenson, from whom the account is taken, spelled the name as "Shalk."

17. The Irish American Bernard F. Mullen (1825–1879) commanded the 35th Indiana from May 1862 to May 1864 when he resigned due to ill health.

18. Here Conyngham inserted page 568 from Stevenson's *Indiana's Roll of Honor*, volume 1.

19. This word was spelled thus in the manuscript.

20. John Crawford Walker (1828–1883) was the 35th's first commander. Disagreements with Governor Morton forced him to resign in late 1862.

21. Thomas Stanley Matthews (1824–1889) was a lawyer from Ohio who rose from lieutenant colonel to command a brigade under General Rosecrans before his resignation in 1863. Conyngham's note, "Now one of the justices of the U.S. Supreme Court," must have been written no sooner than the spring of 1881 when Matthews was narrowly confirmed to serve on the court by a vote of 24 to 23.

22. Horatio P. Van Cleve (1809–1891) of Minnesota was a division commander in the Army of the Cumberland.

23. Camp Wild Cat was located in eastern Kentucky's Laurel County. It was the site of an early engagement in the war (October 21, 1861) in which the Federals were victorious.

24. Fought on October 8, 1862, the Battle of Perryville checked Confederate General Braxton Bragg's invasion of Kentucky. Despite forcing his foe's retreat, Union General Don Carlos Buell's lackluster pursuit led to his replacement by General Rosecrans later that month.

25. Here Conyngham inserted page 570 from Stevenson's *Indiana's Roll of Honor*, volume 1.

26. This was corrected from Conyngham's misspelling of "Tassan."

27. This was corrected from Conyngham's misspelling of "Dufficey."

28. Here Conyngham inserted page 572 from Stevenson's *Indiana's Roll of Honor*, volume 1.

CHAPTER XVII

1. Conyngham incorrectly referred to Father Thomas Brady as "John Brady" throughout the manuscript.

2. Peter Paul Lefevère (1804–1869) was Detroit's Belgian-born coadjutor bishop during the Civil War.

3. This was his only change to the newspaper account. Conyngham changed the text here from "far bitterer" to "far more bitter."

4. Conyngham may be referring to Father Francis Fusseder, the Austrian-born chaplain of the 24th Wisconsin Infantry Regiment.

5. Here Conyngham refers to the Grand Review of Grant's and Sherman's armies in Washington, DC, held on May 23 and 24, 1865. As part of

Sherman's Army, the 15th Michigan would have marched on the second day of the review.

CHAPTER XVIII

1. The others were Paul Gillen (chapter 14), James Dillon, Peter Cooney (chapter 16), Julian Bourget, Zepherin Lévêque, and Joseph Carrier (chapters 4–6).

2. English Combatant [Thomas E. Caffey], *Battle-Fields of the South: From Bull Run to Fredericksburgh; With Sketches of Confederate Commanders, and Gossip of the Camps* (New York: J. Bradburn, 1864).

3. Mooney was actually removed from his chaplaincy shortly before the battle by Archbishop John Hughes of New York, who personally traveled to Washington, DC, to do so. Mooney's immediate successor was Father Bernard O'Reilly, S.J., who served a short time as the 69th's chaplain before leaving for Europe. O'Reilly was replaced by another Jesuit, Father Thomas Ouellet (chapter 12), who served in the Irish Brigade for most of the rest of the war.

4. Including Corby, seven Notre Dame priests served. Please see this chapter's first endnote for their names.

5. The deleted word "chaplains" was restored for clarity's sake here.

6. Private Thomas E. Caffey, a native of London, England, and member of the 18th Mississippi Regiment, Company D (James I. Robertson, Jr., "The War In Words," *Civil War Times Illustrated* 23, no. 2 [April 1984]: 52).

7. Here Conyngham inserted pages 194 to 196 from Caffey's *Battle-Fields of the South*.

8. Conyngham replaced the phrase "the ancient Irish" with "Catholic."

9. The Irish Brigade suffered almost five hundred casualties during the course of this campaign (Susannah J. Ural, ed., *Civil War Citizens: Race, Ethnicity, and Identity in America's Bloodiest Conflict* [New York: New York University Press, 2010], 106).

10. The extraneous word "hear" was deleted.

11. After achieving success in the war's western theater, Major General John Pope (1822–1892) was promoted to command the Union's Army of Virginia. His forces suffered a tremendous defeat at the Second Battle of Bull Run in August 1862.

12. Thomas J. Jackson (1824–1863), better known as "Stonewall," commanded a corps in Lee's Army of Northern Virginia. Jackson appears frequently in Conyngham's narrative of Father James Sheeran's Confederate chaplaincy (see chapters 21 through 24).

13. This was originally misspelled as "Fair Fax."

14. This incident is strikingly similar to one that Conyngham initially depicted and then deleted at the beginning of his account of Father Jeremiah Trecy's chaplaincy (see chapter 1).

15. Conyngham's placement of Corby in Watertown suggests the draft of this chapter was written sometime between 1872 and 1877.

CHAPTER XIX

1. Conyngham names this chaplain Henry Gache. Most sources refer to him as Hippolyte Gache or Louis Hippolyte Gache.

2. Cornelius M. Buckley, ed., *A Frenchman, A Chaplain, A Rebel: The War Letters of Pere Louis-Hippolyte Gache, S.J.* (Chicago: Loyola University Press, 1981).

3. Jean Marie Odin (1800–1870) served as New Orleans's bishop from February 15, 1861, until his death.

4. Here Conyngham deleted a harsh phrase: "but, I must say, not very diligent or zealous ones."

5. Confederate Major General John Bankhead Magruder (1807–1871) successfully delayed a much larger Union army during the 1862 Peninsula campaign.

6. Actually the 14th Louisiana Regiment and its chaplain, Father James Sheeran, were also stationed on the Virginia Peninsula at this time (see chapter 21).

7. Sister Mary Blanche Rooney (1824–1884), a Daughter of Charity of Emmitsburg, Maryland, served after the war at St. Vincent's Female Asylum in Washington, DC.

8. These women belonged to the Sisters of Our Lady of Mercy, Charleston, South Carolina (see chapter 27).

9. The previous three paragraphs were taken directly from a text written in a different hand, that of Gache according to the manuscript. In a note to Conyngham at the bottom of one page, dated June 10, 1869, Gache apologizes for not writing more due to his numerous "sick calls and other obligations." Although these paragraphs were originally deleted, Conyngham changed his mind and restored them to the text.

10. The previous two paragraphs were inserted like the previous ones from another crossed-out text in Gache's hand. The manuscript then continues in the usual handwriting.

11. The content of the following paragraph is strikingly similar, albeit much more detailed, to one Gache wrote in a letter to his fellow Jesuit and

friend, Father André Cornette, on November 18, 1862 (Buckley, *A Frenchman, A Chaplain, A Rebel,* 148).

12. Sister Juliana Chatard (1833–1917) was a member of the Daughters of Charity of Emmitsburg, Maryland.

13. This paragraph is yet another insertion from the crossed-out, but later restored, manuscript written by Gache.

14. Union General David Hunter (1802–1886) commanded a raid through Virginia's Shenandoah Valley that was ultimately defeated in the summer of 1864 by Confederate General Jubal Early.

15. Sister Rose Noyland (1844–1909) was a member of the Daughters of Charity of Emmitsburg, Maryland.

16. The previous two paragraphs are in Gache's hand, crossed out but later restored by Conyngham's direction.

17. A note from Conyngham reads: "Father Gache enters so fully into the services rendered by the sisters and the treatment of the Federal prisoners in Richmond, that the author prefers giving his own statement to any personal sketch."

CHAPTER XX

1. This city, located on the Crimean Peninsula along the coast of the Black Sea, was laid siege to for eleven months in 1854–1855 during the Crimean War.

2. This was originally "Yankees." The text was changed by Conyngham.

3. Originally the text at this point read: "so the Yankees get mad and vent their spleen by sending a bomb through the church in the midst of the Mass." The text was changed by Conyngham.

4. Here Conyngham deleted "at 5 minutes to six o'clock."

5. "Another" was originally "at six a bomb." The text was changed by Conyngham.

6. Conyngham deleted the phrase "a la Yankee."

7. Here Conyngham deleted the phrase "through a rat hole."

8. Originally the text read, "A shell, a twenty five pounder, fell. . . ." The text was changed by Conyngham.

9. This could be a reference to Amede A. Hébert of the 3rd Louisiana Infantry Regiment, company A. Hébert was wounded in the trenches before the Battle of Vicksburg and died June 25, 1863, in Vicksburg. There were two General Héberts in the Confederate Army, Louis Hébert (1820–1901) and

Paul Octave Hébert (1818–1880). Conyngham or Heuzé misspelled the name as "Heber" throughout the letter.

10. Heuzé's original letter noted here that "an Episcopalian preacher of N. O. was also there." The text was changed by Conyngham.

11. Athanase, Charles V., and Theodore Babineau all enlisted as soldiers in company A of the 26th Louisiana Infantry Regiment. The three brothers from Lafayette Parish, Louisiana, died in or near Vicksburg in 1862.

12. Here Conyngham deleted the following phrase: "Such ignorance—such indifference among such a population," which he probably deemed too critical of the piety of Louisiana Catholic soldiers.

13. As in the chapter title, Conyngham misspelled his name here as "Henze."

CHAPTER XXI

1. Chapter 23, the third of the five chapters on Sheeran, has been omitted from the text because it was not actually taken from the diary (see chapter 23's introduction). The only published version of the full diary is Patrick J. Hayes, ed., *The Civil War Diary of Father James Sheeran: Confederate Chaplain and Redemptorist* (Washington, DC: Catholic University of America Press, 2016).

2. In editing this chapter, Conyngham may have written the word "in" here. We have deleted it as its placement confuses the sentence's meaning and was probably meant to go before "almost."

3. Major General Richard S. Ewell (1817–1872) was a division, and later corps, commander in Robert E. Lee's Army of Northern Virginia.

4. Colonel Zebulon York (1819–1900) was the 14th Louisiana's commanding officer until he was promoted to brigadier general in 1864.

5. David Zable (1832–1906) served as a major and lieutenant colonel in the 14th Louisiana until 1864 when he took over the regiment from Zebulon York.

6. According to Patrick Hayes, this is probably Dr. Isaac White (1837–1889), who was then serving as a surgeon with the 29th Virginia Infantry Regiment (Hayes, *Civil War Diary of Father Sheeran*, 13–14).

7. Brigadier General Isaac R. Trimble (1802–1888) served under Ewell until his capture at the Battle of Gettysburg. His name is misspelled throughout the manuscript as "Tremble."

8. Sheeran further identifies the soldier as Patrick Sullivan of the 73rd New York (Hayes, *Civil War Diary of Father Sheeran*, 19).

9. Born in Ireland, Colonel Michael Nolan (d. 1863) was the commander of the 1st Louisiana Infantry Regiment until he was killed at the Battle of Gettysburg. In the full diary, Sheeran praised Nolan as "a brave officer and a worthy man" (Hayes, *Civil War Diary of Father Sheeran*, 198).

10. The French-born Jesuit Darius Hubert (1823–1893) served as the 1st Louisiana Regiment's chaplain throughout the war. Conyngham frequently misspelled his name as "Huebert," which has been standardized to "Hubert."

11. Here a passage noting that a Protestant chaplain persuaded the men not to be baptized was deleted, probably due to Sheeran's denunciation of his non-Catholic foes as the "spiritual murderers" of the accused men. "O Protestantism," the passage continued, "how much thou hast done to offend God, injure man, and serve the evil one."

12. This and all instances have been corrected from Conyngham's misspelling, "Warrentown."

13. General J. E. B. Stuart (1833–1864) was the dashing commander of the Army of Northern Virginia's cavalry.

14. Misspelled by Conyngham as "Bristow" throughout the text, this has been corrected to "Bristoe."

15. General Ambrose Powell Hill, Jr. (1825–1865), would eventually rise to command a corps in Lee's Army of Northern Virginia.

16. This was originally "surprising."

17. Major William Monaghan was a New Orleans resident of Irish birth who later became colonel of the 6th Louisiana Infantry. He was killed in action in late August 1864 near Shepherdstown, West Virginia. Conyngham misspelled his name throughout as "Monahan."

18. This was originally misspelled as "Drainsville."

19. Actually, these sisters belonged to the Daughters of Charity, located in nearby Emmitsburg, Maryland. Protestant Americans and even some Catholics such as Sheeran frequently referred to all sister nurses as "Sisters of Charity" even if they belonged to other female religious communities.

20. The three priests mentioned here were Father James A. Ward (1813–1895), a native of Philadelphia and rector of the local Jesuit novitiate; Father Angelo M. Paresce (1817–1879), the Jesuit provincial born in Naples, Italy; and Father Bernard Maguire (1818–1886), the Irish-born Jesuit and former president of Georgetown College (Hayes, *Civil War Diary of Father Sheeran*, 63). Conyngham refered to Father Paresce as "Principal" instead of "Provincial."

21. Conyngham deleted the time of the march but it has been restored for clarity.

22. Conyngham spelled the name "McGarney," but Sheeran's diary records the surname as "McGary" (Hayes, *Civil War Diary of Father Sheeran*, 70).

23. This was misspelled as "Heedgersville."

24. Even though he was born in the North in Pittsburgh, Father Thomas Albert Andrew Becker (1832–1899) supported the Confederate cause and was briefly imprisoned during the war for failing to say prayers for the U.S. government. In 1868 he became the bishop of Wilmington, Delaware, and in 1886 he became the bishop of Savannah, Georgia (Hayes, *Civil War Diary of Father Sheeran*, 71).

25. Born in Ireland, Father Michael A. Costello (1833–1867) had been pastor of St. Peter's Church in Harpers Ferry since 1857 (Hayes, *Civil War Diary of Father Sheeran*, 77).

26. Captain Patrick R. O'Rorke commanded Company F of the 1st Louisiana Volunteer Infantry Regiment. Conyngham also spelled his name as "O'Rourke" in other chapters, which we have standardized to "O'Rorke."

CHAPTER XXII

1. James Nelligan (c. 1830–1871), an Irish auctioneer living in New Orleans before the war, would later be promoted to colonel of the 1st Louisiana Regiment.

2. Sheeran spelled the name "McCormack" in his diary (Hayes, *The Civil War Diary of Father Sheeran*, 92).

3. The Seventh Day Baptists observed the Sabbath on the seventh day of the week, Saturday.

4. Senator Thomas Jenkins Semmes (1824–1899) was a prominent lawyer from New Orleans who served as a Confederate senator from early 1862 to the war's end. He helped design the Confederacy's seal, with its motto *Deo Vindice* meaning "God will vindicate." References to his mother, Mary Matilda (Jenkins) Semmes (1800–1881), and his sisters, Mary Virginia (1821–1897) and Clara Elizabeth (1830–1908), appear in Sheeran's diary (Patrick J. Hayes, ed., *The Civil War Diary of Father Sheeran: Confederate Chaplain and Redemptorist* [Washington, DC: Catholic University of America Press, 2016], 247–48).

5. John Mitchel (1815–1875) was a celebrated Irish patriot, pro-slavery editor, and champion of the Confederate cause. Captain James Mitchel (1840–1908) was the only one of his three sons to survive the war. Conyngham misspelled their surname with an extra l.

6. This was originally written as "Bunkers."

7. Conyngham had mistakenly written "May" here.

8. Conyngham spelled the name as "Heassett."

9. Conyngham replaced "Yankees" with this word.

10. Despite his forces turning back Stonewall Jackson on March 23, 1862, Major General James Shields (1810–1879) had actually been wounded the day before the battle and was not in command. Although very popular with Irish Americans, his overall wartime career was unsuccessful, leading to his resignation in March 1863.

11. This was originally written as "Newmarket."

12. According to the full diary, after receiving 1st Lieutenant Robert R. Scott, Co. H, 8th Alabama Infantry Regiment, into the Catholic Church on April 20, 1863, Sheeran then officiated at his wedding ceremony to Margaret McDougal of Fredericksburg that same day (Hayes, *Civil War Diary of Father Sheeran*, 151). Unfortunately for the young couple, Scott was grievously wounded in early July at the Battle of Gettysburg and died later that month.

CHAPTER XXIII

1. Patrick J. Hayes, ed., *The Civil War Diary of Father Sheeran: Confederate Chaplain and Redemptorist* (Washington, DC: Catholic University of America Press, 2016), 157–68.

CHAPTER XXIV

1. Father Malachy Moran, O.S.B., served as pastor of St. Mary's Church in Hagerstown, Maryland, from 1862 to 1864.

2. Father Sheeran was not shy about reprimanding his own men or officers when he felt it necessary. Here Conyngham deleted: "On the 13th heavy pickets were thrown out and numbers of the men behaved themselves very badly. On the 15th after Mass Father Sheeran had all the officers of his regiment called together and rebuked them severely for their conduct." In this case, Sheeran was so incensed by their "scandalous" conduct that he threatened to quit the regiment altogether (Patrick J. Hayes, ed., *The Civil War Diary of Father Sheeran: Confederate Chaplain and Redemptorist* [Washington, DC: Catholic University of America Press, 2016], 220).

3. General Robert D. Johnston (1837–1919), born in Lincolnton, North Carolina, briefly led a division in early 1864 before assuming command of a

brigade in Early's army during the 1864 Shenandoah Valley campaign. The surname "Johnson" has been corrected to "Johnston" throughout the manuscript.

4. Bishop John Quinlan of Mobile, Alabama.

5. Father William Harris Duncan (1835–1894) served as vicar general of the Diocese of Mobile, Alabama. After the war, he joined the Society of Jesus and ministered in Boston and Washington, DC.

6. Note from Conyngham: "Father Bliemel was shot dead at the battle of Jonesboro near Atlanta, while preparing a dying soldier.—Author."

7. In addition to serving as a Confederate chaplain, Father Thomas O'Reilly (1831–1872), of County Cavan, Ireland, is most famous for intervening with General Sherman to spare the churches of Atlanta from destruction.

8. Father Anthony Carius (1821–1893) was then a priest of the Diocese of New Orleans.

9. Born in Londonderry, Ireland, Father William J. Hamilton (1832–1883) was the first priest to visit the infamous prison at Andersonville, Georgia.

10. Mary L. Gleason (c. 1843–1926) was the daughter of Irish immigrants Patrick and Arabella Gleason. She frequently exchanged letters with Sheeran during the war and accompanied him on his return to Richmond after his visit to Bragg's army. Mary married Zebulon York, former commanding officer of Sheeran's regiment, the 14th Louisiana Infantry, on August 24, 1885, in New Orleans. The Gleason family appears frequently in Sheeran's full diary.

11. Bishop Augustin M. Verot (1804–1876) led the diocese of Savannah, Georgia, as well as the vicariate of Florida during the Civil War. An ardent Confederate, he wrote a tract in 1861 defending slavery while calling for reformation of its worst excesses.

12. This was misspelled as "Dufast."

13. Born in County Wexford, Ireland, Father Peter Whelan (1830–1871) was most famous for his missionary work at Andersonville Prison, where he became known to history as the "Angel of Andersonville." Conyngham spelled the name "Whalin."

14. Born in Kerry, Ireland, Father Jeremiah F. O'Neill (1792–1870) was known as the "Pope of Savannah" for his great influence with and tireless efforts on behalf of the city's Catholics. We have corrected this and other places where Conyngham spelled the name as "O'Neil."

15. Father Charles C. Prendergast (c. 1828–1896) served for many years in the Diocese of Savannah.

16.   Born in Ireland, Francis Xavier Garland (1805–1854) was the first bishop of Savannah, Georgia.

17.   Father Leon Fillion (d. 1865) was born in Angiers, France, and served as one of two vicar generals of the diocese during Bishop Lynch's mission to Europe on behalf of the Confederacy in 1864–1865. Conyngham's misspelling of his name ("Sillian" or "Sillion") has been corrected to "Fillion."

18.   Bishop Patrick N. Lynch (1817–1882) was the Irish-born leader of the diocese of Charleston throughout the war. In 1861, he famously engaged in a public newspaper debate with Archbishop Hughes over the merits of southern secession and later served as an unofficial Confederate emissary in Rome in the last year of the war.

19.   Conyngham originally wrote "1863" here and in Patrick Hayes's version of the diary the date is given as 1862. The city's "great fire" actually took place on December 11, 1861. The fire burned more than 540 acres in the city, taking with it a number of Catholic buildings including the Cathedral of St. Finbar (David C. R. Heisser and Stephen J. White, Sr., *Patrick N. Lynch, 1817–1882: Third Catholic Bishop of Charleston* [Columbia: University of South Carolina Press, 2015], 82–85).

20.   The story of the Sisters of Mercy of Charleston is explored in chapter 27.

21.   Lizinka Campbell Brown Ewell (1820–1872) married General Ewell in 1863.

22.   This battle was actually known as the Battle of Walkerton or Mantapike Hill. It was part of the infamous Kilpatrick-Dahlgren Raid, an effort by Union cavalry to rescue prisoners of war held in Richmond, which, according to Confederate authorities, also aimed to burn Richmond and assassinate Confederate President Jefferson Davis. The actual Battle of Mine Run took place from November 27 to December 2, 1863.

23.   Major General Robert E. Rodes (1829–1864) led a division in the 2nd Corps of the Army of Northern Virginia. We have corrected Conyngham's spellings of the name as "Rhodes" or "Rhode" throughout the manuscript.

CHAPTER XXV

1.   Unfortunately, it is not clear who this person is, and Patrick Hayes's published edition of Sheeran's diary contains no reference to him meeting the son of a famous New Orleans doctor. This sentence may refer to a

conversation Sheeran had with a "son of a celebrated doctor in Mobile [Alabama]," that took place on April 17, 1864 (Hayes, *Civil War Diary of Father Sheeran*, 347–49).

2. Although only mentioned in Conyngham's manuscript a few times, Dr. Stephens, who is identified in a deleted phrase as "lately promoted to Division Surgeon," incurred the wrath of Father Sheeran on many occasions in the full diary. It is unclear, however, who this bumbling surgeon was, and Sheeran may have purposefully refrained from using the doctor's real name.

3. This was misspelled by Conyngham as "Coal."

4. Here Sheeran describes the Battle of Cold Harbor, which took place from May 31 to June 12, 1864.

5. Jubal A. Early (1816–1894) was a corps commander in General Lee's army, assuming independent command in the Shenandoah Valley in mid-1864 in an effort to draw Union forces away from Richmond. Although initially successful, he was eventually defeated by General Philip Sheridan.

6. These were actually the Daughters of Charity.

7. This was the Jesuit, Father Joseph O'Callaghan (1823–1869) of St. John's Church, Frederick, Maryland. Prior to his residence in Frederick, O'Callaghan had served as the president of Loyola College in Baltimore from 1860 to 1863. According to some sources, he briefly served as chaplain of the 69th New York National Guard in the summer of 1863. Conyngham misspelled his name as "Callahan."

8. Here Conyngham deleted a long passage describing Sheeran's condemnation of an officers' dance to be held on the evening of July 15 by the ladies of Leesburg, Virginia. Sheeran thought it inappropriate, accusing the officers planning on attending the dance of "reckless carelessness . . . in the very face of the enemy." Discussing the matter with General Johnston, Sheeran said he hoped that "the Yankees will throw a shell among them when they are making fools of themselves dancing." Sheeran happily noted that he "succeeded in breaking up the party."

9. This was misspelled as "Schnecker" in the manuscript.

10. In another deleted passage, Sheeran once again threatened to resign, this time over the "profanity of the officers calling at Headquarters." Upon receiving General York's promise that he would not swear anymore, Sheeran decided to remain.

11. Colonel James A. Mulligan (1830–1864), a prominent Irish nationalist from Chicago and commander of the 23rd Illinois Regiment known as the Irish Brigade of the West. Conyngham had incorrectly identified him as "W. Mulligan."

12. This sentence was originally deleted by Conyngham but has been restored for clarity so as to explain his brief absence from the army at this time.

13. Oilcloth is a cloth, often of linen, with a coating of linseed oil to make it waterproof.

14. Hayes noted that Sheeran (and therefore Conyngham) mistakenly reported that Captain James Brady was a member of the 16th Massachusetts. It is corrected here to indicate his service in the 26th Massachusetts Volunteer Infantry. Brady, as Conyngham indicated, was wounded at the Battle of Winchester on September 19, 1864, but survived the war (Hayes, *Civil War Diary of Father Sheeran*, 475).

15. General Alfred "Nattie" Duffié (1835–1880). Conyngham spelled the surname as "Duffer."

16. "To" was originally deleted but has been restored for clarity.

17. Colonel John S. Mosby (1833–1916) was a feared and effective Confederate guerilla leader operating in northern Virginia.

18. A notorious Confederate prison in Richmond, Virginia, housing Federal prisoners of war.

19. Conyngham subsequently abbreviated this man's surname as "Fitz," which we consistently rendered in full as "Fitzgerald" for clarity.

20. Father Michael Müller (1825–1899) was a Redemptorist priest then serving at St. Mary's Church in Annapolis, Maryland (Hayes, *Civil War Diary of Father Sheeran*, 486). Conyngham recorded the name as "Miller."

21. We have corrected Conyngham's spelling of "marshall" to "marshal" here and throughout the chapter.

22. The German-born Father George Ruland, C.Ss.R., was the Redemptorist's provincial in the United States.

23. Built in 1798 to guard Baltimore Harbor, Fort McHenry was used by the federal government as a military prison during the Civil War.

24. Brother Denis Halpen, C.Ss.R. (1817–1886). Conyngham referred to him as "Father Dennis."

25. Conyngham presents a much abbreviated account of Sheeran's time behind federal lines, his imprisonment, and his subsequent personal conversations with General Sheridan, in which the priest strongly denounced his imprisonment without trial. After his final discussion with the general, Sheeran lamented, "I had to dirty my hand by shaking his, stained as it is with blood, rapine and every species of injustice." For Sheeran's full account of his two unpleasant talks with Sheridan, see Hayes, *Civil War Diary of Father Sheeran*, 545–50.

26. The last five words were added in later, perhaps after Conyngham consulted Sheeran's diary.

CHAPTER XXVI

1. Here Conyngham deleted the word "Jesuitical."

2. Before replacing the end of the sentence with the "robbing . . . purity" text, Conyngham had originally written "striving like demons to convert one another all for the love of God."

3. See Gerald J. Griffin's poem, "The Sister of Charity," in Gerald Griffin, *The Poetical Works of Gerald Griffin* (Dublin: James Duffy, 1854), 169–71. Here Conyngham reproduces the first four lines of the poem's second and seventh stanza. An Irish poet and novelist, Gerald J. Griffin (1803–1840) probably was inspired to write this particular poem by his sister Anna's decision to join the female religious community of the same name.

CHAPTER XXVII

1. Conyngham is probably referring to battles fought in December 1864 and January 1865 for control of Fort Fisher, which guarded Wilmington, North Carolina.

2. Confederate authorities used Charleston's race course to house captured Union enlisted men at the end of the war. After the city's capture, local African Americans reburied the more than two hundred prisoners who died there and held a large parade and ceremony in their honor, which is now considered to be the first Memorial Day celebration in American history.

3. This appears to be a literary reference to the work of Irish novelist Laurence Sterne (1713–1768), *The Life and Opinions of Tristram Shandy, Gentleman.*

4. Private Samuel J. Benton of the 54th Massachusetts shot and killed Corporal William Wilson in a "private quarrel." Benton was sentenced to be hanged. The sisters' petition, it seems, contributed to Benton's sentence being commuted.

5. This was originally "1868," but Benton's trial and pardon took place in late 1865.

6. Mother Mary Teresa Barry (1814–1901) moved from Ireland to the United States at the age of three. After helping to found the Sisters of Our Lady of Mercy in Charleston, she served as Mother Superior of the Sisters of Our Lady of Mercy for most of her life. Under her guidance, the community cared for orphans, taught in parochial schools, and ran their own hospital. Before her death, the community had spread into neighboring Georgia and North Carolina.

7. Like Mother Barry, Sister Mary Xavier Dunn (1813–1887) was also born in Ireland. Devoting herself to the care of the sick throughout her life, she tirelessly cared for soldiers from both sides during the Civil War. St. Francis Xavier Hospital, named in her honor, was opened in 1882.

8. Louis Asty de Rathier DuVerge (c. 1839–1894) of the 30th Massachusetts Infantry Regiment, Company H. It is possible this incident took place after the war, as he was not made a full captain until December 2, 1865.

9. In 1864, six hundred Union prisoners were moved to Charleston by Confederate officials hoping to exchange them for a similar number of Confederate men held by the Union. The breakdown in the prisoner exchange cartel meant that the exchange never happened and in fact the Union soldiers were effectively human shields meant to discourage their troops from shelling the city. In retaliation, Secretary of War Stanton ordered six hundred Confederate soldiers rounded up from northern prisons and sent to Morris Island to discourage Confederate artillery from attacking Federal positions there. This group of southern prisoners became known as the "Immortal Six Hundred."

10. John E. Michener (1838–1879) was released on October 16, 1864, as part of an exchange for a Mississippi cavalry captain.

11. Stephen H. Ballard (1836–1890) was second lieutenant in the 6th Michigan Cavalry.

12. Thomas Jordan (1819–1895), a Virginian and West Point graduate, saw service at First Bull Run and in the western theater before being assigned to command the third military district in South Carolina in 1864.

13. Born in Ireland, Father John Moore (1834–1901) received his doctorate in theology from Urban College in Rome. He helped Father Leon Fillion administer the diocese of Charleston during Bishop Lynch's months-long absence in Europe at the end of the war. In 1877, he became the bishop of St. Augustine, Florida.

14. This was misdated originally as "1864."

15. Father Patrick O'Neil (1810–1865) was the popular Irish-born pastor of St. Patrick's Parish in Charleston from the late 1830s through most of the Civil War. O'Neil died on January 10, 1865, after contracting pneumonia on a sick call. Father Moore succeeded him as St. Patrick's pastor.

16. This paragraph was immediately followed by the sentence: "In order to make some of the following letters intelligible, I must state that the sisters made application to Congress for the compensation for the injury done their convent during the bombardment." While the placement of this statement does not make much sense, Conyngham is clearly referring to letters found earlier and later in the chapter that were compiled as a petition asking for the

U.S. Congress to compensate the sisters for damage to their orphanage. The Sisters of Mercy finally received compensation years after the war was over, although the amount granted was only part of what they had asked for from Congress (see this chapter's conclusion).

17. This may have been Thomas Young Simmons (1828–1878), captain of Company B, 27th South Carolina Infantry.

18. William Finton (c. 1837–1864) emigrated from Ireland and worked as a day laborer in Calais, Maine, before the war. Enlisting in Company A, 9th Maine Infantry, on September 22, 1861, he was wounded and captured at Fort Wagner on July 18, 1863. He eventually died of disease on December 22, 1864.

19. The Catholic church in Jackson, Mississippi, was burned by Union forces under Sherman in 1863 during Grant's campaign against Vicksburg. Finton's confession of guilt is curious, because the 9th Maine Infantry was then on assignment in South Carolina.

20. Baltimore Smith (c. 1822–1873), a carpenter from Cincinnati, Ohio, mustered into Company I of the 54th Massachusetts Colored Infantry Regiment on May 13, 1863. He was wounded and captured at the Battle of Fort Wagner on July 18, 1863, and on his parole in 1865 he was discharged for his wounds at Alexandria, Virginia.

21. William Merrill (c. 1840–1862) of Danville, New Hampshire, was a private in Company B of the 3rd New Hampshire Infantry. Captured on June 16, 1862, at the Battle of Secessionville, South Carolina, he died in Charleston on July 2.

22. This was probably Andrew J. Lawler (c. 1835–1864), a resident of Boston, Massachusetts, and an officer in the 28th Massachusetts Regiment.

23. John T. Robeson (1837–1906) served as an officer in the 7th Tennessee Cavalry (U.S. Volunteers) during the Civil War. Conyngham spelled the name as "Robison."

24. Lewis S. Payne (1819–1898).

25. This was "enemies" in the article. Major General Quincy Adams Gillmore (1825–1888) was then in command of the Department of the South and 10th Corps besieging Charleston. Conyngham spelled the name as "Gilmore."

26. Lieutenant Henry Tyson Kendall (1842–1916) was captured at the Battle of Spotsylvania Court House on May 12, 1864. Conyngham wrote the middle initial as "F."

27. Joseph V. Kendall (1844–1917) was captured on the same day as his brother Henry. Conyngham misspelled his middle initial and surname as "B. Kendal."

28. William H. Telford (c. 1840–1909). Conyngham spelled the name as "Talford."

29. This was an "A" in the manuscript.

CHAPTER XXVIII

1. Dr. Richard Richey McMeens (1820–1862). Conyngham spelled the name as "McMeenes."

2. Named after Ohio Governor William Dennison, Camp Dennison was established near Cincinnati in 1861 to train Ohio's Union soldiers. We have corrected Conyngham's misspelling "Denison" throughout the manuscript.

3. Dr. George Suckley (1830–1869). Conyngham spelled the name as "Sukely."

4. This was probably the Irish-born Dr. Abraham McMahon (1823–1905).

5. This was possibly Dr. Lincoln Ripley Stone (1832–1907), who later became surgeon of the 54th Massachusetts Colored Infantry.

6. Sister Anthony O'Connell (1814–1897), born in Limerick, Ireland, had charge of several orphanages before the Civil War. She eagerly took up hospital work during the war, becoming the leading figure in the Sisters of Charity of Cincinnati's nursing efforts. See Judith Metz, S.C., "Sister Anthony O'Connell: Angel of the Orphan, the Sick, the Wounded, and the Outcast," *U.S. Catholic Historian* 35, no. 4 (Fall 2017): 53–78.

7. General William S. Rosecrans was more commonly nicknamed "Old Rosy."

8. In 1862, Albert N. Reade (1815–1896) became the United States Sanitary Commission's chief inspector in the Department of the Cumberland. A lifelong Presbyterian, his high regard for the sisters' hospital work showed they were valued as capable nurses by many army doctors of all religious backgrounds.

CHAPTER XXIX

1. Mother Mary Jerome Ely (1810–1885) served as the superioress of the New York Sisters of Charity three times: from 1849 to 1850, 1861 to 1870, and 1876 to 1885. She was a prominent figure in Catholic education and charity in New York City throughout her lifetime.

2. Born in Ireland, Father William Starrs (1807–1873) served for many years as the vicar-general of the New York diocese and the superior of the Sisters of Charity.

3. Though a Democrat, Edwards Pierrepont (1817–1892) supported both the Union and Lincoln during the war.

4. Edwin M. Stanton (1814–1869) became the U.S. Secretary of War in 1862 after President Lincoln removed Simon Cameron from office.

5. A footnote marked with an asterisk at this point in the text reads, "These words are interlined in the original."

6. William A. Hammond.

7. McDougall (1804–1885) was a longtime surgeon of the U.S. Army. He served as medical director of the Army of the Tennessee (1862) and medical director of the Department of the East (1862–1864).

8. One of the earliest members of the Sisters of Charity of New York, the Irish-born Mary Ulrica O'Reilly (1815–1888) led the sister nurses working at St. Joseph Military Hospital from their arrival in late 1862 until May 1864 when she was reassigned to New Haven, Connecticut.

9. Born in Vermont, Frank Hastings Hamilton (1813–1886) was a renowned physician who became the medical inspector of the U.S. Army in 1863.

10. John William Severin (J. W. S.) Gouley (1832–1920) served as a surgeon in the Central Park Military Hospital. His wartime service extended from 1861 to 1864.

11. Father Maurice W. Koeder (Kaidor), O.S.B., was born in Kammern, Prussia, in 1837. Ordained in 1860, after his brief service at St. Joseph's Military Hospital he served as rector of Melrose, New York, from 1864 to 1866. Conyngham misspelled his name as "Kaider."

12. Born to Irish parents in New York City, Father Edward McGlynn (1837–1900) served as chaplain of St. Joseph's through the end of the conflict. After the war, he controversially supported public schools and the socialist teachings of Henry George, leading to his temporary excommunication from 1887 to 1892.

13. Overlooked by Ellen Jolly in her monumental study of Civil War sister nurses, Mary Prudentia Bradley entered the Sisters of Charity novitiate in 1862. She died on May 28, 1864, shortly after having professed her vows.

14. Father John B. Biretta was an Italian-born Franciscan stationed at the Sisters of Charity's Font Hill motherhouse at the beginning of the Civil War.

15. Psalm 51.

16. Born in South Carolina, Sister Mary Rosina Wightman (1825–1894) entered the Sisters of Charity of New York in 1848. In 1891, she became the community's mother general, serving for two-and-a-half years. Here Conyngham corrected the misspelling "Sr. M. Rosina Whitman" that was in the original newspaper article.

17. Here Conyngham corrected the misspelling "Dr. Ganley" that was in the original newspaper article.

18. Here Conyngham corrected the misspelling "Dr. Ganley" that was in the original newspaper article.

19. John J. Milhau, Jr. (1828–1891) became a surgeon in the U.S. Army in 1851. His extensive wartime service included the Seven Days Battles, the Second Battle of Bull Run, and Gettysburg.

20. Born in Lurgan, Ireland, Charles Devlin (1805–1881) immigrated to New York in his late twenties and soon made a name for himself as a contractor and Democratic political operative.

21. This Thanksgiving celebration must have taken place in 1862 as it mentions the hospital's first head surgeon, Dr. Hamilton, who received a new assignment after only a few months. For more on this Thanksgiving feast and the sisters' strained relationship with Hamilton, see Marie de Lourdes Walsh, *The Sisters of Charity of New York, 1809–1959* (New York: Fordham University Press, 1960), 171–73.

22. This is perhaps a reference to Dr. David E. Tully (1818–1916), a Presbyterian and chaplain to the 77th New York Infantry.

23. Note from Conyngham: "Dr. Clements had brain fever, but is now, I believe, quite established in health."

24. Originally misspelled *firlefauz* in the newspaper; *firlefanz* is a German word for showy but worthless finery.

25. A *fata morgana* is a reference to an optical illusion or a mirage.

26. This is perhaps a reference to sister nurse Mary Scholastica Quinn or Ann Cecilia Nealis. Both served during the war as members of the Sisters of Charity of New York.

27. Note in newspaper article: "'Louy' was the name of his ring dove."

28. Private John Schiffler was badly wounded near Currituck, North Carolina, in July 1863. Sent north to St. Joseph's Hospital in November, he was finally discharged from the sisters' care on September 1, 1864. Conyngham misspelled his name as "Shaffler."

29. Beginning with this sentence, the rest of the chapter is a handwritten manuscript in the hand of the main writer of the *Soldiers of the Cross* manuscript.

30. Conyngham's note: "This poor man meditated suicide, but his mind was soon relieved from such gloomy thoughts by the sisters."

31. Portions of this paragraph are badly damaged in the original manuscript. The missing words have been supplied from the twentieth-century typescript.

32. Conyngham continued his narrative by attaching a newspaper article titled "The Cradle of Charity," which had appeared in a New York newspaper. As it relates the postwar history of the Sisters of Charity and not their Civil War service, it has been omitted.

CHAPTER XXX

1. Mother Mary Ignatius Walker, born in New York, became the superior of the Sisters of Mercy, St. Louis, on July 7, 1868, taking over from Mother Mary de Pazzi. Mother Ignatius served in this role for only a year until she left to establish a new community in Louisville, Kentucky. Thus Conyngham's initial research and writing of this chapter occurred sometime between 1868 and 1869 (Mary Isidore Lennon, *Milestones of Mercy: Story of the Sisters of Mercy in St. Louis, 1856–1956* [Milwaukee: Bruce Press, 1957], 247–48).

2. The Society of St. Vincent De Paul was founded in 1833 in France by Frederic Ozanam. Its members dedicate themselves to direct service to the poor. By 1845, the first chapter in the United States was established in St. Louis. Local chapters provided aid to poor families whose men had enlisted in the Union army, and Vincentians paid regular visits to army camps and hospitals to help care for the sick, write letters, or distribute Catholic reading material to the men. In 1861, the Society produced the *Manual of the Christian Soldier*, a book designed to help Catholic soldiers practice their faith in the field (Daniel T. McColgan, *A Century of Charity: The First One Hundred Years of the Society of St. Vincent De Paul in the United States*, vol. 1 [Milwaukee: Bruce Publishing, 1951], 240–42).

3. The philanthropists mentioned are believed to be John E. Yore (c. 1831–1867) and Richard Francis Barry (c. 1817–1892). In 1861, the two were instrumental in founding a soup kitchen located near Immaculate Conception Church in St. Louis. The soup kitchen was under the auspices of the Sisters of Mercy and the St. Vincent de Paul Society. Both Barry and Yore were officers in the society. Conyngham spelled Yore's name as "York."

4. Conyngham meant a *lettre de cachet*, or an order for someone's arrest and imprisonment.

5. Conyngham may be referring to the Sisters of Charity of Saint Augustine, a French community that sent four of its members to run a hospital in the diocese of Cleveland, Ohio, in 1851.

6. This is "weakly" in the manuscript.

CHAPTER XXXI

1. Born in County Monaghan, Ireland, Mother Augustine [Ellen] MacKenna (1819–1883) moved with her family to America after the Irish Potato Famine. She received her habit from Archbishop John Hughes in 1856.

2. A graduate of West Point and a career army officer, John G. Foster (1823–1874) was a veteran of the Mexican War. His capture of Fort Macon led to his promotion as commander of the Department of North Carolina in 1862.

3. Misspelled by Conyngham as "Newberne" or "New Berne," the spelling "New Bern" has been used throughout.

4. Jabez Baxter Upham (1820–1902), born in Claremont, New Hampshire, studied medicine at Harvard and in Europe prior to the outbreak of the Civil War. After serving at the hospital with the sisters, he resumed medical practice in Boston before moving to New York City.

5. An extra "was" that was in the manuscript has been deleted here.

6. Conyngham is referring to popular anti-Catholic convent tales then widely in print in antebellum America. The most infamous such account was *Awful Disclosures of Maria Monk, or, The Hidden Secrets of a Nun's Life in a Convent Exposed* (1836), an alleged true account of sin, depravity, and murder said to have taken place in a Canadian convent. Although its author, Maria Monk, was exposed as a fraud, her story and other similar convent narratives were still very popular and widely accepted as accurate by many Protestant Americans.

7. Here Conyngham later added, but then deleted, the phrase: "They lived and succeeded by the force of their good and gentle example."

CHAPTER XXXII

1. This word is rendered "it" in the manuscript.

2. There is no record of the Sisters of Mercy of New York serving at Gettysburg. Indeed, they had already left their hospital in New Bern, North

Carolina, and returned home by May 1863. The anecdote may actually have come secondhand from the Daughters of Charity, whose nearby convent in Emmitsburg allowed them to send a number of sisters to care for the wounded after the battle.

3. The word "not" was deleted here for clarity.

4. Mustered into service at Albany, New York, in December 1861, the Rocket Battalion's two companies served in North Carolina in 1862. When the unit's rocket artillery proved ineffective, it was disbanded with companies A and B becoming the 23rd and 24th New York Independent Battery Light Artillery respectively.

5. This name was added by Conyngham as part of his editing process. No soldier named Arthur matching this description could be found in either of the Rocket Battalion's two companies.

6. Given that this letter is written from Lowell, Massachusetts, and the young soldier's father said he was a member of the 44th, this soldier was probably Private Charles Augustus Bradt (1844–1863), a member of Company C of the 44th Massachusetts Infantry. His nine-month regiment was stationed in the Department of North Carolina, where he fell ill and died of typhoid fever while under the sisters' care on February 19, 1863.

7. The soldier was Charles Pullin (c. 1833–1862) of Harnedsville, Pennsylvania, who enlisted in October 1861 as a corporal in Company H of the 85th Pennsylvania Infantry Regiment. Pullin died of battle wounds at Stanley Hospital on December 14, 1862.

8. A postscript deleted from the manuscript read:

> "I will give you my address.
> Direct ~~those~~ to
> Anna Pullin
> Harnedsville
> Somerset County
> Pennsylvania."

9. Charles Bayard Springer (1836–1862) enlisted as a sergeant in the 9th New Jersey Infantry, Co. I, in October 1861. Promoted to lieutenant the following March, he died of bilious fever at Hammond General Hospital on July 31, 1862.

10. The postscript was deleted from the manuscript by Conyngham. It read: "N.B. You will please to write as soon as possible and I will send a handsome thanks. Direct as before. Bridgeport Glincester Co New Jersey."

CHAPTER XXXIII

1. A note at the top of the manuscript reads, "These are her Sketches of the Sisters of the Holy Cross. The other furnished by the Nuns themselves." While the person "her" refers to is unclear, the "other" may refer to a three-chapter-long draft account of the Holy Cross Sisters during the war addressed in the introduction to this chapter.

2. Here Conyngham quotes the penultimate stanza in Griffin's poem "The Sister of Charity."

3. According to most accounts, it was Governor Morton who first approached Father Sorin and Mother Angela about sending sisters to nurse the Union wounded. Receiving his request on October 21, Mother Angela took five other Sisters of the Holy Cross with her to Cairo, Illinois, where General Grant gave her further instructions about where her sisters were most needed.

4. Eliza Maria Gillespie (1824–1887) was in religion known as Mother Mary of St. Angela or popularly as "Mother Angela."

5. Most sources credit the Sisters of the Holy Cross with sixty-three Civil War nurses. However, it is quite possible that, just like the Daughters of Charity, there were members of the community who nursed soldiers for a time without official government recognition.

6. This was probably James Simons, the medical director of the Department of Cairo, Illinois.

7. The Battle of Belmont (November 7, 1861), fought in Mississippi County, Missouri, was General Grant's first real experience of combat in the Civil War.

8. Dr. Edward C. Franklin (1822–1885) was medical director of the Mound City, Illinois, hospital.

9. William H. Osborn (1820–1894) served as the Illinois Central's president through the end of the Civil War.

10. Perhaps a reference to Sister Mary Francis de Paul Sullivan, born in County Cork, Ireland, and one of the original group of Holy Cross Sisters sent to attend Federal wounded and sick soldiers.

11. The battle occurred from February 12 to 16, 1862, near the border between Tennessee and Kentucky.

12. *Hors de combat* is a French term literally meaning "outside the fight," referring to combatants incapable of fighting.

13. The original unclear word here appeared to be "treats" although "traits" makes more sense in context.

14. The Sisters of the Holy Cross wore a series of beads (similar to the rosary) to aid in praying the chaplet of the Seven Dolors. Each section of seven beads represented one of the sorrows of the Blessed Virgin Mary.

15. More familiarly known as the Battle of Shiloh (April 6–7, 1862), this two-day fight badly bloodied General Grant's army, which suffered over thirteen thousand casualties. Many of the over eight thousand wounded men were sent to Mound City, where the sisters were hard-pressed to care for them all in the wake of the war's bloodiest battle to that time.

16. This was probably Edmund C. Rogers, an 1853 graduate of Albany Medical College who served as an assistant surgeon in the 80th Illinois Infantry Regiment.

17. "Low Sunday" is a term for the first Sunday after Easter.

CHAPTER XXXIV

1. This version of this chapter is a shortened version of a previous draft's two chapters of material. Many anecdotes were eliminated; some substantial changes were made to various passages, especially about the Holy Cross Sisters in Washington, DC; and all mention of the Holy Cross Sisters on the *Red Rover* was removed.

2. Sister Mary Fidelis Bridget Lawler, born in Ireland in 1831, was the first of two Holy Cross sisters to die while nursing the wounded and sick during the war.

3. The Chapel of Loretto was built on the campus of Saint Mary's in 1859.

4. This was Bishop Martin J. Spalding of Louisville, Kentucky.

5. This was probably Dr. James F. Weeds (1832–1875).

6. Sister Mary Elise O'Brien was born in Ireland in 1838. She died on July 9, 1862, when she was only in her second year as a novice.

7. The following sentence was deleted from the manuscript: "Like Sister Fidelis she was buried at Notre Dame St. Mary's, where still their modest graves may still be seen."

8. This was the German-born Dr. John G. F. Holston (1809–1874). Conyngham rendered the name as "Holstern."

9. This was the Battle of Fort Charles fought on June 17, 1862, near St. Charles, Arkansas. Colonel Graham N. Fitch (1809–1892), who had served in the House of Representatives and Senate before the war, helped lead this combined Union navy and army operation whose purpose was to gain con-

trol of the White River. Although the operation was successful, the U.S.S. *Mound City*'s steam drum exploded, badly scalding its commander and killing over one hundred Union sailors.

10.   Joseph Fry (1826–1873) was a graduate of the Naval Academy at Annapolis. After serving in the antebellum navy, he resigned his commission when his adopted state of Louisiana seceded from the Union in January 1861. Despite his capture at Fort Charles, he returned to Confederate service and served along the Gulf Coast until the end of the war. A note in the manuscript completes his story: "The Confederate officer, Colonel Fry, was the Captain Fry of the Virginius, who was captured in November 1873 by the Spanish gun boat [the *Tornado*] and shot by order of General [Juan N.] Burriel at Santiago de Cuba."

11.   Augustus Henry Kilty (1807–1879) was a long-serving veteran of the antebellum U.S. Navy by the time of the Civil War. Although he lost his left arm as a result of his wounds from the Battle of Fort Charles, Kilty survived the war, serving as the commandant of the Norfolk Navy Yard before retiring with the rank of rear admiral in 1870.

12.   A marginal note in the manuscript reads: "Captain Fry died an exemplary Catholic and a most edifying death when shot at Santiago. If the above statement made by the sister herself, that when [in the] hospital he was not a Catholic be correct, he must have subsequently become a convert."

13.   Born in Ireland, Francis Noel Burke (1830–1907) received his medical degree from the Medical College of Ohio in 1856.

14.   Mary Augusta Anderson (1830–1907) was born in Alexandria, Virginia, and entered the Sisters of the Holy Cross in 1854. She replaced Mother Angela as the head of St. Mary's Academy and in 1882 became the first superior general of the Sisters of the Holy Cross. In 1894, she sent a questionnaire to surviving Holy Cross Sisters who had been nurses during the war, asking them for their memories of their Civil War service. Their responses can be found at the archives of Saint Mary's College.

15.   This was "1863" in the manuscript.

16.   In 1863, the navy converted the Commercial Hotel in Memphis into the Pinkney Hospital, named in honor of Union naval surgeon Ninian Pinkney. The Sisters of the Holy Cross helped staff this institution as well as the U.S.S. *Red Rover*, a hospital ship ferrying wounded Union soldiers up and down the Mississippi from January 1863 until December 1864. Moored at Mound City, the ship continued to house wounded men until November 1865. About 2,500 men were brought on board the *Red Rover* during its wartime career, and 90 percent of the patients recovered from their wounds

or illness (M. Georgia Costin, *Priceless Spirit: A History of the Sisters of the Holy Cross, 1841–1893* [Notre Dame, IN: University of Notre Dame Press, 1994], 186–87).

17. Due to damage to the manuscript page, sections of this paragraph in brackets were supplied from a previous draft of this chapter.

18. A previous draft of this chapter reveals that this hospital had been built to spare the Church of St. Aloysius, a Jesuit-run parish, from being turned into a hospital by the federal government. See George M. Anderson, S.J., "Bernardine Wiget, S.J., and the St. Aloysius Civil War Hospital in Washington, D.C.," *Catholic Historical Review* 76 (October 1990): 734–64.

Selected Bibliography

GENERAL REFERENCE WORKS

Herbermann, Charles George, ed. *The Catholic Encyclopedia: An International Work of Reference on the Constitution, Doctrine, Discipline, and History of the Catholic Church*. 15 vols. New York: Robert Appleton Company, 1907–12. http://www.newadvent.org/cathen/.

The Metropolitan Catholic Almanac and Laity's Directory. Baltimore: Fielding Lucas, John Murphy, etc., various years, 1850–1861.

Sadlier's Catholic Directory, Almanac, and Ordo. New York: D. J. Sadlier, various years, 1864–1896.

Wagner, Margaret E., Gary W. Gallagher, and Paul Finkelman. *The Library of Congress Civil War Desk Reference*. New York: Simon & Schuster, 2002.

Warner, Ezra J. *Generals in Blue: Lives of the Union Commanders*. Baton Rouge: Louisiana State University Press, 2013.

———. *Generals in Gray: Lives of the Confederate Commanders*. Baton Rouge: Louisiana State University Press, 2013.

ONLINE DATABASES

American Civil War Research Database. Historical Data Systems. Accessed May 1, 2018. http://www.civilwardata.com/.

"Civil War (1861–1865) Military Records." Ancestry.com. Accessed May 1, 2018. https://www.ancestry.com/cs/civilwarrecords.

"Civil War Records." Fold3 by Ancestry. Accessed May 1, 2018. https://www.fold3.com/browse/249/.

"The Civil War Soldiers and Sailors System." National Park Service. Accessed May 1, 2018. https://www.nps.gov/civilwar/soldiers-and-sailors-database .htm.

The Hierarchy of the Catholic Church. David M. Cheney. Accessed May 1, 2018. http://www.catholic-hierarchy.org/.

"Union Civil War Surgeons." Ruth Lilly Medical Library at the Indiana University School of Medicine. Accessed May 1, 2018. http://www.biblio server.com/19centurydocs/index.php.

CATHOLICS AND THE CIVIL WAR

Blied, Benjamin J. *Catholics and the Civil War.* Milwaukee: St. Francis Seminary Press, 1945.

Bruce, Susannah Ural. *The Harp and the Eagle: Irish-American Volunteers and the Union Army, 1861–1865.* New York: New York University Press, 2006.

Conyngham, David Power. *The Irish Brigade and its Campaigns.* Edited by Lawrence Frederick Kohl. New York: William McSorley, 1867. Reprint, New York: Fordham University Press, 1994.

Gleeson, David T. "For God, Erin, and Carolina: Irish Catholics in the Confederacy." In *The Green and the Gray: The Irish in the Confederate States of America,* 150–86. Chapel Hill: University of North Carolina Press, 2013.

Hope, Arthur J., C.S.C. *Notre Dame: One Hundred Years.* Notre Dame, IN: University of Notre Dame Press, 1943.

Kurtz, William B. *Excommunicated from the Union: How the Civil War Created a Separate Catholic America.* New York: Fordham University Press, 2016.

Longley, Max. *For the Union and the Catholic Church: Four Converts in the Civil War.* Jefferson, NC: McFarland & Company, 2015.

Macnamara, Daniel George. *The History of the Ninth Regiment, Massachusetts Volunteer Infantry.* Boston: E. B. Stillings, 1899.

Miller, Randall M. "Catholic Religion, Irish Ethnicity, and the Civil War." In *Religion and the American Civil War,* edited by Randall M. Miller, Harry S. Stout, and Charles Reagan Wilson, 261–96. New York: Oxford University Press, 1998.

Miller, Robert J. *Both Prayed to the Same God: Religion and Faith In the American Civil War.* Lanham, MD: Lexington Books, 2007.

Rable, George C. *God's Almost Chosen Peoples: A Religious History of the American Civil War.* Chapel Hill: University of North Carolina Press, 2010.

Schmidt, James M. *Notre Dame and the Civil War: Marching Onward to Victory.* Charleston, SC: The History Press, 2010.

Sorin, Edward, C.S.C. *The Chronicles of Notre Dame du Lac.* Edited by James T. Connelly. Notre Dame, IN: University of Notre Dame Press, 1992.

CIVIL WAR CHAPLAINCY AND CHAPLAINS

Armstrong, Warren B. *For Courageous Fighting and Confident Dying: Union Chaplains in the Civil War.* Lawrence, KS: University Press of Kansas, 1998.

Brinsfield, John W., William C. Davis, Benedict Maryniak, and James I. Robertson, Jr., eds. *Faith in the Fight: Civil War Chaplains.* Mechanicsburg, PA: Stackpole Books, 2003.

Buckley, Cornelius M., ed. *A Frenchman, A Chaplain, A Rebel: The War Letters of Pere Louis-Hippolyte Gache, S.J.* Chicago: Loyola University Press, 1981.

Corby, William, C.S.C. *Memoirs of Chaplain Life: Three Years with the Irish Brigade in the Army of the Potomac.* Notre Dame, IN: "Scholastic" Press, 1893. Reprinted and edited by Lawrence Frederick Kohl. New York: Fordham University Press, 1992.

Fabun, Sean. "Catholic Chaplains in the Civil War." *Catholic Historical Review* 99, no. 4 (October 2013): 675–702.

Germain, Aidan H. "Catholic Military and Naval Chaplains, 1776–1917." PhD diss., Catholic University of America, 1929.

Hayes, Patrick J., ed. *The Civil War Diary of Father James Sheeran: Confederate Chaplain and Redemptorist.* Washington, DC: Catholic University of America Press, 2016.

McAvoy, Thomas T. "Peter Paul Cooney, Chaplain of Indiana's Irish Regiment." *Journal of the American-Irish Historical Society* 30 (1932): 97–102.

Shattuck, Gardiner H., Jr. "Holy Joes: The Experience of Clergy in the Armies." In *A Shield and Hiding Place: The Religious Life of the Civil War Armies,* 51–72. Macon, GA: Mercer University Press, 1987.

Sheeran, James B., C.Ss.R. *Confederate Chaplain: A War Journal.* Edited by Joseph T. Durkin. Milwaukee: Bruce Publishing, 1960.

NURSES, WOMEN RELIGIOUS, AND THE CIVIL WAR

Barton, George. *Angels of the Battlefield: A History of the Labors of the Catholic Sisterhoods in the Late Civil War.* Philadelphia: Catholic Art Publishing, 1897.

Costin, M. Georgia. *Priceless Spirit: A History of the Sisters of the Holy Cross, 1841–1893.* Notre Dame, IN: University of Notre Dame Press, 1994.

Howe, Barbara J., and Margaret A. Brennan. "The Sisters of St. Joseph in Wheeling, West Virginia, During the Civil War." *U.S. Catholic Historian* 31, no. 1 (Winter 2013): 21–49.

Jolly, Ellen Ryan. *Nuns of the Battlefield.* Providence, RI: Providence Visitor Press, 1927.

Maher, Mary Denis. *To Bind Up the Wounds: Catholic Sister Nurses in the U.S. Civil War.* New York: Greenwood Press, 1989.

McNeil, Betty Ann, D.C. *Balm of Hope: Charity Afire Impels Daughters of Charity to Civil War Nursing.* Chicago: DePaul University Vincentian Studies Institute, 2015.

Metz, Judith, S.C. "Sister Anthony O'Connell: Angel of the Orphan, the Sick, the Wounded, and the Outcast." *U.S. Catholic Historian* 35, no. 4 (Fall 2017).

———, ed. *Sisters of Charity of Cincinnati in the Civil War: The Love of Christ Urges Us.* Cincinnati: Sisters of Charity of Cincinnati, 2012.

Schultz, Jane E. *Women at the Front: Hospital Workers in Civil War America.* Chapel Hill: University of North Carolina Press, 2004.

Sweeney, Helen. *The Golden Milestone, 1846–1896: Fifty Years of Loving Labor among the Poor and Suffering by the Sisters of Mercy of New York City.* New York: Benziger Brothers, 1896.

Wall, Barbra Mann. "Grace Under Pressure: The Nursing Sisters of the Holy Cross, 1861–1865." *Nursing History Review* 1 (1993): 71–87.

———. *Unlikely Entrepreneurs: Catholic Sisters and the Hospital Marketplace, 1865–1925.* Columbus: Ohio State University Press, 2005.

Index

Entries in bold are biographical entries supplied by the editors.

absolution on the battlefield
  given by Father Corby at Gettysburg, xiv, 234
  given by Father Gillen, 189, 194, 199–200
  given by Father Ouellet (Willett), 175
  given by Father Trecy at Stones River, 60
African Americans, 44, 64, 72, 105, 157, 336, 357, 395, 455n.10
  in U.S. Army (U.S. Colored Troops), 335, 341–43, 474n.2 (chapter XXVII)
Alabama troops (CSA)
  3rd Infantry, 440n.18
  4th Cavalry, 446n.7
  5th Infantry, 313
  8th Infantry, 291, 469n.12
alcohol
  abuse of, 194, 314, 341
  chaplains promote abstinence from, 161, 216
Anderson, Sister Mary Augusta, 429, **485n.14**
Andrew, Governor John A., 144, 151, **453n.5**

anti-Catholicism, xv–xvi, 156
  lessened by the war, 129–30, 178, 251–52, 256–57, 395–96, 424–35
  Maria Monk, 481n.6 (chapter XXXI)
  in Massachusetts, 142–43, 453nn.1–2
anti-Protestantism
  of Conyngham, xv–xvi
  of Father Sheeran, **467n.11**
Army of Northern Virginia, 302, 463n.12, 466n.3, 467n.15, 472n.5
Army of the Cumberland, 67, 132, 134, 214, 228, 358
Army of the Mississippi, 85
Army of the Potomac, 21, 30, 152, 182, 188, 190, 197, 201, 234, 240
Army of the Tennessee (CSA), 445n.16
Army of the Tennessee (USA), 30, 478n.7
Atlanta Campaign, xv, 135–37, 230
Augur, General Christopher C., **442n.40**
  letter from, 26–27

Babineau, Athanase, 266, **466n.11**
Babineau, Charles V., 266, **466n.11**
Babineau, Theodore, 266, **466n.11**
Ballard, Stephen H., 339–40, **475n.11**

Banks, General Nathaniel, 193

Bannon, Father John, 114, **451nn.5–6**
(**chapter VII**)

baptism, sacrament of, 60, 68, 236,
252, 381, 416, 459n.32, 467n.11
Father Brady, 229–30
Father Carrier, 109
Father Christy, 68, 123, 131–32
Father Gache, 251–56
Father Sheeran, 273, 308, 467n.11
Father Trecy, 60, 68–69, 73, 75
Sisters of Mercy, Charleston, 335, 343
Sisters of Mercy, New York, 394–95
Sisters of Mercy, St. Louis, 381–82,
384–86
Sisters of the Holy Cross, 416–18

Barry, Colonel William F., **442n.37**
letter from, 24–25

Barry, Mother Mary Teresa, **330**, 335,
346, **351**, **474n.6**

Barry, Richard Francis, 382, **480n.3**

Beauregard, General Pierre Gustave
Toutant, 45, 237–38, 303, 340,
443n.45
letter from, 27–29

Becker, Father Thomas A. A., 280,
468n.24

Bedini, Archbishop Gaetano, 165,
455n.3

Belmont, Battle of, 412, 429, 483n.7

Bergrath, Father Innocent A., **205–6**,
208, 460n.8
prevented by his bishop from joining the army, 206–7
serves troops on both sides in Eastern Tennessee, 207–8

Bickham, William D., 61

Biretta, Father John B., 370, **478n.14**

Bixby, Doctor George H., 97–98,
450n.6

Blair, General Frank Preston, Jr., 90,
105, 109, 115, 117, **450n.22**

Bliemel, Father Emmeran, O.S.B., 18,
299, **441n.24**, 470n.6

Boglioli, Father Charles, C.M., 18,
441n.20

Bolles, Miss
conversion of, 108–9

Bonner, Stephen Purcell, 102, **451n.1**
(**chapter VI**)

Bourget, Julian P., 16, 84, **449n.6**,
463n.1

Bradley, Sister Mary Prudentia,
369–70, **478n.13**

Bradt, Private Charles Augustus, 404,
482n.6

Brady, Father Thomas, 17, **225–26**, **231**
death of, 231
hospital service in Chattanooga,
230
hostility of southern Catholics
toward, 227–28
joins other chaplains in Chattanooga, 229

Bragg, General Braxton, 45, 63, 69–70,
73, 75, 207, 216, 298, **445n.16**

Brown, Father Henry V., 17, **440n.15**

Buell, Don Carlos, 47–48, 216, **445n.21**

Buford, General John, 86

Bull Run, First Battle of, 124, 151, 154,
156, 188–90, 200, 234, 270

Bull Run, Second Battle of, 276–78

Burke, Doctor Francis N., 428, **485n.13**

Burnside, General Ambrose E., 19–20,
208, 391, **441n.29**

Butler, General Benjamin F., 148, 270,
442n.41
praises Catholic chaplains, xvii, 27,
235

Caffey, Private Thomas E. (English
Combatant), 463n.2, **463n.6**
description of chaplains in Confederate service, 236–38

Camp Dennison, Ohio, 355, 477n.2

Carius, Father Anthony, 18, 299, **441n.22, 470n.8**

Carrier, Father Joseph C., C.S.C., 16, **79–80, 119–20,** 448n.1
  arrives at Vicksburg, 87–90
  friend's sketch of, 81–83
  incompleteness of diary, 83, 110
  letters to Father Sorin, 112–13, 116–19
  meets General Grant, 94–96
  praise for, 84–85

Casey, Doctor Newton R., 84, **449n.7**

Cass, Colonel Thomas, 144, 148, **453n.4**

Catholic chaplains
  neglect in Civil War scholarship, xi, xiv, 435n.2
  overview and numbers of, xii
  stop soldiers' gambling, 158–59, 174, 286

Catholic sisters
  equal treatment of all soldiers, 326, 333, 381, 393
  lessen prejudice among Protestants, 324–26, 395–99
  neglect in Civil War scholarship, xi, xiv, 435n.2
  overview and numbers of, xii–xiii
  reluctance to help Conyngham, 15–16
  role in conversion of soldiers, 255–56, 381–82

Chancellorsville, Battle of, xv, 244, 293–95, 438n.17

Chatard, Sister Juliana, 257, **465n.12**

Cheatham, General Benjamin F., 63, **447n.22**

Chickamauga, Battle of, 75–76, 131, 229, 448n.17, 460n.8

Christy, Father Richard C., 16, 59–60, 68, **121–22,** 138, 229, 453n.19
  at Chickamauga and Chattanooga, 131–32

nearly drowns, 127–28, 135–36
  ordination date, 452n.4
  reported absent without leave, 132–34, 452n.1
  at Stones River, 128–29

Cleburne, General Patrick R., 63, **447n.21**

Collins, Father Edward, 355

confession, sacrament of, 52, 75, 189, 191, 238, 240, 242, 305

Confiteor, 60, 446n.16

Father Bergrath, 207

Father Brady, 227

Father Carrier, 86, 92–94, 96–98, 101–3, 109, 113

Father Christy, 132

Father Cooney, 214–15

Father Corby, 238, 240, 242–44

Father Egan, 182–84

Father Gache, 251–53, 260–61

Father Gillen, 188–92, 194, 196

Father Heuzé, 266

Father Ouellet (Willett), 174–75

Father Scully, 142, 153–57, 189

Father Sheeran, 271, 273, 280, 283–87, 289–90, 299–300, 305–6, 308, 314, 316, 318

Father Tissot, 166–67

Father Trecy, 51–52, 57–58, 60, 62, 75

Connecticut troops
  7th Infantry, 343

conversions, 33, 108–9, 129, 131, 167, 178, 251, 297, 305, 307, 326, 395, 417–18

Conyngham, David Power
  apologetic tone and message of, xvi–xvii, 13–14
  biography of, **xiv–xviii,** 437n.12
  solicits additional information in *The Pilot* for his work, 354

Cook, Major McKinney L., 107–10, **451n.4 (chapter VI)**

Cooney, Father Peter Paul, C.S.C., 16,
61, 129, **211–12, 223–24,** 229
promotes temperance, 216
as regiment's banker, 216–18
says Mass before Stones River, 59
soldiers' regard for, 213–14

Corby, Father William, C.S.C., xiii–
xiv, 16, **233–34, 245–46, 436n.8,**
444n.2, 456n.4 (chapter XII)
celebrates Christmas Midnight
Mass (1861), 239
resigns due to poor health, 245
shot at while helping wounded at
Fredericksburg, 244

Corcoran, General Michael, 151, 154,
195, 198, 234, **454n.15**

Corcoran Legion, 23, 188, 197–98, 245,
454n.15, 459n.31. *See also* Gillen,
Father Paul E.; New York troops,
155th Infantry, 164th Infantry,
170th Infantry, 175th Infantry,
182nd Infantry

Corinth, Battle of (October 1862),
54–56, **446n.11**

Cornette, Father Andrew, S.J., 17,
441n.19

Cornyn, Doctor Florence M., 93,
450n.2

Costello, Father Michael A., 281, 319,
468n.25

Couch, General Darius, 192, **457n.7**
(chapter XIV)

Cretin, Bishop Joseph, 79, 82

Crittenden, General Thomas L., 75,
220, **448n.16**

Cullen, Cardinal Paul, 169, **456n.9**

Dana, Captain James Jackson, 193,
457n.10

Daughters of Charity (Emmitsburg,
Maryland), 14, **437n.12, 467n.19,**
472n.6, 481n.2 (chapter XXXII)

Davis, President Jefferson, 156, 290,
471n.22

De Camp, Doctor Samuel Grandin
Johnston, **443n.50**
letter from, 32–33

de Chaignon, Father Anthony, S.J., 18,
441n.26

Deserted House, Battle of, 199

Devens, Colonel Charles, Jr., 193, 195,
458n.14

Devlin, Charles, 372, **479n.20**

Dillon, Father James M., C.S.C., 16,
188, 198–99, 239, **459nn.26–27,**
459n.29

d'Orléans, Francois, Prince de
Joinville, 167, **455n.4**

Dranesville, Battle of, 196, **458n.23**

Dufficy, Major John P., 222

Dufort, Father, 300

Duncan, Father William H., 298,
470n.5

Dunn, Sister Mary Xavier, 335–37,
343–44, 347, **475n.7**

DuVerge, Louis Atsy de Rathier, 336,
475n.8

Dwyer, Doctor John, 34, 188, **443n.55**
letter from, 197–200, **458n.24**

Early, General Jubal A., 310–17, **472n.5**

Egan, Father Constantine L., O.P., 17,
181–82, 185
cares for wounded, 185
prepares souls of condemned
soldiers, 182–83
school of logic, 184

Elder, Bishop William Henry, 106, 263,
451n.3 (chapter VI)

Ely, Mother Mary Jerome, 364–65, 374,
376, **477n.1 (chapter XXIX)**

Ewell, General Richard S., 271, 274–76,
296–97, 305, 307, 309, **466n.3,**
471n.21

Ewing, Captain Charles, 86, 88–89, **449n.13**

Ewing, General Hugh, 86, 88–94, 96, 99, 102–3, 111, 113–19, **449n.13**

Ewing, General Thomas, Jr., **449n.13**

Fillion, Father Leon, 301–3, 305, 340, 350, **471n.17**, 475n.13

Finton, William, 342–43, **476nn.18–19**

Fitzgibbon, Captain Thomas C., 69, **447n.3**

Fitzpatrick, Bishop John B., 144, 148, **453n.6**

Fordham University (St. John's College), 88, 163–64, 170–71

Fort Cass, 152

Fort Charles, Battle of, 425, 484n.9, 484nn.10–11

Fort Corcoran, 152, 189–90

Fort Donelson, Battle of, 41, 414, 483n.11

Fort Fisher, 331, 474n.1 (chapter XXVII)

Fort McHenry, 318, 473n.23

Fort Monroe, 148, 158

Fort Union, 40, 444n.7

Foster, General John G., 176, 391–92, 394, **481n.2** (chapter XXXI)

Fourteenth Army Corps. *See* Army of the Cumberland

Foxe's Book of Martyrs, 125, 452n.8 (chapter VIII)

Franklin, Battle of, 76, 220

Franklin, Doctor Edward C., 412, 419, **483n.8**

Fredericksburg, Battle of, 243–44, 288–89

Fry, Colonel Joseph, 425–28, **485n.10**, **485n.12**

Fusseder, Father Francis, 61, 229, **446n.17**, **462n.4**

Gache, Louis-Hippolyte, S.J., 17, **249–50**, **261**
as chaplain to Federal prisoners, 258–61
describes war in private letters, 253–61
joins the army, 250–51
lessens prejudice in army, 251–53
praise for Catholic sisters, 256–58

Gallagher, Father Hugh Patrick, 123, **452n.3**

Gallitzin, Father Demetrius A., 123, **452n.2**

Garesché, Julius P., 58–59, 192–93, **446n.15**

Garland, Bishop Francis X., 300, **471n.16**

Garretty, Captain Michael, 194, **458n.16**

Georgetown University (College), 87, 467n.20

Georgia troops (CSA)
39th Infantry, 445n.18

Germans, 183, 206, 227, 251, 373–76, 484n.8
Catholic, 102, 473n.22
See also Bergrath, Father Innocent A.

Gillen, Father Paul E., C.S.C., 16, **187–88**, **204**
absolution before battle, 189, 191
at Ball's Bluff, 194–95
bravery of, 197
death of, 203
door-to-door salesman, 187
joins army, 189
newspaper obituaries, 200–203
unique mode of travel, 193, 199, 457n.11

Gillespie, Doctor Charles B., 34, 122, 124, 130, **443n.56**, 452n.6

Gillespie, Father Neal Henry, C.S.C., 409

Gillespie, Mother Angela (Eliza Maria), 409–10, 412–13, 419, 421–22, 428–30, **483nn.3–4**

Gillmore, General Quincy Adams, 345, **476n.25**

Gleason, Miss Mary, 299–303, **470n.10**

Goddard, Calvin, 68, **447n.1**

Gouley, Doctor John W. S., 368, 371, **478n.10**

Grand Army of the Republic (GAR), 161, 224, 246

Granger, Father Alexis, C.S.C., 85, **449n.12**

Grant, General Ulysses S., 126, 228, 245, 308, 310, 448, **449n.4**, 483n.7, 484n.15
and the Sisters of the Holy Cross, 410, 412, 483n.3
at Vicksburg, xvi, 80, 83–86, 89–90, 94, 96, 101, 103, 107, 111, 113

Griffin, Gerald (poet), 411, **474n.3** (chapter XXVI), 483n.2

Guiney, Colonel Patrick R., 184, **457n.7 (chapter XIII)**

Halpen, Brother Denis, C.S.C., 318–19, **473n.24**

Halpin, Captain William, 47, **445nn.18–20**

Hamilton, Doctor Frank H., 368, 373, **478n.9, 479n.21**

Hamilton, Father William J., 299, **470n.9**

Hammond, Surgeon General William A., xvi, **443n.49**
letter from, 31

Hancock, General Winfield Scott, **442n.35**
letter from, 23–24

Hardie, Assistant Adjutant General James Allen, 182, **456n.1 (chapter XIII)**

Hays, General Harry T., 28, **442n.42**

Hébert, Amede A., 266, **465n.9**

Hébert, General, 266, **465n.9**

Heuzé, Father Charles P., 114, 263, 267, 451n.2 (chapter VII)
anti-Yankee sentiment, 465nn.2–3, 465n.6
describes bombardment of Vicksburg, 264–65
gives last rites to dying Catholic soldiers, 265–66

Hill, General Ambrose P., 275, 281, **467n.15**

Hinckley, John, 159–60, **455n.12**

Hiss, Joseph 143, **453n.2**

Holston, Doctor John G. F., 424, **484n.8**

"Holy Joes," xii. *See also* Catholic chaplains

Hood, General John Bell, 76, 230, **448n.20**

Hooker, General Joseph E., xv, 295, **441n.30**
letter from, 20

Hubert, Father Darius, S.J., 17, 28, 273, 275–76, 279–83, 289–90, **467n.10**

Hughes, Archbishop John J., 31, 156, 164, 368, 389, **443n.48**

Hunter, General David, 259, **465n.14**

Hurlbut, General Stephen A., 87, **450n.17**

Indiana troops
7th Battery, 223
35th Infantry (2nd and 61st Irish Regiments consolidated), 211–23, 461n.17, 462n.20
37th Infantry, 136
44th Infantry, 53

Illinois troops
  1st Artillery, 346
  19th Infantry, 359
  23rd Illinois (Irish Brigade of the
    West), 472n.11
  80th Infantry, 484n.16
  90th Infantry (Irish Legion),
    458n.17
  92nd Infantry, 195
Ireland, xviii, 40, 61, 143–44, 169, 333,
  451n.5 (chapter VII), 456n.9,
  461n.7
  people born/raised in, xiv, 37–38,
    141, 147, 181, 185, 187–88, 202, 211–
    13, 225–26, 269, 444n.8, 450n.1,
    452n.3, 453n.4, 457n.7 (chapter
    XIII), 457n.4 (chapter XIV),
    458n.18, 467n.9, 468n.25, 470n.7,
    470n.9, 470nn.13–14, 471n.16,
    474n.6, 475n.7, 475n.13, 476n.18,
    477n.6, 478n.2, 479n.20, 481n.1,
    483n.10, 484n.2, 484n.6, 485n.13
  people went to after the war, 17, 267
  Sisters of Mercy founded in, 379,
    389
Ireland, Father John, 52, **446n.5**
Irish Brigade, xv, 23, 197–98, 234, 238–
  45, 290, 463n.9. *See also* Corby,
  Father William, C.S.C.; Massa-
  chusetts troops, 28th Infantry;
  New York troops, 63rd Infantry,
  69th Infantry, 88th Infantry
Iuka, Battle of, 52

Jackson, General Thomas J.
  (Stonewall), xiv, 17, 242, 271–76,
  280, 285, 287, 290, 311, **463n.12**,
  469n.10
  death of, 293–95
Jacquet, Father John Mary, 73, **448n.11**
Johnson, General Richard W., 214,
  461n.11

Johnston, General Albert Sidney, 41,
  444n.9
Johnston, General Joseph E., 95,
  450n.4
Johnston, General Robert D., 297,
  469n.3
Jonesboro, Battle of, 18, 470n.6
Jordan, General Thomas, 340,
  475n.12

Kendall, Lieutenant Henry T., 347,
  476n.26
Kendall, Lieutenant Joseph V., 347–50,
  476n.27
Kenrick, Archbishop Francis P., 189,
  457n.1
Kenrick, Archbishop Peter R., 379
Kentucky troops (USA)
  2nd Infantry, 451n.1 (chapter VI)
  15th Infantry, 47, 445n.19
Kerrigan, Colonel James E., 192,
  457n.6
Kilty, Captain Augustus H., 425–28,
  485n.11
Know-Nothings. *See* anti-
  Catholicism
Koeder (Kaidor), Father Maurice W.,
  368, **478n.11**

Lambert, Father Louis A., 86, 92,
  449n.14
Lawler (Lalor), General Michael K.,
  92, **450n.1**
Lawler, Captain Andrew J., 344,
  476n.22
Lawler, Sister Mary Fidelis, 422, **431**,
  484n.2
Lee, Colonel William R., 194–95,
  458n.15
Lee, General Robert Edward, 242–43,
  270, 280, 296–97, 307, **442n.44**
  letter from, 27–28

Lefevère, Bishop Peter Paul, 226, **462n.2**

Leray, Father Francis Xavier, 18, 263, **441n.21**

Lévêque, Father Zepherin, C.S.C., **440n.9**, 463n.1

Libby Prison, 195, 317, 473n.18

Lincoln, President Abraham, xvi, 103, 211

Logan, General John A., 94–95, 104, 111, 228

Loras, Bishop John Mathias Pierre, 39, **444n.4**

Louisiana troops (CSA)
  1st Brigade (Louisiana Tigers or Hays's Brigade), 28, 275, 284–85
  1st Infantry, 17, 272–73, 275, 281, 284–85, 441n.22, 467nn.9–10, 468n.26, 468n.1
  2nd Brigade, 28, 281, 285
  3rd Infantry, 465n.9
  5th Infantry, 271
  6th Infantry, 271, 467n.17
  7th Infantry, 271
  8th Infantry, 17, 271
  10th Infantry, 17, 249–51
  12th Infantry, 62, 65, 446n.18
  13th Infantry, 62
  14th Infantry, xiv, 17, 270–72, 278, 289, 464n.6, 466nn.4–5, 470n.10
  20th Infantry, 446nn.18–19
  26th Infantry, 466n.11
  30th Infantry, 441n.23

Luers, Bishop John Henry, 84, 86, **449n.5**

Lynch, Bishop Patrick N., 301, 329, **471nn.17–18**, 475n.13

MacKenna, Mother Augustine, 390–91, 407, **481n.1**

MacNamara, Michael H., 34, 142, **443n.59**

Magruder, General John B., 251, **464n.5**

Maguire, Father Bernard, S.J., 279, **467n.20**

Maine troops
  2nd Infantry, 190
  9th Infantry, 476nn.18–19

Martin, Father Michael F., 195, **458n.18**

Mass, celebration of, 44, 49, 73, 98, 106, 108–9, 114, 142, 155–56, 183, 188–89, 191, 203, 229, 263–64, 369–70, 451n.6, 465n.3
  Christmas 1861, 238–39
  for soldiers in camp or on battlefield, 58–59, 61, 63, 65, 74, 76, 86–89, 91, 94, 96, 100–102, 113, 116, 129, 145–46, 148, 152, 166–68, 173–74, 176, 190, 192–97, 199–201, 207–8, 233, 235, 242, 244, 251–52, 271, 273, 279, 283–90, 298–300, 302–3, 305–6, 310, 313, 316, 318, 460n.8, 469n.2
  for souls of departed soldiers, 296

Massachusetts troops
  7th Infantry, 192
  9th Infantry, 17, 141–42, 144–48, 151–60, 181–82, 184–85, 189–90, 354, 443n.59, 455n.12, 457n.7 (chapter XIII)
  10th Infantry, 192
  15th Infantry, 194–95
  20th Infantry, 194, 458n.15
  26th Infantry, 316, 473n.14
  28th Infantry, 456n.4 (chapter XII), 476n.22
  30th Infantry, 475n.8
  44th Infantry, 404, 482n.6
  54th Infantry, 474n.4, 476n.20, 477n.5

Matthews, Colonel Thomas Stanley, 220, **462n.21**

McAtee, Father Francis, S.J., 17, **440n.14**

McCall, General George A., 196, **458n.21**

McCann, Captain Joseph Richard "Dick," 70, **447n.6**

McClellan, General George B., xvi, 192, 240–41, 243, **441n.28**
letter from, 19

McCook, General Alexander M., 214, 221, 447n.2, **461n.13**

McDougall, Doctor Charles, 367, 372, **478n.7**

McDowell, General Irvin, **442n.34**
letter from, 22–23

McElroy, Father John, S.J., 144, **454n.7**

McGee, James E., 34, 172, 176, **443n.58**

McGill, Bishop John, 156, 256, 330, **442n.43**

McGlynn, Father Edward, 364, 368–70, 375, **478n.12**

McGraw, Captain Patrick, 190, **457n.4**

McMahon, Doctor Abraham, 355, **477n.4**

McMahon, Father Laurence, 355, 456n.4 (chapter XII)

McMeens, Doctor Richard R., 354, **477n.1 (chapter XXVIII)**

McMillan, Doctor Charles, 88, **450n.18**

McPherson, General James B., 89, 94, 96, 105–6, 111, **450n.20**

Meade, General George G., **441n.31**
letter from, 21

Meagher, Father Michael, S.J., 164, **455n.1**

Meagher, General Thomas F., xv, 169, 230, 242, 244, **456n.6 (chapter XI)**

Merrill, William, 343, **476n.21**

Michener, Captain John E., 337, **475n.10**

Michigan troops
2nd Infantry, 169
6th Cavalry, 475n.11
10th Infantry, 58, 446n.14
14th Infantry, 57, 70, 447n.3
15th Infantry, 17, 225–31, 462n.5

Mignault, Father Joseph E. "Napoleon," 101–2, **450n.19**

Miles, Bishop Richard P., 206, **460n.4**

Milhau, Doctor John J., Jr., 371, **479n.19**

Minnesota troops
1st Infantry, 193
5th Infantry, 446n.5

Mississippi troops (CSA)
18th Infantry, 463n.6

Missouri troops (CSA)
1st Brigade, 451n.5

Missouri troops (USA)
6th Cavalry, 79–80, 90
7th Infantry, 105
10th Cavalry, 450n.2

Mitchel, Captain James, 285, **468n.5**

Mitchel, General Ormsby M., 44–48, **444n.14**

Mitchel, John, 285, **468n.5**

Mooney, Father Thomas H., 200, 234, **459n.32, 463n.3**

Moore, Father John, 340, 343, 347, 350, **475n.13**

Monaghan, Major William, 278, 284, **467n.17**

Moran, Father Malachy, O.S.B., 296, **469n.1 (chapter XXIV)**

Morgan, General John Hunt, 63, 70, **447n.5**

Morton, Governor Oliver P., 211, 213, 355, 409, 412, **461n.6**, 462n.20, 483n.3

Mosby, Colonel John S., 317, 319, **473n.17**

Mound City, Illinois, 84, 86–87, 414
   flooding of hospital, 419–22
   Sisters of the Holy Cross, 412–19,
     428–29
Mount Saint Mary's Seminary (Emmitsburg, Maryland), 37
Mullen, Colonel Bernard F., 217,
   220–22, **461n.17**
Müller, Father Michael, C.Ss.R., 317,
   473n.20
Mulligan, General James A., 314,
   472n.11
Murphy, Charles J., **459n.36**
   obituary for Father Gillen,
     200–201
Murphy, Colonel John McLeod, 188,
   190–91, 195–96, 199, 201, **457n.5**
Murphy, Colonel Robert C., 48–49, 51,
   445n.22

Nachon, Father Francis, S.J., 18,
   441n.25
Nash, Father Michael, S.J., 17
Nash, Michael, 214–16, **461n.10**
Nealis, Father John T., 74, 207, **448n.12**
Negley, General James S., 126–27,
   452n.9 (chapter VIII)
Nelligan, James, 284, 288, **468n.1**
New Hampshire troops
   3rd Infantry, 476n.21
New Jersey troops
   9th Infantry, 482n.9
New York troops
   1st Mounted Rifles, 376
   6th Infantry (Wilson's Zouaves),
     440n.12
   12th Infantry, 280–81
   14th Brooklyn (Militia), 190
   15th Engineers, 188, 190–91, 196–97,
     199, 201, 457n.5
   22nd Infantry, 189
   24th Infantry, 191

   25th Infantry, 457n.6
   31st Infantry, 440n.14
   33rd Infantry, 190, 457n.4
   34th Infantry, 190
   36th Infantry, 192
   37th Infantry (75th Militia or Irish
     Rifles), 163–70, 440n.10, 443n.57
   42nd Infantry (Tammany), 193,
     458nn.16–17
   63rd Infantry, 459n.26
   69th Infantry, 151–52, 154, 169,
     171–76, 189, 200, 234, 443nn.57–
     58, 454n.15, 457n.2 459n.32, 463n.3
   73rd Infantry, 466n.8
   77th Infantry, 479n.22
   82nd Infantry, 164
   88th Infantry, 233, 245, 456n.4
     (chapter XII)
   100th Infantry, 345
   155th Infantry, 197
   164th Infantry, 197
   170th Infantry, 188, 197–99
   175th Infantry, 459n.25
   182nd Infantry (69th New York
     National Guard), 188, 197–98,
     443n.55, 459n.25, 472n.7
   Rocket Battalion (23rd and 24th
     Light Artillery), 482n.4
Nolan, Colonel Michael, 272, 275, 278,
   281, 283–86, 289, **467n.9**
Notre Dame. *See* University (College)
   of Notre Dame
Noyland, Sister Rose, 259, **465n.15**
Nugent, Colonel Robert, 169
nuns. *See* Catholic sisters

O'Brien, Sister Elise, 424, 431,
   484nn.6–7
O'Callaghan, Father Joseph, S.J., 313,
   472n.7
O'Connell, Sister Anthony, 65, 354,
   361, **477n.6**

O'Connor, Bishop Michael, 123

O'Higgins, Father William T., 17, 61, 129, 229, **440n.16**

O'Meagher, Doctor William, 34, 164, 172, **443n.57**

O'Meara, Captain Timothy, 194–95, **458n.17**

O'Neil, Father Patrick, 340, **475n.15**

O'Neill, Chaplain William J., 183, **456n.5 (chapter XIII)**

O'Neill, Father Jeremiah F., 300, **470n.14**

O'Reilly, Father Bernard J., S.J., 189, **457n.2, 463n.3**

O'Reilly, Father Thomas, 299, **470n.7**

O'Reilly, Sister Mary Ulrica, 364, 367, 371, **478n.8**

O'Rorke, Captain Patrick R., 281, 284, **468n.26**

Odin, Archbishop Jean Marie, 250, **464n.3**

Ohio troops
10th Infantry, 17, 57, 129
47th Infantry, 451n.1 (chapter VI)
51st Infantry, 223
65th Infantry, 214, 461n.10
80th Infantry, 443n.46
104th Infantry, 137

Orléans, Prince Robert of, 167, **455n.4**

Osborn, William H., 412, **483n.9**

Osterhaus, General Peter J., 117, **452n.8 (chapter VII)**

Ouellet (Willett), Father Thomas, S.J., **171–72, 179,** 239, 242
early chaplaincy, 173–74
leaves regiment for hospital service in North Carolina, 176
as regimental banker, 175, 177
rejoins 69th New York, 177–78

Overland Campaign, 184–85, 245, 259, 308–10, 472n.4

Owen, Colonel Joshua T., 193–94, 458n.13

Paresce, Father Angelo M., S.J., **467n.20**

Payne, Lewis S., 345, **476n.24**

Peninsula Campaign (1862), 238, 240–41

Pennsylvania troops
2nd Reserves, 196
17th Cavalry, 317
18th Cavalry, 319
42nd Infantry (Bucktails or 13th Reserves), 193, 458n.20
50th Infantry, 347
69th Infantry, 193–95
77th Infantry, 126
78th Infantry, 16, 59, 122–23, 124–38
79th Infantry, 126
85th Infantry, 482n.7
118th Infantry, 183, 456nn.4–5 (chapter XIII)
119th Infantry, 317

Pepper, George W., **443n.46**
letter from, 29–30
tribute to Sisters of Charity, 30

Perryville, Battle of, 220–22, **462n.24**

Pierrepont, Edwards, 366–67, **478n.3**

Pinkney, Doctor Ninian, 98, **450n.7,** **485n.16**

Poe, Colonel Orlando M., 169, **456n.7**

Pope, General John, 242, 274–76, 359, **463n.11**

post-war Catholic Civil War monuments, xi, xiv

Prachenski, Father Joseph, S.J., 17, **440n.18**

Prendergast, Father Charles C., 300, **470n.15**

Price, General Sterling, 52, 54–55, **445n.3**

Pullin, Charles, 405–6, **482n.7**

Purcell, Archbishop John Baptist, 64, 73–74, 102, **447n.26**

Quinlan, Bishop John, 41, 43, 298, **444n.8**, 470n.4

Reade, Doctor Albert N., 360, **477n.8**
Ready, Colonel Charles, 63–64, **447n.24**
Regan, Sergeant Daniel J., 153–54, **454n.1**
Rhode Island troops
  2nd Infantry, 192
Richardson, General Israel, 168–69, **455n.5 (chapter XI)**
Robeson, Consul John T., 345, **476n.23**
Roddey, Philip D., 53–54, **446n.7**
Rodes, General Robert E., 305–6, 310, **471n.23**
Rogers, Doctor Edmund C., 419, **484n.16**
Rooney, Sister Mary Blanche, 254, **464n.7**
Rosary, 153–54, 198, 305, 332, 385, 423
Rosecrans, General William Starke, **441n.32, 445n.1, 452n.14, 477n.7**
  at Chickamauga, 75, 208, 460n.8
  conversion of, 187
  at Corinth, 55–56
  and Father Cooney, 214–15, 217, 223
  and Father Trecy, xvi, 16, 38, 48, 51–52, 56–57, 59, 68, 228
  letter from, 21–22
  relieved from command, 75, 448n.17
Rousseau, General Lovell, 129, 222, **447n.2, 452n.12**
Ruland, Father George, C.Ss.R., 318, **473n.22**
Ryan, Captain John, 62–65, **446n.18**

Saint Palais, Bishop Jacques-Maurice des Landes d'Aussac de, 206, **460n.3**
scapular, 96, 102, 109, 172, 177, 401
  saves life of General Stanley, 76, 448n.21
Schalk, Emil, 216, **461n.16**
Schiffler, Private John, **479n.28**
  letter from, 374–76
Schofield, General John M., **442n.36**
  letter from, 24
Scott, Lieutenant Robert R., 291, **469n.12**
Scully, Father Thomas, 17, **141–42, 161**, 184, 189, 242, **454nn.3–4**
  captured, 155–56
  at chaplain's meeting, 149–51
  visits Boston, 154–55
Semmes (family), 284, **468n.4**
Seven Days Battles, 155–56, 198, 241–42, 253–54
Sheeran, Father James B., C.Ss.R., xiv, 17, 28, **269–70, 319–20, 436n.9**
  arrested while with Federal army, 317–18
  attends to wounded after Fredericksburg, 288–89
  discourages gambling, 286
  with General Early in the Shenandoah Valley, 310–15
  meets Generals Ewell and Jackson, 271–72
  meets General Sheridan after being released from prison, 319, 473n.25
  ministers to wounded after Chancellorsville, 295–96
  during Overland Campaign, 308–10
  rejoins Army of Northern Virginia, 304
  reprimands his troops, 469n.2, 472n.8, 472n.10

during Second Manassas Campaign, 273–78
takes leave of absence in West, 298
visits Bragg's army, 298–99
Sheridan, General Philip H., 315–17, 319, **442n.33**
letter from, 22
Sherman, Ellen Boyle Ewing, 85–86, 95, **449n.10**
Sherman, General William Tecumseh, xv, 230, **448n.19**
in Atlanta Campaign, 76, 135, 137
at Vicksburg, 84–90, 93, 97, 111–13, 115–16
Shields, General James, 287, **469n.10**
Shiloh, Battle of, 18, 142, 356, 380, 416, **484n.15**
Simons, Doctor James, 342, **483n.6**
Sirwell, Colonel William G., 124, 130, **452n.7**
sisters, *See* Catholic sisters
Sisters of Charity of Mount Saint Vincent, Cincinnati, **353–54, 361,** 447n.27
begged to stay by soldiers and Doctor Reade, 359–60
care for African American refugees, 357–59
dispatched to care for wounded in South, 356
not subject to Dorothea Dix's authority, 357
Sisters of Charity of Mount Saint Vincent, New York, **363–64, 378**
celebrate Thanksgiving Day 1862, 372–73, 479n.21
New York City officials request their services, 364–67
omitted section on post-war history, 480n.32
soldier testimonials in favor of, 374–77

Sisters of (Our Lady of) Mercy, Charleston, **329–30, 351,** 464n.8, 475n.16
care for northern prisoners, 331–35, 341
soldiers' testimonials in favor of, 336–40, 343–50
Sisters of Mercy, New York, **389–90, 407**
devoted service lessens prejudice against them, 394–99
soldiers initially afraid of, 392–93
thanked by deceased soldiers' families, 404–7
wartime anecdotes related to Conyngham by, 399–401
Sisters of Mercy, Saint Louis, **379–80, 386–87**
care for imprisoned women, 386
inspire conversions, 382–83, 385
praised by soldiers, 382–83
Sisters of the Holy Cross, **409–10, 431–32,** 483n.5
attend Memphis hospital, 429–31
beads worn by, 484n.14
death of sisters in hospital service, 422–24
divine source of their dedication and endurance, 413–14
inspire conversions, 417–19
and Kilty-Fry incident, 425–28
letter from sister on prejudice overcome, 424–25
multiple draft chapters of, 439n.20, 483n.1, 484n.1
at St. Aloysius Hospital in Washington, DC, 431, 484n.1, 486n.18
soldiers' reverence for, 415–16
volunteer at request of Governor Morton, 412

Smith, Baltimore, **476n.20**
Smulders, Father Egidius, C.Ss.R., 17,
   28, 284, 286, 290, 296, 305, 310,
   318, **440n.17**
Society of St. Vincent de Paul, 382,
   480nn.2–3
Sorin, Father Edward, C.S.C. (Presi-
   dent of Notre Dame), 85–86, 88,
   233, 245, 409, 411–12, 483n.3
South Carolina troops
   27th Infantry, 476n.17
   Kershaw's Brigade, 455n.5 (chapter
   X)
Spalding, Bishop Martin J., 423, 354,
   440nn.2–3, 484n.4
   letter from, 14–15
Spalding, Doctor David C., 58,
   446n.14
Springer, Sergeant Charles B., 406,
   482n.9
Spring Hill College, 250, 441n.19
Stafford, General Leroy A., 28,
   442n.42
Stanley, General David S. 48–49,
   51–52, 68, **445n.23**, 448n.21
Stanton, Secretary of War Edwin M.,
   335, 366, 475n.9, **478n.4**
Starrs, Father William A., 365, 389,
   478n.2
Steele, General Frederick, 93, 117,
   450n.3
Stephens, Doctor, 309, 472n.2
Stone, Doctor Lincoln R., **477n.5**
Stone, General Charles P., 193–94,
   458n.12
Stones River, Battle of, 58–62, 128–29,
   134, 214, 461n.9
Stuart, General J. E. B., 274, 285,
   467n.13
Suckley, Doctor George, 355, **477n.3**
Sullivan, Patrick, 272, **466n.8**

Sullivan, Sister Mary Francis de Paul,
   413, **483n.10**

Tassin, Lieutenant Augustus G., 222
Teeling, Father John, 17, 156, **455n.7**
Telford, Captain William H., 350,
   477n.28
Tennessee troops (CSA)
   9th Cavalry, 447n.6
   10th Infantry, 440n.15, 441n.24
Tennessee troops (USA)
   7th Cavalry, 476n.23
Thomas, Adjutant General Lorenzo,
   442n.38
   letter from, 25
Thomas, General George H., 75–76,
   448n.18
Tissot, Father Peter, S.J., 16, **163–64**,
   170, 440n.10
   character of, 167
   prayer for flag raising, 168–69
   as regiment's banker, 166
Townsend, Assistant Adjutant
   General Edward D., 335, 357
Trecy, Father Jeremiah F., 16, **37–38**,
   77, 129, 229, **446n.20**
   becomes 4th Cavalry's chaplain,
   67–68
   leaves army, 77
   and Native Americans, 39–41
   opposes advance on Christmas
   Day, 58
   as Rosecrans's personal chaplain,
   57–59
   says Mass before Stones River, 59
Trimble, General Isaac R., 271, 274,
   285, **466n.7**
Tullahoma Campaign, 130, 452n.14
Tully, Chaplain David E., **479n.22**
Turgis, Father Francois Isidore, 18,
   441n.23

University (College) of Notre Dame,
    xiv, 80–81, 119, 187–88, 198, 201,
    203–4, 211–12, 224 233, 235,
    245–46, 409, 411, 431
Upham, Doctor Jabez Baxter, 391,
    481n.4
U.S. Army (regulars)
    4th Cavalry, 16, 38, 57, 62, 67–68, 76,
        129
    15th Infantry, 57
    16th Infantry, 68
    19th Infantry, 69
U.S.S. *Ben de Ford*, 148
U.S.S. *Cambridge*, 148
U.S.S. *Carondelet*, 201
U.S.S. *Mound City*, 425, 484n.9
U.S.S. *Red Rover*, 89, 96–98, 112,
    484n.1, 485n.16

Van Cleve, General Horatio P., 220,
    462n.22
Van Dorn, General Earl, 54, 446n.10
Van Vliet, General Stewart, 193, 457n.9
Verot, Bishop Augustin M., 299–300,
    470n.11
Vicksburg, Battle of
    Father Carrier's ministry at, 91–110
    Father Heuzé's description of the
        siege, 263–67
    pursuit of Confederates after,
        114–19
    surrender of, 111–13
Virginia troops (CSA)
    1st Infantry, 17, 285, 455n.7
    29th Infantry, 466n.6

Walker, Colonel John C., 220,
    462n.20
Walker, Mother Mary Ignatius, 381,
    480n.1
Walsh, Father Thomas E., C.S.C., 203,
    460n.37
Ward, Father James A., S.J., 279,
    467n.20
Weeds, Doctor James F., 423, 484n.5
Whelan, Bishop James, 206, 460n.6
Whelan, Father Peter, 300, 470n.13
White, Doctor Isaac, 271, 466n.6
Wightman, Sister Mary Rosina, 371,
    479n.16
Wilderness, Battle of, 184, 245, 259,
    308
Wiles, William M., 53, 446n.6
Willett, Father Thomas. *See* Ouellet
    (Willett), Father Thomas
Wisconsin troops
    17th Infantry, 446n.17, 450n.19
    24th Infantry, 446n.17, 462n.4
Wright, General Horatio G., 315–16,
    442n.39
    letter from, 26

Yandell, Doctor David Wendell, 41–43,
    444n.10
Yore, John E., 382, 480n.3
York, Colonel Zebulon, 271, 275–76,
    309, 312, 314, 466n.4, 470n.10

Zable, Major David, 271, 284–85,
    466n.5

DAVID POWER CONYNGHAM (1825–1883) was an Irish journalist, novelist, and staff officer in the Union army during the Civil War.

DAVID J. ENDRES is dean of Mount St. Mary's Seminary of the West/ Athenaeum of Ohio and associate professor of church history and historical theology.

WILLIAM B. KURTZ is the managing director and digital historian at the John L. Nau III Center for Civil War History. He is the author of *Excommunicated from the Union: How the Civil War Created a Separate Catholic America.*